D0504298

HIGH MOUNTAINS AND COLD SEAS
A BIOGRAPHY OF H. W. TILMAN

HIGH MOUNTAINS AND COLD SEAS

A Biography of

H. W. TILMAN

by

J. R. L. ANDERSON

LONDON
VICTOR GOLLANCZ LTD
1980

© J. R. L. Anderson 1980

ISBN 0 575 02806 8

NOTE

Quotations from H. W. Tilman's own books are re-
printed by permission of the publishers as follows: The
Cambridge University Press for *The Ascent of Nanda Devi,
When Men and Mountains Meet, Mount Everest – 1938, Two
Mountains and a River, China to Chitral, Nepal Himalaya,
Mischief in Patagonia*; Bell & Hyman Ltd for *Snow on the
Equator*; Granada Publishing Limited for *Mischief among
the Penguins*; Hollis & Carter Ltd for *Mischief goes South*;
The Nautical Publishing Co. Ltd and Ziff Davis
Publishing Co. for *Triumph and Tribulation*. Extracts from
books by Eric Shipton, *Nanda Devi* (Copyright Eric
Shipton 1936) and *This Untravelled World* (© Eric Shipton
1969) are reprinted by permission of Hodder &
Stoughton Ltd.

PRINTED IN GREAT BRITAIN
BY EBENEZER BAYLIS AND SON, LTD.
THE TRINITY PRESS, WORCESTER, AND LONDON

For
Joan and Pam

CONTENTS

LIST OF ILLUSTRATIONS

Unacknowledged photographs are from the Tilman collection

PLATES
(Following page 96)

John Hinkes and Adeline Tilman (*née* Rees), H. W. Tilman's parents
Berkhamsted School OTC in camp, 1914, showing H.W.T.
H.W.T. as a cadet at Woolwich, 1915
Mount Kenya (*photo Camera Press*)
Mount Kiliminjaro (*photo Camera Press*)
The Mountains of the Moon (*photo Camera Press*)
The West peak of Nanda Devi rising over the South Face
One of the few pictures showing H.W.T. in a state of physical exhaustion: on the ascent of Nanda Devi with W. F. Loomis, 1936
The twin peaks of Nanda Devi
Nanda Devi expedition, 1936, showing H.W.T., W. F. Loomis, T. Graham Brown, C. S. Houston, Peter Lloyd, N. E. Odell, Arthur Emmons, H. Adams Carter

(Following page 192)

Everest from the Tibetan side
Everest expedition, 1938, showing C. B. M. Warren, P. Lloyd, H.W.T., P. R. Oliver, F. S. Smythe, N. E. Odell, E. E. Shipton
H.W.T. at the outbreak of war in 1939
H.W.T.'s father as a member of the Mersey Docks and Harbour Board
Albania, 1944
H.W.T. after receiving the Freedom of the City of Belluno, 1945
H.W.T. on the approach to Rakaposhi
On the road to Kashgar, 1947
The Fluted Peak in the Langtang Himal, Nepal, 1949
The south-west and south faces of Rakaposhi

(Following page 256)

H.W.T., *Mischief*'s skipper

9

Mischief on her return from the Antarctic, 1967 (*photo W. G. Lee*)
The Calvo glacier leading to the Patagonian ice-cap
H.W.T. in *Mischief*'s saloon, 1966 (*photo W. G. Lee*)
Ice off Bylot Island
The galley on *Mischief* (*photo W. G. Lee*)
Penguins and elephant seals on Possession Island (in the Crozet group)
Patanela on the way to Heard Island
Sea Breeze in the Needles Channel, 1970 (*photo W. G. Lee*)
Sea Breeze in Torssukatak Fjord, West Greenland, 1970
Crew of *Sea Breeze*, 1970 (*photo W. G. Lee*)
H.R.H. The Duke of Edinburgh presenting H.W.T. with the Fellowship of the Royal Institute of Navigation
Sea Breeze in ice off West Greenland
Baroque in Magdalena Fjord, North-west Spitzbergen, 1974

(*Following page 304*)
Adeline (Mrs Reid Moir) with Toffee, 1973
H.W.T. on board *Sea Breeze* in 1971 (*photo W. G. Lee*)
Baroque off Angmagssalik, East Greenland, 1976
The Mawddach estuary showing the house, Bod Owen (*photo W. G. Lee*)
Bod Owen
The last voyage: the departure of *En Avant*, Southampton, August 1977

MAPS

INTRODUCTION

THIS IS THE biography of a very private man, who contrived to live a long life on a physical scale unmatched by anyone in this century and by few in any century. H. W. Tilman's life defies comparison. His land travels in Central Asia and Africa were less important than those of the great nineteenth-century explorers—Livingstone, Stanley, Younghusband and their peers—because they took place later when more of the world was known; nevertheless Tilman helped to fill in some blank spaces on the map and his journeys earned him the highest award of the Royal Geographical Society, the Founder's Medal. Those earlier great travellers did not go out of their way to climb mountains. Tilman did, and he must be reckoned among the top twenty of the world's outstanding climbers. When he climbed Nanda Devi in 1936 it was the highest summit then achieved by man, and he was the natural choice to lead the British Everest Expedition in 1938.

There have been other great mountaineers. In his fifties, when Tilman considered that he was too old to go much above 20,000 feet, he took to the sea, and for the next quarter of a century he sailed a succession of ancient Bristol Channel Pilot Cutters, none built later than 1906, to the Arctic and the lonely wastes of the Antarctic; when he circumnavigated Spitzbergen in 1974 he was seventy-six and his cutter *Baroque* aged seventy-five. He was invited to join an expedition to Smith Island in the South Shetlands, off the Antarctic Peninsula, when he was seventy-nine, and had hopes of spending his eightieth birthday if not actually on Smith Island (where landing is so difficult that it might have proved impossible even for Tilman at that age), at least in the high latitudes of the far south.

He saw active service in two world wars, winning the MC and bar in the first and the DSO in the second. In so for as he had a profession other than traveller and writer he was a soldier, having gone straight from school in 1915 to the Royal Military Academy at Woolwich, to be commissioned as a regular officer in the Gunners. In January 1916, a month before his eighteenth birthday, he was on the Western Front. His letters home from the Somme and other battlefields, published here for the first time, contribute many insights into the life of a young subaltern in the First World War. In 1919 he left the Army to farm in Kenya and explore mountains in East and Central Africa. When he wanted to come home in 1933 he took the unusual route of crossing Africa from Uganda to the west coast by bicycle, a feat that may have been repeated since but which was certainly a "first" when he did it. Climbing and travel in Africa were followed by remarkable expeditions to the Himalaya and the Karakoram, culminating in leadership of the British Everest team in 1938.

On the outbreak of war in 1939 he immediately rejoined the Army in his old rank of lieutenant, though he was soon promoted captain. After fighting in France and being evacuated from Dunkirk he soldiered in Iraq and the Western Desert, commanding a battery in the battle of Alamein and fighting through to the end of the African campaign in Tunis. At the age of forty-five he volunteered (and somehow got accepted) for parachute training and service behind the enemy lines, first with the partisans in Albania and then with the Italian resistance forces in northern Italy. As soon as he could get there after the war he was back in Central Asia, climbing mountains, exploring and mapping little-known passes wherever he could go from China to Chitral. When the attitude of post-war China and Russia made his kind of wandering in Central Asia impossible he turned to Nepal, where, with an American party organised by Oscar and Charles Houston (father and son), he was the first Westerner to travel to Thyangboche and the southern approach to Everest, the route by which it was ultimately climbed by Lord Hunt's expedition in 1953. After a brief interlude in the diplomatic service as a consul in Burma he returned to a life of travel, combining a voyage to the Pacific coast of Patagonia in the first of his Bristol Channel Pilot Cutters, *Mischief*, with a remarkable crossing of the Patagonian ice-cap. Then came the Arctic and Antarctic voyages and explorations, two shipwrecks, and continued adventuring into old age.

After a lecture on one of his expeditions given to Army cadets at Sandhurst Tilman was asked by one of them, "Please sir, how do I get on an expedition?" "Put on your boots and go," was Tilman's answer. His creed of self-sufficiency is becoming rare in our complex and highly-commercialised society, but it was inherent in Tilman's being, reflecting the virtues in the hard schooling of his generation. He was mountain-explorer as much as mountaineer, scorning technical aids to climbing, and relying on stout boots, ice-axe and rope to get himself where he wanted to go. It is an attitude that may seem old-fashioned now, but it produced some of the triumphs of climbing history and lighted the way to the great summits of the earth.

Briefly, after the ascent of Nanda Devi, Tilman was the most famous mountaineer in the world, and he remained in the public eye as leader of the 1938 Everest expedition. But he had no use for, nor art in, publicity and he preferred anonymity. When war came he wished to be a front-line soldier, rejecting the suggestion that he might be an instructor at a school of mountain warfare. He met his mountain warfare at first hand in Albania and the Dolomites. After the war his early voyages in *Mischief* attracted attention, and among sailors he became a legendary mariner, as he remained a legendary climber among mountaineers. He wrote fifteen books, his early ones, *The Ascent of Nanda Devi* and *Snow on the Equator*, being near best-sellers. His *Mischief* books attracted some general readership, but his later sea books, much concerned with the minutiae of navigation in ice, could scarcely hope for wide readership outside a specialised sailing world. His exploits attracted little public attention, partly at least because he sought none. Even so, it is strange that in the sixties, when Francis Chichester and Alec Rose were given knighthoods for sailing single-handed round the world, and other adventurous voyagers became world figures, Tilman, whose voyages outdid most, remained largely unknown. Crowds assembled to welcome the sailing heroes of press and television but Tilman would slip into Lymington after a voyage to the ends of the earth as if he were returning from a weekend cruise.

He hated the idea of sponsorship, and with the exception of the Everest expedition and small grants from scientific bodies towards the cost of his travels in the Karakoram and in Nepal, he financed all his journeys and voyages himself. He could afford to, for although never really rich his father left him comfortably off; he was businesslike in selling his land in Kenya; and his personal tastes were so austere that he could and did travel on a shoe-string. Some of those who climbed or sailed with him thought that he carried austerity to unreasonable lengths, but he did not even consider himself austere; simply, he wanted little, and in any circumstances was content to make do with what he had. These are perhaps unusual characteristics but they are not inhuman, and Tilman was far from unfeeling. He could be stern with others because he was severe on himself, but he had a fund of kindness and he was always generous in offering opportunities to the young. He could be taciturn to the point of total silence and could sit for hours with a friend he knew well without feeling the need to say a word, but he was not unsociable and he could keep the small communities of his shipmates or fellow-climbers bright with laughter at his wit and pointed comments on human affairs.

He had the reputation of being a woman-hater. He did not seek the company of women, but his misogyny was more myth than real. He was devoted to his sister and his two nieces, and to any woman whom he met he was the soul of courtesy and consideration. In our century there is often felt to be something unnatural in a man or woman who does not pursue sex; if a man is not much drawn to women he is assumed to be homosexual. There was no trace of homosexuality in Tilman, and if he was not much interested in sex it was because sex did not interest him. Tilman did not consider that women can neither climb nor sail: he had genuine admiration for the climbing and sailing achievements of some women, but he himself preferred to climb or sail with men.

A biographer should declare an interest, and I have several. For the last fifteen or so years of his life Tilman was my friend, and we corresponded a good deal although we seldom met. My son, Richard (Major R. A. L. Anderson, Royal Signals), became a disciple of Tilman's when he heard him give a lecture at school, and Tilman kept a kindly eye on Richard's own expeditions to the Hindu Kush and Himalaya, offering constant encouragement. This is merely one instance of his generosity to younger climbers and sailors. So although I have been critical when Tilman's attitude or behaviour seems to me to merit criticism, I cannot, and do not wish to try to hide my admiration for the man.

A biography depends on its sources. In theory the best sort of biography should be autobiography, for a man may be expected to know best what happened to him, how he felt, thought and acted at various times of his life. It does not always work like that; memory is often unreliable, and a man is not always the best witness in his own case. Tilman's stern regard for truth and dislike of frills would have made him a good autobiographer, and I spent several months trying to persuade him to write his own life story. I failed; and perhaps my efforts then are among the reasons why the invitation to write about him came to me. To attempt to reconstruct any life of eighty years is a daunting task, and Tilman's life, covering such widely-spaced activities in such diverse fields, has been exceptionally difficult to piece together. On the surface it is fairly well documented; there are his books, his diaries and logs, and several thousand letters. The books should in theory provide a sure guide to his life and he thought they did, giving their existence as one of the reasons why he would not write an auto-biography. But they are not always easy to interpret. His style can be of masterly lucidity, but it can also be elliptic, and his habit of under-statement often makes it difficult to determine precisely what he did, or why he did it. His diaries are illuminating, but often they are little more than rough notes which he wrote up later in his books. In 1967 he was asked by Dr Gene M. Gressley of the University of Wyoming, which has a considerable collection of the archives of exploration, if he would add his papers to the archive. He replied typically, "I should have no objection to your having my mountaineering diaries, which are of no use to me." Later he added his sea diaries, the whole collection forming a valuable record of his adventures from the reconnaissance, with Eric Shipton, of Nanda Devi in 1934 to the Heard Island expedi-tion in 1965. Through the kindness of Dr Gressley and of Dr David Pluth, a young American scholar and climber who is planning to produce an edited version of the diaries, I have been given photocopies of these documents; and Tilman's nieces have given me access to some remaining diaries of other periods. Unhappily, there is virtually nothing about Africa, and for the thirteen years he spent in Africa I have relied on the record in his book *Snow on the Equator*, on Eric Shipton's writings, and on the reminiscences of surviving contemporaries of Tilman's Kenya days, now half a century ago, who without exception have been generous in trying to help. In war, letters are subject to censorship and to the constraints on the writer of his own appreciation of the danger of letters falling into enemy hands. I have been helped enormously in working out Tilman's movements in two world wars by Brigadier R. J. Lewendon and Brigadier C. J. Codner of the Royal Artillery Institution, whose Historical Section has an invaluable collection of records.

The most important source for the interpretation of Tilman's life is his letters, first to his parents, then to his sister Adeline Reid Moir (who died in 1974) and to numerous friends. Tilman was an almost compulsive letter writer, and in his letters, especially those to his sister, he comes nearer to expressing spontaneous thoughts and feelings than in the books. His letters were faithfully preserved by his sister, and after her death by her daughter Pam Davis. There are inevitable gaps but taken as a whole the letters, starting from his schooldays, are a wonderful flow of report and comment over nearly seventy years. Whenever I have had a choice of quoting from letters or books I have chosen the letters. But the books are also valuable, and if my quotations send readers back to them, they will enjoy a rewarding experience.

My debts to the many people who have helped me are acknowledged separately. But this introduction would be incomplete without a special acknowledgment of thanks to those who made the work itself possible. I am not quite of Tilman's generation, but I am sixty-nine and at one time it seemed likely that my chances of starting, let alone of finishing, the book would be seriously diminished by illness. That the book exists is due to the unfailing support and encouragement of my wife Helen and my family, of my publisher Livia Gollancz, and of Tilman's two nieces, Pam Davis and Joan Mullins. Pam in particular (since Joan lives in Ireland) has borne patiently with my endless questions, and interrupted a busy life as wife and mother to do so; as befits a Tilman, she is also a leading competitor and instructor in gliding. My three doctors, Dick Squires, Joe Smith and Christopher Paine, and the staffs of various hospitals in Oxford, have helped not only with their skills but by their constant understanding, as have my friends Peter Lloyd (President of the Alpine Club), Robin Hodgkin, Scott Russell, and W. G. and Mary Lee, of Lymington. Lee, who took many of the photographs in this book, has been a tower of strength in sharing his first-hand knowledge of Tilman and his boats. Peter Lloyd (who climbed with Tilman on Nanda Devi and on Everest), Scott Russell (who went with Shipton to the Karakoram in 1939), and Robin Hodgkin, another distinguished climber, have been invaluable guides through the intricacies of Himalayan and Karakoram geography and the records of great climbs. I need scarcely add that any errors or infelicities which remain are mine alone.

It is almost axiomatic that a married author's introduction to a book should include an acknowledgment to "my wife, who did the typing". (Oddly, few husbands seem to get similar acknowledgments from women writers.) My acknowledgment to Helen is not axiomatic. My debt to her is total, for typing certainly, but far more for ceaseless help and advice with a mass of correspondence, for dealing with people, for driving me to places when I could not drive myself, for everything that makes marriage (even when it involves the trials of writing) still the best of human partnerships.

Finally, a note on technique. In reading biographies I am irritated when a biographer says of his subject that he "must have thought" or "may well have felt" this or that; worse, when bits of imaginary dialogue are put in from conversations of which there can be no possible reporter. I have attributed nothing to Tilman for which there is not direct evidence, either in his own writing or in first-hand personal recollection, and I have given the source. Occasionally I have used an apocryphal story about him because it is such a good story that it has seemed worth telling, but in such cases I have made clear that it is apocryphal. Orthography has presented numerous problems, most of them insoluble. Asiatic place-names and the names of fjords in Greenland are not spoken to be written in the Roman alphabet and there are usually alternative spellings, equally right or wrong. I have tried to be consistent, but do not pretend that my spellings are better or worse than others. The political map of Africa in the 1920s and 1930s was very different from the Africa of today; Tilman travelled through the Belgian Congo and other territories whose names have disappeared from the map. Here I have used the names he used, adding the modern names at the first mention. Heights are given in feet, distances in miles and depths in fathoms, because that is how he thought.

Where I have interpolated anything in Tilman's letters or other writings for the sake of clarity or explanation, it is enclosed in square brackets. When round brackets are used they occur in the original text.

ACKNOWLEDGMENTS

I HAVE WRITTEN in my introduction of some of those whose constant help, encouragement and advice made this book possible but my debt to many others is immense. And it reflects on the kindliness and courtesy of H. W. Tilman himself in his dealings with other people throughout his life that everyone to whom I wrote asking questions about him replied, even when, as happened sometimes, I asked questions that could not be answered. Those who helped particularly with information about Tilman's schooldays and family background include Mr John Spencer, headmaster of Berkhamsted School, Colonel A. L. Wilson, who was at Berkhamsted with Tilman, Mr A. J. Hayes, Mr T. Eland, Mr J. Bellis, Mr J. S. Rebecca, whose knowledge of the local history of Wallasey was invaluable, the Merseyside Chamber of Commerce and the Superintendent Registrar for Liverpool.

For the reconstruction of Tilman's service in two world wars I have already recorded my debt to Brigadier R. J. Lewendon, of the Historical Section of the Royal Artillery Institution, and Brigadier C. J. Codner, secretary of the Institution, but many others gave material help. These include General Sir Jack Harman, KCB, formerly Adjutant-General, Mr R. H. Forey of the Army Historical Branch of the Ministry of Defence, Dr John Ross, Mr E. H. Cookridge, Colonel D. Smiley, Major Peter Kemp, and Lieutenant-Colonel Neil Maclean. *A History of the Scarborough Pals' Battery (C Battery, 161st (Yorks) Brigade, RFA)*, compiled by Sydney Foord, MBE, MM, and Thomas Northern in collaboration with members who served with the Battery, and a memoir of Major Richard Archer Houblon who commanded I Troop, RHA, are important sources relating to the First World War— and moving tributes to the courage of men who were brave and endured as a matter of course. Copies of relevant extracts from the War Diaries of the artillery units with which Tilman served were supplied by the Royal Artillery Institution. Mr Anton Logoreci generously contributed his expert knowledge of Albania, both in letters and in his book *The Albanians* (Gollancz, 1977), and Signora Giuliana Foscolo, who lived through the Nazi occupation of Belluno and at great risk to herself gallantly sheltered Tilman and his companions during their guerilla operations, let me draw freely on her rich store of memories.

For Kenya and East Africa, sometimes with recollections of more than half a century ago, my helpers include Mrs Marjorie Sneyd and her son Mr Richard Sneyd, Mr H. A. Carr, Mr J. E. Barlow, Mr J. T. Wilson, Mr J. Howard, Mrs Avril Royston, Mr P. Le Pelley, Mr Charles Gardner, Mrs Horace Dawson, Mr R. J. Butterfield, Miss J. Waddington, OBE, Sir Michael Blundell, KBE, Mrs M. Wilkinson, Mr R. Cashmore, Mr C. Wilks, OBE, Mr R. Wainwright, CMG, and Mr S. H. Fazan, CMG, CBE. Mr E. F. Given, CMG, and Mr D. F. Parkinson, CMG, provided reminiscences of Tilman in Burma and Dr J. S. Watson, Principal and Vice-Chancellor of the University of St Andrew's, helped with details of Tilman's relations with the university and his honorary degree. The Royal Geographical Society provided the citation for the award of the Founder's Medal.

On the mountaineering side of Tilman's life some of my major helpers have already been recorded. The Alpine Club provided a copy of his application for membership and many other details, and generous help was also given by Dr Charles S. Houston, Dr Charles Warren, Mr Walt Unsworth, editor of *Climber and Rambler*, and Mr Showell Styles. For sailing I have drawn much from Mr Colin Putt, Mr Warwick M. Deacock, Mr M. W. Richey, MBE, Director of the Royal Institute of Navigation, Mr Frank George and Mr K. W. Rhodes. Dr R. Haworth was especially helpful with details of the Three Peaks Race. In a more general context I owe a great deal to Miss Mabel Pugh and the Rev. Wynn Rhys.

In addition to letting me use their own memories many of my helpers also lent original letters from Tilman. Where I have quoted directly from such letters the source is acknowledged in the text, but the value of the correspondence goes far beyond direct quotation for it helped to provide the essential framework for the reconstruction of a life of eighty years.

I was given unrestricted access to all Tilman's papers, letters and books by his nieces and next-of-kin Joan Mullins and Pam Davis, and have quoted freely from them. There is an important point to be made about my quotations from his letters home. I have confined extracts to matters directly relating to his adventures and this may give a wholly false impression that his letters were somewhat self-centred. In fact they are instinct with love for his family and there are constant references to family affairs, showing that throughout his war service and wide-ranging travels his father and mother, his sister Adeline, his nieces and their families were always close to his heart.

The extract I have quoted from *Il Nuovo Adige* of February 1946 relating to Tilman's service with the Italian Partisans is from a type-script in English that I found among his papers. The faded paper and rusted paper-clip suggest that the translation was given to him at the time and I regret that after the lapse of more than thirty years I have been unable to identify the translator. I hope that he or she will forgive me, and, indeed, share my pride in being able to use this extract to remind a new generation of the heroism shown around Belluno.

A Note on Maps
The selection and construction of maps used to illustrate this book presented many problems that are insoluble in terms of finite book production. Tilman's travels covered such an immense area of the globe that to attempt to map them fully would require a large atlas. More-over, there are particular problems of scale—if the little known areas of Africa, Central Asia, the Arctic and Antarctica that he explored are to be shown in any detail their geographical setting in the larger regions of the world cannot adequately be conveyed; if their setting is to be mapped, then detail must be ignored. One is left with a variety of compromises, all more or less unsatisfactory. I have tried to show the extent of his travels and voyaging at the expense of much omission, but showing, I hope, enough essential detail to give sense to the picture. Above all I have striven for uncluttered clarity, and where this has meant omission I have been compelled to accept it. I am profoundly grateful to the production department of Gollancz and to the carto-graphers, Oxford Illustrators, for the trouble they have gone to in trying to meet my needs. The map showing the route out of the Nanda Devi basin taken by Tilman, Dr Charles Houston and Pasang is based on a sketch by Mr W. G. Lee.

HIGH MOUNTAINS AND COLD SEAS

I

Beginnings

HAROLD WILLIAM TILMAN was born at Wallasey, Cheshire, on
14 February 1898, the third child and younger son of a prosperous
Liverpool merchant. The first of his male forebears of whom anything
is now known with certainty is his grandfather, William Tilman. The
family seems to have had some earlier connection with Coventry, but
from the middle of the nineteenth century they lived in Liverpool.
William Tilman began his working life in modest circumstances,
apparently as a cobbler's assistant. He married Caroline Hinkes, and
when their son John was born in 1861 the father was described on the
birth certificate as "shop man". He seems to have prospered, for a
Liverpool street directory of 1867 lists him as carrying on business at
29 Ranelagh Street as a boot and shoe manufacturer. Later he moved
his business to 77 Great George Street, but by 1880 he must have
retired, for a Wallasey directory of that year records him as "gentleman". He moved to 87 Union Street, Egremont, Wallasey, and died
there in 1893.

John Hinkes Tilman was what would be called a self-made man, a
copybook example of the rewards that come from the Victorian
virtues of prudence and industry. At the age of about fourteen he went
straight from school to a job, probably as office boy, with a firm of
Liverpool sugar merchants. He was soon promoted and became a
salesman, and then in 1895 he and a partner, Mr George Rome, set up
for themselves as sugar brokers, trading as Rome and Tilman. The
business was highly successful. J. H. Tilman was also a shrewd investor,
and when he died in 1936 he left a fortune of £109,629, a sum
equivalent to something like a million pounds in the depreciated
currency of our own times.

He married Adeline Rees, who came of a long line of Cumberland
hill-farmers. Some of the family went to Wales, which brought her into
the orbit of Liverpool and her future husband. Her family was hard-
working and prosperous, providing at least one magistrate for Wales.

After living for a time at Rock Ferry, Birkenhead, the Tilmans moved to Wallasey, first to Radnor Drive and then to the big house called Seacroft in Grove Road, which was to be J. H. Tilman's home for the rest of his life.

As well as running his own business, J. H. Tilman took a prominent part in the wider concerns of the sugar trade. He was chairman of the Sugar Association of Lancashire from 1900 to 1901, in 1911–12, and for a third time in 1931–32. He was a director of the Association for over thirty years. In 1922, finding that looking after his by then considerable investments was taking more and more of his time, he retired from sugar-broking, leaving the firm to be carried on by his partner, George Rome. However, he remained closely associated with the sugar trade and the work of the Sugar Association, an important body independent of all dealers, concerned to supervise all aspect of sugar-importing through Liverpool and the Lancashire ports. In 1926 he was elected a member of the Mersey Docks and Harbour Board, a real accolade for a Liverpool businessman. He was justifiably proud of his membership of the Board, and took a keen interest in its affairs.

He was not an easy man to work for. I am indebted to Mr T. Eland, of Aughton, Lancashire, for an office boy's view of him. Mr Eland started his long career with the Sugar Association as an office boy in 1929. When he applied for the job he was interviewed by J. H. Tilman and the secretary of the Association. He writes:

> They had prepared an exhaustive list of questions relating to academic achievement, home background, athletic pursuits and other interests. I was accepted, and commenced work on a wage of ten shillings a week. I was extremely thankful, since a permanent occupation was very hard to come by during the years of the depression.
>
> My first instruction from Mr J. H. Tilman was to meet him every morning at James Street station at precisely two minutes past ten. I was to meet him at the "Underground" in order to collect his attaché case, which usually contained library books. It was my duty to be there on time, and to exchange books at Potter's Private Library. . . . He was an avid reader of books—five or six a week was not an unusual number. I had to return books to the library each

week and collect books which he had either listed, or given verbal instructions about. . . .

Mr Tilman was a very astute gentleman, possessed of considerable business acumen. When he gave orders they were obeyed to the letter. . . .

Occasionally he would storm into our office and in stentorian tones shout, "Eland! Get me to the Dock Board!" On arrival he would ask, "Why is the pilot boat at the stage in weather like this?" It meant little that gale force winds were forecast—in fact they had only come in to change crews. It seemed to me that he carried with him an all-pervading aura of authority. Although only a small man— about 5 ft 4 ins in height—he was blessed with a good pair of lungs, and was certainly able to make his presence felt.

Mr Tilman was in touch with his stockbroker every day, and died a wealthy man. He favoured good discipline, and if we met in the street would not even acknowledge my presence with a nod. Through all this, however, I had a great deal of respect for the man. He was completely honest and fair in all his business dealings.

Alfred J. Hayes, also of the Sugar Association of Lancashire and later its secretary, has similarly sharp memories of J. H. Tilman. "He lived, ate and slept business, and thought anything else, apart from doing good works, a waste of time."

It is not a wholly attractive picture, but there was more to J. H. Tilman than a ruthless business man. Mr Hayes also recalls what happened when Tilman's former partner, George Rome, retired in 1930 and the sugar-broking firm, then Rome and Company, was in danger of going out of business. It was a time of world slump, and office staff in Liverpool who lost their jobs were unlikely to find other work. J. H. Tilman came to the rescue. He offered the office manager, Mr J. E. Bellis, a loan in order to keep the firm going, which he did until the sugar trade was taken over by the Government under war-time regulations in 1940. And in his will J. H. Tilman left Mr Bellis a legacy sufficient to write off the loan.

This picture of J. H. Tilman is taken, as it were, from the outside. Within his family it was different—he is remembered by his grand-daughters as an always kindly grandfather, with a wonderful sense of fun. And the unity of the family, always a warm, affectionate world of its own, shows him a benign patriarch.

27

Like other successful businessmen of his time, J. H. Tilman was a good churchgoer. He was brought up a Congregationalist, but he and his family later became Anglicans, though remaining always on the Low Church side of the Church of England. His Nonconformist conscience, Victorian belief in good works—call it what you will—was no suit of Sunday clothes to be taken off when he got home. There was no National Health Service then, and hospitals depended on voluntary support. He gave generously to local hospitals in his lifetime, and on his death left the Victoria Central Hospital, Wallasey, £1,000, and the Hahnemann Hospital, Liverpool, £500—considerable sums in the thirties. There were also substantial legacies to other bodies concerned with social or charitable work. His personal creed may have been a hard one, but it was not conscienceless, and he was no hypocrite.

He had probably left school at fourteen, but his prodigious reading (a habit inherited by his son) made him well-informed on an immense variety of subjects. On internal evidence from his son's letters (scarcely any of his own have survived) he knew a fair amount of Latin, and had quite good French. He could appreciate fine furniture—his home at Wallasey was full of beautiful things, and while this certainly reflected the taste of his wife it also showed that whatever might be the surface appearances, the making of money in him was not quite an end in itself.

There were three children: a daughter, Gertrude Adeline, born while the Tilmans were still living at Rock Ferry in 1892, and two sons, Kenneth, born in 1896, and Harold William, born in 1898. His sister Adeline, shortened to "Adds", was to play an enormously important part in H. W. Tilman's life. Kenneth, who preceded his brother to Berkhamsted, left school in 1913 intending to make a career in the Merchant Navy. Naturally he joined the Royal Navy Volunteer Reserve which soon after the outbreak of war in 1914 was embodied in the Royal Navy. He was one of the earliest members of the Royal Naval Air Service and became a flight-lieutenant. He stayed on in the Navy after the war and in 1924 was killed in a flying accident in the Mediterranean.

With such a father, dominant, self-willed, successful, one might have expected all sorts of psychological tensions in the home. Instead, they were an extraordinarily happy family, the children devoted to their parents, the brothers devoted to their sister, and she to them. J. H. Tilman and his wife may have come from different backgrounds but their marriage was a thoroughly good one, bringing much happiness to both. Of course there were troubles. When the stock market fell J. H. would be plunged in gloom, announce that he was ruined, and that the family would have to give up everything. His wife knew how to handle him through such crises. The market duly rose again, the maids were not sacked, and everything went on as before.

Before he became famous, Harold William Tilman was something of a disappointment to his father, who would have liked his surviving son to follow him in business. But their relationship was complex. The father had great pride in his son's record in the First World War, and his later achievements as a climber. The son, for his part, had immense respect for his father, and from his schooldays showed a determination —which J. H. appreciated—to stand on his own feet. Financial matters, which might have caused much misunderstanding and bitterness between father and son, in fact did not, because of the son's sensitive knowledge of his father. In all financial dealings with his father H. W. Tilman acted—as the lawyers would say—at arm's length. During the First World War, when young Tilman found that the pay which he could not spend at the Front was mounting up in his bank account, he asked his father for advice on investment—he would never have asked for money to invest. When he wrote home from the Front asking his father to give a present of ten shillings to a former Army servant he carefully enclosed a cheque for ten shillings. When, after the war, Tilman senior put up some money to help his son buy a farm in Kenya, there was a formal legal agreement between them. The outcome was mutual respect which, added to real affection, was strong enough to keep bridges between the two of them intact, and prevent profound differences in outlook on life from developing into rows. Indeed many of J. H. Tilman's qualities were manifest in his son, qualities which might undergo mutation but which as fundamental human character-istics were very much the same in both. Physically, too, H. W. Tilman took after his father, though he grew to be considerably taller, standing 5 ft 8 ins against his father's 5 ft 4 ins. Like his father he was stocky and small-boned, with enormous strength concealed in his wiry frame, and his strength was moral as well as physical.

Harold William Tilman went first to a preparatory school at New Brighton and then to Wallasey Grammar School. In 1909, at the age of eleven, he followed his elder brother Kenneth to Berkhamsted. The headmaster then was the Rev. T. C. Fry, DD, who was considered one of the outstanding headmasters of his day, and it seems to have been mainly on account of his reputation that J.H. chose Berkhamsted for his sons. In 1910 Dr Fry became Dean of Lincoln and was succeeded as headmaster by another remarkable man, C. H. Greene, father of Graham Greene the novelist, Sir Hugh Carleton Greene, who became Director-General of the BBC, and Dr Raymond Greene, the distinguished mountaineer. It is curious that what was then a relatively small school should have produced three such outstanding climbers as H. W. Tilman, F. S. Smythe and Raymond Greene.

Both brothers went into School House at Berkhamsted, and in 1913 H. W. Tilman was awarded a Foundation Scholarship which exempted him from all tuition fees, and he also became a prefect. He was a good all-rounder, playing games and drilling with the OTC with the same enthusiasm that he gave to his work. He played football for the school's First XI, became Captain of Fives, and was particularly good at gym.

Colonel A. L. Wilson, Royal Engineers, who was at school with him, recalls an impression of shyness that was really reserve. "One didn't get to know him easily," Colonel Wilson wrote. "He was physically a fine specimen, and clearly very well co-ordinated as regards eye and muscle. He was likeable, but a bit remote." That description of Tilman as a schoolboy fitted him all his life.

He took his School Certificate in 1913. He was then in the Science Vth and his school report for that summer term survives. It shows something of the breadth of his interests, and all-round ability. He was top in algebra, divinity, history, geography and French, and did well in chemistry and physics. His conduct is described as "Very good". Being on the science side of the school, and having reached the fifth form, he had abandoned Latin, but like most boys of his time Latin had been well drilled into him in earlier years, and he kept a fondness for an apt Latin tag throughout his life.

Next term he went into the VIth Form and could reasonably have expected to crown a successful school career with a university scholarship. But on 4 August 1914 Great Britain declared war on Germany.

That autumn of 1914 was the Rupert Brooke period of the First World War, a time when practically every young man wanted to show

30

that Britain was capable of all the military valour of her past. The wars and frontier campaigns of the nineteenth century were fought by professional soldiers, whose countrymen might glory in a victory or call for political heads to fall after a defeat, but the vast mass of the population of the British Isles, safely defended by the Royal Navy and the sea, knew nothing whatever of war. A great war in Europe was splendid and romantic—it was meant to be over by Christmas, and some who passionately wanted to prove themselves as soldiers feared they might not have time to join in. Looking back on the agony and blood-stained mud of Flanders it seems inconceivable that anyone could have welcomed war, but the nation as a whole was excited by it, and Rupert Brooke could write

> Now, God be thanked Who has matched us with His hour,
> And caught our youth, and wakened us from sleeping,
> With hand made sure, clear eye, and sharpened power,
> To turn as swimmers into cleanness leaping. . . .

Tilman, in his seventeenth year, was determined to leave school as soon as possible to join the Army. He was good at maths and physics, and the right thing seemed to be to try for a commission in the Gunners. He sat the exam for cadetships at the Royal Military Academy at Woolwich in November 1914, and passed in 55th out of 111 candidates —a position respectable enough, if scarcely distinguished. (The Royal Military Academy at Woolwich, known to the Services as "The Shop", was established to give specialised training to officers for the Royal Artillery and the Royal Engineers. After the Second World War it was amalgamated with the Royal Military College at Sandhurst.)

If the British in 1914 were partly intoxicated with the idea of war as a great national cleansing they also underwent a period of national madness concerning German spies. Anyone with a German or even German-sounding name was suspect, and much injustice was done to individuals. Language teachers were naturally in the front line as victims, and a master at Berkhamsted school was among the sufferers. In his last term at school Tilman wrote home:

You know I was talking about Dr —— in the hols, one of our

language masters. Well, the little squit was arrested. Charles [the headmaster, Charles Greene] like an idiot baled [*sic*] him out for £100 and he is now put under the five mile limit. We have got a new man in his place. He will probably be arrested again and sent to a concentration camp.

(The "five mile limit" imposed under the Defence Regulations was a requirement that an alien should not travel more than five miles from his place of residence without permission from the police.)

Before leaving school, Tilman wrote cheerfully of his promotion to corporal in the Officers' Training Corps: "By the way, before I forget, the victory of the Allies is assured—Captain Hopkins with marvellous discernment has given me command of a section in No 1 Platoon. Vive Hoppy! Vive Corporal Tilman!"

The new term at Woolwich began in January. There were no uniforms available for the first term men, known as "Snookers". On 17 January 1915 Tilman wrote home:

I arrived here about 4.30 last night. The station you go to is Woolwich Arsenal and you have to get an old cab to go up to the Academy. . . .

I am of course amongst the "Snookers" and the Senior and Second Term men keep us in our places. We are not allowed to put our hands in our pockets, or leave our coats unbuttoned, or turn any coat collar up. You have to be awfully smart on parade. There is a parade before each meal close to the gun park, and at the luncheon parade the blighter literally crawls round you inspecting you, and the least speck of dust on your clothes, or an unshorn face, and you parade next morning as a defaulter.

While drilling in mufti as the "Snookers" are, there are other regulations to be observed; trousers must not be turned up at the bottom and bowlers must be worn if you go outside, and also gloves.

The Church of England men go to our own chapel on Church parade. The Presbys, about ten, fall in and are marched down to the town as a squad in order to get to church. Reveille is at 6.15 except Sundays, when breakfast is at 9. Lights Out is at ten.

As far as I can make out the training consists of the following: squad drill and signalling, FA (field artillery) training, riding, sword drill, French, workshops (forge, etc) tactics and administration, gym, map-reading and various lectures.

I am told that it is absolutely essential to have a trouser press, especially when we get uniform. Could you send mine along somehow? Will you also go through the pockets of my black waistcoat and send me the stamp book?

I can get down into Woolwich pretty nearly every day at off times. The bike will be very useful for this, as it's a long way. It is not much of a town as it is pretty nearly all barracks.

The grub is excellent. For breakfast this morning we had bacon and kidneys, tea or coffee, brown or white toast, marmalade and jam. For lunch roast beef, Yorkshire pudding, roast potatoes, cauliflower, plum pudding, sauce, cheese. Drinks were beer or ginger beer. For dinner we have several courses—the number you get depends on what servant you have, sometimes you can get five.

Tilman, having gone to Woolwich with a cadetship secured by competitive examination, was training for a Regular Army commission. He worked with a schoolboy's enthusiasm, and had a schoolboy's attitude to anyone outside his own House. On 6 March 1915 he commented scathingly on a batch of "Kitchener's Army" officers sent to Woolwich on a course:

The young officers, or "Wetters" as we call 'em, are some of our newly commissioned brethren in "Kitchener's Army". As they have probably never seen a gun in their lives before or never moved faster than a crawl, they have been sent here for a six weeks' course to give them a faint glimmering of their duties and to make them tolerably smart. To watch them doing gun drill is simply priceless. The Sergeant-Instructor was telling us that to get in a battery with some of them (as we shall probably have to) would be as good as suicide. However, six weeks at "The Shop" may wake them up.

In the same letter he described equipping himself with binoculars:

We have had our field glasses ordered so that they will be ready when we pass out. Ross, the Army opticians, are the makers. There were two kinds, one £5 7s 6d, the other £6 1s 10d, the only difference being that the latter had simultaneous adjustment for the

2

eye-pieces. The magnification is 6. I got the cheaper, with graticules, which is 15s extra. It is absolutely necessary for RA officers.

By April he was a "Second Termer", and wrote: "One batch of 'Snookers' arrived on Thursday. It gave us 'Second Termers' immense pleasure to watch them arriving, looking very much at sea."

All guns in the Royal Artillery then were pulled by horses, and riding and learning to look after horses was an important part of the training at Woolwich. Tilman rode every day except Saturdays, doing his best (he told his parents) "to attain to such mystic virtues as 'good hands', 'independent seat', etc." The riding instructors were not always polite to the young gentlemen cadets. "One of the riding men called us the Royal Flying Corps Balloon Section," he observed ruefully. At the end of April he was ordering spurs, and proudly recorded that his intake were starting their "Third Term" work a month earlier than the previous lot. Things did not always go his own way, and in May he was punished for untidiness on parade. "I hadn't brushed my tunic properly and was naturally jumped on," he told his parents frankly.

Kit required much attention. As well as spurs and field glasses he had to acquire a revolver, a sword, and field boots, puttee leggings, Service dress, riding trousers and the type of overcoat known as a British Warm. The Army gave him an allowance of £50 towards the cost of all this. He made the grant cover most of it, though he was a bit concerned about the cost of swords. "I don't know the exact price of the swords we get," he wrote. "£4 10s is about the average price for a sword, but as we get 'em sort of wholesale I should think they would be considerably cheaper."

The independence and self-sufficiency manifest throughout his life was as strong in him as a cadet at Woolwich as it was later—he was determined to manage on his pay and allowances. Although his father was by then a wealthy man, the young Tilman asked little from him. His letters from Woolwich are full of estimates about the cost of things he needed, but that is because making ends meet interested him, and he knew would interest his father—he was not expecting his father to pay for them. Only rarely in his letters home is there a request for a subsidy, and then it seems almost an afterthought. To a letter of 23 May 1915 he adds, "PS. Could Pater please send me another £1 when he writes?"

Observations commonplace in the letters of 1915 are sharp reminders of how the world then differed from that of the later twentieth century. A junior officer did not just buy a pair of boots—they were made for him. Tilman reported being measured for his field boots and leggings, adding that he was also measured for a pair of brown brogues. Anxious perhaps to make clear that the shoes were not an extravagance, he explained, "You have to have these last to mess in, as we don't wear mess kit nowadays."

On 6 June 1915 he described one of the first Zeppelin raids on London:

> Great doings here last week. About midnight last Friday a sort of young aerial battle was heard in progress, and some even went so far as to say they heard the buzzing of the gentle Zepp. At any rate they were tooling all round here, and at Gravesend they did a fair amount of damage to docks and things. All work at the Arsenal was suspended for about two hours so as not to give the show away. We live in stirring times.

On 28 July Tilman was commissioned as a second lieutenant in the Royal Field Artillery.

Soldiers were not supposed to be sent to the front before the age of 18, and Tilman, at $17\frac{1}{2}$, was posted to 2A Reserve Brigade RA at Fulwood Barracks, Preston. He was still in a mood of schoolboy exultation at being at last a real soldier and he was chafing to be off to France, but he accepted the delay as inevitable. And Preston was not a bad posting, for it brought him much nearer to his home at Wallasey.

1915 was not a good year for the Allies in the war against Germany. It saw the failure of the Anglo-French offensive on the Western Front. The British broke through the German line at Loos, but reinforcements were slow in coming up, and when the Germans counter-attacked the British had to fall back. The Germans were effectively dug in from the Rhine to the Belgian coast, and if the line was sometimes dented here and there the Allies failed to make any material progress. There were appalling casualties for no apparent purpose, and a new horror was brought to warfare when the Germans first used poison gas at Ypres. There was disaster on the Eastern Front when the Germans overran

Poland and forced the Russians to retreat, losing something like a million casualties and prisoners. The British campaign at the Dardanelles and Gallipoli was another costly failure.

The shortage of shells for the guns provoked outrage—and brought Lloyd George to the Ministry of Munitions, with far-reaching political results later. There was a coalition government at home, and the military high command was placed in the hands of General Haig and General Robertson. Bickering by politicians and generals symptomised a deep-seated malaise in the conduct of the war. The ghastly casualty lists of 1916–18 were still to come, but many thousands of homes were suffering loss.

The trouble was that although *at* war Great Britain as a nation was scarcely yet *in* the war. Although George V had been on the throne for five years the golden Edwardian autumn lingered in people's minds and social habits. The Army, regular soldiers and newly-enlisted men alike, was still composed entirely of volunteers—conscription in Britain did not come until 1916. Income tax was still 3s 6d in the pound. Patriotic response to the appeal for recruits brought thousands of skilled men into the Army, and in the factories there was no one to replace them. Trade unions resisted the dilution of labour (permitting unskilled men to be trained for craftsmen's jobs) and the women who flocked into factories, fields and offices later had not yet shown that they could do what had been traditionally regarded as men's jobs. The malaise of 1915 is well summarised by A. J. P. Taylor in his *English History 1914–45*:

> The war still seemed a long way off: something "over there", as symbolised by the leave trains departing each night from Victoria Station. At home, life rolled on almost unaffected. There was plenty of food, and, indeed, of everything else. Statesmen still appeared in top hats. Business men rarely lapsed into bowlers. Some standards were slightly relaxed. Short black jackets took the place of tail coats for evening dress. Some men wore unstarched collars at the weekend. Maidservants, instead of footmen, handed round the sandwiches at afternoon tea and were to be seen even in west end clubs.

But Second-Lieutenant Tilman, hugely proud of his Regular Commission, was still in his Rupert Brooke mood, longing to be off to the front. The "life as usual" aspect of Britain in 1915 is evident in his letters. He continued to be concerned with kit and in October was delighted to acquire a prismatic compass for £2 10s—"I didn't think it worth while paying £5 for the oil-balanced sort." The payment of an Army ration allowance of £5 put his financial affairs "on a sound basis once more", and he celebrated by buying "a most awfully natty cane". That letter (3 October 1915) continued: "I must come home and let you see it before I lose it. Alec* will be relieved to hear that I've invested in a new pair of gloves." He wanted his golf-clubs sent to him, and gently reproved his mother for addressing his unit as "Reserve Battalion": "We're 2A Reserve *Brigade*, not Reserve *Battalion*. Only the infantry have Battalions."

The sad need for replacing subalterns in France was growing, and in November Tilman suddenly had hopes of being sent out, although he was under age. His father was asked to postpone sending the golf-clubs, and a letter home on 9 November 1915 went on:

Our names (three under-age Shop fellows and some others) have been sent up to the War Office with a view to attending a course of instruction in France. Quelle stroke!! It will be tophole if we are accepted, but the objection is that the Colonel has also sent our ages. Gott strafe the Colonel! With luck, however, they may take us, we are living in hopes.

Those hopes, however, were dashed. On 18 November he wrote home: "This afternoon a WO wire came instructing three fellows to proceed overseas for instruction, but not a word about us three Shop fellows, so that's a wash out. We are frightfully sick with life. PS. Will you send my golfing kit off at once?"

At the end of November he was given the job of taking a draft of forty horses to a big remount camp at Ayr. In a letter on 28 November he described the journey:

We left [by train from Preston] at a quarter to five (three hours late). Watered and fed at Carlisle at midnight. It was bitterly cold. The horses' noses froze into the bucket, an icebreaker was requisitioned to get them out. We arrived at Ayr 9 o'clock next morning. We spent most of the journey in the brake van and railwaymen's refreshment taverns, as there was no heat in the carriages. A

* Alec Reid Moir, who later married Tilman's sister Adeline.

staff captain gave me breakfast at his house, very decent of him. His wife was there.

The golf-clubs came in handy, for apart from odd jobs like conducting drafts of horses or recruits there wasn't much to do. He went to Manchester to collect a party of volunteers and was irritated by the number of men who, invited to express a preference for some particular arm of the Service, elected what he called "departmental" jobs, such as the Army Service Corps, Army Veterinary Corps and Postal Section. But already he was getting to know the Army, and in a letter home (19 December) added the comment, "However, only about one in five thousand will get what they asked for—they'll be shoved into artillery, cavalry and infantry."

He had Christmas leave from 23–29 December and on getting back to Preston after Christmas he was put in charge of a draft of 250 men to be taken to 6A Reserve Brigade in Glasgow. Writing to his sister Adeline on 9 January 1916 he described their arrival: "We got in at 10 o'clock on Saturday night. The population of Glasgow lined the streets. . . . The Maryhill Barracks are about three miles from the station, right through the main streets. Strange to say I lost no one on the way."

In mid-January he got another weekend leave and went home to Wallasey. That leave was never finished. Just before 8 o'clock on the Saturday evening (15 January) a telegram was delivered to Second-Lieutenant Tilman at home. It was from his Commanding Officer at Preston, and read, "Return here at once for the front." He was still one month short of his 18th birthday. The crying need to replace casualties in France inhibited any over-conscientious study of the calendar at the War Office.

II

1916

TILMAN'S SERVICE AT the front in 1916 was dominated by the great Allied offensive on the Somme, first by preparations for it, then by the battle.

He travelled to London from Preston on the Sunday that was supposed to have been part of his weekend leave, spent the night at the Euston Hotel, and had Monday morning to himself for shopping. He caught an afternoon train to Southampton and at 10 o'clock that night embarked for Le Havre. He was posted to No 2 General Base Depot at Harfleur, to await allotment to a unit. On 18 January 1916 he wrote home:

> Bit of a swell crossing—I made a strategic retreat, but was not actually ill. . . . We're in canvas and wood huts here. We tossed for beds, I got the floor, however. We old campaigners—a fire, a few rugs and cushions, and a roof, and we don't worry! I'll write again when I get posted to a battery.

After four days he was posted to B Battery, 161st Brigade, Royal Field Artillery, moving up the line to his unit on 22 January.

The 161st Brigade was attached to the 32nd Division, holding a line to the south of the British sector in France. The Brigade was very much a part of "Kitchener's Army", having been raised as a direct result of his appeal for volunteers. Towns and country districts were invited to form "Pals' Battalions", in which friends and neighbours could serve together. Recruiting went so well that soon there were not enough potential units of other arms to support the new infantry, and early in 1915 the War Office asked all Lord Mayors of cities and Mayors of boroughs to help to recruit special Artillery and Engineers units to supplement the Pals' Battalions. The 161st Brigade was a Yorkshire formation, two of its four batteries having been raised at York, one at Scarborough, and the other at Wakefield. Throughout the battle of the Somme Tilman fought with C Battery, known as the "Scarborough Pals' Battery". Whatever his feelings as a young Regular cadet about "Kitchener's Army" he rapidly developed affection and respect for the men who formed it. The British Army on the Somme was still almost wholly an Army of volunteers—there had not yet been time for many of the conscripts of 1916 to be trained to join it. The British Regular Army then policed much of the world, and without its spare-time Territorial soldiers and the volunteers who flocked to join them it would not have been able to fight as it did in France. It was an Army of amateur enthusiasms and amateur keenness not to let down the professionals. It was partly this keenness that produced the dreadful casualty lists—men simply rushed into danger. Young officers, eager to set an example to their men, were particularly prone to ignore personal risks and the rate of casualties among officers at times was pro-portionately six times as high as that for other ranks.

The 161st Brigade RFA was commanded by Lieutenant-Colonel A. S. Cotton, DSC. The brigade had not been long in France when Tilman joined it, having arrived at Le Havre at the end of December 1915. It was first sent to Bresle, north-east of Amiens, and then moved a little farther north-east to the neighbourhood of Albert, on what was then a fairly quiet section of the front.

Throughout the First World War the motive power for all the Royal Artillery's guns was the horse. The Royal Field Artillery was armed with the 18-pounder quick-firing gun and the 4·5 inch howitzer. Both weapons were drawn by teams of six horses and RFA units were expected to be able to move their guns at the pace of marching infantry. The Royal Horse Artillery, to which Tilman was later transferred, provided artillery support for the faster-moving cavalry. For greater mobility the RHA was equipped with the lighter 13-pounder gun, which was also drawn by a team of six horses. Wagon lines, where the horses were rested and groomed, were vital to the life of the artillery, serving each unit as a sort of temporary depot from which guns were deployed to the batteries using them.

Tilman's posting to B Battery lasted for some eight weeks (though he was away for part of the time on a course). The battery occupied a position in a side valley of the River Ancre, and Tilman wrote home on 26 January 1916:

Here we are at last, writing by the light of the bursting shells, we don't think! We are down on the extreme south of the line. It's moderately quiet, I mean compared with Ypres or La Bassée. The shelling moderately continuous all day, with occasional bits of rifle fire and machine guns. We're in action behind a low crest, and are at present busy providing the [gun] emplacements with cover. To me the position seems hopelessly obvious, but they say our own planes can't spot it, and at any rate the Germans have not found it yet. All the dugouts are in a shallow ravine about 50 yards to the left. We're jolly comfortable and live more or less like lords. Bullets which just miss our first-line parapet come over the crest and down the ravine, otherwise it's very jolly.

This morning I went round the trenches with the Battery Commander, an awfully decent Captain. You'll be glad to hear we used the periscope instead of our own eyes in most cases. Most of the trenches are very decent, in others the mud just reaches the top of your puttees. Those are about the worst.

This afternoon we did our daily hate, loosing off our allowance of 28 rounds, HE [heavy explosives] and shrapnel. We were going for a farm behind their lines—infantry HQ, we thought. I forgot to tell you—this morning I watched one of our planes brought down fairly near by shrapnel. I believe either the pilot or observer were hit.

There is one man from Berkhamsted in our Battery, and Gamble, a man I knew at Berkhamsted, is in our infantry brigade, doing great stunts with a Lewis machine gun.

The letters are almost all written in pencil, often no doubt under difficulties, and the writing—sometimes hard to read over 60 years—occasionally shows signs of strain. But Tilman was never anything but perky and cheerful, still seeing war as a great adventure—or at least persuading his parents that that was how he saw it. Most of the letters are to his parents, but some are to his sister Adeline. Being on active service and subject to field censorship none of the letters from the front has an address other than BEF or sometimes simply "France". His location on the front at different times has been worked out by relating the dated letters to the *History of the Scarborough Pals' Battery*, by Sidney Foord and Thomas Northern, and to the *War Diary of the 161st Brigade*.

On 4 February Tilman wrote from the north of Albert that things had "livened up considerably" and described their first gas alarm. He

2*

ended his letter, "By the way, a few things I should like very much if you could send them: *The Bystander* (when you've finished with it—other fellows in the Mess get *The Sphere* and *Tatler*) and in the way of occasional eatables, chocolate, a cake, Patum Peperium, those little soft Dutch cheeses I used to get. Candles we get over here." One of the remarkable things about the First World War (to anyone who served in the Second) was the efficiency of the post.

In that first week of February 1916 Tilman was involved in a night attack. In a letter on 11 February he described this:

At about 11 pip emma we rose to join in a party started by the Hun. This lasted for about an hour. We have not heard definitely what the row was, but believe it was a cutting-out raid made just on the left of our sector. He fires on a fairly long front on our front line for about an hour, then on a front of about 100 yards, lifts on to the second line, and a party of about 20 men then crawl over into our front line, do what they can, and then nip back again.

We lost our best sergeant the other day, up at the OP [Observation Post]. A whizz-bang came through the window as he was looking out. It's always the way—the best fellows get done in, the rotters escape.

On 14 February he celebrated his eighteenth birthday with a party in his dugout and a bottle of champagne. His celebrations included a trip to a nearby village to get a bath. Writing to his sister, he explained, "It's a village that gets strafed fairly often. One time the bathers had to retire to the cellars in nature's garb. Needless to say I didn't linger over mine, but it's awfully good to be able to get one at all."

The work of a gunner subaltern often involved close liaison duty with the infantry battalion their battery was in position to support, to relay requests for the shelling of a farm building or other fortified strongpoint, and to let the guns know what the infantry was doing, so that a barrage could be lifted over them. It was dangerous work, for it meant living in the forward trenches, and going out with a field telephone to a Forward Observation Post. A good deal of this work came Tilman's way, and he wrote home:

I have just returned from another tour of liaison duty. I was glad to get back to the battery, as the trenches have become pretty rotten lately, and the wind, rain etc, have half filled them, and made them fall in in parts.

Our Colonel is a bit of a lad. At the beginning, when he was a Major in charge of a battery he got a name for killing off his subalterns. He was fitted out with a new lot of subs several times over. He himself is a DSO, and never been hit. At present he leaps about on the parapet, stands up at the Observation Post (he doesn't spend the day there—you do that) runs guns into the open and beats the gong. When you go round the trenches with him you feel like that worn out knight's charger in *Punch*—"I wonder what the —— fool's going to do next?" We were all horribly bucked when a man told us (probably a lie) that when the Colonel was going through the wood one day a whizzbang burst near—and down went the old boy, flat as a pancake. Previous to this he had given us the impression that he never even ducked to one.

It was bitterly cold with deep snowdrifts and he was thankful when the battery was withdrawn for a rest. Although he had to spend it on another course, there were compensations, including a night out in Amiens—"The Hotel de l'Univers do you awfully well. Sheets and baths and a six-course dinner were almost too good to be true."

By the end of February he was back in action again and in the middle of March was transferred to C Battery of the 161st. Geographically the move was not far, but C Battery covered a different sector of the front slightly to the north, and supported a different battalion of infantry. On the whole Tilman liked the change. He wrote home on 19 March, "The messing is much better, and if not on duty we play bridge at night till about 11.30, sometimes later. Would Mater like to join us for a weekend?"

On 27 March he was wounded and taken to a field hospital a few miles behind the line. He wrote home next day:

I was very slightly hit with a bit of a rifle grenade yesterday, it's only a flesh wound in the thigh, and I hope to be back in the line in a few days' time. I was going along the front line yesterday where it has all been bashed in, no proper trench left. They evidently saw or heard us, and sent over a rifle grenade, which burst about five yards away, getting me, but missing the Machine Gun Officer of the Inniskillings, who was with me. I got here last night, and am having a very jolly time. Pity it wasn't bad enough for a Blighty case.

The wound was rather more serious than he implied, and he was transferred from the field hospital to a casualty clearing station at Villers Bocage, near Amiens. On 31 March he wrote to his parents:

It will take a bit longer than I expected, but I don't think I shall have to go down to the Base—I hope not, I hope not sincerely. I'll probably be able to get back to duty some time next week. Meanwhile, I'm having a first class time, having a most glorious slack. Besides, there are some awfully decent Sisters down here, and that makes a lot of difference. The other place I was in, farther up, had nothing but orderlies, very efficient and all that, but not quite the same thing.

It's perfectly heavenly to look through the window and see troops on their way up to the line. There they go, the brave boys—How I wish I was with them! . . . By the way, en passant, will you tell Alec we have seen five battalions go past, and out of the whole lot I think three officers were marching, the rest were riding. And yet they call themselves "the poor old footslogging infantry!" Will you ask Alec for his reasons in writing?*

He was worried that his parents might have seen his name in a casualty list before getting his letter telling them that his wound was only slight. His fears were justified—they had a telegram from the War Office reporting that their son had been wounded, and were frantically worried until his letter reached them. Concern, however, was offset a little by the splendour of getting a lift back to his battery in a Staff car—motor cars were fairly rare in the Army in those days, and normally used only by senior officers.

Tilman was back at the front on 8 April 1916, in time to take part in the great Allied offensive on the Somme.

Most military historians now agree that this attack achieved nothing except slaughter, and that few strategic gains could have been made even if it had ended in victory for the Allies. The region was peculiarly unsuited for an offensive: the Germans were well dug in on a ridge

* Captain Alec Reid Moir, Adeline Tilman's fiancé, was now a staff officer.

44

overlooking the river valley, and the Allies had to attack uphill. The standard military thinking of the time held that a war was to be won by attack; the opposing line should be broken, and then cavalry could be sent charging through the breach to "roll up" the enemy. These tactics had succeeded in the nineteenth century, but took no account of the fundamental changes in the technology of battle such as the vastly increased firepower of artillery, the devastating effects of high explosive, and the fact that a machine gun can enable a single well-protected infantryman to hold up an entire company. High explosive helped the defence as well as the attack—it might blast in some enemy trench, but it left huge craters which provided machine-gunners with shelters almost as good as trenches. And shells so tore up no-man's-land between attackers and defenders that it became extremely hard for troops to advance at all, and virtually impossible for cavalry to charge.

Second-Lieutenant Tilman would not have been thinking much about grand strategy as he returned to C Battery of the 161st after his spell in hospital at Villers Bocage—he is likely to have been more concerned about whether he would find a parcel from home. He did, and it contained a good supply of his favourite cheese, some of which he generously sent over to his old Mess at B Battery. Tilman's new unit—C Battery—was stationed in dugouts near a small lake by the village of Aveluy, a little over a mile from the outskirts of Albert. As the weather improved with spring, living conditions got better, and there was the prospect of swimming in Aveluy Lake. Albert was considered a good billet, although the town had been severely damaged by shellfire. In a way, perhaps, it was too good a billet, for things seem to have become rather slack, and one of Tilman's first jobs on return from hospital was to take over the wagon lines for a fortnight to try to improve discipline. He wrote home on 24 April:

Things seem to want gingering up very considerably here. I came down in place of a man gone on leave, and the first day three brasshats came round. They had a whole heap to say—I had nuffin', and at the end of a gruelling half-hour I had the air of one who has been caught in the machinery. In consequence I have sworn death and destruction to the NCOs and other ranks abiding at the wagon lines. I've got a priceless billet—feather bed, curtains, pictures, ornaments, and in the Mess on the same floor grub, drinks, cigarettes and Decca gramophone.

He worked hard at cleaning up the stables, and on 29 April wrote:

The gingering up process pursues its relentless course. After about the first day I was heartily loathed. Shaving for Early Stables at 6 a.m. was not at all popular, but as there is not much active service about just at present, one or two peace rules can be introduced with advantage. The tendency is to get awful slack with regard to some things out here. It's jolly hard to keep discipline up to scratch— I think the Guards Regiments are about the only ones who've succeeded.

Life has been considerably brightened by several encounters with the jolly old Town Major. I try and cadge old iron off him for making hoof picks—he warns me of the penalties of looting. I try and cadge old bricks for repairing standings—he strafes my pirates for pulling walls down while obtaining same. I retaliate by pinching a civilian cart; the town is roused, and to the accompaniment of blood-curdling threats the cart is restored to its owner. This sort of thing is great mental relaxation to both the TM and myself, and passes the time pleasantly enough. Meanwhile, the war goes on.

PS. Will you send my old stiff hat, the one with the badge? I might as well wear it out here.

In May he got some leave, and after a visit home he called at his old school at Berkhamsted. He was disappointed to find few of the masters he remembered—they had all joined up. By the end of May he was back at the front, finding "everything as before". There is a gap of ten days in his letters, which he explained on 8 June:

Sorry I've been such a time writing, but we've been fighting battles, or rather, one battle. We had some great fun before the battle, with the open sight touch. I had two private bombardoes on an old machine-gun emplacement in the Boche front line. I don't think it did any Boche any harm as there were probably none there, but it pleased us no end. It was the first time our gunners have seen their target!

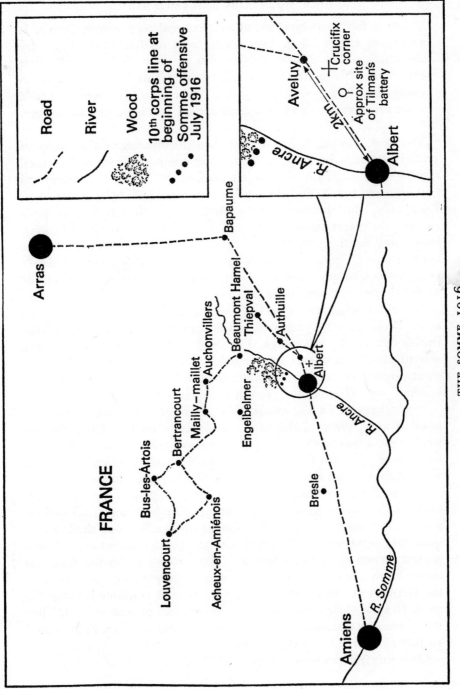

THE SOMME 1916

Just before zero hour about four colossal mines were sprung. It was most entertaining. Everything went off like clockwork, very slight casualties. Alec's division just on our right got all their objectives. It's perfectly splendid getting this jolly old ridge so easily. Our battery is bringing two Boche guns in tonight. No idea what the next item on the programme is—just have to wait and see.

The next item on the programme was the opening of a tremendous artillery barrage in preparation for the coming offensive. The shell shortage was over: Lloyd George's work at the Ministry of Munitions had achieved much, and there were huge stocks of shells at the front. Unhappily, the weather deteriorated, and although it was mid-summer there was pouring rain, and the whole front was muddy, even before any further churning up by high explosive. Pleas for puttees became more frequent—"Fox's spiral sort". Oddly, Tilman didn't seem to acquire any gum-boots until some weeks later. When at last he did they were "most awfully useful".

The 161st Brigade was part of the 32nd Division, which, with two other Divisions—the 36th and 49th—formed the Xth Corps of the British Army. The task assigned to the Corps in the coming offensive was to attack north-east in wooded country round Authuille, some eight kilometres north of Albert. Their front ran roughly from the southern edge of Authuille Wood to the River Ancre.

In preparation for the attack Tilman's battery was moved from its position near Aveluy Lake to a new location on the Albert–Aveluy road, near a wayside Crucifix. The new site was not as comfortable: there were only two dugouts for the whole battery, living conditions were cramped, and the guns were installed in ruined houses.

The preliminary bombardment that was supposed to shatter the German defences opened on the morning of 24 June and continued for a week. C Battery had already brought up nearly 7,000 shells for its guns, and night after night throughout the bombardment ammunition parties carried up more. This was a dangerous job, for the road was under heavy enemy fire, and darkness gave only minor relief, for once the German gunners had the range they could continue shelling the road. In spite of this, the guns were never short of ammunition. They were in action continuously day and night, and between 24 June and 16 July 1916 fired some 16,000 rounds.

On 6 July Tilman wrote home:

From the 24th [June] to the 1st was a pretty strenuous week for the gunners, and from the 1st onwards for everybody. During the seven days, besides continuous bombardment night and day, we let loose various kinds of frightfulness on the unfortunate Allimand (pronounced *Alleymande*) including gas and smoke, both of which I regret to say left him absolutely frigid, in fact he seems to thrive on it.

Wire cutting, the 18-pounders' job during the preliminary, is absolutely our bête noire. If you are at the OP you observe till your eyes nearly drop out of your head, if you're at the battery you fire all day till your head sings, and at the end there's nothing to show for it —no Boche killed, no trenches blown in, only, if you're lucky, a few strands cut, and a few stakes bowled over. It's no *bon*, and tends to promote profanity.

I happened to be in the OP when the infantry went over the top. You could see practically nothing for smoke.

The front line is popularly supposed to present no difficulty; such was not the case on this particular front. Our divisional infantry went back to recover a few days ago, and the artillery hope to be relieved soon.

You must know more about the whole stunt than we do—we get no papers now, and hear absolutely nothing. . . .

This is an extraordinary country. Civilians are still allowed to live in the line. Can you believe it? Next to our telephone dugout was a cottage in excellent repair, with an old woman living in it. By chance or design she happened to be away last Saturday—when she came back in the evening her jolly old house was *non est*. It had had an argument with numerous 5·9s and come off second best. Here we live in mouldy cellars, OPs [Observation Posts] are next to impossible to find, the trenches are exceeding long and winding, the weather is outrageously hot, bathing is difficult, and the battery position is a household word in Hun artillery circles. Otherwise we are all right.

PS. My balance at Cox's is really getting excessive £80 odd. This needs blowing. Shall us? LET's—when we get leave!

Sergeant Sydney Foord, MBE, MM, takes up the story in the *History of the Scarborough Pals' Battery*:

On the morning of 1 July the great attack was launched. At 4.30 am a preliminary bombardment started, and then at zero hour, 7 am, the infantry launched their attack. The 32nd Division had Thiepval as their objective, and this proved to be an invulnerable point. Standing on a high ridge it bristled with machine guns, and these took heavy toll of our attacking infantry. . . . Every attack was repelled, despite the fact that reserves were poured into the battle.

The scene at Crucifix Corner on the evening of the first day of the Somme battle was one never to be forgotten. The Crucifix itself was one of particular beauty and remained undamaged as it stood sentinel over the long road leading to Aveluy. In the shade of the Crucifix was a large open space from which trenches led to various parts of the sector. During the late afternoon and early evening of this warm summer day the walking wounded had been streaming down the communication trenches, and by sundown the stretcher cases were being brought in in ever-increasing numbers. There they were, all gathered round the Crucifix, the symbol of the supreme sacrifice. . . .

On that dreadful July day in 1916 the British Army on the Somme suffered 60,000 casualties—probably at least one-third of them killed. There were a few breathing-spaces, but the Battle of the Somme, aiming for that decisive breakthrough which never came, dragged on until November, when mud and winter combined to force a halt. Tilman fought through almost all of it.

During the night of 3 July he and his gun-crew had their first serious encounter with poison gas. They had met gas before, but in relatively slight concentrations, and mostly in the form of chlorine-derived tear-gas, which, although searing and horribly unpleasant, is seldom fatal in small quantities. The Germans had now developed a much more lethal gas shell, releasing phosgene. On that first night the battery was bombarded with the new gas-shells three times and from then on gas-shells came over night after night. Tilman described them:

The Allemand has started a new frightfulness—started shelling batteries not with lachrymatory (tear) shells, but pukka gas shells, and a new kind of gas at that. It put us back a whole heap first night, but as long as you've the old "helmet-gas" on it's as harmless as scent. Without this [gas helmet] it attacks the heart, and tends to promote sudden death.

50

Minor troubles continued in spite of everything else. He went on: "The wretched man who runs our Mess went down with 'shell shock' the other day, likewise with 200 francs belonging to the Mess. We are sadder and wiser in consequence, and have decided to get somebody immune from 'shell shock' to run the accounts."

The German defences at Thiepval remained intact, and for all the huge volume of artillery support the infantry made little progress. One problem was that barbed wire proved remarkably resistant to high explosive, and even when fences were destroyed the tangle of twisted wire left littering the ground between shell-holes was a serious obstacle to advance. The gunners had practical reason for loathing the job of wire-cutting.

On 18 July Tilman's battery—with the rest of the Division—was relieved and sent to join the reserve Army near the Belgian frontier for a short rest. They were soon in action again, but the four days' march through the French countryside was a pleasant change from the hell of the Albert–Aveluy road. The weather improved, and Tilman enjoyed the march north. On 29 July he wrote:

Our division is still resting, but I am in the line with another division for four days, preparatory to taking over. It's very quiet here after the south, and the country is horribly flat and dull, nothing but coal mines. The only thing is it's a fair-sized salient, so when there's any strafing you get it from three sides. . . . Yesterday we had the pleasure of being sniped by a 42 howitzer. There were four of us, so the Allemand has evidently plenty of ammunition.

There was time for a certain amount of parade-ground smartness, and, towards the end of August, Tilman was detached from his battery to act as a liaison officer with the infantry. "Nothing to do but walk round the line and visit the different companies. Not an unpleasant occupation, as each visit generally entails a consumption of 'Quick ones' and 'Half 'uns'. By the time you've visited the last you feel equal to capturing the Boche front line singlehanded."

In September 1916 the Divisional Artillery was reorganised to turn 4-gun batteries into 6-gun units. Several of the existing artillery brigades were consequently broken up, but Tilman's 161st brigade survived, and his battery acquired from the 168th brigade an officer and a detachment of NCOs, gunners, drivers and horses. The new arrivals somewhat watered down the strongly local links of the original Scarborough battery, but as they came mostly from around Huddersfield it remained a staunchly Yorkshire unit. Tilman had slightly mixed feelings about what he called "strongly local" units. They had advantages in comradeship and team spirit, but could become a little dull for anyone who did not come from the same home town. He doesn't discuss the reorganisation in his letters home—it would have been subject to strict censorship, because German Intelligence would have been keenly interested in any such change in the Order of Battle—but probably he welcomed it.

Tilman's references in his letters to death and wounds are laconic, in keeping with the iron self-control he exercised throughout his life. He does not enlarge on the nightmare of warfare on the Western Front—his letters lose the naïve ebullience with which he went to the front, but they never lose a schoolboyish determination to regard everything as a bit of a lark. Perhaps that is how he kept going. Letters meant a great deal to him throughout his life, and he remained exemplary in replying to them. And that First World War postal service was an immense comfort—in spite of complaints like "No mail for three days", letters and parcels got through with what now seems astonishing regularity, usually within a week. His parents and his sister were models as suppliers of parcels. Goodies in the way of food were always welcome, but he asked his people not to send bacon, Oxo or cocoa, which were available in the rations. Frequent requests in his letters home were for puttees, and brown leather bootlaces ("strong"). He smoked cigarettes then, apparently liking best the Egyptian blends of cigarette tobacco that were popular at that period. The pipe to which he became so attached for most of his life came after the war.

The Army in 1916 reflected the society of its period—there were the gentry, and the rest. Officers were gentlemen, and even the most junior subaltern was allotted his servant (sometimes called batman). To be an officer's servant was not usually resented by the soldier detailed for the job—if he did resent it he could usually get out of it. Some men rather liked the job—it might exempt them from other fatigues, and if an officer was respected his servant had a certain standing among his mates. Tilman took his servants for granted, and mentioned them only occasionally in his letters. His first servant was a Regular soldier with over ten years in the Army. When he was classified unfit for active service and sent home, Tilman wrote asking his father to send him a present of ten shillings, enclosing a cheque for the purpose. Half a sovereign was quite a useful present then, and not ungenerous for a second-lieutenant. In the middle of 1917 the man was regraded fit for active service and Tilman met him again. He would have liked to get him back as his servant, but could not contrive it.

He sacked his next servant and rather regretted it. Apparently he acted in a fit of temper—he was living in cramped quarters, the weather was bad, and he'd just heard that some leave he was hoping for had been cancelled. "I got up so early this morning and in such a vile temper that I sacked my servant before I knew what I was doing," he explained. "Easy enough to do, but difficult to replace." The sacked man's successor seems to have been more or less satisfactory, save for a habit of waking his master in the morning by punching him in the tummy.

A Naval Division fought with the Army on the Western Front, and rumour had it that the shooting of the Army's guns was improved by borrowing some Naval gun-layers for the heavy artillery. Tilman senior dared to relay this to his son, and got a stinging rebuke:

Anyone could lay a rotten heavy—it takes a Gunner to lay a field gun. The nearest the Navy has ever got is the 15 inch howitzer, manned by Royal Marine Artillery, and they're nothing to write home about. The only qualifications for a heavy gunner are a certain amount of beef, and must be able to write—the latter in order that they can write "A present for Bill" or some such rot on the mouldy shell. They always do that, they think it's funny. As they haven't the vaguest idea where the shell's going to there's a remote chance that it will fetch up somewhere at the address given—that is, of course, if they remember to loose her off somewhere in an easterly direction. The beef is required to load her. This they do with about a hundred cranes and derricks and a few thousand perspiring navvies.

After a few days out of action in mid-September they were sent back to the front, temporarily attached to another division—"so instead of being harassed by one HQ we are now chased by two," he observed. A week later things got even worse when the 161st became for a time an unattached brigade. On 7 October he wrote:

We are at present a brigade at large, wandering aimlessly on the face of the waters, at the beck and call of any old brasshat. Some old boy rings up, "Hello—send me some reinforcements will you?" The other bloke murmurs, "Certainly, General. You can have the 161st Brigade, glad to lose 'em," or words to that effect. And off we pole to some other mouldy position, which is invariably mouldier than the last. And what makes it so monstrous is the fact that we always seem to relieve some unit which is going to Paris for a month's rest, or England to refit, or the Riviera to recuperate—and they wonder why we're so rude to 'em. Also for our brigade leave has stopped. . . . It's a vile district. If you dig down you're flooded, and the Boche does not encourage you to build a young Tower of Babel, so you have to strike the happy mean. If we stay here for any time the jolly old boots-gum-thigh will be all the vogue.

On 26 September Thiepval fell, after withstanding everything the British Army could throw at it for nearly three months. Its defences were described by the Commander-in-Chief, Sir Douglas Haig, as being "as nearly impregnable as nature, art and the unstinted labour of nearly two years could make them". When finally the fortress fell the British line all but surrounded it.

The fall of Thiepval, however, put an end to his hopes for leave. He was making plans for getting home in October when his brigade was ordered south again, and leave was cancelled. The Germans had withdrawn only a few miles, and still held the important Beaumont Hamel–Auchonvillers road, a little to the north-west. The British aim was now to cut this road and the German supply lines to both sides of it, and to advance on the west bank of the River Ancre. Beaumont Hamel had been one of the objectives in the original British offensive in July, but then the attack had failed. Now there seemed a better chance of breaking through. Tilman's battery was to give artillery support to the advancing infantry.

They were back almost where they had started in July, but about 4 miles to the north-west of Albert instead of a mile or so north of the town. The guns took up position in an orchard at Engelbelmer, in the open, without gunpits. Conditions that dismal autumn were atrocious, for it rained most of the time and the ground rapidly became a sea of mud, as sticky as treacle. The wagon lines were some 6 miles away at Louvencourt, and in the wretched weather, conditions at the stables were almost as bad as at the guns. Work at the guns was made more difficult by the fact that a battery of heavy artillery, firing 60-pounders, was stationed just behind the orchard at Engelbelmer, and every time the big 60-pounders fired, C Battery's field guns suffered a sort of minor earthquake that made accurate gun-laying almost impossible. They found a new position in some old gunpits a short distance away. The pits were in bad condition, deep in mud, and much broken by shell-fire from the earlier battle.

The move to the old gunpits had one slight advantage for the battery in that they were able to find living accommodation in some ruined houses. The weather stayed vile, seriously hampering the offensive. On 8 November Tilman wrote:

> The trenches are in great form, this last rain and gale have brought the sides in, and made them impassable in places. One has to chance one's arm and go over the top to get to the OP in the support line. It's as safe as houses, really, as the Boche here is wonderfully tame. I think anybody would be after four months on and off bombardo, always expecting an attack. I think he's all for the old 30 ft dug-out, and the sight of people walking about on top leaves him cold.
>
> We were trying to do some wire-cutting this afternoon, but it was so cold and so boring that it finally degenerated into a rat hunt with a stick and a ·25 automatic. One rat killed, one wounded.

Tilman's writing—clean, spare English, with few adjectives, spiced with a slightly vinegary humour—is that of all his later books. He seems to have fashioned a style that suited him in his last years at school, and he used it throughout his life. It is not a style for heroics—he was contemptuous of heroics. In his letters from the front, as with his accounts of adventures later, you have to read between the lines to come upon the vein of courage that he displayed almost casually. There is an example in a letter written on 14 November 1916, describing the night following a day of battle:

> A magnificent beano started here yesterday, and is still in progress. The weather is holding up splendidly. The show went down well, and the prisoners are coming in in thousands.
>
> The night of the 13th the Colonel (Cotton *is* a sportsman) took out a small private party to bring wounded in. It was great fun, and we

got about 25 in during the night, which was not bad considering the distance they had to be carried. The Boche was strafing promiscuous like, but only one of our crush was hit.

During our wanderings I hit on a Boche machine gun and got old Cotton to help carry it home. About halfway back to our former front line it got so infernally heavy that we left it. As it was then about 4 am we were beginning to lose touch. However, when we got back and had had one or two quick ones we were feeling pretty well, and the Colonel was no end sick at leaving it. So today we went back for it, but nahpoo. Some blighter had got there first and snaffled it, which was not to be wondered at considering what a top-hole trophy it was. However, we collected some common or garden trophies such as Boche helmets, bayonets, etc., and then retired, and on the way back had the luck to find another wounded fellow in a shell hole. He was no end bucked, as he had been 24 hours without being spotted, and was rapidly becoming a doubter.

The Colonel, Tilman and the men with them had been scouring no-man's-land through a November night after a day of heavy fighting, carrying wounded, climbing in and out of shell-holes in the dark. The "doubter" in Tilman's last sentence is a piece of his characteristic understatement.

The tank was a British invention, though developed and exploited later by others. When the prototypes were on the drawing board they were given the code-name "Tank" to disguise their intended real use as armoured fighting vehicles. Tanks first appeared on the Western Front in September 1916. There were not many of them, and they broke down fairly frequently. Nevertheless, their tracks enabled them to crawl over shell-holes and their weight crushed barbed wire. They succeeded in penetrating the German lines in a few places, but were not followed up—no one at that time had much experience in their use. Fortunately the Germans had no more idea than the British, and seem to have regarded the first tanks as rather useless oddities. Tilman did not see his first tank until November 1916, when he wrote, "I saw a jolly old Tank on its way to their meet the other night. What a turn! They make extraordinarily little noise." A few days later he saw another: "It would make you howl with laughter to see it coming up the straight, trenches, barbed wire, etc., leave him absolutely cold."

By mid-November the great offensive of the Somme was over; it had petered out in the mud and misery of winter. From mid-July to mid-October Tilman's battery had been in the north around Bethune, but he had fought through both the opening and the closing battles of the Somme. At least on his sector of the front he had the satisfaction of advancing a few miles in the valley of the Ancre, but the Germans did not withdraw far, and Allied gains in territory were minimal. The cost can never be fully calculated: the British lost some 420,000 men in killed and wounded, the French about 200,000, the Germans something between 450,000 and 600,000—even taking the lower figures, over a million men, mainly young, were killed or maimed. Tilman had a worm's-eye view of battle—he was not a Staff officer and he had no concern with strategy; he commanded his section of Gunners, served in the trenches when he was liaison officer with the infantry, risked death from snipers or "promiscuous strafing" every time he had to make his way to a forward Observation Post. Day after day he was wet, cold and half-submerged in mud, and he had also to endure the sight of hundreds of pathetic French civilian refugees streaming from their ruined villages and farms. Somehow in his schoolboyish way he kept cheerful, saw things with a touch of humour, and above all he inspired his men.

The success, limited though it was, of the British advance on Tilman's sector of the front led temporarily to even worse conditions for the long-suffering C Battery. On 25 November they moved forward to Mailly-Maillet north of the Beaumont Hamel–Auchonvillers road, where they took over the guns of a Territorial battery. Conditions there were worse—if possible—than almost anything they had met previously. The guns were in water in places a foot deep, and only three of them could be fired. And since water filled the pits in which the shells were stacked, firing off anything was a doubtful operation. Temporary relief, however, was near. On 5 December the battery was taken out of action and withdrawn for a rest to St Ouen, near Pontoise to the north-west of Paris.

Tilman got his long-postponed leave, had a few days at home, and a fine supper at the Savoy in London on his way back to France—"starting with oysters". He returned to his unit, and wrote, on 29 December:

We had a great Christmas, and the men a better. We gave them a huge blow-out, more power to them.

We're having a splendid time, although it's a bit wet, and muddy in the horse lines. Plenty of football and boxing for the men. We got into the final in the former, got a draw, but were beaten two-nil on the replay. . . . We're going into the line again on the 1st, in the same place as we left. Nothing like starting the New Year well.

PS. An air cushion would go down excellently as a football if it failed as a pillow.

III

1917–18

SECRET. From Lieutenant-Colonel commanding A Group RFA of 161 Bde RFA to Officer Commanding 22 Btn Manchester Regiment and 22 Bde RFA. 2/Lt Tilman of A Group RFA has been instructed to report to Btn. Headquarters at Stewart Work at Zero Time Z Day with 2 telephonists and 2 runners. This officer has been instructed to select OPs in MUNICH TRENCH after it is captured and consolidated. He is to work in conjunction with a similar FOO [Forward Observation Officer] detailed by 22 Bde RFA.

THIS FLIMSY SCRAP of paper surviving from 9 January 1917 put Tilman in hospital for three months and secured him an immediate award of the Military Cross.

Much misery had been endured by Tilman and his battery before the wound which put him out of action. On New Year's Day 1917 they left their (relatively) comfortable Christmas quarters for their old position to the left of Mailly-Maillet on the Auchonvillers Front. The wagon lines were at Acheux-en-Amiénois, about four miles to the west, but heavy snow made conditions there so appalling that the horses had to be moved north to Bus-les-Artois, where the men had the luxury of Nissen huts and the horses temporary stables of canvas on a timber frame. At the guns conditions for the gunners were worse than those for the horses in their canvas shelter.

An attack was being planned on a strongly defended trench held by a Bavarian unit, code-named by the British MUNICH TRENCH. The attack was to be made by the Manchesters of the 91st Infantry Brigade. Tilman's job of going forward with the infantry at least made a change from working the guns in frozen snow.

At 6 a.m. on 11 January the Manchesters went over the top. The guns from Tilman's battery which had been pounding the German trench lifted as the infantry advanced. The trench was taken, and Tilman with his little party of telephonists and runners went forward to select an observation post and lay wire for the field telephone. The *War Diary of 161 Brigade RFA* records events tersely: "2/Lt H W Tilman C/161 went forward to the captured position to lay a telephone line and was wounded. He, however, continued with his work until communications were established. For this service he was awarded the MC."

He was severely wounded this time, and had to be carried back by his men. He was taken first to a field dressing station, then to a casualty clearing station farther back, and from there to a base hospital at Le Touquet. On 18 January he was evacuated to Somerville College, Oxford, which had been partly turned into a hospital for wounded soldiers. He couldn't walk, but he could still write cheerfully, and on 21 January he wrote home:

Owing to a number of movements have not heard from you now since I left the battery, so am somewhat out of touch. I hope things have been OK and you've had no alarms. . . .

We had a splendid crossing yesterday, quite calm, although it took the best part of twelve hours. We got in about 5 pm. I think I ate more that day than I've ever eaten on any other boat, it was so jolly comfortable.

I've had the luck to get quite a lot of kit over, and am writing for the rest. If you were thinking of coming down, I shouldn't just yet, it's hardly worth it. I shall probably be up in a few days. After I've been here a bit I'll be able to let you know how things are. So just sit tight and have as easy and comfortable a time as I'm having.

Two days later he was still making light of his wound, expecting to be "up and about early next week", and looking forward to being discharged. He asked for some slacks to be sent him to be ready for getting up, and a couple of books, *Animal Management* and *Field Artillery Training*. But his condition was more serious than he tried to pretend, and on 27 January he wrote:

I'll just explain why I'm not up, a sort of history of the case, you know, not too technical, although I'm getting a bit of a high flyer at medical terms. Soon after I got here they took the stitches out of the wound (pronounced properly, please*) which had healed.

* Like the past tense of "wind", then an in-word at the front.

Unfortunately there was a whacking great blood clot inside, dying to get out, so the wound burst open again. Since when they've been busy getting the blood out, which is now nearly finished, when I hope it will begin to heal. Only for this I would be up by now. Apparently the Le Touquet people, not too cleverly, sewed it up so close and tight that absolutely nothing could get out.

No need for parcels, fruit, etc.

On the same day he wrote to his sister, thanking her for a letter written just after she had heard that he was wounded and forwarded from France. She had written hopefully, "Is there the foggiest, vaguest chance of Blighty? I bet you will have a try." To this he responded:

Monstrous! I shudder to think of Cotton's remarks should he see it! May I hasten to remove the impression that seems to exist that I'm a confirmed and highly successful wangler? To a man with a highly developed sense of duty, like myself, to have to leave France was a wrench that time alone can heal! M'm. . . . Yes, I think so.

Although he had been given an immediate award of the Military Cross he did not know about it until the end of January, when he had a note conveying the Brigade Commander's congratulations, and he didn't hear officially until February, when he wrote to his parents:

Isn't it great about the jolly old MC! I had no more idea than you had that I was for it, as of course I poled off straight away. I suppose it's for the FOO stunt on the 11th, though I don't quite see why. What pleases me is that it is an immediate award by the Corps Commander, and not given out as a divisional allotment like a good many are.

His parents gave him a watch (with a guard) as a congratulatory present, and the whole family subscribed to give him a silver cigarette case. Thanking them, he wrote of the watch, "The guard is most effective, so effective in fact that only with great difficulty can one discern the time. However, I've taken it off now, and will keep it for use on service, when it will do splendidly."

He was promoted from a wheelchair to crutches, which he could manage satisfactorily "after a short course". He wrote to his father about the investment of £60 accumulated in his bank account from his pay, and finally decided to put it into War Loan. In the middle of March he was discharged from hospital and allowed to go home. Three weeks later he was back at the RFA depot in Preston, awaiting a medical board, before which he appeared on 14 April, and, as he put it, "had no difficulty in wangling GS"—i.e. being passed for General Service.

He got some leave and attended the Investiture for the conferment of his Military Cross, and on 30 April was back in Preston for posting. On 15 May 1917 he was again at the base depot in Le Havre, on his way to rejoin his old unit. On 23 May he wrote to his parents:

After five days' travelling, once more in my home from home. I very nearly got hung up in a rest camp with the draft till someone was ready to receive them, but a combination of circumstances and subterfuge enabled me to get rid of them. Next afternoon sailing through a station I saw our division entraining. We managed to stop the train by waving sticks at the engine driver, so I got out, caught a train going the other way, and found my battery just commencing to entrain at the next station.

We left about ten that night and arrived up north about nine in the morning. After a march of about 10 miles we got to our wagon lines, quite decent, and under canvas, about five miles from the line. The battery is going up into action in a day or two. Even Cotton deigns to call it "Perilous! Perilous!" so it ought to be fairly fruity.

The battery has changed very much, only the Major remains. Of the rest of the old firm, two wounded, two sick, and one promoted. The Brigade also has changed considerably. They had stirring times in the advance, at one time a section was wired-in in front of the line of resistance, only outposts in front.

PS. An occasional parcel would not be amiss, please. What about the soap?

1917 was another grim year for the Allies. True, in April the United States entered the war against Germany but although American strength offered long-term hope to the Allied cause, the immediate effect was a new demand on the British and French for military supplies to equip American troops. And America's coming into the war was balanced—to many it seemed over-balanced—by the Russian revolution and the collapse of the Eastern Front. The Battle of the Somme had left the British Army unbroken, but not unchanged. The last vestige of the Rupert Brooke attitude to the war was gone, replaced by a dour determination to hang on, by distrust of generals who seemed able to think of nothing but sending yet more men to pointless slaughter, but redeemed by a wonderful sense of comradeship among the junior officers and other ranks who had to do the fighting. Unlike the Second World War, in which the British Army could feel that it was fighting to destroy the bestialities of Nazism, soldiers in the First World War were given no clear aims—except to win. Since victory in a battle amounted all too often to no more than gaining a few yards of blood-stained mud it looked as if the hell of trench warfare would go on for ever.

While Tilman was in hospital in England there was a renewed French offensive on the Aisne. The 161st Brigade was detailed to provide artillery support and Tilman's old C Battery moved towards St Quentin, some 50 miles east of Amiens, to take over a position from the French. The *History of C Battery* describes it as "one of the best-equipped positions we had yet been in, with well-constructed and spacious gun pits, and living and sleeping accommodation alongside. Accustomed as we were to rely on candles it was luxury indeed to have electricity throughout, and enough fuel to have fires going all day long." The British were also impressed by the way the French gunners lived—coffee and cognac at reveille, steak and chips at 5 p.m. "with an issue of wine to round off the day". These exceptional conditions were explained by the fact that the front was curiously quiet—the Germans had in fact withdrawn to a new defensive line farther east, and when the Allied infantry attacked on 17 March they were able to advance until nightfall without even making contact with the enemy. The battery followed the infantry in advancing across what had been no-man's-land, finding movement difficult and hazardous, because the Germans had blown all road bridges and booby-trapped the roads. Conditions were made even more difficult for the gunners' transport by hordes of fleeing French civilian refugees. The battery was soon in action again, and suffering casualties, once more digging themselves into the mud.

The French offensive failed. The next move was to be an attempted breakout from the Ypres salient held by the Allies. Tilman rejoined his battery when it was moving north to take part in the Battle of Messines Ridge, one of the preliminary engagements in the main Ypres offensive, and one of the few unqualified Allied successes on the Western Front in 1917. The ridge, 150 feet or so in height, lay a little to the south of Ypres and north of the River Lys. It was a strong natural position, and the Germans had fortified it even more strongly. Worse, it dominated all the neighbouring countryside, and from it the Germans could observe all British troop movements with impunity. For nearly two years the Royal Engineers had been tunnelling discreetly into the ridge, and by June 1917 had planted about 1,000,000 lbs of high explosive. Six brigades of the Royal Field Artillery, several 6-inch howitzer batteries, and a 60-pounder battery of Heavy Artillery moving by night, were brought up to support the assault. The mines were exploded in the early hours of the morning of 7 June, the guns all went into action, and within three hours the whole of the ridge was in Allied hands. The explosion when the mines went off was heard in England; over 7,000 prisoners were taken, and large quantities of German artillery and ammunition were seized. The Germans were pushed back only about two miles, they entrenched themselves in prepared positions, and the attack ground to a halt. Nevertheless, the capture of the ridge was an important gain.

As soon as Messines Ridge had been carried, Tilman's brigade was pulled out and sent to a position near De Panne, on the Belgian coast and close to the French frontier. This was on the extreme left of the Allied line, a position that had been held by the French, and Tilman's gunners took over from the French. The move was intended as part of a major seaborne assault, a combined operation with the Navy, on the Belgian coast beyond Nieuwpoort. This stretch of coast was in German hands, and the gunners were to support the operation by bombarding the German positions. Tilman's battery installed its guns in a field between two roads leading to Nieuwpoort. Conditions in the area were fairly quiet, and a farmer and his wife were hoeing potatoes in the field while the guns were being brought in. The wagon lines were at Koksijde, a couple of miles away, where again things were relatively quiet, with civilians leading more or less normal lives. The gun crews on their farm were well placed for milk, fresh eggs and fruit. On 19 June Tilman wrote home:

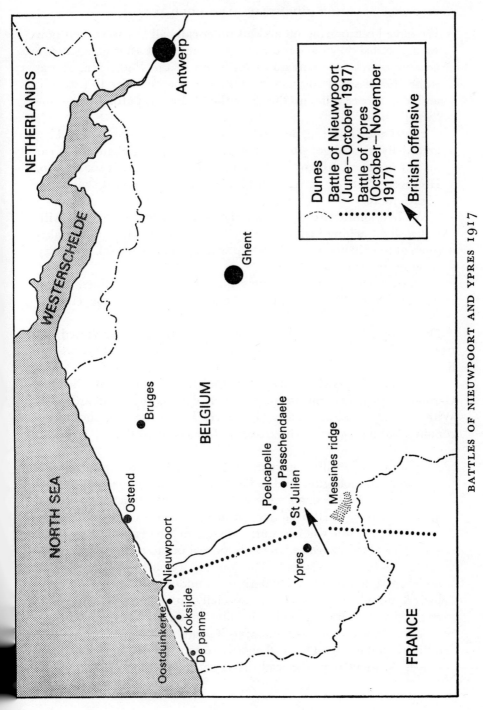

BATTLES OF NIEUWPOORT AND YPRES 1917

We have been moving on and off practically all last week, but now we are settled down in our own wagon lines. . . . Last evening after a 20 mile march we went down for a dip in the North Sea. It was rather priceless, as you had to climb over barbed wire to get to it, and about three miles up the shore the Boche was putting over some "woolly bears".

It was a top hole dip, but with my usual luck I ran into a whacking great jellyfish and got stung all over. I was hopping about like a cat on hot bricks till about 1 a.m. when I managed to get some sleep. However, c'est la guerre. I think it must be a new form of Boche frightfulness.

We had another [dip] this afternoon, and I pulled through with just a slight aching behind the knee. Still, you can imagine it takes some of the abandon out of the dip when you have to pick your way between the jellyfish.

The French have left us some quite decent wagon lines. I also managed to snaffle a French sword and bayonet—more souvenirs.

On 5 July King George V and the King of the Belgians visited the troops, and Tilman's battery provided a guard of honour at the wagon lines.

The seaborne operation was planned for the middle of July, but the Germans struck first on 10 July with a devastating bombardment. With his senior colleagues away on leave, Tilman was temporarily in command of the battery. The *History of C Battery* records:

At 7 a.m. the shelling started, and having brought up a 17-inch howitzer, 15-inch guns and a large number of specially mounted naval guns, the Germans were able to concentrate a heavy fire of armour-piercing shells into our defences. . . . For hours the shelling continued, and the whole countryside to a depth of six miles was laid waste. The battery teams, 18 in all, turned out to carry ammunition up to the battery positions. The journey was a hazardous one, as both Koksijde and Oost Dunkirk were under heavy fire. C Battery had a number of casualties, especially among those who were engaged in bringing up and unloading ammunition.

A wagon team had just unloaded its ammunition and was setting off back to the wagon lines when a salvo burst in the road alongside. Driver A. Stevenson, the lead driver, was blown off his horse and killed. With great presence of mind Sergeant H. Holmes, who was in charge of the team (although severely wounded in one arm and a piece of shrapnel through his face and jaw), galloped alongside the team, turned them round a sharp corner, and brought it to a standstill. . . .

The results of this bombardment were devastating. In the first hour one half of the field guns of the two divisions engaged were put out of action, the 1st Division losing most in the sand dunes. . . . The German bombardment destroyed every bridge across the canal and isolated the battalions north of the Yser. An attack followed. The 1st Northamptons and the 2nd KRRC of the 1st Division, cut off from any chance of retreat and with no room to manoeuvre, set themselves to sell their lives at the highest cost. When night came four officers and seventy men swam the Yser and came safely to our lines. They were all who escaped. Seven hundred of the Northampton Regiment and 400 KRRCs were captured.

The 32nd Division, though isolated, had more room to manoeuvre and after heavy fighting all day round Vauban's Redan this magnificent earthwork and the bridgehead of Nieuwpoort were still in our hands. . . .

The enemy's bombardment was followed by an intense concentration of gas shells on and around the battery position. Throughout the night he kept up this gas shell attack, during which the battery was continuously in action.

Tilman's own account on 14 July, subject to censorship, is laconic as always: "Awfully sorry I've been unable to write for so long, but as you see from the papers we've been as it were well in the party. . . . As you can imagine the coast has for us for the time being lost its charm." After congratulating his mother on her prowess in a game of golf, he continued:

On the 10th I fear we met our Waterloo. What a party! It beat everything in the way of Boche bomboes we have struck, it brightened our ideas considerably. I was OC battery at the time. The Boche could not have known it (perhaps he did, though!) I was also unfortunately at the OP which was blown in as a preliminary. As you see, I did not follow the O Pippers'* example, although an

* He is referring lightly to the dreadful rate of casualties among artillery officers manning Observation Posts.

officer of the heavies, who was also there, did. Unfortunately, this is only the beginning, the party is not nearly over yet. The Major is back now. Poor old Cotton was recalled after about four days and is now in his element.

There was a heroic little action by a detachment of Tilman's gunners on 21 July. A sub-section of the battery, under the command of Sergeant Foord, took a gun into an independent position among the sand dunes at Nieuwpoort Bains, only a little way from the front line. The sergeant and his men had to lie hidden in the dunes all day because they would have been clearly visible to the enemy, and could man the gun only at night. They occupied this exposed position for eight days and nights. During this time the main body of the battery came under fire from mustard gas for the first time. This was a new kind of gas, not fatal but liable to cause severe burns and sometimes blindness.

In the early hours of Monday, 6 August—in 1917 the August Bank Holiday—the battery suffered another disaster. The previous day had been relatively quiet, but in the evening the battery opened fire on the German trenches, and kept up the bombardment for about an hour. By 10.30 p.m. the firing was called off, and the gunners settled down for the night. The gun crews were living then in low shelters built of corrugated iron, and about a dozen of these were grouped together under a hedge alongside the guns. Suddenly the German artillery opened fire, scoring a direct hit on the shelters. Five men were killed outright, and another five seriously wounded (one of them dying next day).

Tilman had a brief break at the wagon lines, and on 10 August he wrote:

Things are still very lively up at the guns, and the other day Fritz blew our No 1 gun head over heels, clean out of the gun pit, a distance of about four yards. Some shell! Unfortunately we've had rather a lot of casualties. My batman, a priceless possession, one of the best, lost his hand. I was round to see him today in hospital, he was in wonderfully good cheer. He was a valet at the British Embassy in Washington avant la guerre, so you can guess what sort of a servant he made. I feel quite lost without him.

Almost as an afterthought, he added,

68

I've reserved the last piece of news for a fresh sheet. Incredible though it appears, I seem to have been lucky enough to gather in a bar to the old MC. Heaven alone knows what for, thousands of others have an equal right to it. I fear it is one of those beastly fireman stunts you read about. Not a word, please, till it's gazetted. "Some have greatness thrust upon them". C'est la guerre.

The award was promulgated in a special Order on 15 August 1917, and the citation was "for gallantry and devotion to duty in action", but did not specify further. Tilman professed that he didn't know why it should have come to him, but it seems probable that it was for his courage and the inspiration he gave his men when he was acting in command of the battery during the ferocious shelling in July.

There is a falling off, both in number and in length, in his letters from the front in 1917, and a change in style. He still uses phrases such as calling a battle "a party", but the schoolboyishness of 1916 is gone. He retains his humour, and his eye for telling little incidents, and seldom mentions the blood and suffering by which he was surrounded. But there is strain in his writing, even in his handwriting: words are omitted in haste, and whole pages of some of his letters are missing. Of course, they may have gone astray over sixty years, but equally he may have had to put letters into envelopes in such a hurry that he didn't notice if the whole letter went in. His accustomed jauntiness, though, never quite deserts him. He was delighted with a new pair of boots sent out from England, and reports treating them daily with castor oil obtained from medical stores. And he is always solicitous about his family, commiserating when one of them has a cold, congratulating Mater or Pater (sometimes "The Guv" or "Guvo") on little triumphs at golf or bridge, and never failing to send love to his beloved sister Adds. He was promoted full lieutenant with effect from 1 July 1917, and as he did not learn of this until August he was pleased to have some weeks of back pay in his new rank.

His battery continued to have a bad time. On 2 September they moved their guns to a new position where the gun crews had concrete pill-boxes to shelter in when not manning the guns. One of these concrete shelters received a direct hit, and four gunners who had been playing cards inside it were all killed. There was not a mark on any of them—they were killed by concussion and shock from the explosion. During the three months Tilman's battery was in the Nieuwpoort sector they suffered sixty casualties. The normal number of men in the gun line at any one time was 35, so that the battery's gun crews were effectively wiped out almost twice over in three months.

At the end of September Tilman was offered a temporary job which would have taken him out of the line, as orderly officer to the Brigadier commanding the Division. With typical reluctance to accept anything he regarded as a soft option he declined, preferring to stay with the battery, which, with the rest of the 161st Brigade, was sent to the Ypres front on the 17th. They were almost glad to leave the Nieuwpoort dunes where they had suffered so severely, and felt that Ypres could be no worse, and perhaps not so bad. These feelings did not last.

The guns were sent to positions on Pilckheim Ridge, a little to the north of Ypres, and the wagon lines were at Vlamertinge, a couple of miles to the west. Tilman's battery went into action at a place on Pilckheim Ridge called Varna Farm. There was no shelter for the horses, and the gun crews had nothing but what they could contrive for themselves with sandbags. Conditions were made worse by the fact that the Germans were now using aircraft in tactical support of their front line troops, so that, in addition to being shelled, men at the gun positions had to reckon on being bombed as well. This meant that not a single candle was allowed at night.

The weather was dismal too, incessant rain turning the heavy clay soil into a peculiarly vicious and sticky mud. On 20 October Tilman scribbled on a half sheet of notepaper, "Just a very hasty line to let you know I'm still alive and kicking. We are engaged in a batthole [*sic*] au moment. It is some party all right, mud and filth and shells up to the eyebrows." He ended with his usual "Best love to Adds".

On 22 October three Divisions of the British Fifth Army managed to advance a little and capture the village of Poelcapelle, to the north-east of Ypres. There they were held up, almost as much by mud as by the Germans. On 26 October they tried to advance again, but could make next to no progress. To give the infantry closer support the guns were ordered forward, Tilman's battery being sent to prepare a new position on the Ypres–St Julien road, leading to Poelcapelle. This was only 500 yards from the German front line, exposed to heavy shelling and within range of machine-gun fire. The road by which ammunition had to be got to the guns was under continual fire, and ammunition parties —the shells carried by packhorses—could move only at night and in the thick mist that mercifully shrouded the early morning.

The whole area was a morass of shell-holes, some of them feet deep in water, and foetid with the decaying corpses of men and horses. To make a hard-standing from which a gun could fire, water had first to be drained as far as possible from a shell-hole, then planks had to be laid on the mud. It was impossible for horses to pull the guns, and they had to be manhandled into position. That the guns were brought into action at all, and served with shells to fire, was an achievement for which the battery commander, Major E. A. Chisholm, was awarded a bar to *his* MC. There was a heavy price in casualties, among them Sergeant S. Foord, author of the first part of the *History of C Battery*, who was severely wounded and evacuated to England.

The war went on unchanged, but for Tilman a good many things were about to change. His much-loved Colonel Cotton, who had commanded the 161st Brigade from its landing in France, was promoted Brigadier-General and put in command of the Divisional Artillery. Tilman himself, who had always wanted to belong to the Royal Horse Artillery, had been recommended for the transfer which was to be acted on in November. Meanwhile he went on serving his guns on the Ypres–St Julien road. Thomas Northern, who continued the *History of C Battery*, wrote of this period:

> Six eight-horse gun teams were called out to serve the gun position at Varna Farm and the new forward position near Poelcapelle. Reveille was at 3 a.m. when there was a mug of tea, if the picquet had been able to make and conceal a fire. We then saddled two horses each with a pack and rode up to the Buffs' dump and loaded each horse with eight shells. Leading our horses three miles we made our way through St Julien, past torn up railway lines, derelict tanks, dead animals and men and smashed wagons, along the remains of a road, splashed from head to foot by equally mud-smothered horses, and sometimes dragged backward or forward by their frantic struggles at gun flashes, near bursts, and the dreadful sights and smells they encountered. The last few yards along what had been a willow-lined lane, now hough deep in mud, brought us to the

unloading point, where the imperturbable Lieut. Tilman super-intended operations, often under enemy fire. Unloaded, we mounted, and the horses that had stumbled their way up made good speed and no mistakes on the way down. By 10 o'clock, having watered and fed our horses, we were getting a much appreciated breakfast, prepared by our cook and shoeing smith. . . . In this way in three weeks we carried up over 4,000 rounds of ammunition.

On 18 November 1917 Tilman left C Battery to join I Battery of the Royal Horse Artillery, attached to the 1st Cavalry Division. His father wrote to Brigadier-General Cotton to thank him for the interest he had taken in his son, and on 1 December the Brigadier replied:

Many thanks for yours regarding your son—he is a real good boy, and I regret that he has left 161 Brigade. As a matter of fact, although I sent in his name for appointment to the RHA as a particularly promising officer, I recommended his being retained with 161 Brigade, as we could not afford to lose him. However, the powers that be decided otherwise, and no doubt the boy is delighted—I well recollect my own delight on first appointment to the RHA, but in this war the RFA has borne the heat and burden of the day, and in my opinion should not be drained of their most promising officers. I was more than sorry to leave my old Brigade, but glad, of course, to get promotion. I had watched them develop into quite one of the best Brigades in France, or so I thought, and so did our infantry, who know best when all is said and done. It is boys like yours who earned us this reputation. I am sure he will continue to do well, and trust that he will come through safe and sound.

After joining the RHA Tilman had no more to do with C Battery; it fought on through Passchendaele, helped to resist the German offensive in the spring of 1918, and took part in the final Allied attack that led to the end of the war. It earned one Victoria Cross and many other decorations.

The historic role of the Royal Horse Artillery was to move with cavalry, but the Western Front 1915–1918, in spite of lingering hopes among some generals of an ultimate cavalry breakthrough, was not a cavalry war. The mobility of the RHA, armed with 13-pounders instead of the heavier 18-pounders used by the RFA, was therefore deployed in sending batteries of horse-gunners to fill any gaps that might appear—they rode with their guns to assist infantry who might suddenly need more artillery support or stayed behind to cover retreats. Tilman's transfer was from preparing and occupying gun-sites that might be in use for some time, to moving constantly from one position to another. On 1 December 1917 he wrote home:

Just another short note to let you know am still going strong. I am more settled down now, as we have just had an officer hit, so I have taken over his section, servant, horses, etc. Things are getting very noisy round here. There was a great party yesterday, Boche troops in the open, and batteries coming into action in the open, but out of range for us, so we simply sat and swore and swore and sat. The best of this business is you're never in one place for long, no chance of getting bored.

He was concerned with getting buttons and badges for his new uniform, also a special type of jacket worn by officers of the RHA. On 5 December he wrote:

We're still somewhat busy round here, and last night we withdrew to a new position. It's not much fun arriving in the middle of a field these cold nights, with nothing ready. The only way to keep warm is to work all night, sleeping is a washout. . . .

Would you now send three pairs of khaki socks, fairly thin (not ribbed) and two suits of Aertex underwear? There is no hurry for these, though. I hoped to get all these things when I got leave, but there is no immediate prospect of this, so I'm getting you to send 'em. I hope to get my jacket sometime, when I shall be able to sport Horse Artillery buttons. Only the senior subaltern has it at present, bar of course the Major and Captain. The former is Archer-Houblon, the latter D'Arcy, a great lad.

He liked his fellow-subalterns—but the one he thought he would like best was killed a few days after they met.

He was moved down to the wagon lines for a spell, where things were relatively quiet, and on 18 December wrote home:

We look like being in action for Christmas this year, but that won't

3*

prevent us having a colossal gorge. Which reminds me that this will have to do in lieu of Christmas cards, as I can't raise one anywhere. The 1st Cavalry Division apparently don't go in for them. So here's wishing you all as jolly a Christmas as poss. If it's anything like the one we intend having it will be a topper.

On 22 December he wrote to his sister asking her to get herself a Christmas present from him, for which he would pay when she told him what it came to, and also asking her to let him know what was his share of family presents, so that he could settle that. On the same day he thanked his parents for a parcel containing salted almonds, a cake, apples and honey, and also for a pair of gloves—"an excellent fit". He went on

This is a pretty quiet sector in parts, notwithstanding that a Boche sniper endeavoured to cut short a promising career yesterday afternoon. The other morning I met, or rather, saw from a trench, the Colonel and Adjutant of the R Fusiliers outside our wire trying to shoot partridges. Of course, the lines are 500 yards apart just there and it was misty, so he wasn't courting sudden death. Still, it shows you it's not exactly Ypres.

The great British offensive from the Ypres salient had slackened off in the mud and rain of winter, with savage losses on both sides, but the front was never quiet. In fact, the Germans were transferring Divisions from what had been the Russian Front, and preparing for a spring offensive which was intended to shatter the Allies—and at one time looked like succeeding. In February Tilman went on a course for Horse Artillery officers, getting a report which was good enough to keep him in the RHA. He was much concerned at this time about whether he could get home for his sister's wedding.

In March 1918 the Germans struck. There were two prongs to the attack: a powerful offensive against the British at Ypres, and another offensive on the Somme. This was intended to split the British and French Armies, and the German High Command hoped to reach both Paris and the Channel ports. For a time the attack on the Somme seemed the more dangerous, and Tilman's battery was ordered south

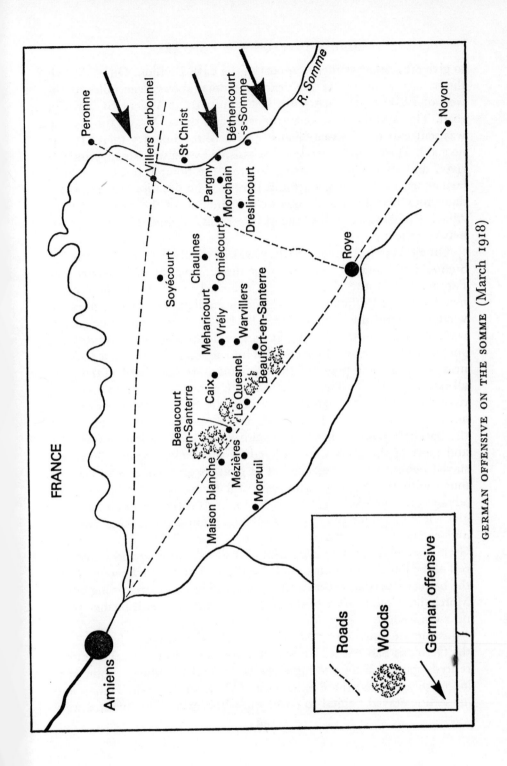

GERMAN OFFENSIVE ON THE SOMME (March 1918)

FRANCE

Amiens

Peronne

Villers Carbonnel

St Christ

Béthencourt
-s-Somme

Pargny

Morchain

Dreslincourt

R. Somme

Noyon

Roye

Soyécourt

Chaulnes

Omiécourt

Meharicourt

Vrély

Warvillers

Beaufort-en-Santerre

Caix

Beaucourt
-en-Santerre

Le Quesnel

Maison blanche

Mézières

Moreuil

Roads

Woods

German offensive

to give additional artillery support to the 24th Division. On 21 March the battery went into action near Soyécourt, about seven miles south-west of Peronne and just south of the important Amiens–St Quentin road. The situation was very confused, and on 22 March the battery was sent east to Mons-en-Chaussée to help the infantry there. It was no good. The German advance was assisted by dense mists covering the river, and they were preparing to cross the Somme in force a little farther south, at Béthencourt and Pargny. The situation was the more dangerous here because it was at the junction of the 24th and 66th Allied Divisions, and the enemy obviously wanted to force a gap between them.

On 23 March Tilman's battery was hurriedly ordered to cross the Somme and move on south to cover the crossings at Béthencourt and Pargny. Again the situation was confused, and the battery commander ordered Tilman to go out with a small patrol to try to discover what was happening. Tilman came back with the news that the enemy was advancing on the crossing at Pargny but did not seem yet to have got any troops across. The guns went into action at once from a position near Morchain and pounded the Germans on the east bank of the river all day long. While daylight lasted no German was able to cross the river, but during the night the Germans did manage to get some men across and established a bridgehead on the west bank. This meant that the battery's position near Morchain would soon become untenable, and most of the guns were ordered to withdraw. Tilman, however, stayed behind with a detachment of gunners and one gun to keep in touch with the infantry, who were still trying to stem the German advance, and give such support as he could. It turned out that he could give a lot: he got his gun to a ridge of high ground overlooking the river and engaged the German infantry over open sights. But when the Germans took Morchain even Tilman had to withdraw and rejoin the rest of the battery a couple of miles south-west, near Dreslincourt. Here the battery stayed in action until dark, shelling the roads leading out of Morchain. Under cover of darkness they withdrew still farther west, near Omiécourt.

Just before dawn on 25 March a patrol was sent out to learn where the Germans had got to. They had taken Dreslincourt, so the battery retired again, this time to high ground around Chaulnes, a somewhat larger village about three miles west of Omiécourt. Again Tilman and his section stayed behind to cover the withdrawal. The infantry were being steadily forced back by the weight of the German advance, and for a time Tilman and his gun were actually in front of the infantry. They couldn't stay long, but went on firing until they had used up all their ammunition, screened to some extent by smoke from a great fire raging at Omiécourt. With the Germans not more than a couple of hundred yards away Tilman and his crew limbered up and rode off after their battery.

Tilman (Tilly to his mates in those days) was in his element. I Battery was a crack unit of the RHA, and its commander, Major Archer Houblon, was a soldier of resource and daring. Although they were not now working with cavalry, the battery was engaged in a type of warfare for which the Horse Gunners had been trained—a war of swift movement, rapid limbering up and quick action. Tilman, with his eye for country and unshakeable determination to stay in action, was an ideal young officer for the difficulties of a confused retreat. And his coolness under fire was an inspiration to his men.

The main difficulty for the gunners was to discover where the Allied infantry were, and where they most needed support. German intelligence was undoubtedly good—they had chosen a vulnerable sector to attack, with the Allied infantry opposing them drawn from both British and French units. The retreat continued. Again the battery found its position in advance of the infantry, and on 26 March it was ordered to withdraw another five miles westward to Vrély, to cover the infantry retreat through the neighbouring village of Meharicourt. The gunners held the Vrély line for two days, expecting reinforcements of French infantry, but they did not arrive. The battery withdrew another mile or so west, and went into action again near the Caix–Le Quesnel road, an important link with the main road from Amiens to Noyon. Here a French battalion was trying to dig in and was thankful to see the guns.

There was wooded country to the east and south, around Warvillers and Beaufort-en-Santerre and the Germans were advancing from the woods. The battery was engaging the enemy coming from the east when a runner brought an urgent appeal for help from infantry trying to stem the German advance from Beaufort Wood to the south. Tilman, a sergeant and one gun crew were detached from the battery and sent with one gun to the crest of a ridge overlooking Beaufort Wood. From this ridge they opened fire on the German infantry and for a time defeated every attempt to advance from the wood. But the Allied infantry could not hold anything that could be called a line and were being driven steadily back, leaving the guns exposed in front of them. Tilman and his gun held one small section of the ridge, but German machine-gunners were coming up on the high ground behind him. In this perilous situation the battery commander ordered another subaltern, Lieutenant J. Casey, to stay behind with one gun to help Tilman, and to cover the withdrawal of the rest of the battery with its remaining guns. This they did effectively, and the main body of the battery got away to a new defensive position. The problem now was, how were Tilman, Casey, and their two gun crews to get away? Several horses had been killed, and there were not enough left to move the guns quickly. In the nick of time a battery of 18-pounders from Tilman's old Royal Field Artillery came to the rescue. Their commander saw what was happening and directed an accurate barrage on the Germans advancing towards Tilman and Casey. With this cover from their friends Tilman and Casey were able to limber up with their remaining horses, and withdraw in good order with their guns to rejoin the main body of the Battery.

They stayed near Beaucourt Woods all the rest of that day (March 26) engaging low-flying German aircraft with Lewis guns. The Allied infantry were still in retreat and at dusk the battery had to withdraw again, coming into action just before nightfall near Maison Blanche, on the main road to Amiens, only 13 miles away. The Germans, however, were in strength, and had the advantage of good cover in wooded country. When they had reached the woods to the west of Maison Blanche the battery was ordered to withdraw to high ground north of Moreuil, some three miles south of the Amiens road. They stayed in action in this area for the next three days, supporting a successful Allied counter-attack on the night of 30 March. At the beginning of April the battery was temporarily withdrawn from the line. Its guns had been in action so continuously that they were all but worn out, most of them needing either replacement or major repair.

There is only one surviving letter of Tilman's over this period. It is written on a page torn from a field notebook, and is barely legible. Dated 24 March, it says:

Sorry to have left it so long but as you see we're scrapping. At the present moment I have not eat [*sic*] for 24 hrs and have neither washed nor shaved nor taken off my boots for days. Wouldn't have missed it for a lot. Today has been great fun, we have had the Boche in view most of the time. The weather is priceless. This is *war*.

After a week out of the line, refitting, the battery was sent back into action in a hurry, covering 37 miles in one day. However, things quietened somewhat, and on 12 April he wrote, "We are now having a jolly time in a topping little village, though we're sort of on our toes the whole time. Looks like no more leave. Everyone seems determined to finish it one way or the other this summer. What ho! for some more open warfare!"

The open warfare that Tilman had just experienced was the beginning of the end for Germany. Marshal Foch, now in supreme command of the Allied forces, recognised that it saved casualties to give ground instead of getting bogged down in trench fighting. The German offensives on the Somme and in the north were held. The war was coming to an end, and Germany's allies were crumbling. There was still some heavy fighting on the Western Front as the Allies advanced towards Germany, but although German soldiers still fought stubbornly they could no longer stem the offensive. The Austro-Hungarian Empire collapsed, and then there was political revolution in Germany, a republic was proclaimed, and the new Government hastened to seek peace. On 11 November 1918 the armistice was signed.

Through that summer Tilman was in and out of the line. He had his long-delayed leave, spent some time assembling drafts for his battery, but whenever his guns were in action he was generally with them. In August he went on a five weeks' course at the Cavalry Corps School near Dieppe, which he enjoyed but found expensive. He was back with his battery in time for the final offensive, writing on 11 October, "We've been having continuous marching and fighting—very much more of the former than the latter." He was now advancing through French territory held by the Germans throughout the war, and added, "The French people all hang out sheets, towels, etc. from their windows to make sure they don't get strafed. They're no end bucked to see us." That is his last surviving letter from the front.

Hoping to be the first British guns into Germany his battery made a forced march through the Ardennes, which he found "awfully pretty but dashed hilly", to cross the frontier on 1 December. On 3 December he wrote from Bonn, "The people here seem more or less apathetic, the majority seem quite pleased and are out to help, one or two don't care about it. . . . One knows so little German it's rather hard to find out what they think about the war. . . ."

Five days later (8 December 1918) he enjoyed a final small triumph:

Our dreams have been realised—a castle on the Rhine! We are now a mile or two north west of Bonn and living in a schloss, well, hardly a schloss, sort of villa, they call it. Anyhow, it's very nice indeed, priceless bedrooms, and a topping big dining room, all done in oak and lit by about 50 electric lights, all cunningly placed. It's about two miles from the Rhine.

By 28 December they were "in the throes of demobilisation. The Major spends all his days in the office, wrestling with forms."

The war was over, but Tilman, like other members of his generation, had as a result known no youth. He had spent his eighteenth birthday on the Western Front at a time when the average life of a subaltern in the trenches was around eleven days. He had survived, but like others who came out on the right side of the statistics, Tilman always gave a slight impression that he was more conscious than are most of us of living on borrowed time and asking himself the question "Why was I spared when so many of the best of my contemporaries were not?" For those who experienced the trenches, merely to be alive had a special value. This does not on its own explain Tilman's complex personality and extraordinary self-sufficiency, but the experiences of the First World War remained a profound influence on him for the rest of his life.

IV

Kenya

To GET OUT of the Army Tilman had to resign his commission, a process which took until May 1919, when he earned a pleasing tribute from his CO, Major Archer Houblon, who wrote, thanking him for his work with the Troop and concluding, "Well, old bird, be good and look after yourself, make tons of money, marry young, and live happily ever afterwards."

Tilman was to ignore the advice about matrimony, and meanwhile he had to decide what to do. His school record suggested Oxford or Cambridge, and he would have had no difficulty in going to either. Nor, like some ex-service undergraduates, was he particularly old. But through the experience of the Western Front Tilman had not only grown up, he had grown out of tolerance for any ordinary way of life. His father would have liked him to go into the sugar trade, or at least to make a start at a university, but Tilman was determined not to. He had clear ideas on what he wanted, expressed in a poem by Max Plowman which he liked to quote:

> "Young soldier, what will you be
> When it's all over?"
> "I shall get out and across the sea,
> Where land's cheap, and a man can thrive."

He chose to go to Kenya.

It was then the protectorate of British East Africa, but in 1920 it became the colony of Kenya. The Government wanted settlers, and encouraged ex-servicemen to apply for grants of land. Not all these schemes were well thought-out. One for disabled ex-officers provided land for growing flax. But it didn't occur to the Government that while flax had commanded enormous prices during the war when every sort of canvas covering was at a premium, demand would inevitably collapse after the war.

Tilman did not go out under this scheme but under another, by which grants of one square mile of undeveloped land were made available to ex-service applicants by what he described as "a lottery". It was more a system of first come, first served, but there was a considerable element of lottery about the land you got, and where you got it. Tilman was fairly lucky, his square mile being well-watered, wooded country on the south-western edge of the Mau Forest, some 15 miles from Kericho, the administrative headquarters for what was then the Lumbwa Reserve. His land stood at about 6,500 feet, and although almost on the equator the height made for a pleasant climate, with daytime temperatures equivalent to a hot summer's day in England—around 80° F—and night temperatures falling to about 50° F, making a wood fire companionable to sit by, and a woollen pullover comfortable to wear.

Shipping was desperately short in 1919 and Tilman was lucky to get a passage to Mombasa on a cargo ship. Probably his father's interests in Liverpool shipping helped. However, it was not a comfortable voyage: he shared a steel deck-house with four other passengers, and found the heat in the Red Sea all but unendurable. He sailed in late August and arrived at Mombasa in October 1919, still three months short of his 22nd birthday. No correspondence with his father about this period survives. I have been told of J. H. Tilman's uneasiness at his son's apparent unwillingness to settle to a steady job but I doubt if there was anything approaching a row between them. Given the father's pugnacious business ability it was natural enough for him to deplore a preference for the Kenya bush to a well-run office, or even Oxford, but whatever his feelings he had a deep instinctive understanding of his son. He probably helped him to get a passage and he certainly behaved with considerable generosity towards him later. Tilman himself never expressed anything but love for his parents. The end of the war was a time of strain for many families, but whatever the strains within the Tilman family its essential unity was not impaired. His sister Adeline Reid Moir was now in America, where her husband embarked on a business career, and Tilman's letter to her on 26 October 1919 shows all the old, slightly bantering affection:

I'm writing this from the site of my future farm, at present a square mile of African bush of the most prodigious thickness. We are 50 miles from the railway by a most precarious road, 15 miles from the township of Kericho, which consists of a Post Office. I have no doubt whatever that with the expenditure of a few thousands and in the course of a decade or so the farm will be in a position to keep its owner.

However, it's a ripping country. We are half a degree south of the equator and 6,500 ft up. The mornings are all English summer days, every afternoon it rains merrily. Am at present staying with Buchanan, one of the eleven who has already started work on his land. As a matter of fact, he's been making 3 miles of road and a 60 ft bridge to take us on to the "main" road. I'm giving a hand, and trying to pick up the language and a few hints before starting on my own.

We live in tents, rise at crack of dawn, breakfast, and then harry a gang of 30 Lumbwa "boys" till it begins to rain about one o'clock. Lunch and then odd jobs between storms till 4.30. After tea the rain generally stops and we push off for a walk in the bush. At sundown we get into pyjamas, cardigans and coats, light a huge fire, bath, dinner, smoke, turn in. Of course, on my own place I shall have work and worry ad lib. There are only pigeons and partridges to shoot round here, but a few days' safari south is a great game country, including elephants.

I think you and Alec ought to chuck New York and come out here. Alec's hard-earned would come in useful, he'd make an excellent horny-handed son of the soil, you would lend the softening influence to see that we didn't become too horny-handed, ride a horse, see that we got some decent grub, and invite people to stay with us. If the altitude and rainfall don't appeal to you we sell out at enormous profit and buy a farm at a lower altitude, where you could roast to your heart's content. Drop me a line when you intend coming. Love to Alec, hope he's not becoming indecently wealthy.

This lighthearted letter skated over some formidable problems facing the new settler. There was a road of sorts to Kericho (the "main road" of the letter) but it was an unsurfaced earth track—and four miles away from Tilman's land, with the Itare River between the road and the potential Tilman farm. The river could be forded in the dry season, roughly from November to March, but after rain the river was too deep to ford. Transport from the railhead at Lumbwa nearly 40 miles away was by ox-cart, and might take three or four days. The motor lorry was to come, but in Tilman's early days as a settler oxen and human porters offered all the motive power there was.

Ron Buchanan, who became a close friend, was another soldier-settler; he had worked in Nairobi before the war, and having served in the King's African Rifles he knew something of the native languages. His cousin Robin Sneyd and a man named McWalter made up the small group of ex-service settlers in the immediate neighbourhood, within a couple of miles of one another.

The bridge that Tilman helped Buchanan build was across the Itare River. The Itare is a tributary of the Sondu, which flows into Lake Victoria some 40 miles from the soldier settlements. There were plenty of trees to provide timber, but neither Buchanan nor Tilman knew which trees were most suitable as piers for bridges. So they had to rely on local knowledge, offset by a tendency on the part of local labour to select those trees which were easiest for felling rather than most suitable for standing in water. For lashing the bridge timbers they used barbed wire, because it could be bought cheaply from Army surplus stores. Both hated it. In his book about his life in Kenya, *Snow on the Equator*, Tilman observes, "We found it just as intractable and spiteful to handle here as it had been in France."

The first bridge lasted only a year. Nevertheless it worked, and could be repaired or replaced as necessary. They went on using improvised bridges over the Itare to bring supplies to the settlements, and to take produce from them, until they abandoned the Itare crossing for a better bridge of steel and concrete over the River Kiptiget, another tributary of the Sondu on the other side of their property. This gave them and their neighbours what they regarded as a better approach to the main road.

After staying with Buchanan for a time Tilman moved into a tent on his own land, and then built a mud and wattle hut. He found this convenient and cheap, although the earth floor had disadvantages, encouraging a fierce growth of vegetation like the earth in a green-house. On the other hand when white ants destroyed the timbers (as they did fairly regularly) a new house could be put up quickly. He lived contentedly in a series of mud huts until he built a more sub-stantial house of burnt brick, firing earth for the brickwork on the spot.

For the first year or two he and his fellow planters pinned their main hopes on flax, which was fetching £400 a ton. In his first year Tilman cleared and planted 50 acres of flax but by the time he came to sell it

the price had dropped to £100 a ton. By the next year it fell to £50 a
ton. This made flax hopelessly uneconomic, for machinery is required
for the scutching process and at such prices there was no possibility of
any return on capital. Tilman and his immediate neighbours, however,
had not survived the war without acquiring a certain common sense,
and none put all their assets into flax. From the start they planted
coffee as well, turning more and more to coffee as the market for flax
disappeared. Although later prone to disease, coffee was a reasonably
successful crop, and they contrived to live by it. Had they known it at
the time, they would have done far better with tea, which grew wild on
the land, but in the early 1920s tea was not thought of as a commercial
crop in that part of Kenya. Today it is among the richest of tea-
growing areas.

Mrs Marjorie Sneyd, widow of Robin Sneyd, has given a vivid
description of life on the soldier-settlements near Kericho in the early
1920s. She refers to Tilman, who became godfather to her son Richard,
as Bill, and writes:

> I first went there on a visit in January 1922. During the flax-growing
> period we had a manager in charge of the flax processing, Eric
> Weatherhead. He lived with Ron Buchanan. So our total white
> population after we were married [in 1923] was five men, one
> woman, and later two baby boys. As Bill says [in *Snow on the Equator*]
> we really were a "family".
>
> Our land was surrounded by six miles of Native Reserve, which
> divided us from the nearest white settlers. At that time Bill was very
> anti-social. I was given solemn warning by my husband and the
> other men that he was very annoyed at the prospect of having a
> woman in their midst! However, with his usual good sense he bowed
> to the inevitable, and we were always very good friends. Actually,
> he invited me to his house during my previous visit, so I can claim
> to be the only woman who ever set foot in House No 1.
>
> Before we were married the men always met every Sunday
> afternoon in one of their houses. McWalter had a tennis court,
> otherwise they played bridge. That continued more or less regularly
> for the bachelors, but they all came to tea with us every Saturday
> without fail. Bill used to attend the occasional farmers' meeting at
> Kericho, but avoided any social event which included women if he
> could.

In 1923 ours was the only car, though I think the others had them in the next year or so. We only used cars for long distances, never on the farm, as petrol was very expensive and tiresome to get. The state of the roads meant that we exchanged visits with our farther-away friends only on special occasions.

Kericho consisted then of the Post Office, the District Commissioner's house and office and a few *dukas* [native shops run by Indians]. The doctor also lived nearby, and that was also the nearest telephone, though later a planter living ten miles away, and between us and Kericho, had one.

A Boy was sent every week to fetch the mail, which included copies of the weekly *East African Standard*. There was no air mail then, of course, and letters from England took a month, and arrived irregularly. The Post Boy could bring small items from the *dukas*. An ox-wagon was sent about once a month, weather permitting, and brought flour and sugar by the sack, and 4-gallon tins of paraffin.

The 40-mile journey to Lumbwa Station, also by ox-wagon, was only undertaken when something had to be collected, or coffee or flax dispatched. Coffee was sent to an agent in Mombasa, where it was shipped to London and sold by auction.

Bill was a great reader, and had a collection of books which he read and re-read. We had a subscription with The Times Book Club for three books a month (to keep) which were enjoyed by all.

. . . The Kisi Hills were our "horizon". There was no official time, except in Nairobi and on the railway, and when the sun set behind the Kisi Hills we set our watches to 6 p.m. and that was *our* time! Being almost on the equator the length of days altered only by ten minutes or so throughout the year.

Tilman's apparent dislike of women was already notable in his early twenties. It is a puzzling aspect of his personality because there is no obvious reason for it—so far as is known he had no unhappy love affair, and he was not in any way inclined to homosexuality. His reactions as a younger man seem to have been wholly normal—when he was wounded he was delighted to get to a hospital where he was looked after by nurses instead of RAMC orderlies, and when the war gave him a chance of some social life during his Cavalry Corps course he enjoyed taking a girl out to dinner. Yet from his first days as a planter in Kenya he acquired the reputation of a man who wanted

86

nothing to do with women, and that reputation grew with time. In a sense it was false, for he was devoted to his mother and his sister, and fond of his two nieces. Yet he did go out of his way to avoid having anything to do with women outside his family, and later in life, when he was a famous member of the Alpine Club, he resigned (though perhaps with his tongue in his cheek) over the club's decision to admit women. He was persuaded to re-join on being elected an Honorary Member—one of the greatest distinctions that a mountaineer can achieve. And—as Mrs Sneyd's recollections show—when he did happen to meet a woman no man could be kindlier or more courteous. He had indeed a kind of eighteenth-century courtesy towards women which made a meeting with him memorable. Perhaps he rather enjoyed his legend, but it remains an odd legend all the same, for there was no touch of the curmudgeon about him, and rudeness was alien to his whole nature. There was certainly a streak of monasticism in him, and he could sit for hours with some friend he knew well without feeling the slightest need for conversation, enjoying a wordless companionship that asked nothing and gave much. How much of this sense that to be alive and not in pain was as much as any man could wish, and that to wish for more was to lack self-discipline, went back to the war, one cannot tell. Probably the war had a great deal to do with it. The Army was a male community, you had to trust your mates and they to trust you, and if you survived it might be because of that mutual trust. Apart from Mrs Sneyd, Tilman's neighbours in the Kenya settlement were all ex-soldiers. That was how he wanted things.

He may have thought that he wanted nothing else than farming, but if so it was not true. In clearing the bush for his farm he had plenty of physical activity, and he was marking time happily enough. He read prodigiously—family tradition has it that he read through all the volumes in Dent's Everyman's Library, but whether he actually achieved this or not he certainly read most of them, and a good deal else as well. And he read to *learn*—his own later writings are dotted with proverbs, wise saws and ancient instances culled from his immense reading, some simply remembered, some carefully written down in a note-book. All this passed the time, but he had not yet found anything that he particularly wanted to do with his life. He knew what he did *not* want to do—settle to an office, or to any sort of humdrum existence. But he had not yet discovered anything that he passionately wanted to do, and this lack of any aim in life provoked a constant restlessness, satisfied for a time by building a new house for himself, or going hunting, but not satisfied for long.

In March 1924 his elder brother Kenneth was killed in a flying accident in the Mediterranean. Kenneth had stayed on in the Navy after the war as an officer in the Fleet Air Arm. In an exercise off Majorca his aeroplane overturned after take-off from the deck of a ship and fell into the sea. He was picked up quickly by an escorting destroyer, but although artificial respiration was continued for four hours he did not recover—he was drowned by the time he was picked up.

Kenneth's death was the first breach in the ranks of a closely united family, and affected them all deeply. Tilman went home to be with his parents—his first visit in five years. His sister Adeline returned from the United States. During that visit Tilman and Adeline took a short holiday together in the Lake District. It was one of the turning points in Tilman's life, for it was on that holiday that he discovered the enchantment of the hills. He did not pursue mountains immediately. He had his farm in Kenya to look after, and he went back to Africa. But his whole way of life was changing.

The next milestone was a visit to him in Kenya by his father, in 1926. Mrs Sneyd tells me that when J. H. Tilman wrote to say that he would like to visit Kenya, Tilman's own feelings were mixed—he was pleased that his father should want to visit him, but he was bothered about what his father might think of the somewhat primitive economy of his farm. He need not have worried. The visit (again according to Mrs Sneyd) turned out to be a great success, confirming that whatever differences they may have had J. H. Tilman had a much deeper understanding of his son than the outside world realised. His own progress in life had all been through self-advancement, and although his son's performance was very different from his own he could admire the energy and hard work that had gone into hacking a more or less profitable farm from virgin bush. Further, his business instincts were aroused—he could see a bright future for settlers in Kenya who went about the growing and marketing of crops in an efficient way. One result of his visit was that he went into partnership with his son in buying more land, not in the immediate neighbourhood of the Kericho settlements, but in the Sotik area, on the Masai Plain, some 60 miles to the south-east.

The colonial Government of Kenya was anxious to promote white settlement in this area because it lay between the tribal territories of the Lumbwa and the Kisii, who were inclined to raid each other's cattle, and it was felt that a block of settled farms would act as a buffer against raiding parties. With his father's help Tilman bought nearly two thousand acres of land at Sotik, to be developed primarily for growing coffee. This required an initial investment of some £2,750, of which Tilman was to provide £2,000 and his father £750. In fact his father was ready to help rather more than the strict arrangement between them required, for soon after his return to England he wrote, "I shall hear each month how you are for cash. In case of need I can squeeze some more for a Christmas remittance."

The investment at Sotik meant that Tilman could no longer live on his settlement near Kericho. Shortly before buying the land at Sotik he had gone into partnership at Kericho with his friend Richard Royston, whose home in England was not far from Wallasey. When he decided to move to Sotik Royston was formally appointed manager of the Kericho plantation, at a salary of £200 a year, which Tilman's father underwrote. It was envisaged from the start that Royston might become a partner in the enterprise at Sotik, and this he eventually did, acquiring a half share in the land. Tilman's original settlement near Kericho was eventually sold, but he owned some of the land until the Second World War. The whole area is now one of flourishing tea plantations.

The Sotik estate was a continuous strip, but it consisted of two areas of good land divided by a swamp. The good land became two farms, Kibore and Soymet. When their joint farming venture was in full swing Royston lived at Kibore, Tilman at Soymet. In England, J. H. Tilman took a continuing interest in the venture. He advised his son to aim at producing a standard quality of coffee under his plantation name—"not necessarily a very good or high quality, but the best you can manage". In his view—and he was certainly right—the important thing was that buyers in the London coffee market should know that they could rely on what they were getting when they bought Tilman coffee. If for any reason the quality of a particular consignment was not up to standard, Tilman should try to sell it locally, and not send it to England and he should also avoid the dispatch to England of coffee in small consignments—a minimum of two to two and a half tons would be about right. He himself visited coffee-buyers, and did all he could to promote the sale of Tilman's coffee. All this doubtless interested him as a business man, but for a man in his late sixties, who had no need to work at all, these activities on his son's behalf show both love and understanding.

Tilman was 31 when he transferred himself to Sotik from Kericho, ten years after his arrival in Kenya. In *Snow on the Equator* he observes:

> For those ten years, except for an annual shooting excursion and one brief visit to England, I had kept my nose to the grindstone. I saw no one else except at weekends, so that in spite of the efforts of kind neighbours, there was some danger of my becoming as mossy and as difficult to uproot as some of the bigger trees which had taken us days to stump; of developing into the sort of person who, in another planting community, is called a "hill-topper"; a man who has lived by himself for so long that he dreads meeting anyone, and therefore builds his house on the top of some hill so as to have timely warning of the approach of visitors to escape into the safety of the neighbouring bush.
>
> Another impelling motive for a change of scene was that the daily routine of attending to planted coffee was much less congenial to me than the earlier struggle to carve a home out of the forest and to tame the wilderness; to watch the landscape—a waste of bush and jungle, but a familiar one—change daily under one's eyes; to see a new clearing here, a shed there, paths and roads pushing out in all directions, while seeds, which one had oneself planted, grew into trees big enough to make timber.
>
> I already had some land in the Sotik, thirty miles further from the railway, where this absorbing task could be tackled afresh; where with a newly acquired partner there would be no danger of becoming enslaved by the farm. If either wanted a holiday it could be taken; all that was needed between the two of us was the sort of understanding that John Jorrocks had with his huntsman James Pigg, to wit "that master and man should not both get drunk on the same day."

Tilman at 31 was tough, resourceful and reserved. He continued to read prodigiously, as he did throughout his life, and although he was in no real danger of becoming a "hill-topper" he preferred his own company and a book to most other companionship. He still had no compelling aim in life. He enjoyed pioneering and clearing jungle, but the routine of settled farming bored him. He enjoyed his hunting expeditions, particularly those that took him into unsurveyed parts of the Mau Forest, but he was not an outstanding shot, and while he had no inhibitions about killing game for food he began to dislike the idea of killing for sport. His move to Sotik brought a change of scene, but the area was more settled and much less wild than the Mau Forest. The motor lorry had largely replaced the ox-cart. And Tilman now had an admirable partner to share in whatever work had to be done.

In December 1929 a brief report in the *East African Standard* changed his life. It described the ascent of Batian, one of the twin peaks of Mount Kenya, by a young planter called Eric Shipton. It was not a first ascent—Shipton himself had climbed the peak before with Sir Percy Wyn Harris, then an Assistant District Commissioner in the Kenya administration, and it had been climbed as long ago as 1899 by Sir Halford Mackinder and two Alpine guides. But the mountain was not then much visited, and Shipton's second ascent, with a young lawyer, Pat Russell, still rated a short piece in the paper. On reading of the climb, Tilman wrote to Shipton saying that he had done a little climbing in the Lake District, and asked for advice on climbing in Kenya. "This", Shipton wrote in his autobiography *That Untravelled World*, "was the start of a long and fruitful partnership in many mountain ranges." This is an understatement worthy of Tilman himself. The partnership of Shipton and Tilman was to become the most famous in mountaineering history. Moreover, it created a new kind of mountaineering, a development that has served since to transform the whole approach to mountains, socially, economically, and, in a sense, philosophically.

Mountaineering in the sense of climbing for the sheer joy of it and the achievement of reaching a summit was more or less invented in the first half of the nineteenth century, deriving partly from the Romantic movement that saw sermons in stones, partly, perhaps, from reaction against the "soft" life enjoyed by some of those who benefited from the first industrial revolution. The English were prominent in the new sport, and the Alpine Club, still the doyen of climbing organisations, was founded in 1857. Mountaineering was popularised by the Englishman Edward Whymper in the decade 1860–69, during which he made the first ascent of the Matterhorn (14,750 ft), and it was one of Whymper's books which he read at school that drew Eric Shipton's imagination to climbing. Up to the Second World War mountaineering, if not a rich man's sport, remained an activity for the relatively well-to-do, partly because of the time involved, partly because of the expense. Guideless climbs could be made in the Alps, but an expedition to the Himalaya or the remoter mountain regions of the world required a considerable outlay for stores and equipment, and to pay porters to carry them.

The Shipton-Tilman revolution was to demonstrate that the only real requirement for the enjoyment of mountains was determination to go there. The essentials were tent, ice-axe and rope, and desirable extras were a Primus stove and a spare shirt. Logistical problems and the expense of transporting crates of stores to remote places could be overcome by living off the land; a bag of flour or rice was necessary, and the addition of a handful of dates or a few eggs could make any meal a feast. In Africa, where they began climbing together, there was no tradition of employing mountain people as porters. They would employ carriers when they could, to get supplies somewhere near where they wanted to climb, but on the mountains they carried for themselves. Later, in the Himalaya and Central Asia, where there are immense distances to cover, they would engage local villagers for the traditional tasks of carrying for travellers, but they did not expect them to establish high camps. To help in this they recruited small groups of Sherpas, then becoming known from the experience of the early Everest expeditions as skilled carriers on mountains. But there was a vital difference in their attitude—they did not regard the Sherpas as merely porters, but as climbing companions. It was at least partly due to Shipton and Tilman that the Sherpa Tensing ultimately shared on equal terms with Edmund Hillary in becoming the first men to set foot on the summit of Everest.

Time has vindicated the Shipton-Tilman approach, and the small, lightly-laden two-man expedition is now accepted as a practicable, even preferable, form of Himalayan climbing. This has brought the joy of great mountains within the reach of almost any fit man or woman, to the great benefit of high climbing as an adventurous recreation, and to the enrichment of whole new generations of climbers. That such expeditions are nowadays taken for granted is a measure of their influence.

Eric Shipton (1907–77) was born in Ceylon, the son of an English tea planter, who died when the boy was two years old. He had a wandering childhood, travelling with his mother between England, France, India and Ceylon. This brought about a much-interrupted schooling, with the result that he failed to pass the entrance exam for Harrow, but his travels did have the compensating advantage of introducing him to the French Alps, and at school he made friends with a Norwegian boy who took him home on a climbing holiday. His mother had a number of friends in France, and Shipton spent all the time he could in the Alps. By his late teens he was a climber of considerable experience and outstanding skill.

In 1928, when he was 21, he went to Kenya to learn the business of coffee-planting. He worked on a farm north of Nairobi, and only about twenty miles from the base of Mount Kenya. Naturally, his thoughts turned towards the mountain, and he was fortunate in knowing two fellow-climbers in Kenya, his old Norwegian friend, Gustav Sommerfelt, and Percy Wyn Harris.

Mount Kenya is an immense Gothic cathedral of a mountain, with two spires (or peaks). These are Batian (17,040 ft) and Nelion, about 40 feet lower, named by Sir Halford Mackinder after two leaders of the Masai tribe (though "Batian" should more properly be written "Mbatian"). The mountain has lesser summits: Point Piggott (16,350 ft), Point Lenana (16,000 ft), Sendeyo (15,800 ft) and Tereri (15,750 ft). Sendeyo and Lenana are named after Mbatian's two sons, and Point Piggott commemorates an official of the old British East Africa Company. Batian was climbed by Sir Halford Mackinder in 1899, but in the next 30 years no one made a second ascent, and Nelion had never been climbed. In 1929 Shipton, Wyn Harris and Gustav Sommerfelt decided to attempt them both. They succeeded, climbing Nelion first and then Batian. It was a second climb on Batian that led to the report in the Nairobi paper that prompted Tilman to write to Shipton.

Shipton responded with a friendly note, and agreed to accompany Tilman on an expedition to Kilimanjaro in March 1930. Kilimanjaro (19,710 ft) is the highest mountain in Africa, and is said to have been included in German East Africa (now Tanganyika) by the boundary treaty of 1890 to enable the Kaiser to claim the highest African mountain as German territory. Tanganyika came under British mandate after the First World War.

Although Shipton was nine years younger than Tilman he was by far the more experienced climber, and Tilman accepted his leadership without question. On the face of things, two men could hardly have been less alike—Shipton, young, mercurial, talkative, enjoying company;

93

Tilman in his early thirties, aged by the war which Shipton had been too young to experience, reserved to the point of taciturnity. They shared a love for hills and wild places, and a preference for travelling light. That seemed about all. Yet from the start the two got on together, each finding in the other, perhaps, qualities that psychologically he missed in himself. Shipton had never known a father, and Tilman, nearly ten years his senior, could count as an older brother. Shipton's ebullience perhaps reflected an insecurity from his wandering childhood; Tilman had a rock-like strength on which others could instinctively depend. And both had a wonderful sense of humour: Shipton's an open delight in fun, Tilman's more subtle, even sardonic, but sensitive to any wisp of comedy in life. They found a deeply satisfying comradeship, but it was built up delicately, without needing to rely on any of the accepted formalities. Shipton records of Tilman "it was many years before I called him Bill", and there is a story which Shipton assured me is not apocryphal, which goes:

Shipton and Tilman are resting on a ledge in the high Himalaya after a particularly arduous traverse.

Shipton: We have climbed many mountains together in Africa and in Asia. We have depended upon each other in many dangerous situations. You have saved my life. I have saved yours. Is it not time that you called me Eric?

Tilman: No.

Shipton pursued it by asking Tilman, "Why?" To which Tilman replied after some thought, "Because it's such a damned silly name." Nevertheless, in the end they did call one another Eric and Bill.

The Kaiser may have acquired the highest mountain in Africa, but not a climb of much interest. The ascent of Kilimanjaro is more a rough mountain walk than a climb, and although they enjoyed the wild country and more or less reached the top, Shipton and Tilman on this particular expedition did not formally achieve the summit because they got tired of floundering about in dense fog. The main peak of Kilimanjaro, Kibo, was first climbed in 1889, and by 1930 it had been climbed or walked many times, and so did not offer much in the way of a mountain prize. More interesting was the neighbouring peak of Mawenzi, which although some 2,000 feet lower than Kibo presents a formidable challenge to rock-climbers.

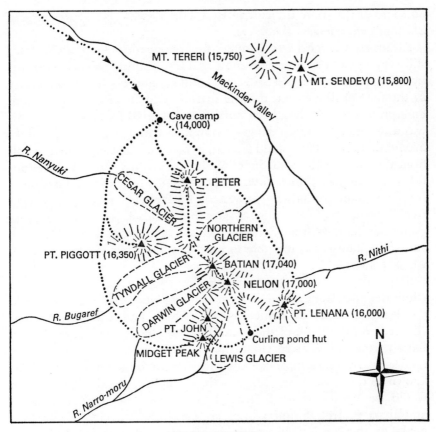

MOUNT KENYA

Having discarded their snow-glasses in the fog of Kibo both Shipton and Tilman suffered severely from snow-blindness after the descent, and as the weather turned to heavy rain (which would become snow at higher altitudes) they considered abandoning Mawenzi. Neither however gave up easily, and in spite of the weather they set off for the peak after a couple of days' rest, starting at 03.15 to reach the saddle (about 16,000 ft) between Kibo and Mawenzi by dawn. Conditions were bad. The volcanic rock of Mawenzi was covered in ice and under the ice seemed dangerously rotten—and it was snowing hard. They went on, and at about four o'clock in the afternoon achieved the summit—the third recorded ascent since the mountain was discovered. The climb down was a race against oncoming darkness, and

95

on some of the more difficult pitches Tilman was glad of the help of Shipton's experienced shoulders.

Although Mawenzi was Tilman's first major rock-climb, and he was still very much a beginner on snow and ice, Shipton was so impressed by his apparently inborn skill as a climber, and his imperturbability in the face of difficulties, that he invited Tilman to accompany him on a project that he had been nursing in his mind for some time. This was a formidable undertaking—a complete traverse of the twin peaks of Mount Kenya, Batian and Nelion, in one go. The two of them set off from the head of the Mackinder Valley on 29 July 1930. They established a base camp in a cave at about 14,000 feet, with a convenient supply of giant groundsel near at hand for fuel. The giant groundsel, a tree-like variety of the ordinary garden groundsel, is among the more grotesque flora of the Central African highlands, and it has the valuable quality of being able to burn in almost any conditions, even when it is wet.

Shipton's plan was to approach Batian from the north-west and to climb the peak from a broken ridge running westwards from Batian to the lesser summit of Point Piggott (which had then never been climbed) on the flank of the great Tyndall Glacier. Having achieved Batian from the western ridge they would go on by another ridge, thence by a saddle almost like a tightrope slung between the two peaks, known as the Gate of the Mist, to the summit of Nelion. The descent would be by the route Shipton had followed in 1929. It was an ambitious project. Shipton later regarded the traverse of the twin peaks as the hardest climb of his life, and from the start he was conscious that in taking Tilman with him he might be acting irresponsibly. He comforted himself by reflecting that perhaps they might only take a look at the western ridge, and that they were not committed to going on. Knowing himself, and by this time knowing a little of Tilman, such comfort was perhaps self-deception.

They spent the first day reconnoitring the western ridge, and in climbing two rock pillars known as Point Dutton and Point Peter, both first ascents. This was partly to give Tilman a bit more experience of climbing, partly to get a better view of the major peaks.

The approach to Batian by the western ridge involved scaling or turning a series of gigantic rock steps, the biggest of which, almost vertical and at least 500 feet high, Shipton called the Grand Gendarme— the name endures. Below it was a lesser, but not much less formidable,

John Hinkes and Adeline Tilman (née Rees), H. W. Tilman's
parents

Above: Berkhamsted School
OTC in camp, 1914. H. W. T.
extreme left

Left: H. W. T. as a cadet at
Woolwich, 1915

Mount Kenya

Above : Mount
Kilimanjaro

Right : The
Mountains of
the Moon

The West peak of Nanda Devi rising over the South Face

Above: One of the few pictures showing H.W.T. in a state of physical exhaustion: on the ascent of Nanda Devi with W. F. Loomis at Base Camp, 1936

Below: The twin peaks of Nanda Devi

Nanda Devi expedition, 1936; *l. to r.* H. W. T., W. F. Loomis,
T. Graham Brown, C. S. Houston, Peter Lloyd, N. E. Odell, Arthur
Emmons, H. Adams Carter

pinnacle, the Petit Gendarme. The first objective was a col at the foot of the ridge, and to get there they had to cross a glacier and go up an ice-filled gully. Crossing the ice required step-cutting. A climber nowadays would wear crampons: they existed then, but neither Shipton nor Tilman had any. Having reached the col they rested to consider the situation. Shipton's autobiography describes it:

> We sat with our legs dangling over the Tyndall Glacier, several hundred feet below. Across the chasm was the great west face of Batian, so close that we might have been suspended from a balloon before its ice-scarred ramparts and hanging glaciers. The upper part of the mountain was in cloud, and we could see little of the west ridge; but this was daunting enough. The Petit Gendarme, towering above us in the swirling mist, looked impregnable. The only way to outflank it was by climbing diagonally up a very steep slope of snow or ice to the right. Snow or ice? It was a matter of considerable importance, for if it were ice the step-cutting involved would take the best part of a day, and, with no protection, a slip would have been impossible to check. Again, no place to take a novice.

The novice himself was untroubled. "For him," Shipton wrote, "the issue was simple: we had come to climb the ridge and, if it were possible, climb it we would."

After this reconnaissance they went back to their cave, and Tilman got up at 2 a.m. next morning to cook breakfast. They left the cave around 3 a.m. to benefit from a bright moon, reached the col by dawn, and set off at once on the long traverse to get round the Petit Gendarme. The surface was ice covered by an inch or two of frozen snow. Where there was enough snow they managed without cutting steps, but in the lee of rocks where the snow was thin Shipton had to cut steps. After some hours they reached the crest of the ridge above the Petit Gendarme, and after a brief rest to eat some chocolate they set off again towards the Grand Gendarme. Deciding that it was impossible to tackle the almost vertical face direct they traversed to the left and found a gully which led upwards. An hour and a half's climbing in the gully brought them to the ridge above the Grand Gendarme. For a moment they were elated, but then they saw that to get any further they would have to climb a rock-step about 130 feet in height and undercut at its base. There was no way of outflanking this rock, for on

4

one side was a sheer drop and on the other the slope led downwards. They must climb the face direct, or admit defeat.

Neither was prepared for defeat. Tilman was in the strong position of not knowing how difficult the climb was. Shipton was on his mettle, and in Tilman he had a companion who inspired confidence. Studying the rock Shipton saw that by standing on Tilman's shoulders he could just reach two small notches, which, he thought, would serve as fingerholds. Having reached them, his right foot found a rough patch of rock-face on which to grip. Inch by inch he worked his way up, the rock-face becoming somewhat rougher and holds more plentiful as he went up. The next problem was Tilman: how was he to follow? Luckily there was a small cleft in the rock into which Shipton could wedge himself securely enough for a belay. Tilman's lack of experience on difficult rock was a severe handicap, and he found it hard to get over the initial overhang. Perseverance did it, and he joined Shipton in the narrow cleft. "The rest," Shipton wrote laconically in his book, "was easy."

It was not as easy as all that. They were at the top of the rock-step, but the rope was not long enough to get down should they have to retreat. So they had to go on, and now they met a new obstacle—mist. They had to advance step by step, hoping that they were going in the right direction. At last they saw the huge mass of the summit loom through the mist, and at 4.30 p.m. Shipton found the summit cairn which he had helped to build on his previous ascent. They had been climbing for over 12 hours. In his autobiography, Shipton described Tilman's performance as magnificent, and added, "He had shown no sign of anxiety throughout the climb, and his stoicism no less than his innate skill in climbing and handling the rope made a vital contribution to our success."

The summit of Batian, however, was only half (although by the route they had climbed, the harder half) of their objective. They were lucky in that the Gate of the Mist between Batian and Nelion did not live up to its name, and the weather cleared slightly as they got there. They reached and crossed the summit of Nelion without stopping and began the descent. There was no chance of getting down before dark, but at least Shipton had done the descent before, and if the weather stayed clear there would be a moon to help them. The moon co-operated, but Tilman slipped and came on the rope. Shipton held him safely, but Tilman lost his ice-axe. And then Shipton was sick—perhaps from nervous exhaustion, perhaps (as Tilman thought) because of some meat essence he had eaten during the climb. They debated what to do and considered spending the night where they were in a bivouac, but a bitterly cold wind discouraged the idea. So they went on, completing the descent by moonlight with one ice-axe between them. In *Snow on the Equator* Tilman wrote of Shipton's performance, "The most vivid impression that remains in my mind of this grim ordeal is how S—— in the feeble state he was in not only climbed, but led the way unerringly and safeguarded his companion."

They spent a happy six days in their camp in the cave, exploring glaciers and climbing rock-towers or pinnacles, including Point Piggott, of which theirs was the first ascent. For Tilman it was invaluable experience—the skill that he later showed on Nanda Devi and Mount Everest was learned on Mount Kenya. His courage and resource were limitless, but he was lacking in climbing techniques; Shipton was a superb instructor.

In climbing one minor pinnacle, a beautiful rock spire rising from a glacier, Tilman had an accident which, but for Shipton, would have ended in disaster. The spire offered a difficult climb, but the rock was sound and when they started it was dry. Soon after they reached the top snow began to fall heavily, and Shipton at once realised that holds which had served well enough when dry would be very different covered in wet snow. The first part of the descent involved negotiating a narrow gully, below which was a sloping ledge. Tilman went first, Shipton looking after the rope, which he secured round a firm rock. Tilman went out of sight in the gully, and suddenly the rope ran taut. Shipton guessed that he had slipped on the fresh snow covering the slope below the gully. He called, got no reply, and assumed that Tilman was hanging unconscious on the rope. He tried to haul up the rope, but Tilman's weight and the friction of rope against rock made this impossible.

Something had to be done quickly. With hindsight, Shipton thought that the best thing would have been to make fast the rope to the rock round which he had hitched it and to climb down himself to find out what had happened. But he didn't want to leave Tilman hanging on the rope—he could not see him, so did not know in what position he was hanging, and there is real danger of an unconscious man's being strangled or suffocated by pressure on his chest if left to swing at the end of a rope. He had some thirty feet of rope in hand from the belay around the rock, and the best thing seemed to be to let it out in the hope that Tilman might come to rest on a ledge. He did so but the rope remained taut. The only thing now was to climb down with the rope secured to his waist, hoping to be able to hold Tilman as he went down. It was a severe physical task, and Shipton achieved it only by his own skill, and by the luck of climbing down a narrow gully where he could press his arms against the rock-face to ease the strain of supporting Tilman's weight. In all this Shipton kept his head. He knew that he could use the friction of rope against rock to help to take the strain of holding Tilman, but he also knew that this was a dangerous aid as the rope might fray beyond its breaking-strain.

As he continued downwards the rope went blessedly slack, indicating that Tilman must have come to rest somewhere. Shipton found a belay for the now slack rope, and hurried on down. As he emerged from the gully he saw Tilman sitting apparently unperturbed on a ledge about fifty feet below. He seemed to answer questions rationally, and said that he could see a way down from the ledge. Having doubled the rope round a belay Shipton slid down to join him, and then found that Tilman had no idea where he was, or how he had got there, and that there was no way of descending from the ledge. Tilman was in fact suffering from concussion. They couldn't stay where they were—somehow Tilman had to be helped back to the place from which he had slipped. Shipton climbed up the doubled rope, one end of which was still fast to Tilman's waist. He knotted the rope to a rock so that Tilman could not fall any further, and then hauled on the part attached to Tilman, who was able to help by pulling on the other part of the rope. In fresh snow and gathering darkness the remainder of the descent was horrible, but Shipton got both of them down safely, though it was dark before they reached their cave. "I have seldom been so glad to arrive anywhere," Shipton observed in his autobiography.

Their next trip together was to Ruwenzori, or the Mountains of the Moon, but that was not until January 1932—Tilman had his farm to look after, and Shipton a job to do. With an able partner on the farm Tilman still found time for other things. He practised rock-climbing on the stone chimney of a neighbour's house, and—so legend has it—kept himself in training by going round the walls of the farmers' club with fingerholds on the picture rail. There was more social life round Sotik than there had been in the Mau Forest, and Tilman made a good friend in another Sotik planter, Horace Dawson. Dawson was more than a planter—he had a number of business interests, including a contract for providing postal services in the region, a fleet of lorries and buses, some ships plying on Lake Victoria, a mill and a garage. Since he too had an able partner he found time for another interest— elephant hunting. Elephants were already protected, but herds sometimes multiplied to the extent of becoming a nuisance. In the Lumbwa valley a herd of some two thousand elephants was doing such damage to native crops that the tribal leaders appealed to the Government for help. Dawson was appointed Elephant Warden for the area, with the task not simply of culling the herd but of driving them across a river some thirty miles away into country where the tribes were pastoralists and there were no arable crops to be destroyed. He invited Tilman to help him. It was exciting work, which Tilman enjoyed, though he didn't stay long enough to clear the valley of all its elephants.

The Ruwenzori range, or Mountains of the Moon, on the borders of Uganda and Zaïre (then the Belgian Congo), had a shadowy existence in European cartography for nearly two thousand years before they were "discovered" (that is, from a European point of view) by Stanley in 1888. They were recorded by Ptolemy (c. A.D. 90–168) who probably derived his information from Greek merchants trading in Egypt, and who was right in regarding their snows as one of the sources of the Nile. But the region was remote and the mountains themselves hard to find because they are normally hidden in mist. The name Ruwenzori was given to them by Stanley because it was what he thought his native guides called them, but the linguistics of the area are complex and the precise meaning of what Stanley thought he heard is a matter of guesswork. When Tilman and Shipton tried to talk of Ruwenzori to the natives accompanying them the word seemed to have no meaning at all, though that may have been because of their pronunciation. Although marked on small-scale maps as a mountain, Ruwenzori is a range rather than a single mountain, and understanding of the region is further complicated in that the main named mountains (Mt Speke, Mt Stanley and Mt Baker) have either several summits, or different names for their peaks. The highest peak, Margherita (16,815 ft) is on Mt Stanley, but Mt Stanley has a second summit not much lower in Alexandra (16,749 ft) and a third in Elena Peak (16,388 ft). The

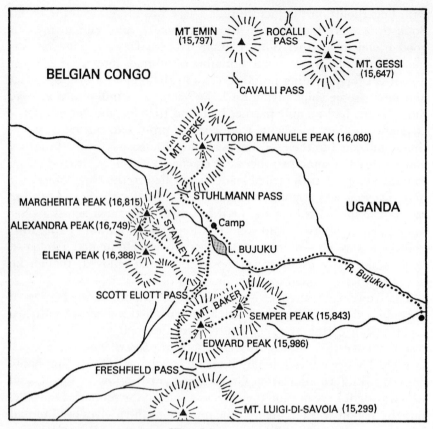

RUWENZORI (The Mountains of the Moon)

summit of Mt Speke is Vittorio Emmanuele (16,080 ft) and Mt Baker has Edward Peak (15,986 ft) and Semper Peak (15,843 ft).

Most of the main peaks were climbed for the first time in 1906 by a big expedition led by the Duke of Abruzzi, a cousin of King Victor Emmanuel III of Italy, who also led important expeditions to Alaska and the Karakoram. In addition to climbing the peaks the Duke of Abruzzi's expedition made accurate maps of the area and accomplished valuable work on its fascinating botany and zoology. After this the Ruwenzori range was little visited until 1926, when most of the peaks were climbed again by a two-man party led by Dr Noel Humphreys. The Tilman-Shipton expedition in January 1932 was the third major mountaineering visit to the region.

As always, they travelled light, buying blankets, cooking pots and food locally, and engaging a small party of fourteen porters to accompany them—thirteen of the men were to carry loads, while the fourteenth was to go ahead with a bush-knife and make a path for the rest. They approached the mountains up the valley of the Bujuku River, and as they gained height entered an extraordinary world. Tilman's own description of it in *Snow on the Equator* can scarcely be bettered:

> The upper slopes of Ruwenzori, from 10,000 ft to the snow-line, comprise a world of their own—a weird country of moss, bog, rotting vegetation, and mud, on which flourish grotesque plants that seem to have survived from a past era; the vegetation of some lost world inhabited by dinosauria, pterodactyls and mammoths. Here are seen gaunt giant groundsel crowned at the top with spiky heads like half eaten artichokes; tough, leafless shrubs with white everlasting flowers called helichrysum; grey, withered and misshapen tree-heaths, tumescent with swollen growths of moss and lichen oozing moisture; monstrous freaks of nature bred from the union of mist and morass; a slimy barrier serving to enhance and make more desirable the fresh purity of the snows that lie beyond.

At around 13,000 feet they found a convenient cave near a rather dismal pool with muddy banks called Bujuku Lake. Here they camped, and having sent eight of their porters down, prepared to go with the remaining six to establish a camp near the Scott Elliott Pass lying between Mount Stanley and Mount Baker. The porters however were reluctant to go higher, so Tilman and Shipton decided to let them stay in the cave while the two of them, carrying their own loads, went off for five or six days. Instead of making for the Scott Elliott Pass they decided to climb the Elena Glacier to the plateau between the Elena and Alexandra summits of Mount Stanley. Apart from the tiresomeness of soft snow the climbing was not difficult, but the mist was so dense that it was extremely hard to know where they were. They pitched a tent on the plateau and were thankful when the weather cleared a little towards evening, and they were able to identify Alexandra Peak. They climbed it next day and returned to their tent, planning to tackle Margherita Peak in the morning. The mist was thick again when they started and having trudged upwards for some hours they were astonished to come across footsteps in the snow. Then they realised that the footprints were their own from the previous day, and that they were simply re-climbing Alexandra!

They went back to their tent, cold and wet, and were so miserable that they got up at 3 a.m. to make tea and wait for dawn. There was the usual mist, but they were determined to have another go at Margherita and set off to navigate as nearly as they could on a compass course. At least they didn't meet their own footprints and by about 11 o'clock in the morning they reached an undoubted summit, but of what they had no idea. At last the weather cleared for about a minute and they were able to see and identify Alexandra Peak, and to satisfy themselves that they were in fact on Margherita. Theirs was the third recorded ascent of the two peaks.

After returning to their cave for a rest day they tackled Mount Speke, achieving the summit peak of Vittorio Emanuele. After another brief rest in their cave they made for Mount Baker, climbing Semper Peak and Edward Peak. Then they made a complete traverse of Mount Baker, passing through an unnamed valley between Mount Baker and Mount Stanley, south of the Scott Elliott Pass. They found the helichrysum invaluable as what they called a "Thank-God-handhold" on the steep cliffs, its tough roots holding where nothing else could.

The physical cost was a sprained shoulder for Shipton and the loss of a wrist-watch by Tilman. It was a remarkable climbing expedition, the porters remaining in their cave while Tilman and Shipton carried everything for themselves on their climbs. They were tough, and happier to be on their own.

V

Across Africa by Bicycle

EVEN WITH THE competent Richard Royston as his partner, Tilman's
share of the Sotik estate could scarcely be left to run itself. Coffee was
their main crop, but they also had a dairy herd producing milk and
butter for the local market, and they had some land under maize,
again for local consumption. All this required a lot of work, since the
Sotik estate was really two farms, Kibore and Soymet; Royston, who
lived at Kibore, could keep an eye on Soymet temporarily, but not all
the time.

Tilman's adventures with Shipton had given him at last a passionate
interest in life, but they had also made him even more restless. He
decided to sell Soymet to Horace Dawson, the farming friend with
whom he had gone elephant-chasing in the Lumbwa Valley. With the
money from the sale he paid off whatever he still owed his father, and
had enough left to go back to England.

No correspondence with his father during this period survives, and it
is not known whether he went home with any idea of staying in
England, or whether he intended to look around for some other job
that would take him abroad again. He was now 34, unsettled, and
still without any clear aim; he knew that he wanted to climb
mountains, but what to do between mountains was another matter.
His father was getting on, and probably wanted to see if there was any
chance of his son's taking up any of his own business interests. Tilman
was ready to discuss anything, but he went home uncommitted.

He came back to find that Adeline's marriage had broken up, and
she had returned from the United States with her two small daughters,
Joan and Pam, to make a home with her parents. Tilman had of course
known of all this by letter. His loyalties were always with his sister,
and the break-up of her marriage brought her even closer to him. And
she was to become ever more important as a pillar of the family,
running the family house at Wallasey as her parents aged and, after
their deaths, maintaining a home for Tilman.

4*

In 1932, the family at Wallasey therefore included two small nieces, who adored their uncle, and for whom he developed a lifelong affection. Tilman was home for Easter, and took advantage of the holiday to go climbing in North Wales with his friend, Dr John Brogden, who was able to leave his practice in Hartlepool over Easter. John Brogden was an experienced mountaineer, who had climbed in Switzerland and Norway as well as in Wales and the Lake District. Adeline, who had introduced her brother to climbing on their earlier holiday in the Lake District, went with them. After spending Easter in Wales Brogden had a few days' holiday left and they decided to spend it in the Lakes, where they planned to climb Dow Crag on Coniston Old Man. The day chosen for the climb was a Sunday, and Adeline wanted to go to church. In her place they agreed to take Vera Brown, a schoolmistress whose father was a friend of Brogden's.

That day was cold and windy, and conditions were far from ideal. Dr Brogden, the most experienced of the three, thought that they could still attempt the climb, and Tilman, who by now had considerable experience of bad weather in mountains, was ready enough to agree. They roped up for the ascent, Brogden leading, Tilman next on the rope, with Miss Brown bringing up the rear. They had almost reached the summit when Miss Brown slipped on wet rock and went over the edge. Her fall dragged Tilman with her, and they were both held by Brogden, Tilman about 10 feet down, Miss Brown below him, hanging over a deep gully. Tilman, realising the strain on Brogden, made desperate efforts to get some sort of hold on the cliff-face. He fought for about half a minute when he heard Brogden shout "I can't hold you any longer", and then all three fell, coming to rest in the gully after a fall of about 60 feet.

Miss Brown was severely injured, both Tilman and Brogden knocked unconscious. Tilman recovered consciousness, but Brogden did not, though he was apparently still alive. As soon as Tilman came to, he tried to get help. He remembered having seen some other climbers a little below them on the ascent, and crawled down a pitch to reach them. He could not find them, so he crawled up again to tell his companions that he was going to look for help. He could do nothing for them where they were, and to get help meant covering four miles of rough hillside to Coniston village. He did not know it at the time, but the fall had fractured some vertebrae. He could not stand to walk, but he could crawl. Four hours later, he got to Coniston and made for the hotel where Adeline was staying. She was waiting for tea, when suddenly she saw an extraordinary blood-covered object crawl through the door like a wounded dog. He was suffering from concussion, but managed to keep conscious until he had given a clear account of where his companions were.

By this time it was dark. A rescue party of quarry workers, led by J. C. Appleyard, secretary of the Fell and Rock Climbing Club, and accompanied by a doctor from Coniston, set off to climb to the gully by the light of storm lanterns. Tilman wanted to crawl back to guide them, and even tried to fight with those who held him. Then he collapsed.

The rescue party found Miss Brown alive, and Dr Brogden dead. With ropes and stretchers they brought down Miss Brown and Dr Brogden's body, getting back to Coniston in the early hours of the morning. Miss Brown was taken to hospital; all agreed that Tilman's crawl had saved her life. Newspapers made much of the story. "Heroic Journey by Injured Companion to Summon Help", was a headline in the *Daily Sketch* of 12 April 1932, and "Injured Man's Heroism" said the *Lancashire Daily Post*. "His heroism was extraordinary. It is a mystery to all of us how he managed to reach Coniston," reported the *News Chronicle* in an interview with one of those to whom Tilman had spoken before he collapsed. For himself, he hardly ever mentioned the event.

Even for a man of Tilman's iron nerve and physical and moral toughness, the fall on Dow Crag and the death of his friend could scarcely be shrugged off. And he was told by his doctors that he would never climb again. He was nursed devotedly by his mother and sister, but it was well into the summer before he began to pick up. At last he could walk, but his back remained bent and he was told that it was unlikely that he would ever be able to reach above his head. In this condition he planned a climbing tour in the French Alps.

He went alone, determined to find out for himself whether the doctors were right, and equally determined to prove them wrong. He acted then as he acted later in mountains and at sea when he suffered some injury—doing his best to ignore it and trusting to willpower to recover. Usually the treatment worked. It did in this case. He made no concessions, even travelling 3rd class* on French trains.

* Second Class on British trains was introduced originally for ladies' maids and other servants attending passengers travelling First Class. It went out of use after the First World War, with the curious result that for the next

He kept a diary of his Alpine tour in a small notebook measuring three inches by five. It is a curious document, mostly written in pencil, the entries laconic, and not always easy to read. It makes no mention of his back injury and the sole indication that he was not always on top of his form is an occasional testiness when other people, fellow inmates in a hut, or other mountaineers who attached themselves to a climb for which he had hired a guide, seem to have been too much for him.

He left England by the night boat on Saturday, 23 July 1932, and got to Paris about 5 a.m. on Sunday morning. He went on by train to Grenoble, describing Third Class travel as "not too bad in spite of a crowded train". He put up at an hotel, where he was charged 10 francs for a bath, but found Grenoble "a pleasant town". He went by bus to La Bérade, where he engaged a guide for ten days, and explored the Alps of the Dauphiné, staying at mountain huts and swimming (though it must have been cold) whenever he came across a convenient tarn. During this time he climbed Le Planet, Les Bans, La Meije, Les Écries, La Grande Ruine and the Pan de Sucre. Sometimes he had a companion with him, sometimes he was with the guide alone. On 5 August, on the Col des Avalanches he wore crampons for the first time and "found them very pleasant to walk in". Then he went on to Chamonix to explore round there. He got some good views of Mont Blanc, and his climbs included the Aiguille de L'M, the Aiguille du Tour, the Col de la Fenêtre and the Col du Chardonnet. On 22 August with a companion and another guide he set out early in the morning to try to climb Mont Mallet. His diary observes, "Difficult icefall to get through, and above that snow very soft. Close under Col de Rochefort guide decided the bergschrund wouldn't go (without seeing it). Also feared danger of avalanches and falling stones." His

---

30 years, until well after nationalisation, there was no Second Class on British trains but only First and Third, the Third Class becoming progressively more comfortable. French railways developed differently and three classes were retained, providing three standards of comfort. Third Class on French trains before the Second World War was cheap but basic transport, with seats that were often wooden benches. It was common for British travellers getting through-tickets for French destinations to travel Third Class to Dover, First Class on the boat and Second Class in France.

companion was tired and not keen to go on, so they turned round and went back. His diary concludes, "Fed up with the whole business. Decided to go home. Mail in the evening helped the decision."

The decision was not only to go home: it was a decision to regard himself as fit for anything again. His niece Pam remembers him both before and after his Alpine tour, how bent he was before he left Wallasey and how he came back ramrod-straight. She adds, "This back injury stayed with him to the end. Whenever he looked particularly grey I used to ask, 'Back trouble again?' and there was the same answer, 'Always with us, like the poor'."

Whether the mail that helped his decision to end the Alpine tour also helped him make up his mind to leave Europe again one cannot say, but if it included letters from Kenya it may indeed have decided him, for he went back to Kenya to prospect for gold.

The finding of gold was first reported in Kenya in 1923, in an area south of the Masai Plains, but nothing much came of it. In 1931 more gold came to light in the Kakamega district, north-east of Lake Victoria. This time it looked as if a potentially valuable goldfield had been discovered, and a geological report commissioned by the Kenyan Government recommended opening the area to prospectors. This led to a considerable "Gold Rush", not on the scale of some of the more famous gold rushes in the world's history, but considerable for the population of Kenya. Whether Tilman actually thought that he would make his fortune out of a gold mine one does not know. More probably he was attracted by the prospect of living rough in the goldfields, and his mind was also turning to the idea of making a living by writing. From his schooldays, as his letters show, he had enjoyed writing, and what better material for writing about than a gold rush? Probably he had a book in mind when he went back to Kenya, though as things turned out it was some years before he started his professional writing career. He returned to Kenya towards the end of 1932, bought a car to get to the goldfields, and formed a gold-mining partnership with his old friend Horace Dawson. Dawson, farmer, elephant hunter and business man of considerable acumen, was game for anything, and naturally he tried his luck in the goldfields. He and Tilman got on well together, and a reliable partner was a valuable asset in the job of staking claims and "trying" crushed rock for traces of gold. Tilman

109

was particularly valuable by reason of his physical toughness and alert mind. And he already had a reputation in the settler community for absolute integrity—a record unsullied throughout his life. Dawson was delighted when he turned up.

There were two main forms of prospecting in the Kakamega gold-fields—looking for gold-bearing rock on land, and panning for alluvial gold in the Yala River. Dawson had already staked ten land-claims when Tilman arrived, and was in process of staking other claims in the Yala, so the partnership gave Tilman an immediate share in the prospecting business. The search for gold-bearing rock might be to investigate an outcrop showing specks of gold-glinting quartz, or it might involve digging down to rock where bits of hopeful-looking quartz were found on the surface. Having found rock containing even the thinnest vein of gold the next job was to try to follow it back to a main gold-bearing "reef". Samples of the rock to be investigated were broken off with a geologist's hammer, and then crushed in an iron pestle and mortar to the consistency of sand. This was then washed in a pan. Gold is heavier than the surrounding grains of rock, so if there was any gold it would sink to the bottom of the pan and show up as yellow streaks on the bottom of the pan when the top "mud" of sand and water was removed. Such streaks of gold were called "tails" or "tailings", and if a good gold tail was found further samples of the rock would be taken to a professional assayer for an estimate of the quantity of gold likely to be found in a given weight of rock. It was hard work, but exciting. Dawson and Tilman found some fine tailings in their pans, but the veins they tried to follow always petered out, and the best reef they found promised only two and a half pennyweights of gold to the ton of rock, a hopelessly uneconomic mining proposition.

Washing for alluvial gold is more suitable for the prospector without a big company and large labour force behind him. This form of prospecting simply requires the "washing" of river-gravel in a fine sieve, in the hope of coming across grains or small nuggets of gold in the process. There was known to be gold in the gravels of the Yala River, but the gravel was in several layers under the banks and river-bed, and the problem was to find a layer of gold-bearing gravel. The Dawson-Tilman partnership never found one.

There was no fortune in gold-mining for Tilman, but he had six good months of outdoor life in the open country he liked, living in a comfortable house of wattle and mud, roofed with grass thatch, built where and when he and his partner wanted. After four months Dawson went back to his farm at Sotik, but Tilman stayed on for a couple of months longer, partly to make sure that they had not overlooked any promising rock on their claims, partly to enjoy a crop of peas and other quick-growing vegetables he had planted when they built their house.

On winding up their gold-mining business (getting £25 for the sale of one of their claims) Tilman and Dawson returned to Sotik. Dawson, who was married, was now living in Tilman's old house at Soymet. The Dawsons remained good friends to Tilman, and he was always welcome to stay with them. He was on excellent terms with the settler community there, and a visit to Sotik gave him a chance to think out what he was going to do next.

Things did not turn out quite as he hoped, because he had a nasty accident riding in a point-to-point at a gymkhana. He was galloping fast, when a herd of oxen wandered on to the course. His horse cannoned into one of them and he was thrown. He was badly cut and grazed, and lost most of his teeth. There are varying legends about what happened next. The best is that he was so angered by the battering of his face and the loss of his teeth that as soon as he had cleaned himself up he drove to Nairobi, sold his car, bought a bicycle and set off to cycle across Africa to the West Coast. What in fact happened was that he went to Nairobi for dental treatment and then, while his face healed, went for a lone climb on Kilimanjaro. When he and Shipton had climbed there in 1930 they had missed the highest point of the main summit (Kaiser Wilhelm Spitze on Kibo) in dense fog. Now Tilman repaired the omission.

He climbed without porters, carrying 40 lbs of kit himself. He had wanted to take a tent, but it was too heavy, so for a bivouac on the mountain he took nothing but a sleeping bag, a good pullover, and some thick woollen stockings. To get to the summit of Kilimanjaro is more of a stiff walk than a climb; even so, it means going up to nearly 20,000 feet, and Tilman was a little nervous because in the past he had tended to suffer from mountain sickness at heights over about 17,000 feet. This time he was delighted to find that, although he suffered slight nausea over 19,000 feet, he was not in fact sick. Having achieved the main summit and three lesser ones (they are humps on the rim of an extinct volcanic crater) he made a bivouac for the night under an overhanging rock. It was not a comfortable night for there was a cold wind, and a wall of stones he built against it was not much protection.

However, he was pleased at having got there by himself, and by his apparent acclimatisation to altitude.

Back in Nairobi he felt that perhaps he had abandoned gold-mining too easily. A new area to the north of Lake Victoria was to be made available for private prospecting, and he contemplated trying his luck there. To fill in time he went duck-shooting with Horace Dawson, crossing part of the new mining area on the way. They collected a number of quartz samples, and all proved worthless. After this disappointment he decided again to go back to England.

But how? Tilman put his thoughts like this:

Being in no particular hurry this seemed the opportune moment for carrying out a scheme with which I had been toying for some time, namely, the finding of an alternative to the usual east-coast route to Europe. I have no great liking for steamer travel at any time, and I was heartily sick of this route, but the alternative had to be at least as cheap—cheaper if possible—a consideration that rather narrowed the field of choice. Journey by air was out of the question;* travelling via the Sudan and the Sahara by car, though doubtless exciting, would also be expensive, and in any case I was not in love with motoring, even in a desert. This overland journey had at that time been done by several people in cars, and it required not only money but also the mechanical ability to cope with the breakdowns that would be certain to occur. Walking, on the other hand, was cheap, and was, moreover, a method by which I was certain of arriving somewhere, but would need more time than even I could afford, so I compromised finally on the humble but ubiquitous push-bike.†

The economics were sound enough, but it may be doubted if Tilman's decision to cross Africa by bicycle was strictly an economic one. He had his book in mind, and crossing Africa by bicycle was not a subject that had been much written about. Having decided on a bicycle, there

* Possible in 1933, but Tilman considered it prohibitively expensive.

† *Snow on the Equator*, containing an account of his bicycle trip as well as descriptions of his climbs, gold-mining, and of his earlier experiences in Kenya, was published in 1937. At least some of it was probably written a good deal earlier. A long article on the bicycle trip was published in two parts by *The Crown Colonist* in 1935.

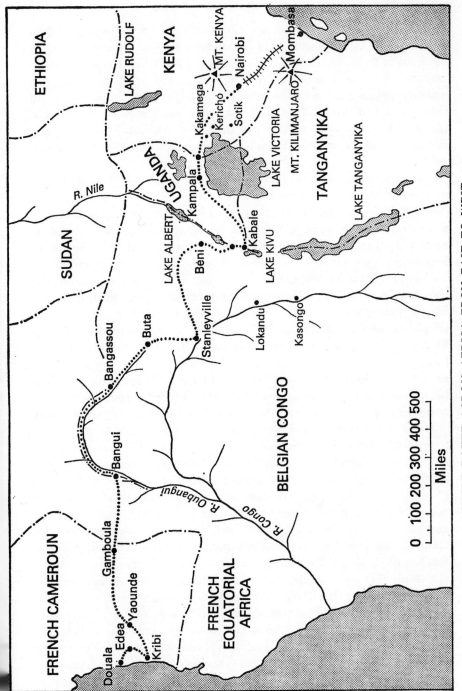

CYCLE ROUTE ACROSS AFRICA FROM EAST TO WEST

0 100 200 300 400 500

Miles

remained the question of route. Going north via the Sudan and Egypt was ruled out by the vast area of Nile swamp known as the *sudd*, and by the need to cross stretches of waterless desert some hundreds of miles in extent. That, he considered, might be feasible in a car, but was scarcely practicable on a bicycle—"apart from the impossibility of riding at all in sand." The most attractive route seemed to be west, through Uganda and what were then the Belgian Congo, French Equatorial Africa and the French Cameroons, a ride of roughly 3,000 miles.

There remained one problem that was real enough then though it may seem less so now—how to avoid the notoriety of a white man riding a bicycle. Tilman felt that this did not matter outside Kenya where nobody knew him, but that in Kenya it did—he wished to attract neither pity nor curiosity, nor to be offered lifts. So on 14 September 1933 he went by train to Kampala in Uganda, and began his bicycle ride a few days later. His dislike of any form of commercial sponsorship was already firm, and he made no effort to interest any bicycle manufacturer in his project by way of offering publicity. He simply bought a bicycle and a couple of spare inner tubes in the bazaar in Kampala. He could have had a Japanese machine for £2, but decided to buy a British-made bicycle for what then seemed the rather extravagant price of £6. As he had not ridden a bicycle since before the war he put in an evening's practice riding round Kampala, and set off at first light next morning before many people were about.

He took no tent, planning to sleep out on a groundsheet under a mosquito net, using an eiderdown sleeping bag. His route took him first to some 9,000 feet on the Uganda–Congo border, and at that height a sleeping bag was comfortable to sleep in. At lower levels it was comfortable to sleep *on*. For the rest he travelled light, as always, taking a rucksack containing spare shirt and shorts, washing things and razor. With about 20 lbs of food, his total equipment weighed about 30 lbs. The food was enough merely to keep him going for the first few days. He planned to live on what he could buy off the country. His staple diet was bananas, not the so-called "sweet banana" sold in England, but the big food-crop banana, sometimes called plantain, which can be baked like a potato, and is delicious. It can also be dried and pounded into meal, which can be made into flat cakes. The banana is a highly nutritious food and it served him well. For variety he bought eggs when he could, and occasionally oranges and pawpaw, a tropical fruit looking rather like a small vegetable marrow but tasting like a melon, and highly nutritious.

He had reasonably good maps of Uganda, but he could get no maps of the Congo, and navigated with a one-page map of Africa which he found in a magazine. It didn't matter all that much, for he could ride only where there were roads or paths through the Congo jungle, and he could navigate locally, making for the next town or village that seemed to be on the way towards the west coast. He did not much mind where he ended up on the coast, provided that it was a seaport whence he could get a ship to Europe. As far as he was concerned this could be anywhere between Accra in the north (in what is now Ghana, then the British colony of the Gold Coast) and Benguela (in Angola) in the south. "This gave me," he wrote in *Snow on the Equator*, "a sufficiently wide target of about 1,500 miles at which to aim, so that my plans had the very desirable quality of elasticity."

Having to navigate from point to point, he decided to make first for Stanleyville, in the then Belgian Congo, now Kisangani in Zaïre. The roads in Uganda were good, and he covered 60 miles on his first day, camping near the shore of Lake Victoria. His camp-site was not a good choice, for it swarmed with mosquitoes and he had to get under his mosquito net as soon as it was dark, and eat his evening meal under the net. He was glad to get away at dawn.

A week out of Kampala he crossed the Ugandan frontier into the Belgian Congo, the frontier then being marked by a solitary wooden post, with no formalities to bother the traveller because there were no habitations, and no officials. He had come through the papyrus swamps of Eastern Uganda, and the rolling downs of the Ankole Highlands. Now came an appalling stretch of broken lava in the area of the Mfumbiro volcanoes, with a "road", if it could be called such, over which he walked and pushed rather than cycled. Nevertheless, it had some lorry traffic, and soon after crossing the frontier he accepted the only lift of his journey, from an Indian lorry-driver bound for Lake Kivu. Tilman excused himself for breaking his self-imposed rule about lifts by reasoning that the lorry's tyres would stand the "road" better than his bicycle's.

The lorry took him to the Lake Kivu–Stanleyville road, meeting the road some 50 miles north of the lake. Here Tilman left the lorry, but since he wanted to see Lake Kivu and was in no particular hurry, he cycled back to the lake, adding about 100 miles to his journey. At the inland port of Kisenyi on Lake Kivu he gave himself the luxury of a night in a small lakeside hotel. This was run by a hospitable but economically-minded Greek, who saw no point in duplicating services provided by nature. When Tilman asked if he could have a bath his host was at first puzzled, then pointed out that there was admirable bathing in the lake. Tilman acted on his advice, going from a clean sandy beach into clear lake water for a swim that he described later as ranking high on his list of "memorable bathes".*

He did not often put up at hotels, for mostly he was nowhere near civilisation, but they made an occasional break from his mosquito net by the roadside. He was sometimes offered hospitality by a Mission Station, or district official, and he was invariably offered hospitality in native villages, whose headman would put a hut at his disposal. He liked the Africans and appreciated their welcome, but the offer of huts was an embarrassment, for he was more scared of a small tick that carries relapsing fever than he was of lions or leopards. Relapsing fever is an illness that can be even more serious than malaria, and a net is no protection against the tick. Moreover, even in those days before the development of modern anti-malarial drugs, quinine offered a fair degree of protection from malaria, but he had nothing to guard against relapsing fever. As the fever-tick infests inhabited places, his only practical safeguard was not to sleep in huts. He preferred to be accepted as the eccentric white man who liked to sleep out of doors, although this usually attracted an audience to observe him. Sometimes a zealous village headman would insist on making a big fire to keep away wild beasts, and on mounting a guard by the mosquito net for extra safety. Tilman accepted these ministrations because he understood the kindliness they reflected, though he would have much preferred to be alone. Sometimes the crowd of followers that his bicycle attracted in the more populated places was real torture to him. But he was firm with himself over keeping his temper, and met politeness with politeness.

His own views on sleeping out were that there was no great danger from wild animals. Lions keep away from men if they can, and although the leopard is more inclined than the lion to raid villages for goats or

---

* To qualify as a "memorable bathe" in Tilman's vocabulary a plunge had to fulfil a number of exacting requirements: he had to be really hot and tired to gain a feeling of exquisite refreshment from the bathe, and the water had either to be clean sea or (if fresh) deep, clear and cool. Finally, he had to be naked.

dogs, a leopard (at least in Tilman's view) will seldom attack a man. His views were justified as far as his own trip across Africa was concerned, for he met no trouble from wild animals. He carried no firearm, partly because he believed that he was in no danger, partly to avoid the fuss that carrying a rifle or revolver may involve on crossing frontiers.

As the crow flies Stanleyville is about 300 miles north-west of Lake Kivu, but the only road then in being covered some 650 miles, first going north to pass west of Lake Edward and the Ruwenzori region, and then on to Irumu near Lake Albert, keeping at first to the floor of the western cleft of the Great Rift Valley. Not far from where Tilman left the lorry on his way to Lake Kivu the road trends westerly, leaving the valley to climb the Kabasha escarpment of the Great Rift. Tilman, having no map, was disconcerted by this westerly trend, for he had expected that the road would continue to follow the valley floor. But it didn't, and as there was no other route for a bicycle he had perforce to follow the road and climb the escarpment, which brought him into open country, with tracks of hippo making for their water-places. It took him two days, mostly pushing, to climb the steep escarpment, but then came the reward of 25 miles of coasting downhill. He had another range of hills to climb before leaving the highlands, and from those last hills he looked down on the Congo forest. In his book he described the scene:

I beheld, far below me, a smooth expanse of dark olive green stretching away into the distance, flat and unbroken like the sea. It was the Congo forest, reaching westwards to the sea and extending to four degrees north and south of the equatorial line. That afternoon I entered what was to be my environment for the next fortnight. Within this tract of low-lying virgin forest, terrifying in its silent immensity, the atmosphere is that of a hothouse, sapping the energy of both mind and body. The only road crossing this sea of vegetation in which I was now submerged stretches endlessly before one like a thin red band at the bottom of a canyon of living greenery. The dark wall of foliage towers up on either hand for nearly two hundred feet, to arch and almost meet overhead, as if to reclaim from the forest the pitiful strip that man has wrested from it. . . .

The only break in the oppressive monotony were the villages, the huts of a road gang, and the rivers. The villages, and the *cantonniers*, as the huts of the road gangs are called, are merely two single lines of huts spread along either side of the road. At the villages there is also a narrow strip of cultivation, perhaps thirty yards deep, over-shadowed at the back by the dark wall of the forest, appearing thus envious of yielding even that insignificant patch to man. . . . This is "ribbon development" *in excelsis*. Everything centres on the road. Away from it is nothing human, except here, in the part called the Ituri Forest, a few pygmies, who live by hunting and who come into the villages to barter skins and meat for maize and bananas.

Tilman met some of the pygmies, finding them tough and alert, standing only 4 feet or less, but strong and wiry, with arms that seemed disproportionately long. They were not shy of other Africans, or of Europeans. They practised then no agriculture, and lived solely by hunting. The forest on this part of Tilman's ride was also the home of the strangely-striped *okapi*, an animal whose existence became known to science only when the Ituri Forest pygmies brought in some okapi-skins to trade.

Twenty-one days on the road, with river crossings made by canoe, brought him to Stanleyville. He had little trouble with his bicycle, though a good deal with his bicycle pump; the connection between pump and tyre valve tended to perish, and although he had some spares they, too, suffered from the heat. There were few other bicycles around from which to borrow pumps, and a flat tyre meant pushing. But he was lucky in finding an occasional Mission Station which possessed both bicycle and pump, and at one exceptional village an African with a bicycle showed him how to pump up a tyre with the aid of a wet rag as a substitute for pump-connector. This was harder work than normal pumping, but after he had mastered the art of wet-rag tyre-inflation he had no more trouble with tyres. He spent one night in Stanleyville, giving himself the luxury of another hotel, this one kept by a Portuguese. He was again in need of a bath, and after being invited to use the lake at Kisenyi he expected to be told to use the River Congo, but they ordered things differently here, and the hotel provided a bath. It also provided another kindly host, who got up specially early to cook Tilman breakfast, and gave him a present of oranges when he left.

From Stanleyville he went north to cross the Ubangi River into French Equatorial Africa. At the Belgian frontier post he expected trouble because he was leaving the Belgian Congo without having entered it—there had been no one to stamp his passport at the Ugandan border. Belgian officialdom, however, was kindly disposed, and accepted his explanation without fuss. French officialdom across the river was very different; although he entered quite legally he was kept waiting over the weekend for Customs clearance for his bicycle. He had a more pleasant encounter later, when he stopped for the night at a village which was also an Army post. Here Tilman's arrival was greeted by the French captain in charge with the offer of a camp bed and an invitation to dinner.

After a long ride across French Equatorial Africa Tilman had yet another frontier to cross into the French Cameroons. After his earlier experience with French Customs he approached the frontier nervously, additionally worried because he had been told that the Customs officer there was mad. There are, however, various forms of madness, and in this case it consisted of waving Tilman through with the utmost courtesy and giving him a present of a big bunch of bananas.

Fifty-six days out from Kampala Tilman saw the Atlantic on approaching Kribi on the Cameroon coast. He had to go on to Douala to get a ship to Europe, but his bicycle ride came to an end at a place called Edea some seventy miles on from Kribi, because there was then no road beyond Edea. But there was a railway, and he and his bicycle finished their long journey by train.

The bicycle survives, and it is still rideable. When Tilman brought it back to England he relaxed his uncommercial approach sufficiently to write to the manufacturers to tell them of his ride. He confessed that he half hoped that they might give him a new bicycle. Instead, he got a polite note expressing the manufacturer's satisfaction that he had enjoyed an agreeable trip.

So a most distinguished bicycle returned to the country of its making, bringing Tilman out of Africa. In his book he summed up, "For fourteen years Africa had been my taskmistress, and now I was leaving her. If she had not given me the fortune I expected she had given me something better—memories, mountains, friends."

VI

Nanda Devi

Eric Shipton had also been tempted to catch gold-fever, and for him it would probably have been a more profitable disease than for Tilman. The farm where Shipton worked was only about 40 miles from Kakamega, and one of his neighbours told him of the discovery of gold there early in 1931. He was invited to join a partnership, and, had he done so, he would have made a fair amount of money, not so much from gold as from the sale of claims already staked when the big gold rush started. However he was also invited by Frank Smythe, among the leading British climbers of the 1920s, to join an expedition to climb Kamet (25,447 ft) in the Himalaya, and Shipton had no doubt of his preference for mountains over gold. The Kamet expedition was a great success; ten previous attempts had failed to reach the summit, but Frank Smythe's party achieved it without much difficulty, getting from base camp to the top in a couple of weeks. Smythe himself and another member of the Kamet party, Dr Raymond Greene, had both been at Tilman's school.

After the success on Kamet, Shipton was invited to join the expedition led by Hugh Ruttledge to attempt Everest in 1933. This was one of the great set-piece mountaineering expeditions between the wars, employing an army of porters and no fewer than 350 pack-animals to carry what was considered necessary equipment, ranging from cases of champagne to boxing-gloves to promote healthy exercise among the party. The whole lavish performance was alien to Shipton's way of thinking, but he was delighted to be invited as one of the climbers. The party also included his Kenya friend Percy Wyn Harris. (It was Wyn Harris who had on this expedition the rather sad distinction of finding an ice-axe that must have belonged to either Mallory or Irvine, who perished together on the mountain in 1924. They were last seen, from a considerable distance, at something like 28,000 feet, and the circumstances of their deaths remain unknown. It seems almost certain that they died from a fall or slip while climbing towards the summit, but it is just possible that they had reached the top and were descending when they died—a remote possibility that can never wholly be ruled out.)

That 1933 expedition failed to reach the summit, defeated like all others by Everest weather and the final 900 feet or so. Shipton did well, and was now reckoned among the finest of the younger climbers in the world. He came back to England with his own ideas on how Everest was to be climbed—by a small party, lightly-equipped, and able to move fast to take advantage of any spell of good weather. In his view the huge, lavishly-equipped expedition, requiring large numbers of porters to establish camps, had a reduced chance of successful climbing, because of the time it took to organise movement on the mountain. He wanted to test his theories of Himalayan climbing by making a reconnaissance of Nanda Devi (25,645 ft), travelling light and living off the country. He set about earning the money to finance himself by giving lectures about Everest. Then, in January 1934, he got a letter from Tilman suggesting that they should have a fortnight's climbing in the Lake District.

Tilman, having abandoned farming and gold-prospecting in Africa, was at a loose end in England. He was doing some writing for specialist journals on his African climbs, and he may have started *Snow on the Equator*, but that was not enough to satisfy his restlessness. In response to his suggestion, he got a letter from Shipton inviting him to spend five months in the Himalaya. He accepted at once, offering to bear half the cost. Looking back, Shipton was conscious of the importance to both of them of these letters. In his autobiography *That Untravelled World* he wrote:

His [Tilman's] return to England was most opportune, and I believe that the course of both our lives would have been profoundly changed if he had arrived a few months later. For, while he would probably not have gone to the Himalaya during the next five years, thus missing the experiences which laid the foundation of much of his subsequent career, I for my part owe the success of the Nanda Devi venture very largely to his support. For the plan I had devised Bill was nearly the ideal partner: he was tough, and always ready for any amount of hardship and privation; indeed, his ascetic tastes often made me feel a positive sybarite. . . . Because I had had a great deal more mountaineering experience he was apparently content to let me assume charge and take the decisions, and we always seemed to be in general agreement about our plans. He was a recluse and a misogynist, and he had no taste for the softer pleasures of life: he had never even been inside a cinema. By contrast he had a sensitive compassion for animals and an effervescent humour which won the hearts of the Sherpas. Nevertheless, he was astringent company, with little use for small talk and none for abstract discussion; and, much as I liked him for his humour and admired his staunchness, our relationship remained practical rather than intimate. As we had done in Africa, we continued to address one another as "Tilman" and "Shipton".

This description of Tilman at the age of 36 by the man who was then his most intimate acquaintance outside his family is interesting, but somewhat misleading. Tilman was not a recluse; he had some almost monastic instincts, but he was ready enough to go out into the world— on his own terms if possible, but if he had to accept conventional social behaviour, then he accepted it. Both by nature and by training as an Army officer he was well-mannered, considerate, gentle and polite. What comes across most convincingly in this description of Tilman by his friend is the absolute trust that each had in the other.

The politics of climbing in the Himalaya need explanation. The great Himalayan range runs roughly north-west to south-east from Kashmir to the borders of Assam and China. In the west, parts of the range are in India, but the mass of the Central Himalaya is in Nepal or Tibet, or on the boundary between the two. Everest is partly in Nepal, partly in Tibet, the northern part of the Everest massif being in Tibet, the southern face of the mountain in Nepal. Until after the Second World War the Nepalese Government forbade any approach to Everest from the south (the route by which it was finally climbed by Lord Hunt's expedition in 1953). Tibet was nearly as inaccessible as Nepal, but not quite, and by patient diplomacy the British Government was able to obtain permission for a number of attempts to climb the mountain from the north. That is why all earlier efforts to climb Everest were made from the north—the British Everest Expedition led by Tilman in 1938 was the last Western European attempt to climb Everest from Tibet. After the Second World War the Chinese closed Tibet and the northern approach to Everest was closed to European expeditions. Nepal, however, became more open and after Tilman's exploration of the Nepal Himalaya in 1949–50 a number of European expeditions began to go to Nepal, culminating in the successful British Everest Expedition in 1953. A Chinese expedition later climbed Everest from Tibet.

In the 1930s large areas of the Himalaya were politically ruled out for climbers. An exception was the Garhwal Himalaya, a small part of the range which came under British rule after the war against Nepal in 1815. Garhwal, tucked in between the western frontier of Nepal and Tibet, later became part of British India. Although small in area, the Garhwal Himalaya contain some of the finest mountains in the range, including Nanda Devi, the highest mountain in what was once British India. There were no political obstacles to British travellers, and this was one of the attractions of the Garhwal region.

Political access is one thing : *physical* access is another. The mountain is so difficult to approach that although it can be seen from a distance, no one before 1905 (outside Hindu mythology) had ever seen its base, and before 1934 no European had ever set foot on the mountain itself. This is because Nanda Devi is enclosed by a ring of precipitous cliffs some 70 miles in circumference, nowhere much lower than 17,000 feet, and some of them rising to peaks of over 21,000 feet.

The Garhwal Himalaya are enshrined in Hindu mythology as the birthplace of the sacred river Ganges, whose first tributaries rise from the snows of Nanda Devi and from the Badrinath mountains to the north-west. It is the gorges of the glacier-fed streams of Nanda Devi that make the approach to the mountain so difficult. One of them is the Rishi, which later joins the Rhamani to meet the Dhauli River, one of the sacred sources of the Ganges. The first attempt to penetrate the Rishi Gorge was made in 1883 by a party including two experienced Swiss mountain guides and led by W. W. Graham. They were turned back by the tremendous rock-faces of the gorge, some of them apparently sheer for 7–8,000 feet. The next effort to reach the mountain was made in 1905 by Dr T. G. Longstaff, one of the pioneers of Himalayan climbing. He tried to reach Nanda Devi by following another gorge farther to the east than the Rishi. Dr Longstaff was able to climb the encircling cliffs at one point and to look down into the basin, but the descent from some 19,000 feet looked too hard to be tackled. As far as is known he was the first man to see the Nanda Devi basin. Dr Longstaff tried again in 1907, but again had to turn back. In 1926 Hugh Ruttledge made yet another attempt to get to Nanda Devi, trying again in 1927 and 1932. All these efforts failed. Ruttledge did succeed in climbing the rim of cliffs to see the Nanda Devi basin, which he called "The Sanctuary", but he was never able to get down into it.

That was the situation when Shipton conceived the idea of carrying out a private exploration of the Nanda Devi basin. He thought it could be done with two Sherpas, augmented by a few local porters, and he budgeted for a cost of £150 to cover his fare from England to India and back to England by cargo ship, and five months in the Himalaya. When Tilman agreed to join him he enlarged his proposed retinue to three Sherpas. The total cost for the two of them turned out to be £286. Even in the sterling of 1934 this was Himalayan travel of almost unbelievable economy.

Before leaving England, Shipton was able to discuss his plans with Dr Longstaff who, in spite of his own defeat there, recommended that they should try to get up the Rishi Gorge, and this they did. They lived on the same food as the Sherpas, mainly *chupattis* (thin cakes made of flour and water) and *tsampa* (roasted barley meal). *Tsampa* is a Tibetan staple, and is commonly eaten mixed with tea. It can also be made into a porridge, and eaten either hot or cold. To supplement their diet they brought from England some biscuits and cheese, and ten tins of pemmican.* The pemmican was reserved for high camps. Tilman took to their austere diet better than Shipton, eating whatever they had to eat without comment or complaint. His example inspired Shipton to persevere, as he explained in his autobiography: "At first I found this simple fare very bleak, and sometimes, particularly at breakfast or when I was tired, even repulsive; though nothing would have induced me to say so in the face of Bill's stoicism. But I soon became accustomed to it, and before long I ate my portion with ever-increasing relish."

An important innovation of this expedition was that the Sherpas were not taken primarily as carriers or servants, but as fellow climbers, a promotion eminently justified when Sherpa Tensing Norkay,

* Pemmican is fried meat (originally caribou or buffalo), shredded, mixed with fat, and made into a hard, cake-like substance. It keeps indefinitely, and having a high protein-value for weight has long been used on Polar expeditions. The process of preparing pemmican was traditional to the Indians of North America, and the name is an American Indian word.

recruited by Shipton for his Everest reconnaissance in 1935, climbed Everest in company with Edmund Hillary in 1953. The Nanda Devi Sherpas were Angtharkay (who was considered the outstanding Sherpa climber of his generation, and who might have reached the summit had there been an Everest expedition in the 1940s), Pasang Bhotia and Kusang. Shipton paid generous tribute to them:

> Sharing with them our food and tent-space, our plans and problems, we came to know their individual characteristics and to appreciate their delicious humour and their generous comradeship in a way quite impossible on a large expedition. Having spent all their lives among high mountains, they naturally saw no purpose in climbing them; nor did they understand our desire to penetrate unexplored gorges and glaciers or to cross unknown passes, for all these objects abounded in their own land. But whatever task we undertook they tackled with as much zest as though it was their own ambition to achieve it. With such colleagues leadership was hardly called for; indeed, in more than one tight corner, it was theirs rather than ours that saw us through. We owed all our successes to their unfailing staunchness.

The Sherpas called Tilman *Balu Sahib* (Mr Bear), apparently because of his somewhat shaggy appearance. They rapidly developed a mutual liking and respect, Tilman's wry sense of humour appealing particularly to the Sherpa cast of mind. They had no common language except a little Urdu, as foreign to the Sherpas as to the Englishmen. But they had the fellowship of laughter, shared dangers and shared food. That was what mattered.

They went by train to Kathgodam, and then 50 miles by bus to Ranikhet where the march began. The bus fare then from Kathgodam to Ranikhet was three shillings (15p). Travelling light as they were, twelve days took them to a village in the foothills of the Nanda Devi massif. They planned to cross a pass at about 13,000 feet from which they hoped to descend to a place where the Rishi joined the Rhamani, and then ascend the Rishi Gorge. Some local porters engaged at Ranikhet volunteered to come with them. Although it was 22 May the pass was deep in soft snow, and Shipton and Tilman had to go ahead to make some sort of path up which the porters could carry their loads. Twice they went wrong, mistaking snow-covered saddles in the ridge for the pass. At last they found it, and after six days' hard going they crossed the pass and got down into the gorge on 28 May. Here they found a strip of river beach under an overhanging cliff to make their base—the cliff was as good as a roof, and there was a useful birch copse to provide fuel. They discharged the Ranikhet men, who had done extraordinarily well, carrying loads in conditions most of them had never met before. It says much for the spirit of the party that the men left reluctantly, apparently genuinely sorry to have to say goodbye.

Shipton, Tilman and the Sherpas had food for five weeks, and near their base camp they had a peculiarly lucky break—they found a huge rock jammed across the river, enabling them to cross from one side of the gorge to the other by simply walking over the rock. The gorge was an awesome place, the river flowing between immense rock-cliffs, smooth, and apparently almost vertical. The cliffs on the northern shore seemed unclimbable, but there was a narrow gully in the rock of the southern side up which they managed to climb, gaining some 2,000 feet in height. Here they found a ledge leading westwards to a series of ledges offering a route by which they could outflank the great gorge itself. It took them nine days to cover four miles, but at last they climbed down the final precipice and entered "The Sanctuary". Shipton described it:

It was a glorious place, and, of course, the fact that we were the first to reach it lent a special enchantment to our surroundings. The Sherpas, whose appreciation of country was more practical than aesthetic, were particularly impressed with the extensive grassland, which they thought would provide unlimited grazing for yaks. . . . We saw many herds of *bharal* (wild sheep) and though fresh meat would have been most welcome I was not sorry that we had no rifle. Several long glacier valleys ran down from the great circle of mountains between 21,000 and 23,000 ft high surrounding the basin. In the centre of this mighty amphitheatre, standing 13,000 ft above its base, was the peerless spire of Nanda Devi, ever changing in form and colour as we moved.

Along that difficult route from their base camp they had carried enough food for three weeks.

Tilman's training as an artillery officer had given him a basic understanding of trigonometrical surveying, the principles of which are used in range-finding. He had polished up his knowledge by reading, and he and Shipton carried out a remarkably accurate plane-table survey of the whole of the Nanda Devi basin. They did this in two halves, starting with the northern section while their three weeks' supply of food lasted, deciding to come back and complete the work after the monsoon. They left it a little late, for their retreat towards the end of June more or less coincided with the arrival of the monsoon, which transformed the rivers into torrents. However, they were retreating unladen, and although they had some hazardous traverses to negotiate and various side streams in spate to cross, they returned to their base camp under the overhanging cliff without accident.

While waiting for the monsoon to rain itself out to provide better conditions for surveying Nanda Devi, they went exploring in the Badrinath Range, where they reckoned that the effects of the monsoon would be less of an obstacle to mountain travel. All things are relative, and while others might regard swollen mountain torrents and slippery rock as inherently dangerous, Shipton, Tilman and their three Sherpas accomplished two crossings of the Badrinath Range during that July and August, becoming as Shipton recorded "the first outside the pages of Hindu mythology to effect a direct connection between the three main sources of the sacred River Ganges". They also did much valuable surveying of glacier systems previously unmapped. They had one narrow escape from disaster. From the head of a glacier at about 18,400 feet they looked down an ice precipice into what seemed a lush green valley some 6,000 feet below them. Attracted by the valley, and also by the interesting climbing offered by the descent of the ice precipice, they decided to go down. The descent proved extremely difficult and took two days, during which they passed a point of no return by roping down a particularly severe stretch which they would not be able to ascend again. Their beautiful valley then betrayed them by turning out to be no lush glade but a tremendous ravine packed with forest and thick scrub. There was no track, it rained incessantly, and the sides of the ravine were so steep that sometimes they would spend an hour to gain twenty-five yards. After a day and a half of this they were stopped completely by a swollen river which they could neither ford nor bridge. Going back was out of the question, and it took them two more days of struggle along the river bank before they found some narrows that they could bridge with a tree trunk. Then they ran out of food.

Fortunately there was a good deal of bamboo in the forest, and it was the season for young bamboos to sprout. For the next week they lived on bamboo shoots, supplemented by a fungus that they found growing on some of the trees. After a week they emerged thinner but still fit at a tiny settlement, where they were able to buy a cucumber, a few dried apricots and—most valuable of all—4 lbs of *ata* (wheat flour). From the settlement there was a track that took them safely, and a little less hungrily, to the pilgrim route to the Hindu shrine at Kedarnath.

That was at the end of August. At the beginning of September they went back to Nanda Devi and, now knowing their way, returned to the "Sanctuary" by the Rishi Gorge route. They completed their survey of the basin, climbed a number of the encircling peaks, including Maiktoli (22,321 ft—and named by Shipton from a neighbouring grazing alp) and went some way up the south-eastern ridge of Nanda Devi itself, getting to about 20,500 feet. They worked out with binoculars what they thought might be a practicable route to the summit, but did not attempt it because their boots were nearly worn out. They left the basin by a different route, descending a precipice that in Shipton's view was even more difficult than the awful cliff that led them to the treacherous valley in the Badrinath Range where they had run out of food. This time they were better off, only two days' march from a village on the way back to Ranikhet.

Shipton was already well known as a mountaineer, but before the exploration of the Nanda Devi basin Tilman as a climber had scarcely been heard of outside Kenya, although his African climbs had been sufficient to secure his election to the Alpine Club in January 1934, just before he left for India. He was proposed for membership by Shipton and seconded by Wyn Harris. His nomination form has a pencilled note at the foot for the information of the Alpine Club's committee: "Mr Tilman has just returned from crossing Africa from E to W entirely alone on a push-bike. Incidentally, he made a solitary (2nd) ascent of Kilimanjaro and slept in the crater at the top!" After the Nanda Devi exploration an explanatory note about Tilman would not have been needed—he was beginning to be recognised as an outstanding mountaineer. In a foreword to Shipton's book, *Nanda*

Devi, published in 1936, Hugh Ruttledge, who had been a District Commissioner in the Indian Civil Service, wrote:

> I had the good fortune to serve for nearly five years in the section of the Central Himalayan chain with which this book deals. I climbed there with Sherpa, Gurkha, Bhotia and Kumaoni—as well as British—companions, and we made four attempts to enter the great Nanda Devi basin, as better mountaineers had done before us. It is therefore with some knowledge of the facts that I acclaim the success gained by Messrs Shipton and Tilman and their three Sherpa comrades as one of the greatest feats in mountaineering history.

Shipton dedicated his book to Tilman.

They were now making plans to return to India in 1935 to attempt a full ascent of Nanda Devi. These plans were upset by an unexpected decision by the Tibetan Government to permit British expeditions to Mount Everest in both 1935 and 1936. The decision came in March 1935 and the Everest Committee in London felt that there was not time to organise a full-scale attempt to climb Everest in that same year. Instead, the committee invited Shipton to lead a small reconnaissance party to Everest that summer, to be followed by a major expedition in 1936. A party of six British mountaineers was agreed, and Shipton at once asked Tilman to be one of them. Tilman accepted, but, to Shipton's surprise, without much enthusiasm. Shipton thought this was because in Tilman's eyes even a party of six was overcrowded.

The other climbers were Dr Charles Warren, W. G. H. Kempson, E. H. L. Wigram and L. V. Bryant. All had much mountaineering experience in the Alps and elsewhere. Bryant, a New Zealander, was considered among the best of the many fine climbers his country has produced. In addition Michael Spender (brother of the poet Stephen Spender and an outstanding traveller and surveyor, who died in an accident in 1945), was attached to the party as surveyor, with the special task of making a photogrammatic survey of the northern face of Everest. Shipton's brief was to find out as much as he could about snow conditions on the mountain during the monsoon, to explore the west ridge, and, if he could, the western basin of Everest, and to test members of the party as possible recruits for the major expedition now planned for 1936.

5

Whether or not a party of six climbers and a surveyor is a crowd may be open to interpretation, but even with Shipton's views, reinforced by Tilman, on the value of small expeditions over large ones, there seems to be a kind of multiplier at work on anything to do with Everest. To accompany the seven Europeans fifteen Sherpas were engaged, making a total of twenty-two. Angtharkay, Pasang and Kusang, old friends from the Nanda Devi exploration of the previous year, were among them, and so was Tensing Norkay, then an up and coming youngster of nineteen. According to Shipton he was selected because of a most attractive grin.

By Everest standards though, a party of twenty-two was exceptionally small, and under the influence of Shipton and Tilman they carried far less in the way of food and equipment than was customary, proving the Shipton-Tilman theory that by travelling light they could travel fast, and also establishing much closer relations with the inhabitants of the Tibetan villages on the route to Everest than had been done before. From these contacts they learned that the main reason for the Tibetan Government's reluctance to permit Everest exploration was the effect on local people of big expeditions pouring out large sums of money on food and the hiring of porters and pack-animals, with the consequent disruption of the normal life of village communities. It seems a fairly obvious lesson that might have been learned earlier, and it does not seem to have had much immediate effect, for although the 1936 expedition was smaller than some of the previous vast Everest caravans, it was still fairly large. The Everest expedition led by Tilman in 1938 was to be the first really to profit from Shipton-Tilman thinking.

Members of the reconnaissance party assembled in Darjeeling at the end of May 1935. Tilman and Bryant arrived first, and had two days together before the others turned up. The story goes that Tilman and Bryant spent those two days in almost total silence—a story that Tilman himself enjoyed. Both men had a nice sense of humour, and on the expedition itself Tilman, according to Shipton, responded to Bryant with "unwonted conviviality".

After crossing into Tibet Shipton and his party marched to Everest by a rather southerly route, exploring part of the Gyankar range of mountains on the way. The monsoon did not break that year until 26 June. They reached Rongbuk, the traditional starting-place for Everest from the Tibetan side, on 4 July. There is a famous Buddhist monastery at Rongbuk, and here they were blessed by the Lama. After paying their respects to him they went on up the East Rongbuk glacier, establishing a camp at about 19,800 feet. On 8 July they reached 21,000 feet and set about climbing the formidable North Col. Four days later Shipton, Kempson and Warren, accompanied by nine Sherpas, established a camp on the col at about 25,000 feet. Shipton was hoping to carry a light camp to some 26,000 feet and from there to go to 27,000 feet or so to examine snow conditions on the approach to the summit.

Tilman did not go with this high party. His old trouble of altitude sickness had returned and, although his "ceiling" now seemed to be around 23,000 feet, at anything over this height he suffered from violent sickness. Shipton's high plan could not be carried out, for soon after establishing his camp on the North Col a storm blew up and his party had to retreat. A tremendous avalanche swept the col, missing the climbers, but sufficient warning that the col was no place to be in monsoon conditions.

Having wisely abandoned the North Col, Shipton and his party spent the next two months in a general reconnaissance of the Tibetan flanks of Everest, rather similar in method to the Nanda Devi–Badrinath exploration in 1934. At slightly lower altitudes Tilman was in his element, revelling in what Shipton described as "a veritable orgy of mountain climbing". In those two months the party between them climbed twenty-six peaks of over 20,000 feet, Tilman and E. H. L. Wigram achieving seventeen of them. It was a Himalayan frolic unmatched before or since. But it was frolic with a serious side: Shipton and Tilman proved once more how much can be accomplished by small parties carrying a minimum of food and baggage, and they brought back valuable information about the whole region. They explored as far as they could on the western side of Everest, and had they been able to get down into the Western Cwm they might have found the route to the South Col by which Everest was finally climbed eighteen years later. What would have happened had they done so remains one of the fascinating might-have-beens of mountaineering history. But exploration here was impossible, for it would have meant going into Nepal, which at that time was closed to climbers.

Hugh Ruttledge was appointed leader of the 1936 expedition, and

Shipton, Wigram, Warren and Kempson were all among the eight climbers selected to go with him. Tilman was turned down because of his apparent inability to go above 23,000 feet. Having been rejected for Everest in 1936 he climbed Nanda Devi instead, reaching at 25,645 feet the highest summit yet attained by man. The Everest expedition, plagued by bad weather, achieved little, and was driven off the North Col by avalanches. Shipton did not enjoy it, finding what he called its "massive scale" not to his taste. He considered resigning from it before it started, but could not bear the thought of missing a possible chance of climbing Everest. Had he resigned he would doubtless have climbed Nanda Devi with Tilman, sharing in a triumph that his reconnaissance of the Nanda Devi basin had done much to bring about. As Shipton was not available, Tilman stood on the summit of Nanda Devi with Dr N. E. Odell, a Cambridge geologist who had climbed to over 27,000 feet on Everest in 1924 and was the last man to have seen Mallory and Irvine alive on the mountain.

Tilman's ascent of Nanda Devi is commonly reckoned the finest piece of mountaineering before the exploits of the new generation of climbers, with new techniques, after the Second World War. Although men had stood higher on Everest, Nanda Devi, when Tilman climbed it, was the world's highest summit to be attained.

How did a man who the year before had been sick at 23,000 feet climb successfully to nearly 26,000 feet—an arduous, extremely difficult climb at that? Altitude sickness is certainly partly physical, brought on directly by lack of oxygen in the thin air and the resulting strain on heart and lungs, but it may also be psychological, the kind of sickness sometimes felt before an examination. As confidence is gained the feeling of nausea may relax. Tilman had certainly gained confidence since he first experienced mountain sickness in Africa, and his "ceiling" had steadily increased. At first he was liable to feel sick above 17,000 feet, then, on his lone climb on Kilimanjaro, he was able to reach 20,000 feet without actually being sick. On Everest in 1935 he could manage around 23,000 feet before feeling too sick to go on. In 1936 he successfully overcame severe physical hardship and fatigue at over 25,000 feet. To some extent this can probably be accounted for by acclimatisation, which does—at any rate with some people—progress from year to year, but Tilman's performance on Nanda Devi was probably achieved for the most part by the willpower and determination he schooled into himself on the Western Front.

The expedition came about partly by accident. In 1936 Tilman was again somewhat at a loose end. By this time he was becoming well known as a climber and when an Anglo-American expedition to the Himalaya was suggested he was invited. The initiative came from the United States, where the distinguished climber W. F. Loomis wanted to organise an attempt on Kangchenjunga (28,160 ft), the third highest mountain in the world after Everest and K2. Loomis, who had done much climbing in the Rockies and Alaska, where porters are not used, thought that a light expedition of mountaineers, carrying their own food and equipment, would stand a good chance of getting to the top of Kangchenjunga. Dr Charles Houston, another well-known American climber, was keen on joining him. Dr Houston had climbed in Alaska with Professor T. Graham Brown, FRS, a distinguished British physiologist and fine Alpinist, and asked Professor Brown if he could collect four British climbers for a joint expedition. Brown was ready to go himself, and he invited Tilman, N. E. Odell (who in addition to having climbed on Everest had climbed in Labrador and the Rockies), and Peter Lloyd (among the best of an outstanding generation of young climbers from the Cambridge University Mountaineering Club) to go with him.

The idea was attractive, but the American preliminaries seem to have been rather haphazard. Kangchenjunga is on the border of Nepal and Sikkim, and to get to the mountain requires going through Sikkim, then an independent state in treaty relationship with the British Raj in India. Permission to enter Sikkim had to be obtained from the Ruler via the Government of India, which took time. As things turned out it was February 1936 before Loomis came to England to meet British members of the party, and to apply for permission.

With Tilman in the party, Nanda Devi, still unclimbed, was discussed as an alternative objective. There were no political obstacles to getting there, so plans could be switched at short notice. The Indian Government maintained an enigmatic silence and plans for the Kangchenjunga expedition went ahead. Tilman, not being tied to a job, went to India in April to arrange supplies for a march to Kangchenjunga in June. But when he landed in Calcutta he was informed that the party would not be allowed to go to Sikkim.

That left Tilman and his stores in Calcutta some 800 miles from Nanda Devi. The distance did not matter much because the stores could be sent by train to the railhead at Kathgodam, but it left Tilman with time on his hands. He decided to go to Darjeeling to engage six Sherpas and to try them out on a trek. Again he was frustrated, for there were scarcely any Sherpas to be had, almost all the fit men having been taken for the big British Everest expedition, a French Himalayan expedition, and a smaller British party which had managed to get permission to climb in Sikkim. Tilman had to make do with veterans and novices. Two of the veterans, Pasang Kikuli and Kitar, were exceptionally good, having been on Everest, Kangchenjunga and Nanga Parbat.

Loomis was due at Bombay on 21 May. With the rest of the party not due until the end of June, Tilman decided to use the time with Loomis to get stores to a dump in the Nanda Devi basin. This would also serve as a reconnaissance to show whether the route by which he and Shipton had reached the basin in 1934 was still practicable. He arranged to meet Loomis at Ranikhet on 27 May, and sent telegrams ordering loads of food—*ata*, rice and *tsampa*—to be assembled at a place called Joshimath, nine days' march from Ranikhet. Tilman solved the problem of porters with ingenuity and imagination. In 1934 he had met His Holiness the Rawal of the great Hindu temple at Badrinath, and now he sent him a telegram asking him to arrange for fifteen Bhotias willing to go to Joshimath to await his arrival. The Bhotias (the word *Bhot* means Tibet) are hillmen of Tibetan origin, and there was a Bhotia village called Mana, then the last village on the Indian side of the Tibetan frontier, only three miles from Badrinath. Having sent his telegrams Tilman went by train and bus to Ranikhet, taking with him only two Sherpas. He arranged for the other four, whom he did not need on the preliminary trip to the basin, to follow later.

By 16 June Tilman, Loomis, and their Bhotia porters had carried 900 lbs of food beyond the difficult passage of the Rishi Gorge to a dump within sight of the Nanda Devi basin. The only casualty was Tilman himself. On the last day but one they had to cross a difficult traverse of smooth and steeply-sloping rock which Shipton and Tilman had called "The Slabs". Here it was necessary for loads to be hauled up on a rope, and while Tilman was superintending this a heavy piece of rock broke away from the face and crashed down the slope. In *The Ascent of Nanda Devi* he described what happened next:

Whether it hit me, or whether I stepped back to avoid it, is only of academic interest because the result was the same, and next instant I was falling twenty feet on to the slabs, head first and face to the wall, for I distinctly remember seeing it go past. Hitting the slabs I rolled for a bit, and then luckily came to rest before completing the 1,400 odd feet into the river. In a minute or two I was able to sit up and take notice, and having told the load haulers to get on with it, crawled up the slabs to a more secure place and assessed the damage. A sprained shoulder and thumb, a bruised thigh and a cracked rib, and a lot of skin missing, was the sum total. None were serious, and it might have been much worse.

Tilman makes light enough of it, but he had to be hauled up on the rope, and spent the next day in camp while Loomis and the Bhotias completed the food-carrying. He found the descent for the return journey to Ranikhet difficult, for he could use neither arm, and had to be partly carried by one of the Sherpas, assisted by the Bhotias, whom he described as "very solicitous and helpful". He made no concessions for himself, and once clear of the difficulties of the Rishi Gorge he cheerfully acquiesced in making double marches in order to get back quickly to Ranikhet, where they had the use of a bungalow lent by the Indian Forest Service. He may have derived some benefit from bathing in a hot spring much valued by pilgrims, but he seems to have overcome his injuries mainly by determination to ignore them.

The Forestry Service bungalow was a spacious building, and it needed to be, for the stores from England had now arrived. Since they had planned for a much longer expedition there was more than was needed for Nanda Devi, and the first job was to scrap the surplus. Much of it was tinned foods brought for the British and American members of the party, and Tilman was eager to get on with the business of weight-saving before the whole party had assembled and individuals could make special pleas for taking this or that delicacy. Tilman himself, who had lived quite happily on *chupattis* and *tsampa* on his last trip to Nanda Devi, would doubtless have scrapped most of the preserved foods, but he had to consider the others. He summed up his own attitude:

Without wishing to appear over-righteous, I may say that I was indifferent to what we took so long as it was food and not chemicals, and gave value for weight. That this attitude involved no self-sacrifice I might add that in my opinion all tinned foods tasted the same, and that if we had to take 100 lbs of tinned meat the proportion of ham, tongue, chicken, roast beef, bully beef or even sardines was of no consequence.

The theory of the expedition was that it should be lightly-laden, the climbers doing much of their own carrying. In practice, in the India of 1936, total adherence to this principle would have been considered so eccentric as to be almost a cause for suspicion; and there were long marches to be made, which would have involved much waste of time in going forwards and backwards if the base camp and food dumps on the mountain were to be stocked without porters. Ten of the Mana Bhotias who had carried for Tilman and Loomis on their preliminary trip to the basin had agreed to accompany the main expedition, and in addition 37 other porters, from the same local community who had done so well in carrying for the reconnaissance in 1934, were engaged.

All but one of the climbers had arrived by 8 July, and on 10 July the caravan set out on the 10-day march to Joshimath, where they had arranged to meet the Mana Bhotias. The British contingent—Tilman, Professor Graham Brown, Odell and Peter Lloyd—was complete. Loomis, Arthur Emmons, and Dr Charles Houston were the American members of the party, the fourth member of their team—Adams Carter—having been delayed by a misunderstanding: when the plan for Kangchenjunga had to be abandoned he thought that the alternative attempt on Nanda Devi was not to be made until after the monsoon, and had gone off to Shanghai; but by the exercise of remarkable resource and use of the air transport then available he managed to join the expedition at base camp.

Having picked up the Mana Bhotias at Joshimath the party started for the Rishi Gorge on 21 July. As on Shipton and Tilman's reconnaissance they were making for the Upper Rishi Gorge, a little above the Rishi's junction with the River Rhamani. It was monsoon weather, and rained incessantly. To get to the camp under a sheltering cliff near the mouth of the Rishi Gorge they had to cross the Rhamani. On the preliminary food-carrying trip this had not been difficult, but now the river was in spate. Tilman and Loomis made a gallant effort to wade

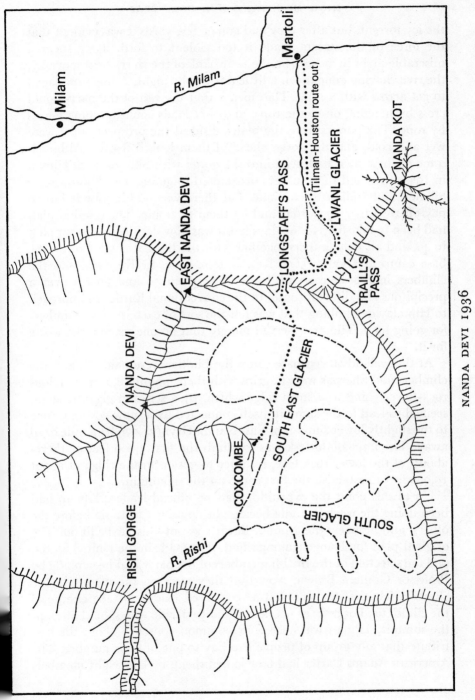

NANDA DEVI 1936

Milam

R. Milam

Martoli

(Tilman-Houston route out)

LWANL GLACIER

NANDA KOT

EAST NANDA DEVI

LONGSTAFF'S PASS

TRAILL'S PASS

NANDA DEVI

SOUTH EAST GLACIER

COXCOMBE

SOUTH GLACIER

RISHI GORGE

R. Rishi

the icy torrent, but after they had gone a few yards it was evident that the force of the stream made it too violent to ford. They spent a miserable night in a camp on the near bank of the river. Next morning, the river having gone down a little during the night, Tilman managed to get across with a rope. That meant that the rest of the party could cross by hanging on to the rope, and that loads could be slung across by rope. The porters from the plains disliked the prospect; they were wet and cold, and the gorge ahead of them looked fearful. Although some of these men had been into the gorge with Shipton and Tilman in 1934, they and their mates now refused to go on. The Bhotias were hillmen and willing to continue, but there was nothing for it but to pay off the other 37 porters and let them go home. The original plan had been to take food for 60 days but it was now decided to cut supplies to 40, and all the climbers together with the Bhotias carried on to the base camp at about 16,600 feet. It took some twelve days, and the climbers had been carrying loads of between 50 and 60 lbs over a precipitous and difficult route. In the conventional European approach to Himalayan climbing that was not the sort of exercise to fit climbers for going high. Tilman observed merely that no one seemed the worse for it.

At the well-advanced base camp the Bhotias were paid off, and the climbers and Sherpas were at grips with their mountain, a tremendous rock-tower rising to a steep ridge which, by a series of gigantic steps, seemed to lead to the summit, itself connected by a snow-covered ridge to the slightly lower summit of East Nanda Devi (24,379 ft) a mile or so away. The immediate task was to climb the first 3,000 feet or thereabouts of the lower rock face, in order to get on to the ridge at about 19,000 feet to establish the first camp on the mountain.

Up to this point the expedition had no official leader. Tilman had been doing the work in India because he could get to India before the others, and he knew the ground. But it was not "his" expedition. The original plan for Kangchenjunga had been made in the United States, and the selection of the British members of the party had been made by Professor Graham Brown. Now that they were on the mountain the climbers felt that they needed a recognised leader to take charge of the climb, to allot tasks as necessary, and to decide who should attempt the summit. Tilman was chosen by common consent—about the best tribute that any group of people can pay to one of their number. The American Adams Carter had now joined them, making eight members of the Anglo-American team and six Sherpas. Only seven of the Anglo-American party could go high on the mountain, for Arthur Emmons had suffered severely from frost-bitten feet during a climb on Minya-konka (24,900 ft) in China, and could not risk a recurrence which might mean the loss of his feet. He planned to concentrate on survey work from the base camp, as well as assisting in administration.

That the climb was going to be difficult was soon apparent. The initial rock was crumbly and often treacherous, offering few secure holds. Peter Lloyd did valiant work, both here and higher on the mountain, for he was brilliant on rock, and wherever there was a particularly difficult stretch to be negotiated his skill was invaluable. Rotten rock was not the only trouble, for when they reached the ridge they found the slope so steep that there was nowhere flat enough for a tent. To establish their first camp they had to dig platforms with trenching spades. The ridge was so steep that it proved impossible to dig out a flat space big enough to take three tents, and they had to construct three separate platforms some distance apart from one another. This made conditions at Camp I far from easy. Nevertheless they established the camp at a height of some 19,200 feet on 8 August. Having worked hard at climbing with loads they decided to make the next day a rest day, and enjoyed good weather for it. But on the day following they were hit by a severe snowstorm and all work on the mountain was held up. On 11 August they were determined to get going again in spite of fresh snow. While the others brought up supplies to Camp I, Tilman and Odell climbed on up the ridge to look for a site for Camp II. The best they could find was a ledge some 20 feet long by 6 feet wide, at a height of about 20,400 feet. It was really no more than a site for a bivouac, but it had to serve, and on 14 August it was occupied by Graham Brown and Houston, who went on to look for a site for Camp III while the rest of the party brought up loads to Camp II. Progress above Camp II required climbing difficult snow-covered rock and a long stretch of exceedingly steep snow, its measured angle of slope in some places being 50 degrees. Above this, however, was a sort of saddle, offering a rather better site for tents than Camp II, and here Camp III was established at about 21,200 feet. By 21 August all seven climbers had been up to Camp III, stocking it with food and fuel for a fortnight.

This was the outcome of leadership and determination, for a disaster hit them that would have stopped many Himalayan expeditions—all the Sherpas fell sick with dysentery, and save for a single load to Camp

III were able to do no carrying at all above Camp II. They had to be sent down to base camp, where sadly Kitar died. The others recovered, but were of no further help on the mountain. Thus the expedition became what had originally been planned—a light party of British and American climbers fending for themselves. They had not only to fend, but to do without, for a case containing all but one ounce of their tea fell over a precipice and climbers want tea more than anything else to quench thirst.

Without Sherpas or tea they carried on. Camp IV was established on a snow shoulder immediately above Camp III, and although this meant a lot of carrying for a gain in height of only about 500 feet, the positioning of Camp IV was vital to final success. For two days (22–23 August) a blizzard held up everything, but on 24 August a bivouac for two men was carried to 23,500 feet, whence it was hoped an attempt on the summit could be made. Odell and Houston were the pair chosen for a first attempt, and they were given two days. They spent the first day climbing to a rather higher bivouac, but on the second day the party lower on the mountain were startled to hear Odell calling for help. At first they thought that he was crying "Charlie has been killed", and made desperate haste to climb towards him. As they got near they learned with relief that Houston was alive but had been violently sick during the night, apparently from some form of food poisoning. Although he was still feeling ill, he insisted on going down forthwith, to give a chance of the summit to someone else before the weather broke again, an attitude that Tilman described as "very unselfish and determined". Tilman himself stayed up in Houston's place, and while the others went down he and Odell found an even higher site for a bivouac and made two journeys to carry up tent and food. Hard as the climbing was, there was an improvement in the quality of the rock, which was now firmer and less friable.

At 6 a.m. on 29 August Tilman and Odell left their tent at about 24,000 feet. It was bitterly cold and the rope that linked them was iron-stiff. They had first to surmount a difficult ridge about 300 yards long, but Odell and Houston had reconnoitred it, and Odell led confidently to a mound of snow which was the highest point that he and Houston had reached. In his book Tilman described what followed:

In front was a snow slope set at an angle of about 30 degrees and running right up to the foot of the rock wall perhaps 600 or 700 feet above us. . . . We were too close under the summit to see where it lay, but there was little doubt about the line we should take, because from a rapid survey there seemed only one place where a lodgment could be effected on the final wall. This was well to the west of our present position, where a snow rib crossed the terrace at right angles, and, abutting against the wall, formed as it were a ramp.

We began the long trudge at eight o'clock and even at that early hour and after a cold night the snow was not good, and soon became execrable. The sun was now well up. After it had been at work for a bit we were going in over our knees at every step. . . . It was like trying to climb up cotton wool, and every step made good cost six to eight deep breaths. . . .

We derived some encouragement from seeing East Nanda Devi (24,379 ft) sink below us, and at one o'clock, rather to our surprise, we found ourselves on top of the snow rib moving at a snail's pace towards the foot of the rocks. There we had a long rest and tried to force some chocolate down our throats by eating snow at the same time. . . . There was a difficult piece of rock to climb. Odell led this, and appeared to find it stimulating, but it provoked me to exclaim loudly upon its "thinness". Over that we were landed fairly on the final slope with the summit ridge a bare 300 feet above us.

Presently we were confronted with the choice of a short but very steep snow gully and a longer but less drastic route to the left. We took the first, and found the snow reasonably hard owing to the very steep angle at which it lay. After a severe struggle I drew myself out of it on to a long and gently sloping corridor, just below and parallel to the summit ridge. I sat down and drove the axe in deep to hold Odell as he finished the gully. He moved up to join me, and I had just suggested the corridor as a promising line to take when there was a sudden hiss and a slab of snow about forty yards long slid off the corridor and disappeared down the gully, peeling off a foot of snow as it went. At the lower limit of the avalanche, which was where we were sitting, it actually broke away for a depth of a foot all round my axe to which I was holding. . . . The corridor route had somehow lost its attractiveness and we finished the climb by the ridge without further adventure, reaching the top at three o'clock.

The summit is not the exiguous and precarious spot that usually graces the top of so many Himalayan peaks, but a solid snow ridge nearly 200 yards long and twenty yards broad. It is seldom that conditions on top of a high peak allow the climber the time or opportunity to savour the immediate fruits of victory. Too often, when, having first carefully probed the snow to make sure he is not standing on a cornice, the climber straightens up preparatory to savouring the situation to the full, he is met by a perishing wind and the interesting view of a cloud at close quarters. . . . Far otherwise was it now. There were no cornices to worry about, and room to unrope and walk about. The air was still, the sun shone, and the view was good if not so extensive as we had hoped. . . . It gave us a curious feeling of exaltation to know that we were above every peak within hundreds of miles on either hand. Dhaulagiri, 1,000 feet higher, and two hundred miles away in Nepal was our nearest rival. I believe we so far forgot ourselves as to shake hands on it.

After the first joy in victory came a feeling of sadness that the mountain had succumbed, that the proud head of the goddess was bowed.

They were back at their bivouac by six o'clock, and squandered the whole of the expedition's remaining ounce of tea (generously left by the others for the summit party) in celebration, saving the tea-leaves for another brew in the morning. There was still food for three or four days at Camp IV, but Graham Brown had already gone down with Houston, and Loomis and Carter had slightly frost-bitten feet, which made it unwise for them to attempt the summit. Tilman was sorry for Peter Lloyd, who was at the top of his form, and he always regretted that they could not make up a second summit party so that Lloyd, who had contributed so much to the expedition's success, could reach the top.

After his election as leader the ascent of Nanda Devi can fairly be called "Tilman's climb", and he was himself one of the two to reach the top. The group had an interesting discussion on whether they should ever disclose to the rest of the world who had got to the summit, leaving the achievement to be regarded as one for the expedition as a whole and not for individual members of it. There is much to be said for this point of view, but its adoption is scarcely practicable. And in this particular case the members of the expedition voted against it on the moral ground that those who had *not* reached the summit might wrongly be acclaimed for having done so, and, if names were to be kept secret, would be unable to set the record straight. So in the expedition's dispatches names were named in the accustomed way.

Accompanied by Charles Houston and the Sherpa Pasang, Tilman added another "first" to the expedition's achievements: they crossed the col on the rim of encircling peaks from which Longstaff had looked down into the Nanda Devi basin in 1905 when he reached the col from the other side but had not been able to descend. Dr Houston writes:

> Bill and I parted from our colleagues after a banquet of fresh baked potatoes and yak butter at the Nanda Devi base camp. They went out via the Rishi Gorge, while Bill and I and Pasang Kikuli climbed wearily up to a steep snow slope a few hundred feet below the pass. Early next morning we floundered in chest-deep powder snow up a very steep slope for endless hours, finally crossing the dramatic pass in cloud, and breaking down the other side. We then had several hours of extremely dangerous ice work over steep slopes precariously covered with powder; I recall being frightened to death before we gave up our efforts to traverse the south of Nanda Kot (over Traill's Pass) and tried to head straight down. We were exhausted before we finally found a small place level enough to camp well after dark. Bill was his magnificent indomitable surly self. It was indeed an epic journey.

After a hazardous descent, during which Tilman was separated from Houston and Pasang by a stream which became an unfordable torrent, the party came out via Martoli. With their crossing of Longstaff's Col it duly became Longstaff's Pass.

Nanda Devi is exceeded in height by many great mountains that have since been climbed, but the exceptional difficulties of the climb, with so much carrying having to be done by the climbers, caused the ascent to be regarded as a triumph of mountaineering. And Nanda Devi was climbed without the aid of oxygen, aluminium ladders, rock drills and pitons that are the staples of modern mountaineering equipment: stout boots, thick woollen stockings, ice-axe and rope were the climbing aids of Tilman's generation.

143

VII

The Karakoram and Everest Again

WHILE TILMAN WAS crossing Longstaff's Pass his father J. H. Tilman died in England. His last letter to his son, written on 28 April 1936, reached him in India when he was recruiting Sherpas for the Nanda Devi climb. In a very shaky hand J. H. Tilman wrote, "I am making steady progress—for four days in succession I have been out in the car." But on the back of the page is a note from Adeline, "Dearest Bill— I'm afraid you must read the other side with kindly eyes. Father is very weak, and literally crawls into the car on his hands and knees. Mentally he is rather muddled, but his spirit is splendid." He lived until 5 September, four days before news of his son's ascent of Nanda Devi was published in the newspapers. On 14 September Tilman's sister wrote:

> The papers here are full of the expedition's success, and we are very pleased for your sake, and proud too. . . . The news in the paper of 9 September which we read at breakfast was by way of an anti-climax—you may have guessed that Father has not been too well recently, but I purposely kept any worry from you. . . . Happily he did not suffer. Of discomfort he had plenty, but he never grumbled, only apologised for troubling us.
>
> Mother has been splendid, and the children a great comfort, and very helpful. . . . But this I must say—Do not hurry home on our account, or in any way curtail your arrangements. . . .

His mother wrote, thanking him for his "comforting and sympathetic letters", and adding, "Your whole trip has helped us to bear our sorrow and loss with greater fortitude. . . . We are all so proud of you." J. H. Tilman died without knowing that his son had just climbed the highest peak then to be achieved by man, but he knew of his magnificent performance in the Nanda Devi basin in 1934, and in the Everest Himalaya in 1935. Whatever his earlier disappointment over his son's

144

reluctance to follow him in business, he lived to realise that his son's own line of activity was making him one of the outstanding figures of the twentieth century. And Tilman could be justifiably proud of his father, who from small beginnings had built up what was then a considerable fortune, which he used generously for the benefit of his family and for the many charities which he supported. With his customary reticence, Tilman makes no reference in his book on Nanda Devi to his father's death, news of which reached him as he emerged from the mountain.

He got back to Ranikhet on 12 September and after winding up the expedition left India towards the end of the month. He had much to do—to help in settling his father's affairs, and to finish writing *The Ascent of Nanda Devi*, which was published by Cambridge University Press in May 1937. He did not give himself much time, for in December 1936 he agreed to join Shipton in an expedition to the Karakoram, which meant getting to Kashmir by the end of the following April. In those few months he also tidied up for publication whatever he had already written of *Snow on the Equator*, which came out in November 1937.

Six months after his father's death his mother died. Her gentleness had always helped to smooth the rough edges of life, and her wisdom had done much to promote understanding between her remarkable husband and her remarkable son. Family continuity was less affected by the death of parents than it might have been, because for years Tilman's sister Adeline had been looking after them, and helping to run the house at Wallasey which remained the family home until after the Second World War. With the death of his parents the family for Tilman became as it was to remain until his sister's death thirty-seven years later: "Dearest Adds"—homemaker, constant support, beloved sister to be written to from wherever he might happen to be, purchaser of pipes and tobacco for dispatch to the ends of the earth—and his nieces, Joan and Pam, Adeline's daughters, after her his closest and dearest relatives. Tilman was left if not exactly rich at least comfortably off and, given his austere tastes and preference for modest expeditions, he could indulge his passion for adventure without having to worry greatly about how it was to be paid for. Perhaps wisely, his father's will did not leave him the whole of his share of family capital outright; J. H. Tilman left a proportion of his capital on trust so that his son could enjoy the income from it without being able to dispose of it all. This was a valuable safeguard for Tilman's later years. In his middle life he had all the income he needed, augmented by substantial sums earned from his books and lecturing.

Tilman had written articles for the *Himalayan Journal*, the *Crown Colonist*, and various magazines and newspapers, but *The Ascent of Nanda Devi* was his first book. It remains one of his best, with a freshness about the writing reminiscent of his boyish letters from the Western Front. The book was well received, and reviewed in the main newspapers and magazines of the United States as well as Britain, the Continent and the Commonwealth. In December 1937 it was a choice of the Book Society, and was later issued as a paperback. The ascent of the highest mountain yet climbed was enough to make the book famous, and Tilman's vivid, mildly ironic style made it highly readable. The chorus of praise was not without a certain amount of criticism. *The Times*, which gave generous space to the book, considered that Tilman's modesty "does not really do the expedition justice", and the complaint that he was over-modest in letting his readers take difficulties for granted was echoed elsewhere. A more serious criticism is that nearly half of the book is not about the mountain at all, but is concerned with the recruitment of porters and descriptions of quite ordinary marches in North-West India. This is made readable by Tilman's pleasant manner but it is mildly disappointing to come to the end of a fairly short book and realise how little one has accompanied the expedition on the mountain itself. The enormous difficulties of the approach via the Rishi Gorge are certainly dismissed too lightly. Doubtless the structure of Tilman's book was influenced by the fact that Shipton's *Nanda Devi*, describing the great reconnaissance of 1934, had been published only the year before, and Tilman would not have wished to trespass on anything he considered to be more properly his friend's territory. His own book therefore suffers to some extent from his own generosity of spirit; nevertheless, it remains a classic of mountaineering history.

Snow on the Equator was also a successful book, well reviewed when it came out, and re-issued in a book club edition after the Second World War. Appearing only six months after *The Ascent of Nanda Devi*, its author's fame as a mountaineer was enough to get *Snow on the Equator* noticed, but it has merits of its own in being among the first published accounts of climbing in the mountain ranges of East and Central

Africa. And the narrative of Tilman's remarkable bicycle ride across Africa is still good reading. With his other books it suffers from his overpowering reticence, at times so unnecessary as to be irritating, but the style is crisp and clear, with many touches of his pleasantly ironic humour. Both books were important to him in themselves, and in bringing him many later engagements as a lecturer.

Leaving his two books to his publishers, Tilman set off to join Shipton in Kashmir. The other members of the party were Michael Spender, who had been with the Everest reconnaissance in 1935 as a surveyor, and John Auden, of the Geological Survey of India. (It is odd that both should have been brothers of distinguished poets.) There were also seven carefully-recruited Sherpas. The expedition which followed was another display of the advantages of travelling light through difficult mountain country. Its main purpose was to explore the northern side of the Karakoram range from which the Shaksgam River flows to Central Asia. It is a sad reflection on the twentieth century that Central Asia was far more accessible to travellers in the nineteenth. You had the physical risks of travel in remote, mountainous or desert regions without benefit of modern antibiotic drugs, and you might have trouble with brigands, but nobody else tried to stop you. In 1887 Sir Francis Younghusband had travelled through the Shaksgam region after a great journey from Peking but he had not been able to map the basin, and the position of the Aghil Pass over which he had reached the Shaksgam remained uncertain. Naturally this area attracted Shipton and Tilman: it offered an immense tract of unmapped high mountain country, and K2 lay on its southern flank. The essential requirement for success was to reach the Shaksgam basin early in the season, before melting snow made the rivers unfordable. This set a number of problems. There are two relatively easy approach routes turning the western and eastern ends of the Karakoram, but both are long and if followed would have meant reaching the Shaksgam basin to find the rivers in spate. In 1929 an expedition sent out by the Survey of India had attempted the eastern approach only to find their way blocked by an unknown river in flood; they named this the Zug ("False") Shaksgam.

Shipton planned a bolder, more direct approach across high passes likely to be still largely blocked by winter snow; to wait for the snow to melt would again mean reaching the Shaksgam basin too late in the year. The crossing was a formidable task in itself, but he also wanted to carry stores weighing several tons to enable his party to live independently in the Shaksgam basin for up to four months. A week out of Srinagar in Kashmir Tilman wrote to his sister from Ladakh:

Four marches out of Srinagar we crossed the Zoji La (11,000 ft) out of Kashmir into Ladakh. At this time of year the pass was still deep in snow, but we started at 3 a.m. and got off the snow by 2 p.m. before it began to get soft. The country this side of the range is very different from Kashmir. It gets little rain, there is rock everywhere, and very little greenery. The villages are Tibetan in appearance and what little cultivation there is, is done by irrigation. . . . There is precious little to be got in the way of food, but I hope things will improve after tomorrow when we get down to the Indus valley.

We are getting on very well. Auden knocks off pieces of rock everywhere and talks most learnedly. He also walks prodigiously fast, and I have given up trying to keep pace with him. Spender is botanising until he can start his survey work, and harps a good deal on food. I do the coolie work such as getting the party up in the morning and cooking breakfast. . . . I still have a cold, but that is not surprising as I crossed the Zoji La in shorts and sandals, and bathe every day.

On 16 May he wrote from Skardu, the capital of Baltistan:

We have been following the Indus valley. . . . We are living fairly well. Eggs are plentiful, chicken, and turnip tops for veg. There are also dried apricots, which are very good. Every village has masses of apricot trees, and this year's crop is now well set. The apricots from here are supposed to be the best in the world, and they certainly taste unlike the ordinary dried apricot as found at home.

Askole, our kicking-off place [for crossing the main Karakoram range into the Shaksgam valley] is five days' march from here.

From Askole he wrote on 26 May:

A local native from Skardu has been assisting us here in buying food so I take the opportunity of sending this back by him. . . . You should get my next letter about the beginning of October.

We got here the day before yesterday and hope to get off today, but it is cold and wet at the moment so it may be a late start. Yesterday was spent in buying 4,000 lbs of wheat flour and persuading 100 locals to come with us. We want them to carry four months' food into the Shaksgam valley, where we shall spend most of our time. As soon as we are across they will come back. We only want them for about 12 days, but it is necessary to carry nearly two tons of flour to feed them. The pass is 19,000 ft and there will be a good deal of snow, and since we cannot give them boots or clothing or tents it is unlikely that we shall get more than 20 of them to cross. This will mean a lot of relaying, but can't be helped. This village is the last that we shall see. It is about 10,000 ft up, but they grow a lot of wheat by irrigation.

Three days later they ran into trouble on reaching the Baltoro glacier. Tilman and one of the Sherpas went down with fever and could not travel for a week, the weather was bad, with heavy snow driven by strong wind on the upper slopes, and the local porters were even more reluctant to go on than Tilman had forecast. Because delay would use up food for the porters Shipton decided to leave Auden and two of the Sherpas to nurse the invalids, while he, Spender and the remaining fit Sherpas went ahead with the porters who were somehow coaxed into carrying on. In spite of all these troubles, just over a month after leaving Srinagar they were in the Shaksgam basin. The invalids caught up with the main party a week later. During the next nine weeks of strenuous climbing, interspersed with dangerous river crossings, they explored and mapped some 18,000 square miles of difficult country and the main objective of the expedition was wholly achieved.

On 10 August Tilman wrote to Adeline from a camp on the Crevasse glacier, the biggest glacier in the region they were exploring:

At last—a voice from the beyond! Auden is leaving a bit earlier, and will post this in Skardu about 25 August. I am travelling with him for a few days, but hope to find a different pass to take me into some country that we want to clear up. I shall have two Sherpas with me, and hope to be down to villages about 5 September and in Srinagar by the end of the month, so that I shall catch the P & O about 9 October, due home 23rd. Eric and Spender, with the rest of the Sherpas, are crossing a pass going north and will be out for another

30 days. I would have stayed on longer myself, but I promised the Everest people I would be home by the end of October.

We have had a very successful trip with regard to what we had in view—that is, we have settled a problem as to where a river went, fixed the position of an important pass, explored this unknown glacier—and, of course, Spender has been mapping all the time. For various reasons, such as shortage of men, shortage of oil, and Eric's keenness on mapping, we have had very little climbing—only two peaks of about 20,500 ft. They were both difficult and gave us good days, but hardly worth coming all this way for. I was hoping that we would try something of about 24,000 ft so that I could see whether last year's effort of mine was only a flash in the pan—a dying kick. However, I mustn't complain, as we have seen some very interesting country, touched Chinese Turkestan, and done some valuable exploration. It is all very useful experience for the future.

Tilman understated what had been achieved; and he did not enlarge on the interesting objective of his journey "into some country we wish to clear up". In 1892 Sir Martin Conway had discovered what he called "The Snow Lake", a huge, nearly flat area of snow from which the trunk of the Biafo glacier flows down the southern flank of the Karakoram to the west of the region the party had surveyed. No one had explored the Snow Lake, and it was thought that it might be an ice-cap, like those in polar regions, from which glaciers might also flow down the north side of the range. After leaving Auden to continue his journey home Tilman and his Sherpas discovered a high pass from which they reached the Snow Lake and explored it to its head. It was completely ringed by mountains and was not an ice-cap, but an immense (though otherwise quite ordinary) névé basin feeding the Biafo glacier. He then turned to another mystery—the "Cornice glacier". Dr and Mrs Workman who travelled in the region in 1908 had reported this glacier as being wholly surrounded by mountains and having no outlet, which would have been remarkable. Tilman reached it over a narrow pass in the West Biafo Wall, and found its outlet in a deep gorge; indeed, it turned out to be not a mysterious disappearing glacier but the upper part of a known glacier that had been on the map for many years. In a discussion at the Royal Geographical Society, after a paper on the expedition read by Shipton, Tilman observed rather mournfully, "When I started I had hopes of being able to vindicate the

Workmans and so confound the scientific sceptics; but, as you have heard, the Cornice glacier behaved normally, and that startling topographic phenomenon, a glacier with no outlet, has gone the way of the lost continent of Atlantis."

If the Cornice glacier failed to remain mysterious Tilman did bring back news of another mountain mystery which, in spite of all the efforts to disprove it, has never wholly been explained away—the Yeti or Abominable Snowman. On his trip to the Snow Lake he came across tracks in the snow which his Sherpas told him were those of a Yeti; moreover they identified them not simply as yeti-tracks, but those of a particular kind of yeti, the smaller man-eating variety as distinct from the larger yak-eating snowman. The tracks were roughly circular, about a foot in diameter, 9 inches deep, and 18 inches apart. In Tilman's view the tracks could not have been made by a four-footed creature, and were *not* those of a bear; they had come across many bear-tracks, and these footmarks did not in the least resemble them. That there were few men to eat in the upper basin of the Biafo glacier did not shake the Sherpas; perhaps the man-eating yeti can travel fast and far. Tilman tried to photograph the tracks but by ill-chance he made two exposures on the same negative, so the photographs were useless. And his measurements could not indicate the precise size of the foot that made the imprint for, in snow, tracks spread. They led to a fascinating correspondence in *The Times* to which Tilman contributed, but they remain unexplained. He summed up in the *Alpine Journal* in 1938, "The past season was a favourable one for snowmen, both in the columns of *The Times* and in their more usual habitat the Himalaya."

Shipton had so fallen in love with the Karakoram that he planned a longer expedition. He proposed to winter in the Shaksgam basin, living and travelling like Central Asian nomads and possibly buying a herd of yak. Winter travel in his view would have advantages over summer exploration, because the rivers, swollen in summer with melted snow and ice-water from the glaciers, would be frozen and easier to cross. As a modification of Central Asian nomadic life he proposed also to use skis, to widen the range of exploration. These bold plans had to be postponed for a reason at which Tilman had hinted in his letter to his sister: the Tibetan Government had given permission for yet another British expedition to attempt to climb Everest, and there was a strong feeling that Tilman should be asked to lead it. The meeting at the end of October with "the Everest people" was to discuss this. Another indication of his growing fame was his election on 5 October 1937—while he was still in India—to the committee of the Alpine Club.

The invitation to lead an Everest expedition in 1938 was formally conveyed to him and announced in November 1937. In keeping with his theories it was to be on a smaller scale than previous Everest expeditions, which would not only save money but avoid upsetting the delicate balance of the Tibetan pastoral economy. For his team Tilman selected Smythe, Shipton, Peter Lloyd, Odell, Warren, and Captain P. R. Oliver. All were climbers. Warren was a doctor, but he joined the expedition as a climber—Tilman took no medical officer as such, and no transport officer or other specialist, regarding all non-climbing members of a mountaineering expedition merely as people for whom additional food and equipment had to be carried. He took no radio, but—at the request of the Everest Committee—he took two types of oxygen-breathing apparatus for experiment. The two types were a "closed" system, with which the wearer breathes pure oxygen through a mask, and an "open" system, developed by Professor George Finch, later FRS, a member of the first Everest expedition in 1922. With the "open" system a mixture of air and oxygen is breathed through a tube held in the mouth, the flow of oxygen being stopped for exhaling simply by biting on the mouthpiece. With the "closed" system, exhaled breath passes into a canister packed with soda-lime, which absorbs carbon dioxide and allows unused oxygen to flow back into the reservoir. Most experts at that time favoured the "closed" system, but the "open" system was of simpler design and weighed less. It was used on the first ascent of Everest in 1953. Tilman agreed that the expedition should test both types but for himself he was hostile to the use of oxygen in any form.

The Everest expedition of 1938 has a rather melancholy place in general history as the last British attempt to climb the mountain from Tibet. As a feat of mountaineering it is more important, for in spite of atrocious weather Tilman got two pairs of climbers, himself among them, to over 27,200 feet. He proved (if further proof were needed) that a light expedition could accomplish just as much on the mountain as a more elaborate one. And he added a fascinating footnote to Himalayan literature by renewing controversy over the existence of the yeti.

Tilman and Shipton got to India in February 1938 and set about recruiting Sherpas, among them their old friends Angtharkay, Kusang Namgyal, Pasang Bhotia and Tensing. Karma Paul, a Tibetan living in Darjeeling, who had been on previous Everest expeditions as interpreter, agreed to come again. Tilman had been suffering from influenza. On 21 February he wrote to his sister from Kalimpong:

> I expect my flu was due to the strain and stress imposed by my vast responsibilities, which just shows how little mental effort I can stand. I am feeling moderately fit now, and shall probably be able to stagger as far as the mountain, and even a little way up it. . . .
> I have got most of the packing done now. We shall want only about 50 mules.

He under-estimated the number of mules as he explained on 1 March:

> The rest of the party arrived yesterday. They had rather a rush to get their stuff packed, as the mules left at crack of dawn today. I hoped we would manage with fifty, but the oxygen and medical dope which Warren brought was more than I expected. Noel [Odell] too is cluttered up with instruments—even my old friend the glacier drill has turned up again. . . .

At Gangtok, the capital of Sikkim, the party was given a send-off dinner by HH the Maharajah. Tilman had to make a speech, and after that he was able to report to his sister "we are on our own at last". They were held up on the march into Tibet by heavy snowfalls, but this enabled some mail to catch up with them, and he was delighted with the publishers' accounts of his two books. The American edition of *Nanda Devi*, he told his sister, "seems to have done quite well", and *Snow on the Equator* had sold 1,350 copies in the first two months of publication.

On 28 March he wrote to his old Kenya friend Robin Sneyd, now settled in England:

We are getting on slowly and shall probably reach Rongbuk about April 5. The slowness is caused by halting at various places to change transport. We only require 58 animals but it generally takes two days to collect them. A curious mixture they are, too, when they come, yaks, bullocks, mules, ponies and donkeys. The last are a sort of miniature donkey, only about 3 ft high. When loaded you can hardly see them. . . . The weather has been a pleasant surprise to me. I was expecting vigorous conditions in Tibet in March, but every day has been cloudless and sunny. A wind generally gets up about midday, but it is warm enough for me to march in shorts, vest and no socks. At night the temp. falls to about 10 deg F, but then the wind drops. I am very well so far. One or two of us have coughs and sore throats, which are no doubt due to the dust raised by the wind. Our last halt was at Tengbye Dzong, where we were entertained by a Tibetan and his wife for lunch and dinner, both accompanied by unlimited *chang* (beer). Fortunately it is very weak, and it takes a great deal to have any effect at all. The food was all Chinese fashion, and we ate it with chopsticks. This hospitality has to be paid for with a present, so it comes rather expensive. Yesterday we, or rather, the Sherpas, caught a lot of fish, which we ate for dinner and breakfast. There are any amount of duck and geese about, but we have no weapons, and in any case are not allowed to shoot. The Brahmany ducks are supposed to be reincarnated Lamas.

They got to Rongbuk, at the base of the glacier, on 6 April, and he wrote again to Sneyd:

Smythe joined us about a week ago. . . . The extra porters came in from Sola Khombu yesterday, and our total strength is now 60. I hope to start carrying up the glacier tomorrow, and as soon as we have got most of the stuff to Camp II we shall send 30 men home and retain only 30 for use on the mountain. We ought to be at III in about a week's time, and will try to see whether conditions warrant an attempt so early. There is a sprinkling of snow on the mountain, but the chief hindrance at present seems to be the wind. It has been exceptionally mild so far for Tibet, but since arriving here it has got

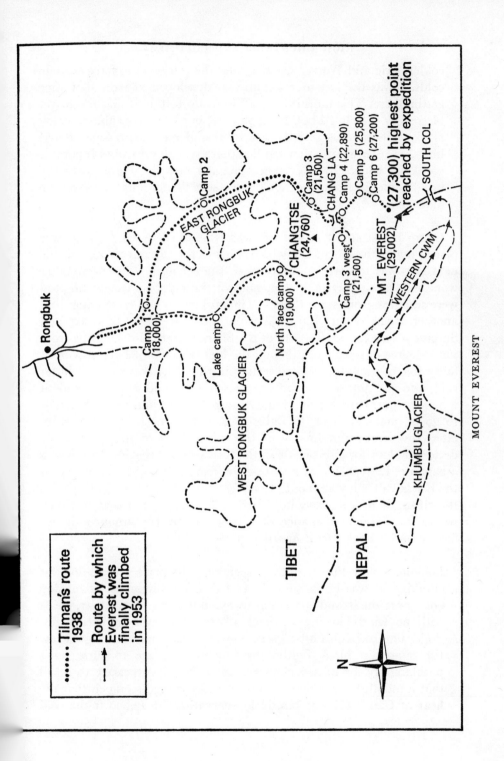

Rongbuk

Camp 2

EAST RONGBUK
GLACIER

○ Camp 3
(21,500)

△ CHANG LA

Camp 4 (22,890)

○ Camp 5 (25,800)

○ Camp 6 (27,200)

(27,300) highest point
reached by expedition

SOUTH COL

CHANGTSE
(24,760)

Camp 3 west
(21,500)

MT. EVEREST
(29,002)

WESTERN CWM

Camp 1
(18,000)

Lake camp

North face camp
(19,000)

WEST RONGBUK GLACIER

KHUMBU GLACIER

TIBET

NEPAL

.... Tilman's route
         1938

——→ Route by which
     Everest was
     finally climbed
     in 1953

N

MOUNT EVEREST

colder. Eric and Warren are sick, and the rest seem to have chronic colds. I was the last to succumb and developed one the day after getting here. This morning we all went up to the Monastery to get blessed by the old Abbot. He is 74 now, but still seems able to enjoy a joke. He gave us a feed—macaroni and meat soup—and I told him that if I was sure they fed like that every day I would become a monk, at which His Reverence laughed heartily. He gave us the usual admonition to be careful, and a selection of pills for use on the mountain.

Camp III at about 21,500 feet was established by 26 April. It was placed under the North Col which leads to the summit ridge, and the next task was to carry a camp on to the col itself. But the weather worsened, it was savagely cold, and all the climbers except Shipton were suffering from some illness—Tilman himself was recovering from another attack of flu; Lloyd, Warren and Oliver all had colds, and Smythe a sore throat. Twenty of the Sherpas were also suffering from some degree of sickness. Although the higher slopes of Everest seemed fairly free of snow the general feeling in the party was that the bitter cold, and the unfitness of most of the climbers and Sherpas, made it unwise to start carrying to a higher camp. Tilman had three choices—to go on and risk lives, to retire to Rongbuk, or to try to find an alternative rest-camp in one of the side valleys of the glacier. He decided to look for a rest-camp in the Karta valley, reached by crossing a pass, the Lhakpa La, at about 22,500 feet. The pass was severe, but the Karta valley lay at about 11,000 feet, and at that lower altitude, in the clean air of a scarcely-inhabited valley, he judged that sick men would have the best chance of getting better. He summed up his feelings in his book *Mount Everest – 1938*:

Looking up at the mountain, seemingly in perfect condition for climbing, it was impossible not to feel some misgivings at turning our backs on it and marching away. But even here, at 21,500 ft with no wind blowing to speak of, the cold was sufficiently intimidating to banish all regrets. The fact that one never again saw the mountain black [without snow] inclines one to curse one's pusillanimity for missed chances; but it is only necessary to recall that a month later, when conditions had changed so much that the heat at Camp III was positively enervating, at 27,000 ft the cold was barely tolerable. There is no question that at this time no man could have climbed on the mountain and lived.

Camp III was not evacuated, and some fit Sherpas were left there with instructions to move the camp a little higher up the glacier if they could. Tilman and the rest of the party, all more or less sick, crossed the Lhakpa La into the Karta valley, where they found a delectable camp site in a juniper-fringed meadow near a little lake. After six days they were all feeling better, except for Tilman himself, who developed pleurisy, which made him sore every time he breathed or coughed. With his customary attitude to such things he did his best to ignore it. They were back at Rongbuk on 14 May and got on with the job of carrying a camp on to the North Col. The weather was worse. There had been heavy snowfalls while they were away from the mountain, and now the wind which had been their enemy before let them down again, this time by reluctance to blow at all. They were relying on wind to blow snow from the rocks on the route to the summit, for in deep snow they would be unclimbable. On 26 May Tilman wrote to Robin Sneyd from Camp III:

We have been working on the N Col and have got everything up there, and hope to occupy tomorrow with 4 of us and 15 porters. There was a lot of fresh snow on it: one party got avalanched, but we held them easily. I felt like death on arrival here, but have been improving since, and I have been twice on the N Col, which is as much as anyone else. My newest trouble is a very painful rib, which makes breathing awkward. Probably pleurisy. I shall probably go up with 3 others tomorrow. . . .

There is too much snow on the upper slabs to make a hopeful attempt—at least, that is what all the experts, FS and Eric say. We shall push up a bit and see what the snow is like. The puzzling thing is the absence of the usual NW wind, which makes me fear the monsoon is at hand. Without the wind it is a question whether the rocks will be cleared of snow sufficiently to give us a chance. On the other hand, the monsoon may be delayed for another fortnight, or may fail altogether. The present plan is that FS and Eric stay down until conditions are more favourable. Peter Lloyd has had a mild attack of flu and has gone down to Rongbuk to recuperate. Whether we shall get a chance or not, God knows, but I don't think we could have done anything by an earlier attempt.

Tilman racked himself over his decision to take time off for convalescence in the Karta valley, and wrote to his sister, "We made a bad mistake in *all* going over to Karta, though had we stayed we should not have had time for a real attempt." So far as I know no one has ever seriously criticised his decision—certainly his fellow-climbers did not. Rest was imperative if the expedition was not to come to an ignominious (or disastrous) end.

The avalanche on the slope leading up to the North Col to which Tilman refers briefly in his letter was potentially serious, but the party was roped, the ropes held, and no one was injured. Tilman was much irritated to discover later that it had been wildly exaggerated by reports in some newspapers, but this was at least partly his own fault for reticence in supplying news. *The Times*, which had contributed to the costs of the expedition, had exclusive rights to messages from its leader. Tilman did what he felt to be his duty in sending back reports, but he hated writing for a newspaper while engaged in leading an expedition, and his messages were sparse. Furthermore, the exclusive arrangement with *The Times* meant that other newspapers had to pick up what they could. If Tilman had sent fuller stories there would have been less inaccurate reporting—but if he had sent fuller stories he would not have been Tilman.

That avalanche prompted a major change in strategy. The eastern slopes of the North Col were notoriously liable to avalanches in certain snow conditions, and Tilman now determined to make a new approach from the west. Shipton and Smythe supervised setting up an alternative Camp III on the western flank of the col, at about the same height as the existing Camp III (21,500 ft). The western approach was a stiffer climb, and harder work, because there was a long stretch of ice up which steps had to be cut. Camp IV was established on the col itself and on 3 June Tilman wrote to his sister, "Four of us, Odell, Oliver, Warren and self, occupied the North Col for 3 days. The mountain was deep in snow, and snow fell daily, so it was rather a waste of time. Self and a Sherpa climbed to about 24,500 to see conditions, and came down again. . . . As I had not yet recovered from manifold infirmities, I was rather pleased."

Camp V was established at 25,800 feet and Smythe, Shipton and their Sherpas carried a two-man camp, VI, to 27,200 feet. The Sherpas then returned to Camp V, leaving Smythe and Shipton to try for the summit. They found it an effort to cook and eat supper, but managed to get down a cup of cocoa and some glucose. They were up before 4 a.m. and started before the sun had reached the rocks above them. The cold was so intense that they feared frostbite and returned to their tent to wait for the sun. Then they set out again, but found themselves floundering waist-deep in soft, powdery snow. An hour of severe effort gained them about one rope's length of progress. Even then they did not give up, but struggled on to steeper ground, where they were in real danger of starting an avalanche. They had gained perhaps 100 feet. At this point they did surrender, and returned to Camp V to meet Tilman and Lloyd coming up. Smythe and Shipton, accompanied by three Sherpas, went on down to Camp IV, leaving Tilman, Lloyd and two Sherpas to spend the night at Camp V. Camp VI was already provisioned, but two oxygen cylinders and a little extra kit had to be got to it. Tilman, Lloyd and the two Sherpas left Camp V (where the night temperature had been $-1°$ F, ($-18°$ C) at 8 o'clock and got all their gear up to Camp VI soon after midday. The Sherpas then went down. Tilman and Lloyd collected enough snow to melt for cooking and then settled into their sleeping bags, for the wind was rising and it was getting very cold. They were some five miles high. Tilman's own account, in *Mount Everest – 1938*, continues:

For supper that evening we each had the best part of a pint mug of hot pemmican soup. . . . We rose early. . . . To say that we rose conveys a wrong impression; we did nothing so violent, but merely gave up the pretence of trying to sleep by assuming a slightly less recumbent position. Then one of us had to take a more extreme step—sitting up, and reaching out for the stove; and for the saucepan full of snow waiting in readiness at the other end of the tent. Once the stove was lit an irrevocable step had been taken, for it had to be tended. . . . In the course of half an hour or so the lifting of the saucepan lid reveals no merrily bubbling water, but a murky pool of slush or half-melted snow, its surface coated with the remains of last night's pemmican. . . . Presently the water bubbles feebly and breakfast is served—a mug of tea, not completely valueless as it contains a good quarter pound of sugar, a few biscuits and possibly a fig. . . .

By morning, the gale of the night had died away, but it was not until 8 o'clock that we considered it warm enough to make a start. . . . The sun was still below the ridge but the morning was fine and calm except for what appeared to be a gentle zephyr from the west. In reality it may have been blowing hard for I suppose if the atmospheric pressure is only one-third of normal, wind strength is also reduced. On our arrival the previous afternoon I cannot say that the rock wall which we proposed climbing as the most direct way to the summit ridge had made a very good impression. . . . But now, in the cold light of dawn, as [it] looked still less prepossessing, we decided not to waste time but to turn the wall on the right where it merged into the easier angle of the face, and where a shallow depression filled with snow led diagonally upwards to the summit ridge. As we moved slowly up the scree towards the right-hand end of the wall I kept changing my axe from one hand to the other thinking it was that which was making them so cold. But before we had been going ten minutes they were numb and I began to realise that the gentle zephyr from the west was about the coldest blast of animosity I had ever encountered. I mentioned the state of my hands to Lloyd who replied that his feet were feeling very much the same. We returned to the tent to wait until it was warmer.

We made a second brew of tea and started again about 10 o'clock, by which time the sun had cleared the ridge, although it was not blazing with the extraordinary effulgence we should have welcomed. In fact at these heights the only power which the sun seems capable of exerting is that of producing snow-blindness. It was still very cold, but bearable. We skirted the snow lying piled at the foot of the wall and took a few steps along our proposed route, where Lloyd, who was in front, sank thigh-deep into the snow. I believe it was somewhere about here that Shipton and Smythe had tried. Without more ado we returned to the rocks. There seemed to be three or four possible ways up, but first we tried my favoured line of which Lloyd did not think very highly. It was one of those places which look so easy but which, through an absence of anything to lay hold of, is not. I did not get very far. A similar place was tried with a like result and then we moved off to the left to see if there was any way round. This brought us to the extreme edge of the north ridge where it drops steeply to the gully coming down from the north-east shoulder. There was no way for us there. Retracing our steps along the foot of the wall

Lloyd had a shot at my place which he now thought was our best chance; but he too failed. . . . I then started up another place which I think would have "gone", although the first step did require a "shoulder". Very inopportunely, while I was examining this, our last hope, there was a hail from below, and we saw Angtharkay, presently to be followed by Nukku, topping the slabs just below the tent. I had left word with him to come up with the oxygen load abandoned by a porter who had failed to reach Camp V with us. We wanted to have a word with him, and of course to go down to the tent was a direct invitation to go down altogether—a course which I am sorry to say was followed without any demur.

They had a difficult descent in a blinding snowstorm, and arrived at Camp IV to find that Pasang Bhotia, who had helped to carry to Camp VI, had suffered a stroke and was paralysed. Another of the Sherpas who had been there had developed pneumonia, and had to be carried down. Since there was not enough manpower to carry two sick men, Pasang had to be left. Tilman now had to exercise authority in a difficult and delicate situation. The other Sherpas considered that Pasang should be left to die, on the ground that in him the mountain had claimed a victim, and if he were taken down another victim might be claimed. Of course Tilman would have none of this, but he was dealing with men's fears and superstitions. It says much for his powers of leadership and for his relations with the Sherpas that he persuaded them to carry the paralysed man from the mountain. Pasang recovered the use of his limbs some weeks later.

A dispirited letter to his sister, written from Rongbuk on 14 June, sums up Tilman's feelings:

We got down here today, and I had your letters . . . Eric and FS occupied Camp VI 27,200 ft and could make no progress above that owing to snow. Lloyd and I took their place on 10 June (Lloyd using oxygen) and we tried to get on to the summit ridge by the NE shoulder at 27,500 ft. However it was very cold, the rocks difficult, and we gave up for lack of guts. In any case we could not have progressed along the ridge owing to the snow. We came back to the North Col and found Odell and Oliver there. The latter wanted to go up but the former judged it useless, as it was, so we all came down. One of the Sherpas had a stroke, and had to be lowered all the way on a rope. Eric and FS were already at III, and now the whole party is here and the attempt for this year abandoned. Eric and FS are convinced the snow does not clear once the monsoon has started, and no one is willing to stay for an autumn attempt. We must chuck it, and try to get permission for next year. . . . Excuse this hurried scrawl, but I have to write an article for *The Times*, who have been complaining about the lack of news. It has been a dim show and I am disappointed, but the weather never gave us a chance. I am pleased personally that with all my infirmities upon me I got as high as the experts.

The last sentence rather contradicts his earlier reference to his own "lack of guts", but that is Tilman. A more fitting epitaph on the expedition was spoken by Peter Lloyd at a symposium at the Royal Geographical Society after the party's return to England: "In appreciation of Tilman's leadership I would like to say that if ever I go to Everest again I very much hope it will be under his leadership."*

Tilman's views on the use of oxygen in climbing are set out in *Mount Everest – 1938*, in which a technical account of the use of oxygen on the expedition, by Peter Lloyd, is contained in an appendix. Tilman wrote:

Mountaineering is analogous to sailing, and there is not much merit to be acquired by sailing with the help of an auxiliary engine. If man wishes gratuitously to fight nature, not for existence, or the means of existence, but for fun, or at the worst self-aggrandisement, it should be done with natural weapons. Obscure though some of them may be, the reasons which urge men to climb mountains are good enough reasons for wishing to climb the highest mountain of all, provided it is done in the normal way of mountaineering by a private party responsible for themselves. The various other reasons which have been adduced in the past, such as demonstrating man's "unconquerable spirit", or increasing our knowledge of man's capacity, should not persuade us to alter our methods, especially when by doing so we stultify the reasons themselves. I take it that when a man has to start inhaling oxygen his spirit has already been

* *Geographical Journal*, vol XCII no 6, December 1938.

conquered by the mountain, and the limit of his capacity has been very clearly defined. . . . In reply to any ethical objections that one may raise, the oxygen enthusiast merely points significantly to one's clothes, well-nailed boots, snow-glasses, or ice axe, all of which he considers sufficiently artificial to condone the use of yet another artificial aid, namely oxygen. And it is a difficult argument to refute. An appeal to common sense merely invites the retort that it is precisely that to which he is making his appeal. "Why," he asks, "jib at using oxygen? If your oxygen could be provided in the form of pills you would use it quick enough, just as some of you use pills to make you sleep." Well, perhaps one would. Oxygen pills, one hopes, would not weigh 25 lbs. But it will be time to decide that knotty problem when the pills are forthcoming, meanwhile, if we are being illogical, which I doubt, let us continue being so; for we are an illogical people, and mountaineering is an illogical form of amusement which most of us are content to have as it is.

After the abandonment of the attempt on Everest the party (except for Warren, who stayed to look after the sick Pasang) left Rongbuk and went home independently. Tilman went off on a private expedition with two Sherpas to try to climb the Zemu Gap on the border of Tibet and Sikkim. The so-called "Gap" is rather a cleft, itself at over 19,000 feet, on the long ridge between the eastern summit (25,556 ft) of the Kangchenjunga massif and Simvu (22,360 ft). It was then little-known territory, and to get to the gap is a formidable climb. It is supposed to have been crossed in 1927, but in Tilman's view some other col must have been mistaken for the Zemu Gap for he did not think that the gap itself could have been crossed in the times recorded. He had tried before to cross it, and failed—he went there in 1936 on his preliminary trek with Sherpas recruited for the Nanda Devi expedition. Now he had another go, and succeeded, making what seems probably the first crossing. On the way he climbed a 21,100-foot peak called Lachsi.

His journey to the Zemu Gap turned his mind once more to the problem of the yeti, for in high snow on the climb to the gap he came upon more mysterious footprints. This time they seemed to be the impress of boot-marks, and at first he was irritated by the thought that some other climber was ahead of him. Later it turned out that there was no one who could possibly have been in the vicinity.

Tilman had been interested in the yeti since coming upon the mysterious footmarks in the region of Sir Martin Conway's "Snow Lake" in the Karakoram, and had made a considerable study of his (or its) history, which was published as an appendix to *Mount Everest – 1938.* The first reference to the creature in Western literature appears to have been in a dispatch from Colonel Howard-Bury in 1921. Colonel Howard-Bury led the first reconnaissance of the approach to Mount Everest, and on the Lhakpa La, the high pass into the Karta valley, he found marks in the snow resembling human footprints, which his porters told him were made by a being they called (or so he translated the name) "The Wild Man of the Snows'. The term "Abominable Snowman" seems to have come from a later translation of *Metch kangmi*, one of the Tibetan names (the Sherpas use *Yeti* or *Mirka*) for the snowman. *Kangmi* means "snowman", and *metch* can apparently be translated as "abominable", though some Tibetan scholars think that it is better rendered as "dirty" or "disgusting", in relation to the snowman, presumably referring to the creature's matted, dirty hair.

If the creature exists, is it a man-like anthropoid or some species of extremely primitive man? The boot-like impressions in the snow found by Tilman on the Zemu glacier in 1938 seem to have inclined him to the view that the yeti has at least elements of human or near-human intelligence. In some notes among his papers, made for the long appendix in his book on Everest (which was not published until after the Second World War) and for a talk he gave about the snowman for the BBC in 1949, he argued that round or roundish pieces of wood have been used for walking in snow since antiquity, and must be among the earliest inventions of snow-dwelling people. To accept the yeti as capable of fashioning and using such devices would explain the more or less circular form of a number of the footprints said to have been made by the creature. "When we consider the simplicity of the device, the intelligence of birds, insects and animals, particularly our own poor relations the simians, the explanation is not so wildly improbable as it may seem," he wrote. He admits the objection that snowshoes are apparently unknown among Himalayan peoples, but counters it by arguing that Himalayan people hardly ever travel on or above the glaciers, whereas the snowman (if he exists) never travels anywhere else.

But does the yeti exist? Efforts to clear up the mystery since Tilman's day have tended to discount his existence, but there remains a considerable body of evidence which has never wholly been explained away. The high snows of the Himalaya are a vast area, still holding much that is unknown. Tilman summed up, "I think he would be a bold, and in some ways impious, sceptic, who, after balancing the evidence, does not decide to give him the benefit of the doubt."

One more piece of (this time certainly real) Himalayan history derives from Tilman's Everest expedition—it was after his expedition that the practice of awarding certain Sherpas "Tiger" badges was officially recognised. He did not introduce the title "Tiger" for Sherpas who climbed exceptionally well—that seems to have been in use at least since 1924. But he did officially dub his outstanding Sherpas "Tigers", and they qualified for extra pay at the then rate of 8 annas a day. This grading has stayed, and to be a "Tiger" became a sort of Sherpa knighthood.

VIII

The Second War

THE CROSSING OF the Zemu Gap left Tilman in his usual state of restlessness after any action. He had to get home for the Everest meeting at the Royal Geographical Society, and he knew that his sister wanted to see him. But also he wanted to explore the Assam Himalaya, and he had devised a private strategy for climbing Mount Everest—a small, light expedition, ready to take advantage of any spell of favourable weather before the monsoon, and to go on trying to climb the mountain every year until it *was* climbed. This, of course, needed permission from Tibet via the Government of India. On 15 July 1938 he wrote to his sister from Sikkim:

> I had a sticky time crossing the Zemu Gap as the weather was rain, snow and perpetual fog. The gap was hairy, much more amusing than Everest.
>
> I hope to go to Darjeeling today, and there settle up porters, etc. Before leaving there I may return to Yatung in the Chumbi valley, three marches from Kalimpong, to see Gould the Political Officer to see if he can suggest any way of getting permission for next year. If I don't do something about it, nobody else will. Anyhow, shall probably not be home before mid-August. Perhaps we could have a holiday somewhere in September, unless you have already taken yours. Don't worry about money—you know I have more than I shall ever need, even if I have to finance the next Everest expedition!

The Political Officer was not hopeful about Tilman's plans for annual Everest expeditions; apparently the Tibetans had been given to understand that the 1938 expedition was likely to be the last for some time, as indeed it was, though for reasons not then foreseen. He was not encouraging, either, about a trip to the Assam Himalaya, for the ill-defined frontier between Assam and Tibet was in dispute, and stray British travellers might raise suspicions. However, the Governor of Assam might be able to help with the proposed trip, so Tilman got in touch with him.

As leader of the recent Everest attempt Tilman was a famous man, and he was at once invited to stay at Government House, Shillong, the capital of Assam. On beautifully die-stamped paper headed Government House, Shillong, Tilman wrote to his sister on 1 August, "You see in what high circles I am moving! I got here this a.m. from Darjeeling after a long journey. The Brahmaputra was in flood, and over a smaller river a bridge had gone, cutting the railway line. This place is about 5,000 ft up, and pleasant open country, with pine forest . . ." His letter goes on to depict a vanished world:

I was received by a tall, good-looking ADC who gave me beer, and then sent down to the bazaar for a black tie for me, because we are officially in mourning for the Queen of Roumania and Government House inmates have to appear correctly dressed. This afternoon I played golf! There is a very good 18-hole course. I was pretty bad, but hit a few snifters.

Tonight we dine out. Tomorrow a dinner party of 11. On 4th I shall probably leave for Calcutta, leave there on 7th, and arrive Simla 9th. Leave there 11th to catch the boat at Bombay on 13th.

I am writing this in my room while a soft-footed slave in scarlet and white lays out my dinner jacket (probably moth-eaten) and prepares my lord's bath. You can't move out of the house without being saluted by several guards and sentries, and the ADC (curse him) likes to call me "Sir". It's all a bit trying, but I shall survive.

Survive he did, but he was only partially successful in getting permission to carry out his plans. The Governor of Assam was helpful, but Tilman wanted to try to climb Namcha Barwa (25,447 ft) which, although near the Assam border, is actually in Tibet, and for permission to enter Tibet he needed help from the External Affairs Department of the Government of India. His pursuit of the British Raj to its summer retreat in the hill-station of Simla was unrewarded. He had more success with the Everest Committee in London, which agreed to apply through the India Office for permission to make Everest expeditions via Tibet in the successive years 1940, 1941 and 1942, but this was used against him as far as his own trip to Namcha Barwa was concerned. In November, when he was back at Wallasey, he had a letter from New Delhi saying that in view of the proposed applications for Everest the Government of India considered it "inadvisable" to try to secure Tibetan agreement for a visit to Namcha Barwa "and we are therefore not forwarding your application to Lhasa". He had better luck with the Governor of Assam, for in February he had a letter from Shillong giving him permission to go to Gori Chen (21,450 ft). There were some fairly stiff conditions: (i) he must adhere to his proposed route for getting to Gori Chen (ii) he must confine his visit to the slopes south of the MacMahon Line which followed the high peaks of the main range and formed the frontier with Tibet (iii) he was "particularly prohibited" from entering the Silung Arbor and Miji Aka country east of his proposed route "as the inhabitants there are dangerous".

These regions were in Assam and technically part of the British Empire, but they were what were known then as "unadministered areas", where the writ of the Raj ran indirectly. The tribes might receive grants or subsidies for good (i.e. peaceful) behaviour, and as long as they kept out of serious trouble they were left to fend for themselves. They might, however, be suspicious of strangers, and the authorities in Shillong had no wish to be involved in sending search parties or punitive expeditions. Tilman accepted the conditions.

It was February 1939—not a happy time for planning expeditions. The crisis over Czechoslovakia in September 1938 had overshadowed Tilman's homecoming, as indeed the earlier international crises of that sad year had overshadowed the whole Everest expedition; like all attempts to climb Everest it had attracted much publicity, but with the Spanish civil war, Hitler's annexation of Austria, and bellicose demands by Germany and Italy to fill the newspapers and dominate radio even an attempt to climb the world's highest mountain could not evoke quite the excitement of the past. Yet life had to go on. War might be in the air, but the horror of war was so widespread and vivid in people's minds that in spite of everything, war still seemed inconceivable. People might be digging air-raid shelters, but when Mr Chamberlain came back from Munich, waving his piece of paper and declaring, "I believe it is peace for our time", most of Britain wanted to believe with him, and at least hoped that he might be right.

Tilman had more first-hand experience of war than most men, and as an ex-Regular he was still on the reserve of officers. He had no illusions about what war meant, but both by instinct and training he remained cool, carrying on with life as normally as possible. He attended meetings of the Everest Committee in London, wrote about the Zemu Gap for the *Himalayan Journal** and was in considerable demand as a lecturer. It is curious that for all his reticence, which might easily appear as shyness, he was a good lecturer, and usually enjoyed it. He took immense pains over his lectures, drafting and redrafting them until they met his exacting demands, and he spiced them with many flashes of dry humour. The excessive under-statement which sometimes mars his books was less apparent when he was there in the flesh, and the slides with which he illustrated his talks spoke for him.

He started to write his account of the Everest expedition, but unlike his Nanda Devi book, which was rushed out by the publishers, *Mount Everest – 1938* was delayed by the possibilities of war, which over-shadowed publishing as they did everything else. It did not appear until 1948, and although much of it was written when events were fresh in his mind it was not finished until nearly ten years later. It may be doubted if his heart was really in it—if he had gone ahead with writing and pressed for publication the book could have appeared without much difficulty in the summer of 1939. Inevitably, *Everest – 1938* lacks the freshness and spontaneity of *The Ascent of Nanda Devi*. Tilman was telling the exact truth when he told his sister that he found his private expedition to the Zemu Gap "much more amusing than Everest". In the early part of 1939 he was more interested in getting to the Assam Himalaya than in writing about Everest.

The international situation affected his planning. Shipton was off to the Karakoram again and wanted Tilman to go with him, but Tilman declined on the ground that if war came he would be cut off from news and too far away to do anything quickly about joining up. If there were to be war, he had no doubts about his own position—he would be in it. He knew too much about war to *want* to be in it, but he could not contemplate being *out* of it. By the spring of 1939 he could certainly have got himself a good military job—to supervise training for mountain warfare, for example. But he went ahead with planning his trip to the Assam Himalaya knowing precisely what he intended to do if war seemed inevitable—rejoin the Army as a regimental Gunner officer. His contingency planning that spring provided for his return to

* Vol XI (1939). An earlier article by Tilman on the Zemu Gap appeared in Vol IX (1937).

6*

England by August at the latest. There was a re-training course for Gunner officers starting then.

The Assam expedition turned out to be a miserable affair. He began with high hopes in April, recruiting three Sherpas in Darjeeling— Wangdi (a "Tiger"), Nukku, who had been with him on Everest, and Thundu—and succeeded in getting the conditions for his journey modified to enable him to have a go at climbing Kangdu (23,260 ft) to the north-east of his principal mountain, Gori Chen. But he had barely got into Assam when news came of the Italian invasion of Albania and the mobilisation of the Italian fleet. He debated whether to turn back, but decided to go on, the Political Officer undertaking to send a runner after him if war came. Then he and the Sherpas all went down with fever. With intervals of lying up to try to recover he struggled on to the foothills of Gori Chen, but Nukku and Thundu were too ill to accompany him and had to be left behind in a village. Wangdi, who had bouts of fever every day but tended to feel better in the evenings, behaved splendidly throughout. Tilman himself became too sick to go on and turned back to collect the invalids to get them home. He found both seriously ill. Nukku died, and Tilman and Wangdi built a cairn of stones, Sherpa fashion, over his grave. Thundu, too weak to walk, had to be carried. Floods made the route by which they had come impassable, and they had to make a diversion through country where it was hard to find porters. At last they got back to settled country, where the Political Officer heard of their difficulties and rescued them with a car. Thundu was taken to hospital, where he recovered. Tilman and Wangdi were taken to the Political Officer's own home, where good food and quinine put them on their feet again. Wangdi went back to Darjeeling and Tilman went home to England— and war. He was 41.

Tilman rejoined the Army in August 1939 and after a short course for Reserve officers he was posted to 32 Field Regiment RA in the rank of Lieutenant which he had held in 1919. The regiment was mobilising at Brighton and he joined it there on 1 September, a subaltern with greying hair wearing the ribbon of the Military Cross with bar.

The main difference between the Army he left in 1919 and that he rejoined twenty years later was the disappearance of horses. Air power, mobile tank warfare, and the vital use of radio would soon show how much in war was changed, but they were not immediately apparent. The absence of the horse was—there were no more stables and horse lines. Instead there was the ubiquitous motor truck. The regiment was armed with the new 25-pounder (Mark 1) field gun, but it was mounted on the old First World War 18-pounder (box trail) carriage, which was quite familiar.

Great Britain declared war on Germany on 3 September. Three weeks later Tilman's regiment, comprising 107 and 115 Field Batteries, embarked at Southampton for Cherbourg, to come under the command of the 51st French Division defending the Lille Sector of the Allied Front. Tilman was Troop Commander F Troop in 115 Battery. In November 1939 he was promoted Acting Captain. There was not much to do except dig gunpits, mount guards, and chafe at inaction.

The strange twilight of non-war in wartime ended in France in May 1940 when the Germans broke through and swept to the Channel coast. The fortresses of the Maginot Line behind which France was supposed to be impregnable were turned by the German advance through Belgium. France was in a state of collapse and it was hard to say where the front was, or even if there was one. The battlefields of the First World War, where entrenched armies fought for weeks to gain a few hundred yards of territory, were a chaos of refugees, advancing German tanks and dive-bombing German aircraft. The task of the British Army in France was simply to save what it could from the mess. Tilman's regiment ceased to be part of a French division and reverted to the command of the British Expeditionary Force. Its job was to help to provide artillery cover for the withdrawal of the 4th British Division to Dunkirk.

It did that job as well as it could be done. Tilman was mentioned in dispatches for going forward at three o'clock in the morning of 18 May to act as Forward Observation Officer on the River Dendre, to try to discover what was happening. The regiment, or what was left of it, was itself evacuated from Dunkirk on 30 May, having destroyed its guns to prevent their falling into the hands of the Germans. Without guns, the gunners fought as infantry. When Tilman finally got home he was still carrying a rifle.

Some 338,000 men (including nearly 140,000 French) were saved at Dunkirk to fight again, but although the BEF brought home most of its men it lost most of its guns, tanks and heavy equipment. The pressing need in that summer of 1940, while England waited daily for a German invasion, was to re-form and re-arm the British Army. Tilman's regiment was mustered at Okehampton in Devon and reorganised into four field batteries—107, 115, 120 and 121. Tilman was appointed second-in-command of 120 Battery. They were armed with 12-pounder quick-firing guns which they took over from the Royal Marines and bolted on the backs of heavy lorries. Thus re-equipped they were sent to Suffolk for Home Defence—not then the kind of "Dad's Army" that symbolised Home Defence later, but front-line gunners sent to resist invasion of the East Coast. In September 1940 Tilman was promoted Acting Major and took over command of 120 Field Battery.

As the likelihood of a German invasion declined, soldiering in England became less to Tilman's taste. The importance of India to the defence of Britain made it inevitable that the Middle East, guarding the sea route to India and the vital sources of oil in Iran and Iraq, would become a major theatre of war. Tilman wanted to serve where his knowledge of East Africa could be put to use, and he applied for posting to a unit in that area. In the mysterious way in which things happen in the War Office he was posted as second in command to 122 Field Regiment RA—destined for Singapore. He protested, arguing that he knew nothing of Singapore and Malaya, and in December 1940, just before embarkation, he was sent to the Royal Artillery depot at Woolwich to await re-posting. In this he was fortunate, for the survivors of 122 Field Regiment after the fall of Singapore all became prisoners of the Japanese. In January 1941 Tilman returned to his old regiment—the 32nd Field Regiment RA—as second in command, and in March he sailed with the regiment for India and the Middle East.

Censorship of soldiers' mail in the Second World War was taken more seriously, and carried out more efficiently, than in the First. Letters from the front in the First World War were all subject to censorship, but while soldiers were naturally forbidden to disclose where they were stationed, no one worried much about saying that a regiment had landed at Boulogne on the way to the front. It didn't matter greatly—radio intelligence was in its infancy, and the Germans knew perfectly well where the main fighting areas were, and the main routes used for crossing the Channel. But in the Second World War, when troopships had to make long voyages to get to India and the Middle East via the Cape of Good Hope, anything that might give an indication of sea routes might expose a convoy to attack. And the development of radio for the swift communication of intelligence made censorship of letters which might disclose troop movements more necessary.

Tilman's letters to his sister, who took the place of his parents as his chief correspondent, are vivid in comment and description, but the locations from which he wrote can be deduced only by correlation with the available war records, and not always then. Sometimes—when stationed temporarily at an established base in India, for instance—he could give an actual address, but for the most part he could not.

He embarked for India at Liverpool on 20 March, and wrote to his sister that evening without being able to tell her that he was at Liverpool, only a few miles from home. He was much concerned about her safety, for Wallasey, in the vicinity of Liverpool and Manchester, was a dangerous place to be. Adeline was serving as an Air Raid Warden and also looking after the local Red Cross organisation. In his letters Tilman discussed the practical things that would have to be done if Adeline had to move temporarily, and—a touch of his father—he suggested that his sister should discover if she would still be liable for rates on a house "which you have been forced to vacate". Soon after getting that letter the house at Wallasey was badly damaged by a landmine, and Adeline had to leave it for a time. She went to Meols, in the Wirral, but she stayed only until the house at Wallasey could be made weathertight. As soon as it was patched up sufficiently to live in she returned, and carried on with her work in the home front line.

Tilman's route to Inda took him via Freetown in Sierra Leone, and Durban.* The night before reaching Freetown, in a letter headed simply "At sea", he wrote, "There is an opportunity to write as we reach a port tomorrow. . . . We get through the time somehow, but I

* Enormous zig-zags across the Atlantic were made by these convoys carrying troops and equipment to India and the Middle East. I, too, sailed for India early in 1941, in a convoy from the Clyde. After calling at Freetown we crossed the Atlantic to within a few hundred miles of Brazil before fetching back across the Atlantic to Cape Town. Troopships might call at either Cape Town or Durban.

feel that enough of my life has been wasted already sitting about as a passenger, without having a further extension of that wasted period in wartime."

He gave up his pipe for Lent, and wrote from Durban, "In spite of Lent having ended I have not started a pipe yet. I made one or two tentative essays but it tasted so foul and I felt so weak in the stomach that I have given it up again. Perhaps on shore I shall start again." The real trouble was that he was suffering from sinusitis, which developed into savage earache a few days before his ship reached Bombay. He felt wretchedly ill on landing, but ignored the trouble and went with his men to the Royal Artillery depot at Kirkee, near Poona. Having seen the regiment settled in he reported sick, and was sent to hospital at Poona. He was X-rayed, his sinuses drained, and he was kept in hospital for about a week. He went back to Kirkee feeling much better.

He hated what he considered to be the luxury of life in India and "felt almost ashamed to address letters to anyone in England". On 25 May he wrote:

This is a most demoralising existence—waited on hand and foot by silent slaves; barbers, tailors, and bootmakers in attendance at one's bungalow; a bungalow with a large luxuriously furnished living room, a verandah to sleep on, a bedroom, a dressing room, and a bathroom. However, the furniture I hope to get rid of except for bare essentials as we are paying far too much for it. I believe we are still on English rates of pay, and of course living out here is very much more expensive. It doesn't matter to me, but the subalterns, especially the married ones, will soon be in debt.

I have found a hill with some 20 ft or so of climbable slabs. The rock is rotten, but in rubbers one can get some exercise and amusement of an evening.

Re-armed with First World War 18-pounder field guns and 4·5-inch howitzers 32 Field Regiment sailed for Iran on 8 June 1941, to serve with 8 Indian Infantry Division. Tilman was now Commander of 107 Battery, which he preferred to being second-in-command of the regiment, a job which in his opinion provided not nearly enough to do. They sailed for Basra in an old coal-fired steamer, and on 14 June he wrote at sea:

This trip is a bit of a change from the last one in the way of food, comfort and accommodation, but I rather prefer it, because with a battery I have something to occupy me in looking after the men. . . . Seven of the men in my battery are giving a hand in the stokehold. The lascar firemen are rather a scratch lot and require assistance. I amused myself last night by doing a 6-hour spell with them— 10 p.m. to 4 a.m. It was not as bad as I expected, but then I didn't have to work as hard as they did. It was grand working with nothing on but a pair of shorts, with sweat streaming down and washing off the coal dust. The cup of tea and wash at 4 a.m. were almost as enjoyable as the same thing after a hard day on the rocks. It was grand getting away from India after only a month there. One can hold up one's head again.

He celebrated his departure from India by returning to his pipe.

The regiment did not stay long in Iran. After a week or so in the south near the Iraqi border they crossed into Iraq and marched up the Tigris valley to enter Syria west of Mosul. The Syrian campaign, where French forces loyal to the Vichy Government in France had resisted the British, was almost over. A light column of troops to which Tilman's guns was attached entered a few Syrian towns without a fight. Tilman made a brief reference to this Syrian adventure in his book *When Men and Mountains Meet* (the title is from Blake: "Great things are done when men and mountains meet") :

We showed the flag to the Sheiks of the Shammar tribe of Bedouin, ate vast trays of mutton and rice with them, and drank little cups of cardamon-flavoured coffee . . . soothed the excited Syrians, and saw that some form of civil government was functioning; and then retired to Mosul to dig ourselves in against the arrival of the Germans. The contingency might be remote, but it served as an excuse for the digging which kept us occupied for the rest of our stay in Iraq.

A German attack on Iraq to seize the oilfields, or to deny their use to the British, may have seemed a remote contingency after the war, but in 1941 after the fall of Crete it was a serious threat. He spent much of October 1941 reconnoitring gun positions on both banks of the River Tigris, and (at least in retrospect) got some fun out of it. He was artillery adviser to the colonel responsible for organising the defences of Mosul. He described their activities:

> We made our HQ in the buildings of a railway station. . . . From this comfortable billet we made extensive surveys of the proposed defences in the colonel's station wagon, accompanied by a bearer with tiffin basket, an orderly with sun-umbrella, the colonel's shotgun, and his dog. If a bustard or a pack of sand-grouse was seen, the siting of company localities, battery positions, anti-tank guns, and machine guns had to wait.

Army mails to the East were irregular and slow. In 1941 it might take up to four or five months for letters to arrive, a situation that was relieved by the introduction of the "Airgraph", a special form on which letters could be written for microfilming and dispatch by air. At the other end the film was enlarged and delivered like a postcard. This was quicker than ordinary Army mail, but had the disadvantage that letters had to be short. Tilman in Iraq was luckier than those serving farther east in that he was getting letters in about two months. On 11 November he wrote to his sister:

> It ought to be possible to do it in less than two months, even though there is a war on. The men have a grouse, and a legitimate one, too, in that they have had no Green Envelopes since they have been here. A Green Envelope is not censored in the unit, and so these are much appreciated by men who naturally dislike putting all their private feelings in letters which will be read by their officers. They used to get a ration of one a week in France.

He planted a garden round his tent, but found difficulty in getting seeds. At the end of November he got an Airgraph from Adeline written on 24 October telling him that she had moved back to Wallasey. He replied, "I think it's no more than one should do, and I dislike those people who go to the country and stay there: it will not do the moneyed people any good after the war. . . . My garden is at a standstill owing to the cold."

In December the Japanese bombed the American fleet at Pearl Harbor, and the war in the Pacific started. The Japanese invasion of Malaya also started. Tilman's initial feeling was that he had made a great mistake in leaving 122 Field Regiment when it went to Singapore. He wrote to his sister, "The 122nd with whom I served for a month must be leading an active life—lucky devils." They were not. Tilman would have hated to be a prisoner of war.

During his service in Iraq Tilman contrived to climb two mountains. The first was a peak of some 6,500 feet in the hills north of Mosul, near the Turkish border. He got to the region in the middle of winter for the strange reason that the charcoal used for cooking and heating came from there, and, with increased demand from the Army, charcoal had quadrupled in price. Whether Tilman thought up an investigation of charcoal production as an excuse for going to the hills, or whether someone in the supply services had heard of Tilman as a climber and thought that he would be the best man to look into charcoal-burning in hill country is unclear. Anyway, he went, found a good-looking peak and duly climbed it, reckoning it to be "of almost Alpine standard".

His other peak was Bisitun (10,000 ft or thereabouts) in the Zagros mountains of Iran, near the Iraqi frontier. He went there on the invitation of a kindly Brigadier, who, knowing Tilman's love of mountains, suggested an inspection of the defences there. Tilman climbed Bisitun alone, spent the night on the summit, and in the morning climbed another peak which he thought looked higher, though when he got there he had doubts. It was a satisfying climb, followed after the descent by a plunge into a clear, cold pool at Tak i Bostan, which he added to his private list of "memorable bathes".

As 1942 wore on he became, at any rate in his letters home, more and more morose. He was tired of digging holes in Iraq, fed up with soldiering that seemed so far away from the war. He was always a conscientious officer, arranging football matches, boat races, canteens, anything he could for his men, but his heart was not in this kind of work. There was local leave for Baghdad, but he had no wish to go there—he was too old and too respectable for a night out in a town, he told his sister, and he did not much like towns, anyway. Life was made more tolerable by fairly frequent moves to new camp-sites, but after a few days one camp became much like any other. On 26 April he wrote home, "I just let the great war go by. Some day we may be asked to lend a hand." They were: in June the regiment left Iraq to join the 8th Army in the Western Desert.

Life in Iraq may have seemed like peacetime soldiering, but in North Africa and the Mediterranean things were different. The earlier British successes against the Italians had been reversed by Rommel and the Afrika Corps, and in June 1942 the Germans seemed to be sweeping relentlessly on Alexandria and Cairo. The seaport of Tobruk was the single British toehold left in Libya, and on 20 June Tobruk fell, and the prize of Egypt seemed within the Germans' grasp.

The British Army was in retreat, and there was need for more and more guns to hold up German tanks, to replace the batteries that had been overrun and captured in Rommel's advance. Tilman's regiment moved quickly, crossing the Syrian desert, Jordan, and Palestine in two days. After one day's halt for repair and maintenance of vehicles they went on across the Sinai desert to Egypt. They were now armed with 25-pounder field guns on modern carriages. To get into action they had first to get to the war, which meant struggling against a mass of vehicles carrying wounded, and administrative and other non-combatant personnel being pulled back from the German advance. It was horribly like the dark days of May 1940 in France.

Once away from the coast road and in the desert Tilman was in his element. He and his battery were detached to form a "Jock Column" with a platoon of Indian infantry and a troop of 2-pounder anti-tank guns. These "Jock Columns" were more or less independent artillery formations, called after Brigadier Jock Campbell, VC, RA, who invented them. Their job was to roam an area of desert to find German tanks or other units, and shell them with the powerful 25-pounders. The infantry and light 2-pounder guns were to protect the 25-pounder gunners, and do anything else that seemed useful. Tilman's column was ordered to "search and destroy" in an area of desert to the west of a huge minefield laid between Mersa Matruh and the Siwa Oasis. His first encounter was with a British 3-ton lorry with a 2-pounder anti-tank gun mounted on it. An officer from Tilman's column went out to meet the visitor to discover what he was doing—and had a 2-pounder shell sent through his own truck. It was a German in a captured British vehicle. This was a constant problem—so much British equipment had fallen into German hands that often what looked like a British gun would open hostile fire.

After the fall of Mersah Matruh Tilman was recalled from his privateering column to join the whole of his Brigade Group in a stand against the German advance. The Germans, with the sun behind them, attacked near dusk, and the British positions were overrun. Guns and gunners were so valuable that when German tanks were less than half a mile away the battery commanders were ordered to save their guns if they could. Tilman extricated his battery, with all its guns. The infantry brigade and the gunners' regimental HQ were all captured.

After this unhappy battle Tilman and his guns were attached to another roving column, with a company of the West Yorkshires. Throughout July they were in action almost every day, sometimes with a column, sometimes recalled to take part in battles in the more normal role of divisional artillery. Some extracts from the battery's war diary read:

4 July One troop advanced 2 miles and came into action but was later withdrawn to main position on being shelled. Considerable enemy heavy bombing of nearby New Zealand units

5 July Situation in north very obscure. Battery was ordered to Deir El Muwassi . . . No link with 5th Indian Div. HQ as their R/T was put out of action by shellfire

6 July X [code-letter for Tilman] went forward 2 miles and observed hostile column of guns to NW but was recalled to Battery. . . . X went out on a bearing 330 deg. for a few miles and fired a few rounds at enemy to N . . . OP and guns were engaged by enemy but withdrawn without loss

7 July X went to yesterday's OP at 07.00 and was met there and fired on by enemy armoured cars . . . about 25 [enemy tanks] were seen advancing towards battery position. These were engaged and halted . . . Bombed and sustained casualties. Lt . . . wounded (died 8 July) Lt . . . wounded, Gunner . . . killed, 2 ORs wounded, 1 vehicle destroyed

13 July . . . Bad march, much winching out of sand

21 July Orders for attack on Deir El Shein Depression . . . considerable hostile shelling in reply . . . fired 120 rounds per gun

And so it went on through the rest of that month.

On 1 August, when his battery was out of the line reorganising, Tilman wrote home:

I spent the afternoon bathing off a white beach, in a sea coloured like the sea in posters. I'm afraid that is the only attraction and distraction here.

I suppose I can't say very much about our five weeks of battle, but I think it was the most trying I have ever had—much more so than our three weeks in France. We always seem to be there when the British Army has its backs to the wall, or is engaged in a long retirement through a back door in said wall. The number of narrow shaves with bomb, bullet and shell make me quite hot under the collar to think on. My own crowd can have the distinction of being the first to be hit on the way up by a bomb splinter, and the day we came out to get blown up on a mine. However it [the blown-up armoured car; he does not tell his sister that he was in it] has been recovered, and will run again. Our first day in action was our worst. We had a 3-hour duel with 25 tanks and a number of assorted guns at about 2,000 yards. How we got all the guns out still fills me with astonishment. Thereafter, after numerous adventures, I finished up with half my own battery and half of another "swanning" about in MEF parlance. . . . I picked up a kitten who enjoyed life in my armoured car very much, paying not the slightest attention to loud noises however close they might be. I last saw her on the way down, when she transferred her affections to another truck, my own being written off.

On the credit side of the severe fighting he managed to feed his battery better than at almost any other stage of the war. He explained this by the fact that they were fighting and moving about so much that there was no HQ to interfere with them, and he gave high praise to the supply services of the Indian Division to which they were attached for contriving to get them what they wanted. No one bothered about whether they were exceeding their tea-ration, and the amount of tea they drank was determined solely by the amount of water they could get hold of. He even managed to acquire some tomatoes and an occasional egg.

He had a narrow escape from one of his own drivers. He told his sister, "I found him a bit too temperamental and excitable. One day in his efforts to get a rifle out of the truck to have a crack at a low-flying plane he shaved my ribs with a bullet. I have a quiet, sedate gentleman now, who shapes quite well. I have taught him the art of *chapatti*-making, so we should get on all right."

That August he made his first acquaintance with the "Jeep", which he described as "great in these sandy wastes".

Rommel's offensive came within 60 miles of Alexandria, but the British stand at El Alamein at the end of July was the turning point in the North African campaign. Rommel failed to break through the British defence; his supply lines were dangerously long, and behind the Alamein defences the British were steadily bringing up reinforcements. A battery commander is not concerned with grand strategy, and there was still plenty of fighting left to do, with which Tilman was directly concerned. His battery's war diary records that on 31 August the sector they were helping to hold was attacked at 04.55 by 200 tanks. On 9 September Tilman was writing home:

It is quieter now. . . . Most of the shelling is done by us, which is as it should be. The fly nuisance has abated a little since we last were here. Then one could scarcely keep glasses to one's eyes when sitting in an OP for more than a few seconds at a time. We all live in holes in the sand without any overhead cover against weather or anything else. However, the temperature at this time is pleasant, and at night it does not go much below 70 deg F 20 C yet.

The days of tomatoes and eggs were for the time over. On 22 September he complained, "All our veg. even potatoes come out of tins. I will never open another tin in my life after this, nor regard anyone who does as anything but an enemy to mankind." A fortnight later things improved slightly, and he reported, "Managed to get some fresh dates and rather high, sour local cheese through a chap returning from Alex."

By early November Rommel could no longer maintain pressure on the British front and began a general retreat. On 11 November Tilman wrote to his sister:

You will be glad to know that as far as I can see the war here is over for us for the time being. We took part in the breakthrough and advanced a bit earlier this month but have now been left far behind in the rush, and look like staying. It was fun while it lasted, and we all got a kick out of advancing for a change. Latterly we have been scouring the desert for prisoners, vehicles, guns, etc. and have collected a heap.

He was within three months of his 45th birthday, and still a Major. Other reserve officers with whom he had served on joining up in 1939 were Brigadiers or Colonels—at least one was a Major-General. Why was Tilman overlooked? It was his own fault: he hated administration and Staff work, and did everything he could to avoid being attached to any sort of HQ. He was in the habit of saying that he had no friends in high places, but it was not true; he had plenty of friends and admirers in positions of influence. What he meant was that he would never use past acquaintance to secure preferment. That is an honourable attitude, but he carried it to a point at which he seemed almost to be in hiding from his own identity. It brought a curious retribution. Time and other men's promotion had left him the senior Major in his regiment, and as such he could no longer be a battery commander but had to become second-in-command—a role he had acted in before, and been thankful to be rid of when he took command of a battery in India.

Sickness came to his rescue when the commander of his regiment was appointed temporarily to the command of divisional artillery, and Tilman became Acting CO. He did not like it much, but it was better than being CO/2.

He had to endure regimental headquarters for another six months, but there were compensations. His commanding officer, with whom he seems to have been temperamentally ill-fitted, returned to the regiment, but was soon posted to another job. This left Tilman again as Acting CO, which he disliked less than being (as he regarded it) a "dogsbody". He continued putting in requests to be allowed to return to a battery, signifying his readiness to forego any further promotion. Higher authority, doubtless getting a little tired of his complaints, offered him a posting as instructor at a school of mountain warfare. If anyone thought that this would make him happy, he was wrong— Tilman's instant reaction was that it would put him in some backwater even farther away from any real war, and that he didn't want the job. Fortunately there was no need for a row, for in the way things sometimes happen in the administrative machine it was discovered that someone else had already been posted to the job. But Tilman's clamour to remain a battery commander meant a note against his name (or so he said) marked "Not recommended for promotion". Certainly he never was promoted, and whatever the mechanics of this ridiculous and patently unfair treatment, he undoubtedly brought it on himself.

He so worried his sister by his complaints against being at RHQ that she thought he had been *demoted*. He explained that it wasn't exactly that, and that the job of CO/2 in fact brought him an extra sixpence a day, which he would gladly forego if he could get back to a battery.

In the intervals of bemoaning his lot the regiment advanced to Tunis. He abandoned moaning when there was fighting to be done, and he took part in the actions to break the German defences on the Mareth Line, in the Gabes Gap and in the Wadi Akarit. His regiment was detached to support the 19th French Corps, and he was delighted to meet units of the French Foreign Legion.

The romantic in him loved Tunis, and the countryside, with some real mountains to look at, was a joy after the desert. He had a meal with his Foreign Legion friends, and enjoyed the food in their Mess— coarse bread, dates and wine. He considered this infinitely preferable to the white bread and tinned rations of the British Army. On 11 May 1943, the day before German and Italian resistance in Tunis ceased, and some 250,000 enemy troops were taken prisoner, he wrote:

We are still nibbling away among the hills and closing in on a large force of Boche; in fact apparently the major portion of his army. I don't think he will resist for more than a few days longer. The weather is grand, the country delightful, and the enemy beaten, so we are all pretty bobbed. I have still got some desert sores, but as we are no longer in the desert I shall have to find a new name for them. Perhaps when this is over we shall have a spell by the sea— that usually cures them. Meantime we have the hills. Zaghouan is one of the most striking of the Tunis hills I have seen. Four thousand feet high, with some fine rock ridges. It looks fine this morning but unfortunately there are still some enemy on it. Perhaps I shall be able to get a day on it later.

He did, or rather, it was a night. He told his sister on 14 May:

We got to the foot at 11 p.m. and started climbing with a half moon. We got onto the wrong ridge, and kept on being driven down by cut-offs. The moon had gone by then, but we had a good supply of German light signals, which I had taken to let off on the summit. They were very useful in showing us when not to go down various bottomless precipices. The green and red lights produced some stirring rock scenery. About 5 a.m. we got to the foot of the final peak, and made it just before 6. There was a tricolour on top, planted by the "Goums" [Moroccan irregulars] who had been clearing up the mountain of Germans. The same "Goums" pinched my coat out of the truck we had left at the bottom. In the coat was a pipe. *Hinc illae lachrymae.*

The pipe crisis was real, for he was reduced to one usable pipe, and one which he described as a semi-pipe—it was broken, but with care could just about be smoked. But with North Africa cleared of the enemy the Mediterranean was usable again by Allied shipping, which meant there should be a better mail service for the troops. He asked his sister in one of many such pleas to try to get and send him two or three pipes—these were difficult to get in England during the war, and pipe smokers had a hard time because briar root from the Mediterranean was unobtainable. He was momentarily happy, feeling, as he wrote, that "Dunkirk was avenged".

He was not happy for long. He begged his sister to send him some books ("no one in the mess reads anything except me"). He asked her particularly to send from his shelves at home *The Wrong Box* by R. L. Stevenson, Lewis Carroll's *The Hunting of the Snark* and Jane Austen's *Persuasion.* At the end of May he was miserable because he was still Acting CO of the regiment, and he did not know what was happening. Early in June the new CO arrived. Tilman quite liked him, but he still hated being second-in-command. With, as he saw it, no prospects in the Army, the future looked bleak.

IX

Albania and Italy

THE CIRCUMSTANCES OF the dramatic change in Tilman's life in the middle of 1943 are still not fully explained. There is a pleasing legend. That one day while acting as CO of his regiment he was brought two letters addressed to the Commanding Officer. Quite properly he opened them. One asked whether Major H. W. Tilman could be recommended for promotion to command a regiment, the other whether there were any officers in the regiment who could be recommended for training for special duties that involved being dropped by parachute behind enemy lines. Tilman (so the story goes) immediately replied to both. To the first inquiry he replied that he could certainly not recommend Major Tilman to command anything except a battery, to the second that there was a Major H. W. Tilman in the regiment who would probably do very well at parachute jumping and operating behind enemy lines, particularly in mountain country. With the Commanding Officer's rubber stamp, and an indecipherable squiggle for a signature, he sent off his replies.

His own account, in *When Men and Mountains Meet*, of how he came to join the Special Services stresses his dislike of being second-in-command of a regiment after having been a battery commander:

> Though the appointment carries with it an extra sixpence a day it is the equivalent of the Chiltern Hundreds as far as any active responsibility is concerned. . . . Having drawn my sixpence a day in such an uncongenial post for several months I was prompted to answer an advertisement in General Routine Orders, which, in the Army, corresponds to the Agony Column of *The Times*. Volunteers were wanted for Special Service of a kind which involved almost complete independence. Better to reign in Hell than serve in Heaven, I thought, as I wrote out my application.

There may be truth in both legend and published version. In his

185

mood of morose despair, Tilman was entirely capable of squashing any chance of his own promotion, and the imp in him would have delighted in recommending himself for a cloak-and-dagger job. It is possible that this is the explanation of the remark to his sister that he was listed as "Not recommended for promotion". It seems fairly certain that he *did* reply to a request for volunteers in General Routine Orders; the Army in wartime was always seeking volunteers for this or that; you applied through the proper channels, your application might or might not be allowed to go forward, you might be accepted for a job you wanted, or you might never hear any more about it. Normally, however, an application to transfer from your unit to some other branch of the Army would require the approval of your Commanding Officer. Did Tilman, as Acting CO, endorse his own application? It is quite possible. What is less easy to understand is how an officer then aged just over 45 was accepted for parachute training and all that went with it. Here it seems probable that even if he made no use of friends in high places, there were people in high places who knew of his qualifications for the job. Anyway, he got it.

The training was at Haifa. He told his sister that he had been sent on a course, but he could not say where, or for what. On 12 July he wrote, "I am still away on the course. . . . We work pretty hard, from 8.30 in the morning until 7.30 at night. It is all interesting stuff, so I am really enjoying it. We walked all night recently, covering about 17 miles. I am still stiff. . . . I am looking forward to the arrival of the pipes. Nothing in that line worth smoking is obtainable here."

On 18 July he wrote, "I am doing the second part of the course now, in a slightly different place. There is far more physical work. . . . The rest of the class of about 50 is half my age, but I can still more or less hold my end up. . . . I am beginning to expect the arrival of the pipes." They didn't come. He got leave in Cairo at the end of the course, and he may have been able to buy a pipe there, for he wrote advising his sister not to send any more pipes for a bit "in view of the circumstances of this new job". He was able to buy a copy of Jane Austen's *Persuasion* in Cairo, and on 1 August he wrote that he was seeing "the last of luxury living for a time. We move on now."

He moved from Cairo to Derna in Libya, where the squadron of RAF Halifaxes dropping agents and supplies to support partisan movements in the Balkans was stationed. His first mission was to be in Albania—code-named "Sculptor", the mission consisted of himself, a

Sapper NCO who was an expert in blowing up bridges, and an NCO radio-operator. Three similar groups, to operate in different parts of the country, were flown in on the same night. One (code-named "Stepmother") was commanded by Captain Peter Kemp, who wrote a book, *No Colours or Crest*, about his experiences. He described his companions assembled at Derna:

> By far the eldest—and the toughest—of us was Major Tilman, commanding "Sculptor" Mission. Short and stocky, with a prominent nose and chin and a small fierce moustache, he was an experienced and enthusiastic mountaineer. . . . He had volunteered for Albania, he informed us, in order to keep himself in practice for his next Himalayan attempt. He took not the slightest interest in politics, and so, while he was always glad to blow up a bridge or ambush a convoy, his passion for climbing left him happily impervious to the bitter quarrels between the different Albanian factions.

Not quite impervious—he cared little or nothing about politics as such, but as a soldier he came to have strong feelings about which Albanian groups merited British support.

The flight left Derna on the night of 9 August 1943. It took about four hours to reach the dropping zone, marked by partisans with signal flares. The four missions were all dropped and safely landed by 3 a.m. though it was not a good drop: the aircraft did not come down as low as usual, and the parachutists landed on the hillside about a mile from the dropping zone. Peter Kemp hit his head on a rock and suffered slight concussion, but recovered after a good sleep. He was the only casualty, and such casualties were rare. The pilots and crews of the Halifaxes developed uncanny skill in flying in and out of steep-sided valleys, and carried out parachute drops with remarkable accuracy. Tilman said later that he had never seen better flying than that of the Halifax squadron from Derna.

On that first night in Albania the new arrivals were met by Major Neil McLean and Captain David Smiley, who had been in Albania on their own for some three months establishing liaison with resistance groups. They had entered Albania from Greece, where they had been serving with guerilla groups operating against the Germans. With two RAF officers, dropped in July, a Sapper officer expert in mine-laying, and a handful of specialist NCOs, they had set up a small HQ for the British Mission in Albania. Tilman described the meeting in his book:

They had been playing a lone hand in Albania for three months and were, I think, as pleased to see us as we were to arrive. We had a warm reception, and having walked from the dropping ground to their village headquarters, we sat down to fried eggs and sweet champagne at three in the morning. My principal feeling was one of intense satisfaction at having at length got back to Europe, even though it was enemy-occupied, after so long in the wilderness. I could almost have hugged the ground.

It was desirably mountainous ground, but few parts of the earth's surface have suffered more from the long violence of human history. Four years of Italian occupation were but one incident in centuries of invasion and oppression, leaving Albania a confusion of feuds and conflicting clan-loyalties, made sharper by the rival political ideologies of modern Europe. Mr Anton Logoreci observes in his book *The Albanians*, "In the conditions prevailing in Albania in 1943–44 the task of deciding who was and who was not fighting the enemy at any given moment would probably have defeated Solomon himself." At the time of Tilman's arrival there were two main resistance movements in southern Albania, where he was operating. These were the Communist-dominated Levizja Nacional Clirimtare (National Liberation Movement) and the anti-Communist Balli Kombetar (National Front). In addition the royalist guerilla movement supporting King Zog, who took refuge in England after the Italian invasion, was more important in the north, and became more prominent after Tilman had left Albania. The Communist LNC, which drew moral inspiration and some practical assistance from Tito's partisans in neighbouring Yugoslavia, was the more sternly-disciplined and effective fighting group, but the Balli Kombetar enjoyed much local support. The aim of the British Mission was to unite these resistance movements in opposition to the enemy. McLean and Smiley had succeeded in bringing their leaders to a conference at which they agreed to work together in fighting Italians and Germans. The British undertook to provide

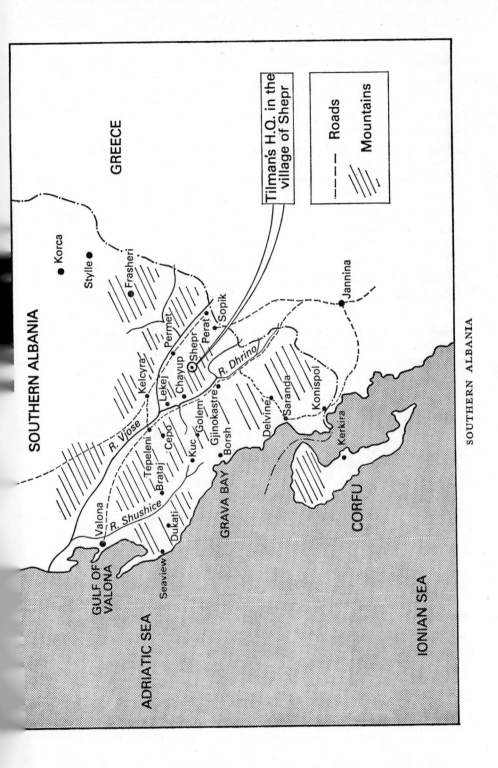

SOUTHERN ALBANIA

weapons, equipment, and technical help through specialist liaison officers.

Orders to the British officers dropped into Albania were simple—they were to take no part in political rivalry between Albanian factions but were to give impartial help to any group or groups prepared to fight the enemy. As time went on, particularly after the Italian collapse and the replacement of the Italian occupying forces by the German army, these orders were often hard to carry out. The alliance on paper between the LNC and the Balli Kombetar broke down. Not only was there open hostility between them, but the LNC went on fighting Germans as well as fighting the Balli Kombetar, whereas some groups of Balli collaborated with the Germans in order to fight the LNC. There were times when Tilman could get through Balli-controlled countryside only by allowing himself to be taken for a German officer. But in August 1943 all this was in the future. The remarkable work of the McLean-Smiley Mission made the British Government decide that their efforts should be reinforced, and when Tilman and his companions arrived it looked as if the British Army had secured some tough, traditionally brave fighters to its side.

The Mission's headquarters were in the village school at Stylle, in the Ostravice Mountains in Southern Albania, a dozen miles or so south-west of Korca (Koritsa), an important road junction near the Greek frontier. Tilman spent a week at Stylle being briefed about conditions in the country and learning his new job. On his last day (15 August) he and the other members of the British Mission attended the inaugural parade of the 1st Partisan Brigade, commanded by Mehmet Shehu, who later became Prime Minister of Albania. The parade was followed by a feast of barbecued mutton. Everybody was in high spirits at the formidable guerilla force being assembled. Next day Tilman and his NCOs left for their own post to support the LNC partisans in the Gjinokastre area, some forty miles south-west of Stylle, across two mountain ranges and the valley of the River Vjose. The party's radio equipment and kit were transported on mules, guided by Vlachs, a Romany race of semi-nomadic shepherds with an age-old tradition as the muleteers of the Balkans. Tilman liked them, and wrote of them, "Showing no interest in politics or war they seem to be the one unchanging, untroubled race in the Balkans which knows enough to meddle only with its own affairs and to let the great world go by."

Italian morale was low, but Italy was still in the war, and behind the Italians loomed the more formidable Germans. The town of Gjinokastre was the headquarters of the Italian Perugia Division of some 5,000 men, supported by a mule-battery of eight 75 mm mountain guns. There were detached garrisons at Permet, between Stylle and Gjinokastre, at Saranda on the coast, and at a few other places. At that stage of the war the Italian troops mostly stayed in their garrisons, but they had still to be reckoned with. Tilman and his party took a cross-country route to the Gjinokastre region, avoiding the Italian garrison at Permet by fording the Vjose River well above the town. They travelled for three days, and Tilman established his headquarters in an empty house in Shepr, a hill village on the eastern slope of the Zagori valley lying between the high ridges of the Nemerke and Lunxheries mountains, both of which rise to over 6,000 feet. From Shepr a mule-track led through a difficult gorge to the Dhrino valley and Gjinokastre, which could be reached by a march of about six hours.

His first action with the partisans was a night attack on a small town across the river from Gjinokastre, occupied by an Italian outpost of some fifty men. An earth-road linked the outpost to the main road, and Tilman's job was to mine the earth-road to prevent reinforcements from Gjinokastre being sent up. The partisans opened fire with rifles and such machine-guns as they had. The Italians replied with machine-guns and mortars from their citadel. Tilman described the battle:

> The darkness was intense, but with so much stuff flying about some of us who were not behind stone walls were bound to be hit. Six of the partisans were killed. The bugle sounded a charge, the attackers closed in through the town towards the fortress, set alight the houses of the most hated Balli and withdrew in good order before dawn. It was a bold but quite futile effort.

Life at Shepr was comfortable, and an Albanian who had once run a restaurant in Tirana, the capital, volunteered to be the Mission's cook. The Mission fed exceptionally well until one day the cook's house was searched by the partisans and some pieces of parachute silk were found concealed there. For this the local partisans sentenced him to be shot. Tilman, with some difficulty, managed to get the man reprieved, but could no longer employ him as cook. Discipline among the partisans was severe—looting, theft, failing to hand over anything captured from the enemy, were all punishable by death, the sentences being carried out summarily. One man was shot for stealing some cigarette papers. Tilman had no part in administering this harsh code of military discipline—he was not in command of the local partisan unit, but simply a British liaison officer giving such help as he could in fighting and organising supplies. Where he could use his influence to obtain mercy he did, but he had only influence to exert.

He was respected as a fighting soldier by the Communist partisans, but his habits sometimes irritated them. Colonel Smiley writes of him at this period:

> I did hear reports that he was unpopular with his Albanian body-guard. We were all given these bodyguards by the partisans, allegedly for our protection, but in fact to make sure we did not make contact with any of the other Albanian political parties such as the Balli Kombetar. The bodyguards had been instructed never to let British officers out of their sight or earshot. Tilman's unpopularity was due to the fact that every morning before breakfast he climbed to the top of his local mountain, Mount Nemercke, a not inconsiderable climb, and the wretched bodyguard had to climb it as well!*

On 7 September 1943 the Italians surrendered to the Allies. Tilman received a radio-signal instructing him to obtain the surrender of the general commanding the Italian division at Gjinokastre, and to arrange for his arms and equipment to be handed over. Accompanied by the leader of the local LNC partisans Tilman went to Gjinokastre and demanded to see the general. The situation was delicate. The general said that he was out of touch with Rome and had no orders, and that he would not permit his troops to be disarmed. The partisans were not in sufficient strength to compel surrender if the Italians resisted, and things were further complicated by the fact that the rival Balli were strong in the neighbourhood. After three days of futile negotiations Tilman and his partisans cut off the water supply to the troops in Gjinokastre. After this the general and his force marched by night to the small seaport of Saranda about 25 miles away, whence they hoped to be taken back to Italy by ship. Here the general finally agreed to surrender, provided that his men could keep their rifles and were permitted to embark. However, only a few of the Italians got away. A

* From a letter to the author.

Everest from the Tibetan side

Everest expedition, 1938; *l. to r.* C. B. M. Warren, P. Lloyd, H. W. T., P. R. Oliver, F. S. Smythe, N. E. Odell, E. E. Shipton

H. W. T. at the outbreak of war in 1939

Right: H. W. T.'s father as a member of the Mersey Docks and Harbour Board

Albania, 1944

Above: H. W. T. (front row, behind notice) after receiving the Freedom of the City of Belluno, 1945

Below: H. W. T. on the approach to Rakaposhi

On the road to Kashgar, 1947. The round structures are the yorts (circular tents) widely used by the nomadic peoples of Central Asia

The Fluted Peak (centre, distant) in the Langtang Himal, Nepal, 1949

The south-west and south faces of Rakaposhi

ship that came to fetch them fouled her anchor, and was sunk by German dive-bombers. The partisans got large quantities of military equipment, but were unable to take away most of it because the Germans arrived first. Prevarication did the Italian general no good, for he and most of his staff were captured by the Germans. Hundreds of miserable Italian soldiers, without food or shelter, roamed the countryside. Some joined the partisans; others were given food by the Albanians in return for work on the land. Tilman thought that this was rather nice of the Albanians.

That winter of 1943–44 in Albania was a confused and horrible time for Tilman and his fellows. The Germans were too strong for any of their main concentrations to be attacked by guerillas, and although the LNC partisans constantly harassed German supply routes and any small detachments they could ambush, such battles did not always turn out well. One was a disaster. Tilman and his partisans watched from a hillside a large German column go by, keeping out of sight because it was too strong to be attacked. A little later a smaller force of Germans came up, and the partisans did attack. Some Germans were killed, but the party did not panic; it went to ground and called up reinforcements. These came in strength, with mortars and 115 mm guns. Tilman's partisans had rifles and two 40 mm anti-tank guns. Tilman, as an artillery officer, took command of the guns and succeeded in hitting a German truck and holding up German movement for a bit. It could not be for long. Both Tilman's guns were knocked out by mortar fire. Gallantry with rifles could do little against well-armed German troops supported by artillery, and the only thing to do was to take to the hills, which had further disastrous consequences, for the Germans made a thorough search of the area, found a monastery that the partisans had been using as local headquarters, and destroyed it.

Open hostility between the LNC and the Balli Kombetar made a miserable winter still more difficult. A cove about 50 miles to the north of Saranda, that the British Mission had been using for landing supplies by sea, was in Balli-held territory, and Tilman had difficulty in getting there, and some narrow escapes from being shot. His Albanian escort had to pretend that Tilman was a German officer. With dogged pertinacity Tilman established another landing place some miles to the south at Grava Bay, and it came in useful, although the Navy never liked it because it was open to the prevailing wind.

7

Blowing up bridges when he could to hinder German troop movements, sending intelligence reports by radio, organising the distribution of supplies to the partisans, and keeping himself and his small mission out of the way of German search parties, Tilman spent an active winter, but he became increasingly unhappy and frustrated by the divisions in the resistance movement. He was saddened by the burning of villages in reprisal for assistance (or suspected assistance) to the partisans. He watched one group of houses "wantonly burned" and wrote in his book:

It is possible to write calmly enough about burning villages, but when we actually see men at work setting fire to one peaceful, familiar little homestead after another, the rising flames, the roofs falling in, and the labour and loving care of years dissolving irretrievably in a few minutes, it is impossible not to experience a hot wave of dismay, revulsion and hate. To watch fires caused by bombing or shelling is bad enough, but guns and planes seem impersonal and their effects do not arouse the same intense feeling.

He got through the winter doing his job as well as he could, but by the beginning of May the Germans were on his track, and it was time for him to go. After lying up in a farmhouse near the coast for two days he was evacuated by sea from Grava Bay on 22 May 1944. On reaching the British base at Bari in southern Italy he was delighted to find some mail, including a precious pipe sent by his sister. He was less happy about British policy in Albania. In concluding his account of his Albanian experiences, he wrote:

I returned convinced that our policy of giving moral, financial and material support to the LNC was just an expedient. Unhappily, the goodwill thus earned was offset by the dislike we incurred by supporting the other two parties [the Balli Kombetar and the Zoggists] . . . Even after two of the three parties had shown themselves to be useless and untrustworthy, we continued to sustain them morally by sending them missions, by refusing to denounce them by name, and by making only obscure references [in BBC broadcasts to Albania] to the deeds and sacrifices of the LNC. The result of this ambiguous policy was that the honesty of our intentions was doubted, and that not one of the parties trusted us. In view of our alliance with Russia a plain man could not conceive that it was the taint of Communism which precluded our giving undivided support to the LNC. By helping the one party we might offend a large number of Albanians and put them in a difficult position after the war, but having once encouraged the resistance movement we were obliged to befriend those who resisted and no one else. . . . The LNC had their faults. . . . Yet the fact remains that the partisans of the LNC fought, suffered and died for professed aims and by so doing helped us. The resolution they showed through many months of hardship, danger and disappointment, the will to win, their faith in themselves and in their cause, all seemed to me to establish their claim to leadership. . . .

That is a soldier's view, expressing a soldier's loyalty to those who fought with him. Tilman's loyalties were unshakeable. He preferred to ignore political judgments—and British wartime policy in Albania was so tortuous and conflicting that it offers only a kind of fog through which to judge. Whether the post-war history of Albania would have been happier if the victorious Communists had come out of the war with a more solid faith in Britain, who can say?

Only one letter of Tilman's from Albania reached his sister—in the nature of things he could not write much because it was hard to get letters out, though he received occasional letters dropped with supplies for the partisans. In this surviving letter he mentioned he had written twice before. Perhaps the earlier letters were lost because of the difficulties of getting through Balli-held territory to the landing place on the coast. The surviving letter he took to the coast himself, observing "I shall accompany this one as far as the sea". It is wrongly dated 20 January 1944, because he refers to receiving a letter from his sister dated 12 February; he discusses Lent, and remarks "Winter seems to start here in March". The letter was probably written some time that month, and the wrong date is a small indication of the strain under which he was then living. Careful as he had to be he could not resist a guarded complaint about the official policy of backing all the partisan movements whether they were fighting the Germans or not. He wrote:

I seem to keep in moderate health and strength and have no worries apart from the common one—mulish and criminal obstinacy on the part of one's superiors. . . . Have you done anything about Lent this year, or has it been done for you by a loving Government? Tobacco very nearly gave me up, had not a supply arrived in the nick of time. But I have given up drinking *raki* [the local brandy] which was a considerable sacrifice when one considers its cheapness, palatability, alcoholic content, the long evenings, the lack of company.

Almost the first thing he did on getting to Bari was to write to his sister:

Here at length is a genuine letter posted by myself, and no phoney cable sent by someone else, or letter posted several months after writing. The reason of course is that I am now back from ops. in the Balkans, in which delightful country I descended like a piece of swan's down as far back as last August. . . . Naturally I cannot go into details, as we are, or are supposed to be, clam-like in our security in this unit.

At the beginning of June he had a few days' leave in Cairo and was there when the news came that Allied troops had entered Rome (4 June). News of the Allied landings in Normandy on D-Day (6 June) reached him just before he left to return to Bari. There he met J. M. L. Gavin, who had been a member of Ruttledge's Everest expedition in 1936, and was now a Lieutenant-Colonel. From Gavin he got news of some of his old mountaineering friends. He liked and respected Gavin, who passed his exacting requirements as a real soldier, but his contempt of others spilled over in a letter to his sister, "I don't like the way most, or perhaps a lot, of climbers cash in on their knowledge to the extent of spending the whole war in comfort and safety."

His prickliness temporarily upset his own prospects. He had come out of Albania expecting to go back after a short interval, perhaps to a different area. But when he was due to return he couldn't go, because dropping missions were temporarily cancelled on account of a burst of German activity. While waiting he seems to have had a difference of opinion with the authorities responsible for the British Mission in Albania over the official policy of giving equal aid to all nominal resistance movements. Precisely what happened is unclear, but in a letter to his sister of 18 July he wrote, "I have parted company with my late employers on a matter of policy and am now trying to find another job. If everything fails I shall go back to the Army. Even CO/2 of a regiment would be preferable to rotting in Bari."

He applied for a transfer to Special Operations in the Far East, and while awaiting the outcome he occupied himself in sailing with Gavin. He enjoyed some rough weather, and was pleased that he was not seasick. He had one sail in a beautiful 12-metre reputed to belong to King Peter of Yugoslavia.

At the end of July he had still not been posted, and wrote on 30 July: "I am still without a job but hope to hear something definite this week. As you can believe, my temper is not of the best during this long period of idleness. I have moved out of the town to a place in the country where it is quieter, and where the food is slightly better. Against this, I lose my early morning bathe."

Things did not go well for him. On 2 August he wrote,

I had hoped to be able to tell you this week of being on the move again, but today I got the answer to my application for a similar job in the Far East—refused on grounds of age and rank. However, I have one, if not two, other irons in the fire. If both those fail I shall find myself washed up high and dry at some RA Base Depot with precious little chance of active employment—even in the despised role of CO/2.

He was spared that fate and a week later was accepted for Special Operations with the partisans in northern Italy, where the Germans, in spite of the surrender of their Italian allies, were holding on tenaciously. Italian partisans had organised guerilla bands and were harassing the Germans wherever they could. They also supplied valuable intelligence to the British and American armies in Italy. Both the British and the Americans sent liaison officers to work with the Italian partisans and to organise the distribution of arms and equipment dropped by parachute. One of their tasks was to locate "safe" dropping areas, and to signal where these were in cipher messages sent by radio. Naturally, Tilman could not tell his sister what his new job was to be, but on 9 August he wrote from the address No 1 Special Force, CMF [Central Mediterranean Forces], "You see the new address. It means I am no longer a lost soul in the Pool. If all goes well I shall spring into action towards the end of the month—if the war isn't over by then. Naturally, I'm pleased, but curse myself for having wasted so much time mucking about with the Far East racket."

In August 1944 the military situation of the Allies in Italy was less happy than it looked on the map. Rome, southern Italy and much of the west coast were in Allied hands, but in the north-east, on what had been the Austrian frontier, German resistance was still strong. Moreover, the Germans wanted to prolong the Italian campaign as long as they could, to tie up Allied armies which otherwise could have sent reinforcements to France and the Low Countries. When Tilman was posted for special operations with the Italian partisans he thought that the war might be over almost before he could get to them. It was not.

The next four months were the most prolonged physical and mental strain of Tilman's life. In the First World War he had endured long periods of danger and discomfort, but the times of *acute* danger were in days or weeks rather than months, and hellish as the mud of Flanders was, he lived in the company of his own countrymen, speaking the same language, knowing what he had to do in the ordered service of his guns. He was often in danger in the Western Desert, but although he might be out of contact with his commanders while serving with a roving column, again it was a matter of days, and he was always part of a great fighting Army. He endured danger in mountains, and later at sea, but he knew what he was doing and could act on his own plans to meet the assaults of wind and weather. In Albania he had fought with his partisans against far better-armed German troops, and then been hunted in the mountains. But his partisans knew their mountains as the Germans could not hope to know them—and there were few roads. He was well-served by the Halifax squadron at Derna, and when he signalled for a drop of weapons or equipment it usually came when and where he asked for it.

Conditions in northern Italy were radically different. There were plenty of mountains in Tilman's area of the Dolomites, but instead of running in long ranges they are relatively isolated groups, with good motor roads in the valleys between them. In Italy there are towns and telephones, and the Germans were well-established—the Belluno Province where Tilman served for much of his time had been annexed by Germany. The partisans cut telephone lines when they could, but this was two-edged—it interfered with German communications, but it also cut off the telephones of one's friends. It was not really good country for guerilla warfare against well-organised regular troops. There were political differences among various groups of Italian partisans, but not to the same extent as in Albania; or rather, though the differences may have been deep, they didn't interfere with co-operation in fighting the Germans. Outside the towns, where Italian Fascists still enjoyed German protection, the Italian people were almost whole-heartedly on the side of the partisans—without this popular support Tilman's mission would have been impossible. But there were still plenty of spies acting for the Germans, and it was dangerous to trust apparent goodwill too far.

These are the expected hazards of operations in enemy-held territory. What made Tilman's first months in northern Italy such a severe personal ordeal was that something went wrong with the arrangements for dropping arms and supplies, and for one hundred and seventeen days he and his companions had to exist without receiving anything. This was depressing enough in itself (nearly four months without a change of shirt); its effect on the partisans was serious. They were poorly armed and short of ammunition, and the promise of support that the arrival of British liaison officers seemed to give raised morale enormously. When support was not forthcoming, morale fell. Night after night Tilman would send radio signals arranging dropping zones. A simple code in the order of certain words in the BBC's radio broadcasts to Italy told him whether to expect a drop or not. Night after night the broadcast would be hopeful, they would man a dropping zone—and nothing came. On one particularly sad occasion supplies *were* dropped, but in the wrong place—straight into enemy hands. To make matters worse, the Americans also had liaison officers working in the field, and some American supplies *did* arrive, to be distributed among partisan units operating independently, and not under the command of the partisan organisation to which the British officers were attached. Tilman's partisans were known as the Garibaldi Division, divided into various brigades. By no means all the partisan leaders were Communists, but Communist influence was strong, and, in Tilman's view, the Communist-led groups were the most efficient, if only because of Communist experience of clandestine organisation. When British supplies continually failed to arrive the Communists felt that it was deliberate policy aimed at weakening them as a fighting force. It took all Tilman's powers of leadership to convince them that this was not so. His diplomacy was assisted by the obvious fact that he himself was sharing all the difficulties and dangers of partisan life, and suffering with them from lack of supplies.

What went wrong remains inexplicable. Tilman put it down to incompetence in navigation—sometimes while waiting for drops that did not come he and his companions could hear planes circling overhead, apparently looking for the dropping zone, and then the planes would go away without dropping anything. The weather was often bad enough to explain failure, but not all failures occurred in bad weather. Perhaps so many of the best RAF crews in that winter of 1944 were flying over France and Germany that supplying partisans in Italy had a low priority. Whatever the reason (if there was any reason other than a chain of accidents) it made hard conditions many times worse for the partisans and the little band of British officers working with them. That the RAF *could* drop accurately and reliably had been shown in Albania, and was shown in northern Italy later. The first successful drop to Tilman's group came on 26 December 1944 when five tons of stores were landed within a couple of hundred yards of the signal fires, and all were safely recovered.

Those four bad months—September to December 1944—began in failure. Tilman, his second-in-command Captain John Ross, RA, his interpreter (an ex-officer of the Italian Alpini), and his wireless operator, left Brindisi for their flight north on 26 August—and came back again because the pilot saw no signal fires. They tried again on 28 August and came back a second time. Not until 31 August did they manage to land in the partisan territory to which they had been sent.

It was not a happy landing. Tilman himself went into a pendulum-swing on the end of his parachute and landed badly, hitting a rock and hurting his back. The radio-operator sprained his ankle, and Captain Ross finished up in a tree from which he and his tangled parachute harness had to be cut down. All landed wide of the signal fires marking the dropping zone, and by the time they had collected themselves the weather had closed in and their plane had gone off without dropping their kit. They had to endure the lack of even the most austere personal equipment for the next four months. But they carried a substantial sum in Italian paper money, divided between Tilman and Ross and stuffed into the pockets of their flying suits, and two volumes of Carlyle's *French Revolution*, which Tilman fitted into his pockets with the wads of notes. The money was useful to the partisans, the books invaluable to Tilman and Ross.

They were dropped on the Altoplano d'Asiago, a wooded plateau between the valleys of the Brenta and the upper Adige, looking down on the flat landscape to the north of Vicenza. Tilman suffered from his back injury for three days. At first he was scarcely able to stand, and could move only by crawling. But he was inspired by living at 5,000 feet and by the wonderful smell of the pine forest in which the partisans were encamped. This was his sort of country, and his indomitable will power in triumphing over injuries worked wonders. On 2 September he walked for 50 yards, on 3 September he did 300 yards, and on 4 September he walked half a mile and climbed a hill to observe the surrounding countryside from the top. After that he walked and climbed as he wanted, and if his back was still painful he never mentioned it.

The Tilman Mission was received by Major Wilkinson, a British officer, already working with the partisans, who was killed in action in March 1945. They lay up for a few days in a hide-out in the woods, hoping for the arrival of their equipment, but it did not come. Captain Ross left on 2 September to get in touch with the Divisional HQ of the partisans. Tilman and the rest of his party followed on 5 September. Major Wilkinson was able to lend them a radio set, and to provide another operator to replace the man who had sprained his ankle on landing and who was still finding it difficult to walk.

In the earlier part of the Italian campaign the Germans had tended to ignore the partisans in north-east Italy, particularly in those areas which they regarded as being annexed German territory. As the war went badly for the Germans the partisans gained heart, and with their strong support in the countryside they began to be a serious threat to the German occupying forces. Tilman was convinced that the resistance movement represented real Italian patriotism. In his view the Italians had never had their hearts in war against Britain and the United States, and as soon as they got a chance to fight on the side of the Allies they fought bravely and well. He developed great respect for their courage and cheerfulness in enduring hardship.

The partisans were loosely organised in military formations—divisions, brigades, companies—but there were also a number of independent groups, and in the nature of things the functioning of any normal chain of command was often difficult. Communications were maintained by young girls on bicycles, who acted as couriers between the various formations. The partisans included bands of men living together in the woods or hills and serving as more or less full-time soldiers, and men doing civilian jobs by day who became active

7*

resistance fighters by night. These semi-civilian partisans were organised by the Gruppo Azione Patriotico (GAP) of which there was a branch in almost every town and village. They were invaluable sources of intelligence, and sometimes had agents working for them within German military and police organisations.

Tilman's first assignment was to the Nanetti Division, which covered a big area from Monte Grappa across to Vittorio Veneto in the south, extending northwards through the upper Piave valley to Monte Marmolada and Cortina. The divisional headquarters were in the Cansiglio Forest, north-east of Vittorio Veneto. However, before Tilman could get to the Cansiglio Forest HQ the Germans conducted what the Italians called a *rastrallamento* (comb-out) in which they dispersed the Cansiglio partisans. These *rastrallamenti* became more frequent; it was a measure of the partisans' success that the Germans were now compelled to take them seriously as a force to be reckoned with.

These repeated German comb-outs made things particularly difficult for Tilman. It was his job to put heart into the partisans (which they didn't need, having stout hearts already), and to supply them with arms and ammunition (which they did need, but which in those four bad months he could not supply). That they accepted him, respected him, and remained ready to work with him says much for his own fortitude and personality. Since for the moment there was no partisan HQ to go to in Cansiglio he decided to attach himself to the Gramsci Brigade, holding out in the mountainous Le Vette area to the north-west of Cesio. Things did not go well.

Tilman had learned guerilla warfare in Albania, and he was now a considerable expert in such fighting. The principle of guerilla tactics is "fight and run": blow up your bridge, arrange an ambush, do as much damage as you can as quickly as you can, and then melt into the countryside. Le Vette is a high plateau standing at about 7,000 feet. It is difficult to get up, and its top is bare of cover. The partisan commander had about 300 men on Le Vette, and since the few rocky paths leading to it could be held by a handful of riflemen it looked a strong, almost impregnable position. Tilman saw that it was a trap. The paths leading up to Le Vette were also the only practicable exits from it, and if they could be held at the top they could be held equally easily at the bottom.

Having dealt with Cansiglio the Germans combed-out the partisans

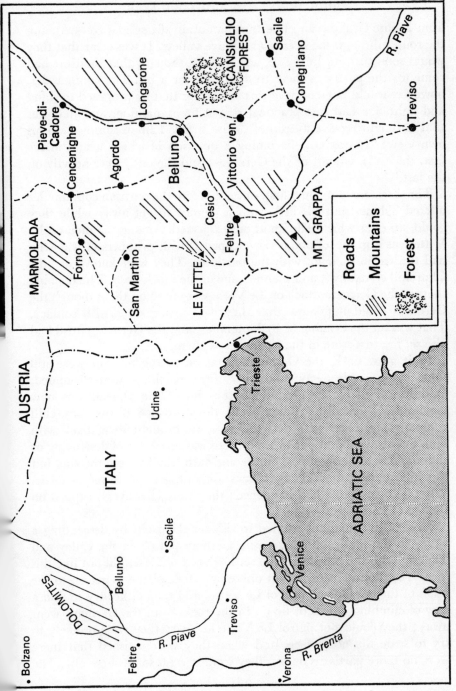

NORTHERN ITALY AND BELLUNO

from Monte Grappa, an important mountain stronghold commanding the routes through the Brenta and Piave valleys. It was clear that they would soon turn on Le Vette, and Tilman thought that the time had come for the partisans there to disappear for a bit. The commander, however, would have none of this, declaring that he proposed to stand and fight. He had one practical reason for remaining, and that was that he might receive a drop of British arms. Tilman summed up his own view: "It was now becoming a question of which would arrive first, the arms, winter, or the Germans; and the odds were heavily on the last."

The Germans did come first, but not before the partisan commander offered Tilman and his little staff a chance to get away while they could, an offer which Tilman at once rejected. Among the men on Le Vette was a group of about ten escaped British prisoners of war who had thrown in their lot with the partisans. They were known as "the Churchill company", and manned one of the block-posts. The opening shots of the German attack on Le Vette were fired on them though the Germans could not know that they were firing on British soldiers. That was on the evening of 29 September, and the German patrol had also set fire to a store in the valley below them.

As it grew dark, the Germans firing on to the plateau were still some 1,500 yards away, and only three partisans were wounded. Withdrawal to higher ground on the rim of the plateau was now inevitable. Typically, Tilman went down to see if the Churchill company had received orders to leave; he brought them back with him. Scouts were sent out to see if there was any hope of destroying or slipping past a German post on the one path leading from the rim, but the information they brought back discouraged plans for a sortie. What Tilman feared had happened; they were effectively trapped on the top of Le Vette.

Most of the partisans wanted to risk breaking out by descending a valley to the south, but there were German patrols in the valley and Tilman, with the precious radio set he dared not lose, did not like this idea. The mountaineer in him offered another plan—to get on to the rocks of the steep north face of Le Vette, and then either try to find a way of climbing down, or lie up in the rocks until the Germans went away; they could not patrol Le Vette for ever, they were unlikely to try to scale the north face, and when they were satisfied that there were no more partisans on top they would go off somewhere else. The

Le Vette men agreed to divide. The Englishmen in the Churchill company asked if they could stay with Tilman, and he accepted them. In the end, a party of sixteen under his leadership set off to try the north face.

Although it was still September, at 7,000 feet it was getting cold, and already there had been some snow. Tilman led his party down the first promising gully, but it petered out and the cliff fell away sharply. There they would have to stay, at least for the night. They had one blanket apiece and no food.

Tilman kept a rough diary in an army notebook, the entries, brief and generally uninformative, describe the ordeal on the mountain:

1 October. 8 a.m. went up to top. Huns on road below. Bad hour—will they come up? Shots. Very relieved at dusk. Fine day, but no sun for us. Some rain at night.

2 October. Woke to a blizzard. Bitter N wind blew all day. Some shots in morning. Decided to beat it at night by ridge to Pass di Fenestri. I went up 17.30. Cries. Man fallen. All frozen limbs. Went down, brought man up. Bad cut on face, shock. Decided against ridge (luckily) as party now not fit. Went down to track. Went on to supposed post—no one there. Took track above Battisti to Pass. Still blowing on top. Ridge looked bad. Joined track from Val Canzoi. Dossed down 05.00 above Battisti track.

3 October. Sent chap down who found Huns had left previous night. Followed.

These bare notes omit the hardship of three nights and days without food at 7,000 feet, where it had already started to snow. Tilman's tactics in hanging on to wait for the Germans to go away were justified, and he lost none of his party. Their descent on 3 October had a happy ending, for they came to a farm which one of the Englishmen recognised as a place where he had been befriended and where they were given a hot meal. Only the day before, the Germans had gone round burning farms to teach the local inhabitants not to be friendly to the partisans.

The resistance groups survived the German comb-outs of the autumn of 1944 with relatively light casualties, though some gallant men were caught and hanged, and others shot in skirmishes. But the partisan organisation was disrupted, there were severe losses of supplies, and even more serious loss of shelter from the systematic burning of barns and cowsheds used as hide-outs. In the summer of 1944 an Allied breakthrough into the Po valley had been expected quickly. It did not come, and with the onset of winter the partisans were advised in British broadcasts to disperse into smaller groups and hold themselves in readiness for a new offensive later. That was not encouraging, and the failure of British air-drops was actively discouraging. Yet partisan morale remained high, thanks to the determination of the Italian people to get rid of the Germans, to the unshakeable courage of the partisan leaders, and to the readiness of the small group of British officers working with the partisans to share in every difficulty and danger. If Tilman and his radio set could have provided arms, equipment, and bundles of winter clothing it would have been an enormous help. As it was, he provided something in the long run even more valuable—a convincing demonstration of the fact that, whatever might be going wrong now, the British Army *was* in alliance with the partisans, and that all would be well in the end. His readiness to march, and hide, and fight, and eat, and work, and sleep with Communists as long as they were fighting Germans was equally a practical demonstration of good faith. As in Albania, he cared nothing about post-war politics. His creed was simple; he was a soldier, and he stood by his friends.

After the disaster on Le Vette, Tilman and his party lay up in a hayloft near Cesio and then had to move on. The Nanetti Division of the partisans, whose headquarters in the Cansiglio Forest had been combed-out soon after Tilman's arrival, was re-establishing itself in the forest, with a new divisional commander, an Italian ex-infantry officer who had become a Communist. Tilman respected him, and thought him an able man. The British mission set out to join the new HQ, a hazardous trip, being passed from friend to friend in various villages, and crossing roads by night. Carlyle's *French Revolution* helped both Tilman and Ross endure the weary hours when they had to hide in barns or attics. The diary gives an impression of those days:

4 October. Went down to next house and had bread, cheese, wine.

Fishing party. Cold. Six small trout. Started down. Various halts . . .
Waiting for pasta. Houses burning. Fresh alarm. Refused to cook
pasta. Packed up. Walked an hour, very dark, raining . . . 10 pm
to a hay loft.

5 October. Rain all day . . . Pasta three times running. Slept in
hay again.

6 October. Another day of rain. More pasta. Bty. [battery for his
radio] no good, only half message sent.

7 October. Fine. Good bty. obtained, but too late for schedule.

He had a conference with a number of partisan leaders to discuss
the situation. The German comb-outs and the lack of British supplies
were having an effect and there seemed a risk of the civilian population's becoming less ready to help. That did not mean a change of
heart—simply that it was becoming too dangerous. Tilman stressed
the need of having smaller bands of partisans requiring food and
shelter.

There was a crisis over the capture of one partisan leader, on whom
the Germans found a number of important papers. All signals for
dropping zones were compromised and had to be changed.

One morning the woman in whose house Tilman and Ross were
staying rushed in to say that a strong column of Germans was closing in
on the village. Tilman and Ross escaped into a wood about half a mile
away, where some girls brought them food and beer. They were well
hidden in the wood, and could watch the Germans, who had some
88 mm guns and began firing over their heads. Neither Tilman nor
Ross believed that their own suspected presence could have brought
out German artillery, and they were right—the Germans were
apparently putting in some firing practice, with the secondary purpose
of trying to overawe the local population. Having watched the Germans
for some time Tilman astonished Ross by putting on a Royal Artillery
fore-and-aft cap which he kept in his pocket, observing that if German
gunners were going to fire in the presence of a Royal Artillery officer,
that officer should be properly dressed. The effect was a little spoiled
by the fact that neither Tilman nor Ross at that time possessed any
shaving kit. It was a nice gesture, which fortunately the Germans did
not observe.*

Some more diary:

* This story is recounted by Dr Ross in an article in *The Gunner*.

14 October. Up early, urged to be careful as Huns said to be coming . . . Gun opened up again . . . Left at 19.00. picked up escort. Crossed bridge over Agordo river, crossed Piave bridge. Bread and meat at a house near Trichiana . . .

16 October. Lay up in a barn. Grapes (the last) bread and cheese for lunch New form of pasta for supper, very filling.

17 October. Good job no plane came last night as signals wrong. [The Germans were watching dropping grounds discovered from the captured papers.]

22 October. NE gale with rain all day. Sat and got smoked in the cookhouse . . . Very cold now that the cows have gone from below us.

28 October. Bathed (cold) and boiled shirt.

The non-arrival of supplies was a constant cause of misery. They would get a "positive" code word on the BBC, which meant "man the dropping zone". They would spend half the night there, and come back empty-handed. *Grappa*, the rough brandy of the country, helped. Sometimes there was *grappa* before breakfast. Getting batteries for the radio charged was constant work, and constant anxiety. The batteries had to be taken to a garage known to be friendly, and obviously the same garage could not be used often. The winter dragged on. Tilman and his companions survived by their wits and the kind of luck that comes to those who trust in the Lord and keep their powder dry. Once a hut in a wood where they were living was betrayed by a spy. There was deep snow on the ground, and a German patrol, dressed in snow suits, closed in invisibly. But instead of rushing the hut, by which move Tilman and the partisans with him would almost certainly have been killed or captured, the Germans opened fire from about 300 yards. That gave the inmates time to escape into the wood. They lost the hut and their supplies, which were burned, but Tilman's radio and some reserve food, which were kept in a hole in the ground that could be quickly covered, were retrieved later. Only one letter of Tilman's to his sister survives from that miserable period. It is dated 15 December and naturally gives no address:

I sent off one note about six weeks ago. I wonder if you have received it? I hope you are getting the regular fortnightly messages. Have had no mail or anything else since we arrived last August, A lot of mail was sent, but unluckily it fell into enemy hands. I expect there were books and possibly a pipe amongst it. Life is a good deal harder and more harassed than it was in Albania, but I have no doubt that we shall get through the winter all right if that should be necessary. There is a lot of snow here now. A few weeks ago I had half an hour on skis and fell about all over the place. It seemed to me to be worse than skating. Hope you are battling along, and that Joan, Pam and Anne are all right.

Adeline faithfully kept her brother's letters, and since the note "written about six weeks ago" is not among her papers it seems likely that it never reached her. The "fortnightly messages" he refers to were stock letters from Special Force HQ sent to relatives of men serving behind enemy lines. A typical one is dated 21 December:

I am glad to be able to let you know that the latest news of your brother Major Tilman received today is that he is safe, well and quite happy. We are now in the midst of Christmas preparations and are hoping to have as happy a time as possible under the circumstances, and although we are not with our families in person we shall certainly be with them in spirit. By next Xmas festivities we sincerely hope that all our wishes come true and we are sharing the joys of peace for all time with our loved ones. I hope it will not be long before he is in a position to write to you himself, but in the meantime, should you be in the least bit anxious about your brother, please do not hesitate to write and let me know and I will be only too happy to let you have the latest possible news as I am in constant touch with him.

Adeline was as faithful a correspondent as her brother, and she replied gratefully to all these second-hand letters. She must have warmed the hearts of those who wrote them, encouraging them in a humane but difficult job. The officer writing that cheerful Christmas letter to Adeline was scarcely reflecting Tilman's real feelings at the time. Tilman's Christmas Day owed nothing to the Army's efforts on his behalf, but the partisans did their best, and produced a special meal. Tilman's diary records it: "25 December. Fine, cold. Patrol. Breakfast biscuits zabaglione (cognac flip) tagliatelli (pasta), chicken, potatoes puree, two kinds of cake, cognac. Speech. Felt very full. Five messages in. Supper (light) 7 pm.

Boxing Day brought their delayed Christmas present of a successful drop. The diary is terse, "26 December. Fine, cold, bathed. . . . Two planes tonight. Planes arrived OK. Worked all night. Slept out." The planes brought five tons of supplies, weapons, ammunition, bundles of warm clothing, even some bottles of whisky.

With the supplies, the planes dropped another British mission. On their arrival Tilman decided to transfer his own from the Nanetti Division of the partisans to the Belluno Division farther north. Characteristically, he observed in his book, "I must confess that when I decided to leave the Nanetti Division to the other mission I was aware that north of the Piave we should be nearer the Dolomites", but there were sound military reasons for bringing more help to the Belluno partisans. Their province, on what had been the Austrian frontier, was directly controlled by the Germans, who had strong forces stationed in the town of Belluno, which was also the local SS head-quarters. There was less scope for going into action against German patrols because they could call up reinforcements too quickly for irregular troops to succeed in getting away. The Belluno partisans for the most part led civilian lives by day, or hid out in cunningly con-trived pits covered by planks topped up with earth containing potatoes, and looking like part of a potato clamp. Their main task in that bleak midwinter when larger-scale action was impossible was to hunt down and kill spies, informers, and prominent Italian Fascists, who, in spite of German protection and savage reprisals, often fell victim to the partisans. Potentially, the Belluno Division was capable of being far more than a thorn in the side of the German occupation forces. When the Allies ultimately broke through into the Po valley, the German field troops would retreat northwards towards the old Austrian frontier. In that retreat, Belluno partisans could play a vital military role in blocking roads and harassing retreating German soldiers. It was vital, therefore, to use the winter to equip the Belluno partisans for the fighting to come.

Tilman left the Nanetti HQ at Cansiglio on 29 December. The journey north at that time was particularly dangerous because the Germans had dotted the area with checkpoints and military posts which seriously hampered partisan movement. Tilman had to lie up for a week in an abandoned building, which gradually accumulated a strange company of hunted men, escaped prisoners of war of various nationalities, most of them trying to make their way into Yugoslavia.

Among them were two Poles, a Russian, a Yugoslav, and a Frenchman. It was a tedious wait, punctuated by alarms, but one of the Poles turned out to be an admirable cook.

On 7 January Tilman crossed the Piave at last, and two days later (9 January 1945) he made contact with officers of the Belluno Division. They were woefully short of arms and ammunition, and his first job was to try to arrange a drop for them. Although the arms were needed round Belluno it was considered too dangerous to try to organise a drop in the vicinity of Belluno itself, and it was decided that he should go to the Forno area, in the mountains to the north-west of Belluno. No drop could be attempted before the partisans of Forno (the Fratelli Fenti Brigade) were ready to receive it. While they were making their arrangements he had to go into hiding. With a guard of three partisans he spent the next three weeks in a bivouac under an overhanging rock on a cliff looking across a ravine to Monte Serva (7,000 ft). It was a remote place. For entertainment there were occasional trips by sledge to the home of one of the partisans, whose mother gave them splendid meals. And he climbed Monte Serva. It took him seven hours and it was not, in his view, a particularly difficult climb, but it impressed the partisans.

On 30 January Tilman and his party set off for Forno, travelling by night and getting to a friendly house in the village of Rivamonte by dawn. It belonged to an old lady who was an active member of the resistance. Her home was a memorable stopping-place, for instead of the normal cowshed she provided beds, with beautifully clean sheets.

From Rivamonte they went on next night to the Agordo valley, getting to a village inn around midnight. Tilman expected that they would have some food and press on, but the partisans had arranged for them to lie up at the inn through the next day. They were comfortable there, but the inn was much visited by German soldiers. However, they stayed out of the way upstairs while the Germans drank below, and Tilman managed a successful radio transmission with Germans actually on the premises.

The last leg of the journey involved six miles of main road to Cencenighe, a hazardous stretch which could not be avoided. They had to jump down a steep embankment to escape a patrolling truck, and at Cencenighe they had to outflank a German barracks, with a guard-post equipped with a searchlight. They were helped by deep snow into which they plunged whenever the beam of the light turned towards them. And although a searchlight seems deadly to a fugitive there is a moment of safety once the beam has passed, for it impairs the night vision of those watching by it. From snowhole to snowhole they worked their way round to the comparative safety of a track leading to the Val di Gares and Forno.

The Val di Gares is a long, narrow valley extending about five miles south from Forno. At the far end is a massive rock complex, rising to the peaks of San Martino, around 10,000 feet. The valley lies between steep walls going up to 7–8,000 feet, and its greatest width is barely half a mile. The Forno men thought that this would be the safest place for an arms drop, and Tilman set about arranging one. Technically, it was an extremely difficult drop—the narrow valley was a hard target to find, and the height of the surrounding cliffs meant that the planes could not fly low. Tilman asked by radio if delayed action parachutes could be used—this would enable loads to be dropped at height without being blown miles off course if the parachutes opened at several thousand feet. The RAF agreed to this, and the first drop was made on the night of 13 February. Recognition signals were flashed, and the loads came down with superb accuracy, repeated by two more planes on 17 February.

Having acquired a considerable quantity of arms, explosives, and other supplies Tilman was anxious to get back to the Belluno area. Safe houses (or cowsheds) to lie up on the journey had to be arranged, which took ten days. Tilman borrowed an ice-axe from one of the local partisans and enjoyed himself on the neighbouring mountains. He set out with his party on the return trip to Belluno on 28 February, deciding that the snow had melted sufficiently to get to Rivamonte via the Cesurette Pass instead of having to use the road. He recorded in his diary:

28 February. Left 11 a.m. Scrambled eggs, milk, farewell. Got to top of pass 14.00 track pretty good except for occasional soft bits. Tried Marlins and Bren. Grappa, wine, cheese. Agordo men arr. 16.00. Got down to Col di P. 17.00. Left 19.00. Meal at Taibon. Left 10 a.m. arr. Rivamonte 1 a.m. Soup, apples, double bed. Very tired for some reason or other.

They were held up at Rivamonte for a week by constant German patrols, and by the problem of getting through the Mis valley, which meant using the road. Finally it was decided that they should go by lorry, concealed under a load of several tons of wood. This required preparation—you can't put two men in the back of a lorry and heave three tons of logs on top of them, not, that is, if you want to deliver them alive. A friendly carpenter made a big, coffin-shaped box, open at both ends. Tilman, Ross, and an arsenal of Marlin automatics went on the floor of the lorry, the coffin went over them, and the logs covered the lot. There were some bad moments when the lorry was stopped at German checkpoints, but the driver's papers were in order (the partisans were practised forgers) and after a glance at the load of logs the German waved them on.

On getting back to the neighbourhood of Belluno Tilman decided to attach himself as liaison officer to the Zone Headquarters of the partisans. He was sad to leave what he regarded as the more active job of working with divisional and brigade groups, but the partisans themselves wanted him at Zone HQ and, with the time for an Allied breakthrough approaching, co-ordination with the Zonal High Command was important. Zone HQ was at a farm in the Alpago, a hilly district east of Belluno, lying between the Cansiglio Forest in the south and Monte Dolada (7,000 ft) to the north. They were 3,000 feet up, with a nice cold mountain stream for Tilman to bathe in.

He liked the HQ staff. Politically, they were a mixed lot, but although Tilman often needed to exercise diplomacy there was none of the political recalcitrance that had so thwarted him in Albania; in Italy, Communists, Socialists, Christian Democrats and people of any other non-Fascist group were ready to work together in the resistance movement. In addition to some dedicated Communists the partisan leaders included a bank manager (who became the first Mayor of Belluno after the war), a Venetian lawyer, an ex-Colonel of the Italian artillery, and a man particularly after Tilman's heart in Attilio Tissi, a rock-climber with a passion for climbs of extreme severity; his route of exceptional difficulty on Monte Agner is still called the "Via Tissi".

Some diary extracts:

11 March. Visited sabotage class in school.

12 March. Changed old radio for new one, good contact. Made some soda bread.

14 March. Tried to make some yeast . . . Bathed under waterfall. Too many people about.

25 March. Bathed . . . Attempted Monte Dolada but failed. Home 16.30.

27 March. Rain all day. Talks over reorganisation . . . Tea, 6 eggs, beer, Ovaltine, long talk.

1 April (Easter Sunday). Coloured eggs. Cake with dove, of peace?

2 April. Climbed Col Nudo (8,000 ft) Snow quite good.

4 April. Fine. Climbed Dolada. No view account cloud.

7 April. Climbed Teverone (c. 7,000 ft). Hard snow, step cutting, amusing ridge.

There were darker things. Some daring partisans put up a big picture of Hitler on a German rifle range, with the inscription "Shoot straight". This so enraged the Germans when they saw it next morning that a group of officers went to tear it down themselves. It was booby-trapped, four Germans were killed and many injured. In reprisal the SS took ten prisoners and hanged them on the rifle range. An inn was blown up, and twelve German officers with it. Laconically, the diary records such events with notes about climbs.

On 26 April the Americans took Verona, commanding the route northwards to the Brenner Pass. This was the breakthrough that the partisans had been waiting for, and Tilman was on the move day and night in helping Zone HQ to deploy resistance forces effectively to block the German retreat. By 30 April the country south of the Piave was in partisan or Allied hands, but there was still a strong German garrison in Belluno. Tilman got news that the Germans were preparing to blow a bridge, now of no use to them, but vital to the pursuing Allies. With his interpreter and a partisan soldier he ran to the bridge to forestall the attempt, and got there first. While he was inspecting the bridge to make sure that no demolition charges had been planted, a partisan on the south bank, assuming that Tilman and his companions were Germans trying to blow the bridge, opened fire with a machine gun. They dived behind the parapet just in time. When their shouted explanations got through to the machine gunner he came over to say how sorry he was. Tilman, having narrowly escaped death, calmly complimented the man on his alertness in guarding the bridge.

A British column of infantry and gunners was on the way from

Vittorio Veneto, but there was still much confused fighting round Belluno. On 1 May the Germans launched an infantry attack, supported by an 88 mm gun, to try to clear the road. Tilman got through to the British commander, and British artillery halted the German attack and dispersed the enemy. A stubborn German unit in Belluno still resisted, but on 2 May the Germans in the town surrendered. Tilman, accompanied by two partisans, all mounted on one captured motor-bicycle entered Belluno that same day, and helped to establish a provisional Italian administration. The last entry in his diary is for 5 May: "Bought a barrel of wine (quintal) for 2,800 lire. Flogged rations for flour and eggs. Dance."

His most important job now was to recommend partisans from the Committees of National Liberation for civilian posts under Allied Military Government. A letter of instructions to him includes this personal note. "I think it only fair to say that the ugly finger of suspicion will point menacingly in your direction if every nominee of the CLNs turns out to be a prominent rock-climber!"

Three weeks after the liberation the newly-installed Mayor and municipal authorities of Belluno made Tilman a Freeman of their city. It was the highest honour they could give him, for the first Freeman of Belluno was Garibaldi, and between him and Tilman the honour had been bestowed on only three other people.

An Italian view of Tilman's services is in an article in *Il Nuovo Adige* of February 1946:

The whole resistance movement around Belluno founded itself on the "Mission Tilman". . . . Tilman was the famous explorer of Nanda Devi fame and the mountains of equatorial Africa, a man who obtained incredible popularity among the Bellunese. Silent, always chewing a pipe, apparently cantankerous and difficult . . . he was the moral force behind the partisans, a man who knew how to accept all, success or failure, bad and good luck, with the same impassiveness, which a superficial observer would have taken for indifference. He was a man accustomed to hard conditions, to all difficulties, never promising anything without performing it, and knowing how to perform it. His Mission was fortunate. Although the Asiago and Cansiglio zones were repeatedly subjected by the enemy to *rastrallamenti* they always escaped, and never abandoned their wireless set, thanks more to the caution and prudence of the leader than to luck. The Bellunese have made him an honorary citizen, and it was certainly not just one of the usual polite and formal honours, for Tilman, with the qualities of a passionate lover of mountains (as he liked to call himself) found himself in sympathy with the mountain folk of Belluno.

A more personal view of Tilman comes from Signora Giuliana Foscolo who, at great risk to herself, sheltered Tilman and Captain Ross at her house Casteldardo in Trichiana. She writes:

A real British Mission had at last reached us on the left bank of the Piave, but when I agreed to receive and shelter the Mission I had no idea that the unforgettable German *rastrallamento* would have begun, and still be going on, all over Val Belluna. On the night of Major Tilman's arrival we had a pleasant dinner together, but next day our Major felt as if he were in a cage because too many partisans had come to meet him and to see the Mission. He had to face so much chatter that he could not bear it and he told me that he wanted to go out for a walk.

The situation was very hard and dangerous. The SS had just burned two houses in our small village of Trichiana, and a young man had been hanged outside a small house adjoining my property, and had been left there for two days, just to frighten everybody. An innocent 17-year-old boy who had happened to walk on the main road had been shot by the SS.... I tried to explain to Major Tilman that he could not, absolutely could not, continue his journey towards the headquarters of the Nanetti Division at Cansiglio. I told him the truth, the whole truth, but he went on smiling, smoking his pipe, never saying a word, and looking at me (a poor stupid female). He was determined to continue his journey, and then he said that he wanted to go out for a walk! I began to think he was mad. I was furious, but I tried to explain the situation politely. Alas, it was hopeless. I was afraid he might escape my attention and go out at any moment. Suddenly I decided to show him my two children, Sandro, aged four, and Maria, aged one. I went to the nursery and told our devoted and very brave nurse Balia, "That damned Englishman wants to take a walk as if he were here for a weekend in peacetime." Our Balia was terrified, but the children smiled so sweetly and so gaily at the Major that he was deeply touched. Moreover I added what he did not yet know, that their father is a Jew [he had escaped to Switzerland] and that the three of us could be deported at any time if we were discovered. I think the Major never forgot that moment because when my husband came back to Italy in May 1945 it was still a time of turbulence so soon after the Liberation, and he had to go to the office of the Allied Military Government in Padua to ask for permission to reach Val Belluna. He was lucky in that Major Tilman was there when he came, and when he began to explain about his wife and children our Major stopped him, said he knew me personally, added a few words of praise on my behalf, and immediately helped my husband to get to us, giving him wise advice on how to overcome difficulties.

After renouncing his walk Major Tilman asked if he could at least see the mountains from some window. I took him upstairs, where from three big windows he could see the view of the mountains he adored. At that moment he felt happy, and exclaimed, "I must confess to you that I came here to be near the mountains I love, and to be far, very far, from Headquarters." He went on smiling at me, not a stupid female now, but a companion, and we became friends at once. I left him there looking at his mountains, while Captain Ross and his men tried to contact HQ to explain that they could not at the moment continue on the route.

Major Tilman asked me if I could give him some English books. I showed him my bookshelf and he was particularly attracted by a big one-volume edition of the *Works of Shakespeare*. I must confess now, as I did then, that I was terribly fond of that book—I had bought it in 1933, when I was twenty, in London for the first time, and eager to learn English. But if it could soothe him in such difficult times I was happy, so I gave it to him.

After the Gramsci Brigade had to abandon Le Vette my heavy Shakespeare had, of course, to be left there and it was burnt by the Germans. It is unbelievable how sad the Major was about it. He wrote to me to apologise, and after the war he sent me a wonderful Shakespeare, which I keep always at my bedside. But before that he dared to ask his HQ, through his wireless, to send Shakespeare's complete works with their next drop. When, at last, the drop arrived, he was desperate that there was no Shakespeare, and he sent me a message to ask if it was possible to spend a few days in Casteldardo. I sent a reply (our bicycle girls were splendid) to warn him that a German soldier had come to visit the house and that I was expecting German troops from one day to the next. But he insisted on a meeting, and he and Captain Ross met me and my brother at a lonely place not far from my house. He had crossed the Piave and risked his life just to apologise again about the Shakespeare, and to bring some tea for me and my brother and some chocolate for my children. Walking back home with my brother around midnight we were so tempted by the chocolate (we had not tasted any chocolate for years) that we decided for prudence sake to eat it ourselves, for fear that the children might talk!

Tilman was particularly proud of the Freedom of Belluno, always including it with his military decorations in reference books. In May 1965 he was invited to a reunion to celebrate the 20th anniversary of the liberation of Belluno. His niece Pam went with him for two days of festivities made poignant by moving ceremonies to commemorate those who had died. She wrote at the time, "Everyone came to shake our hands and wish us well. . . . So many people wished to thank him for his time with them 20 years before, and for his returning to them now. There will always be a welcome in the hillsides for the man who holds such a special place in the history of Belluno and the hearts of its people."

X

Central Asia

Tilman came out of the war at the age of 47 with the DSO, the Freedom of Belluno, the honorary rank of Major, and his restlessness still unsatisfied.

War with Germany ended on 8 May 1945 but the war against Japan dragged on until 2 September. With the end of the war in the West Tilman had little to do in Italy, and it offended him to feel that he was idling while there was still fighting in the East. He tried again for a transfer to Special Operations in the Far East, but was again turned down on the grounds of age. There was nothing for it but to await demobilisation. He took some local leave and enjoyed climbing Presenella (11,500 ft) near the Swiss frontier. He climbed alone because there was no one to go with him and he climbed the mountain twice, the second time by a new route. He filled in more time by visiting some of the famous towns of Italy but did not much enjoy sightseeing, finding places too crowded with soldiers like himself awaiting demobilisation. He was invited to one aristocratic house which he described as "full of art treasures", but of the owner he wrote to his sister, "He himself was a bit decadent, reactionary, and possibly Fascist. Having spent so long with Communists I thought him a candidate for liquidation." The war was still close; not two months before he was flitting from barn to hayloft where poor peasants risked their lives, and savage reprisals on their families, to give him food and shelter.

In July 1945 he was back home. He had no need to find a job, for he had spent little during the war, living mostly on his field allowances, while his pay accumulated in the bank. During the war he had accepted an offer for the land at Kericho in Kenya, getting a good price because the area was prospering with tea. He also had an income from the money inherited from his father. He made generous gifts to his two nieces, and had ample for his own needs.

Those needs were simple in one sense, complex in others. He already

219

had a home with his sister, and he wanted nowhere else. But he did not want to stay at home for long—home to him was always a place to come back to. In 1945 he wanted chiefly to do more climbing and exploring in Central Asia.

It was not easy. In the England of 1945 travel abroad was restricted by the need to get permission and by currency regulations. Passages were hard to come by. Thus debarred from the Himalaya he went instead to Scotland and Ben Nevis in April 1946. While there he slipped, rolled some 200 feet on scree, and broke his arm. Somewhat to his embarrassment he was rescued by a party of Boy Scouts and after his arm had been set went home to Wallasey. His family insisted that he should see a Liverpool specialist who advised treatment that would have limited his movements for a time. Tilman refused to contemplate any such concession to a broken arm and stormed out of the consulting room. The surgeon was equally angry with one whom he clearly regarded as a lunatic.

The arm recovered, but Tilman's battered Trilby hat, which he had owned since before the war and liked to wear on his travels, had not been rescued with him, and although it could be replaced he never liked another hat as much.

To test his arm he thought again of Switzerland and got permission for enough foreign exchange for a short trip to the Alps; with his austere habits he did not require much. Back in England, and satisfied that his arm was not going to inhibit climbing, he battered away at the authorities for the currency and permits for a journey to the Karakoram to explore another area so far unsurveyed.

He had also to finish *Mount Everest – 1938*, held up by the long interlude of war. Much of the book was already written. He brought it up to date by adding a few characteristic animosities against the use of specialised equipment developed during the war, radio for instance! He was prepared to tolerate lightweight radio receivers for getting weather reports, but no more.

He delivered his manuscript to the Cambridge University Press and enlisted friends for proof-reading and correcting. In a preface, written at Wallasey in February 1947, he thanked particularly Dr T. G. Longstaff (then President of the Alpine Club), Dr R. J. Perring and his old friend of Kenya days, R. T. Sneyd. Robin Sneyd acted as a kind of literary executor for him, and helped with the proofs not only of Everest but of a number of his other books.

His plans for the Karakoram made slow progress. He was helped by the fact that surveying unmapped areas gave him a scientific purpose that impressed officials, but politics were against him. The old India of the British Raj was approaching independence and partition into India and Pakistan, and Kashmir, through which he wished to travel, was a troubled area claimed by both sides. Meanwhile he was invited to join a Swiss expedition planning an attempt on Rakaposhi (25,550 ft) at the north-western edge of the Karakoram range, and in Gilgit, then still an Agency of British India. Having accepted the Swiss invitation he received official permission for his proposed journey through Kashmir, but he could not go back on his word to the Swiss.

The attempt on Rakaposhi was planned under the patronage of the Swiss Foundation for Mountain Exploration, and although the expedition was expected to finance itself (Tilman contributed his share of the cost) the prestige of the Swiss Foundation was a considerable help in mounting it in the difficult years immediately after the war. The Swiss members of the party were Hans Gyr and Robert Kappeler, both distinguished Alpine climbers. Tilman was asked to join them because of his Himalayan experience. The fourth member of the expedition was Campbell H. Secord, who had attempted to climb Rakaposhi in 1938.

At the end of February 1948 Tilman was invited to Zürich to inspect the equipment collected for the expedition. He felt that as a guest (even a paying guest) he could not be too critical, but he distrusted the design of the tents chosen and replaced them with three "Meade" tents of his own, and a tent of the "Logan" pattern that had proved useful on Nanda Devi. Sleeping bags of real eiderdown, then virtually unobtainable in England, delighted him. The climbers were all fitted with specially made boots with moulded rubber soles. He was impressed by the performance of the rubber sole, but considered the weight of the boots a disadvantage—his own (size 9) weighed six pounds. Nevertheless, he approved their robust construction, although he formulated Tilman's Law of Weights in Climbing—that a pound on the foot is the equivalent of twenty pounds on the back. He liked a canvas boot-cover which he had not met before, and which he considered of real value in wet snow.

On food his opinions were both philosophical and practical. The

Swiss had not followed his doctrine of "the minimum", which means taking nothing on an expedition but supplies for real emergencies, and relying for food on rice, flour which can be baked on a hot stone into *chapattis*, dried apricots, dates, and anything else that can be bought locally. His practical objections to scientifically-devised packs of tinned and preserved foods were that packaging adds greatly to weight without adding anything to nourishment. And however admirable in theory, boxes containing ingredients for a balanced diet for so many men for so many days are inclined in practice to be rifled, losing their goodies and leaving only those foods that no one particularly likes. He was too polite to say all this to his Swiss hosts, though he managed somewhat to reduce the load. Officialdom then stepped in with more reductions. Food was short everywhere in Europe in 1947, and the Swiss withdrew export permission for all the meat, all the butter and half the cheese allotted to the expedition. It is pleasant to record that the hard-pressed Ministry of Food in Britain generously made up some of the supplies thus lost. And Tilman made the odd discovery that pemmican could actually be obtained in England—and that it was unrationed.

Tilman's First Law of Expeditions is that it should be possible to do all the paperwork required for planning and provisioning on the back of an envelope. For a really big expedition he was prepared to allow up to one sheet of notepaper, but he held firmly that any expedition that cannot organise itself on a single sheet of paper is over-organised.

He reached Karachi by air on 1 May 1947 and the Swiss members of the Rakaposhi expedition followed a week later. They started for Gilgit from the railhead at Abbottabad, then still in the North West Frontier Province of British India. Their approach to Gilgit was via the valley of the Kagan River (a tributary of the Jhelum), and the Babusar Pass (13,000 ft) into the valley of the Upper Indus. They reached Gilgit on 4 June, and Campbell Secord joined them there two days later.

When he marched out of Gilgit in June 1947 to try to find a way to climb Rakaposhi Tilman was beginning a series of travels in Central Asia and Nepal that occupied him for most of the next four years. They were the most extensive Central Asian journeys of any Western European since the legendary Sir Aurel Stein (1862–1943), whose surveys and archaeological work in Chinese Turkestan in the earlier years of this century remain the basis of modern knowledge of the region. Tilman was not an archaeologist but he was an accurate surveyor, and although his Central Asian journeys were not undertaken

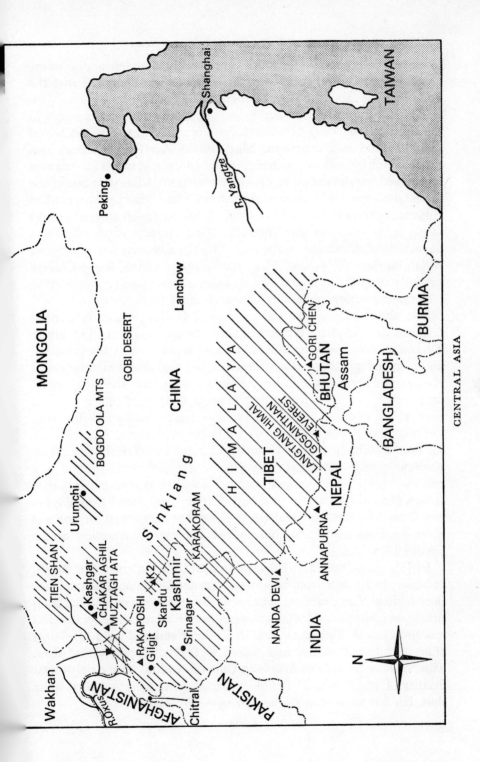

to make formal surveys, he added considerably to understanding of the geography of Central Asia, work for which he was honoured with the Founder's Medal of the Royal Geographical Society.

Tilman's Central Asian journeys were not only the most extensive in the third quarter of the twentieth century; they were also the last of their kind up to the present. Much of Sir Aurel Stein's work was carried out for the British Government of India, and on all his journeys he enjoyed the protection of the Government of India, then one of the three Great Powers in Central Asia. Britain had been as concerned to cultivate spheres of influence in Central Asia as the traditional powers in the region—Russia and China. Tilman's journeys came in the last days of the Raj, but they were helped by the authority and prestige of Britain as the ruler of India. The resurgence of China, Russo-Chinese suspicions and the decline of Britain as an imperial power combined to make such journeys politically impossible after 1948.

The vital listening-post and emblem of British prestige in Central Asia was the Consulate-General in Kashgar, an ancient city in Chinese Turkestan, now Sinkiang, and at various times in history the capital of an independent country of uncertain frontiers conveniently called Kashgaria. Throughout history, Russia, China, and the local tribes-men—whenever they felt strong enough—competed for control of Kashgar. It is on an important caravan route crossing the deserts of Central Asia to Afghanistan, to India, to Russia and ultimately to Europe. During the Raj, Russian, Chinese and British officials in Kashgar treated one another with politeness and suspicion, and in a curious sense all were necessary to one another to maintain a fragile system of security. In 1947 and 1948 Tilman's old friend Eric Shipton was Consul in Kashgar, and while Tilman neither asked for nor was given physical protection, he enjoyed the moral protection of the famous consulate.

In July 1947 India and Pakistan secured independence. The British consulate in Kashgar continued until arrangements could be made for the dividing of its functions between India and Pakistan, and the tran-sition was complicated by their struggle over Kashmir. The remote and romantic British diplomatic post in Kashgar endured for a brief time after 1947 but its status, and indeed its function, really ended then. Tilman was able to cross Asia from China to Chitral on the north-west frontier of India because the old political doors were not then quite shut. His last great land journey (in 1949–50) was in Nepal.

He wrote three books about these journeys, all published by the Cambridge University Press. They are *Two Mountains and a River* (1949), *China to Chitral* (1951), and *Nepal Himalaya* (1952). The four years of his travels were interrupted only by brief visits home, to see his sister, and to finish off the writing of his latest book. Having delivered the manuscript to his publishers he left it to Robin Sneyd and a few other friends to see each book through the press. These books are instinct with his philosophy of travel in particular and of life in general. Setting off for Gilgit and Rakaposhi (*Two Mountains and a River*) he wrote, "I felt uncommonly happy at trekking once more behind a string of mules with their bright headbands, gaudy red wool tassels, and jingling bells, over a road and country new to me, . . . I felt I could go on like this for ever, that life had little better to offer than to march day after day in an unknown country to an unattainable goal."

To travel was one thing, to be a passenger something quite other: "The distinction between a traveller and a passenger is that the one uses travel as an end in itself while the other is merely carried as a means to an end," he wrote in *China to Chitral*. Travel for him was not simply an end in itself; it was at once a way of life, and living in the way he most wanted to live. If a mountain happened to be at hand it was good to climb it, and a mountain made a good goal for a journey. But the journey mattered more than the mountain, and once on a mountain the finding of a way to the top mattered more than actually getting to the summit. Tilman was as keen as the next man on making a first ascent, or achieving a difficult climb, but he was not in the least competitive about it. In his great ascent of Nanda Devi he cheerfully let Houston and Odell have the first chance of getting to the top, and it was only because Houston became ill that he himself went up with Odell. "Playing the game" has become a catch-phrase for qualities of fair dealing and an honourable attitude to opponents; Tilman was one of those rare people who really believed that it was more important to play the game than to win.

His attitude to science was curious—and ambivalent. In theory he was against it, holding that travel and climbing mountains should be ends in themselves. In 1946 when he was trying to organise his own expedition to the Karakoram he was prepared to allow the scientific purpose of surveying unmapped territory to impress officials, but in his own view "scientific purpose" was wholly secondary to travel. Nevertheless he liked accuracy, and was a careful observer, taking much

225

trouble to check geographical locations and work out heights. An example is the care he took to ascertain heights on the march with Shipton to the Bogdo Ola mountains north-west of the Gobi Desert:

We used an aneroid barometer and at specially important points took boiling-point thermometer readings. As there were no basic stations sufficiently near for the reduction of the barometer to sea level, the barometrical readings taken during three days before leaving Urumchi were used as a check. For this period a correct mean height of the barometer was ascertained by using the observations made by Strowkowski over a period of three years in Urumchi.*

He was critical of heights in the Tien-Shan range announced by a Russian expedition in 1946. The Tien-Shan lie partly in Soviet Central Asia and partly in Sinkiang and when Tilman visited the Chinese part of the range he adopted the then generally-accepted view that the highest peak in the range is Khan Tengri at 23,620 feet. The Russian expedition claimed to have discovered a higher peak, just on the Soviet side of the frontier, at 24,180 feet. They also reduced the height of Khan Tengri by nearly 1,000 feet to 22,730 feet. Tilman observed, "The survey of the Tien Shan by Merzbacher [an Austrian explorer] in 1904 was fairly thorough, and the discovery of a mountain 1,500 feet higher than Khan Tengri only about ten miles away is remarkable to say the least."* Tilman was not anti-Russian and he respected Russian mountaineering; his criticism illustrates his concern for geographic accuracy for all his apparent hostility to "science".

The Rakaposhi expedition was the last attempt to climb a major mountain under the British Raj. When Tilman and his companions left Gilgit there was little more than a month to go before Indian independence, but all the old work of Empire went on around them; British officials were settling disputes about water-courses and playing polo (in Gilgit a national sport) as if the imperial sun were not about to set. The Gilgit Scouts, a famous regiment recruited for service on the North-West Frontier, were as brisk on parade as ever, and a number of them volunteered to accompany the sahibs to their mountain as porters. At the end of the expedition Tilman went on to join Shipton in Kashgar and on 1 August he passed the fort at Kalam Darchi, which

* *China to Chitral.*

had been the last outpost of British India. That was the day on which the Gilgit Agency was formally handed over to its new rulers. The fort was still manned by a platoon of Gilgit Scouts. Tilman observed that "although British rule had ended the Subadar in charge of the fort appeared to be in no hurry to haul down for the last time his Union Jack". It is a nostalgic footnote to the last page of British imperial history in India.

Rakaposhi is a difficult mountain. Its north face is formidably steep, and the most hopeful approach seemed to be one of three side valleys— the Jaglot Nallah from the east, the Dainyor Nallah from the southeast, or the Bagrot Nallah from the south. All involve long and exhausting marches, and to get from the head of the valleys on to the summit ridge requires crossing a number of dangerous ice-falls. Tilman's first thought was that the party should make a thorough reconnaissance of all the approaches, but there was not enough time, for he himself was due to leave at the end of July to meet Shipton, and Secord also had to leave at the end of July. In 1938 Secord had got on to the north-west ridge of Rakaposhi from the Jaglot Nallah, and the party decided to concentrate on trying this approach. They were defeated by avalanches. They then tried the Dainyor approach, and were again defeated by conditions on the mountain. There was not time for a full-scale effort from the south, but they did valuable work in mapping the previously unknown course of the Kukuay Glacier. Tilman summed up in *Two Mountains and a River*:

As for our crushing defeat by Rakaposhi, while not wishing to diminish the part played by the mountain in bringing this about I think our chief mistake was in attempting the climb too early in the season. . . . To devote less than two months to a big unknown mountain is bordering on disrespect. . . . Whether either of our two routes would be easier later in the year is unlikely, but they would undoubtedly be less dangerous. . . . Our gamble on the Jaglot approach seems to have been justified, for in August the Swiss had a look at the north side and the Bagrot Nallah, and in their opinion our approach, such as it was, was the best—probably the only one worth trying. Had we carried out our first plan of reconnoitring every side we should have got nowhere. In the Himalaya it seems to be almost impossible to tell whether a given route will go without trying it.

Tilman crossed into Sinkiang by the Mintaka Pass (15,500 ft) over the high country between the Karakoram and the Hindu Kush, and met Shipton and his wife at Tashkurghan, an ancient town once the capital of Sarikol on what is now the Chinese–Soviet frontier. He enjoyed the journey, delighting in the *joghrat* (the Central Asian version of yoghourt) offered to him at every resting place, and in freshly-baked Turki bread. Bread was always important to him, and whenever possible he made his own. He reckoned that with *ata*, dried yeast, a wood fire and a billycan he could turn out a passable loaf anywhere. Later in his life, when he shared his sister's home at Bod Owen near Barmouth, he always made bread for the household. If tobacco ash from his pipe went into the dough—well, it was no more than a little ash from a wood fire.

The second mountain of his 1947 travels was Muztagh Ata (24,388 ft) in Sarikol, north of Tashkurghan. The name Muztagh Ata means "Father of Ice Mountains". He and Shipton planned to climb it with a Sherpa who had been a porter on Everest and recruited by Shipton as a servant at the consulate in Kashgar. Mrs Shipton and a Turki attendant accompanied them to their first camp at some 17,000 feet and then left them. They planned to establish two more camps, at 20,000 feet and 22,000 feet, to make the final climb to the summit from the higher camp. Finding the snow in good condition they decided to have a go for the summit from their camp at about 20,000 feet, but without success. In spite of his recent experience of high altitude on Rakaposhi Tilman suffered from a severe headache, and Shipton also suffered from mountain-sickness. The Sherpa plodded gamely but he too became exhausted, and they had to return to camp. They hoped to make another attempt next day but both Shipton and Tilman found that their toes were frostbitten. That meant immediate descent.

Shipton believed that they had reached the summit dome of Muztagh Ata and were within a hundred feet or so of the top when they had to turn back. Tilman was less sure that they had in fact got quite so high, but whatever height they finally reached it was certainly quite near the summit. Tilman observed:

An inexcusable assumption of the probable snow conditions, over-confidence in our powers, and the unexpected cold proved our undoing, and of these only of the last had we any right to complain. In early June on the North Col of Everest one would not experience such cold. Here it was mid-August, and though Muztagh Ata is in Lat. 38 and Everest is 10 degrees further south one would not expect that to make so much difference. We live and learn, and big mountains are stern teachers.

After three pleasant weeks staying with the Shiptons at the consulate in Kashgar, with much diplomatic entertaining among the British, Russian and Chinese officials, Tilman started for home. He did not want to go back by the way he had come, so he worked out a route that would take him to Tashkurghan via the Kara-tash pass (16,388 ft) and two little-known passes, the Tur-bulung and the Yangi Dawan, to the east of Muztagh Ata. This was all in Chinese territory and he had no trouble, revelling in his caravan of assorted yaks, ponies and donkeys, and in the yoghourt and fresh bread that were the hospitable offering to travellers by the semi-nomadic peoples of the country. After Tashkurghan he again wanted a new route and decided to make for Gilgit by going west of his outward journey and crossing the Hindu Kush by the Wakhjir Pass (16,000 ft). This is a beautiful route that would take him to the source of the Oxus through a little-known area, but it meant crossing briefly into Afghanistan. He had no visa for Afghanistan, and no practical means of getting one, but thought that he could trust to luck and the remoteness of the region to stay out of trouble. He was wrong.

The journey to the Wakhjir Pass was the kind of travel Tilman enjoyed, though he found it perishing cold at the beginning of October. The country was magnificent, the Oxus valley winding between the Pamirs to the north and the Hindu Kush to the south. The Oxus here is the boundary between Afghanistan and Russian Asia, and which of several streams is properly the infant Oxus was of great importance when the boundary agreement with Russia was made in 1872. For decades afterwards there was diplomatic fuss over whether the right river had been chosen. In Tilman's view the stream called Ab-i-Wakhan, rising as a glacier and emerging as a rivulet from an ice-cave below the Wakhjir Pass, is the true Oxus, but in 1872 the Pamir River had been preferred.

From Afghanistan Tilman wanted to make for Gilgit by the Khora Bort Pass, but when he tried to hire yaks for the crossing the local headman refused to give any help for what he regarded an irregular way out of Afghanistan. He insisted that Tilman must go forty miles out of his way to the Afghan frontier post at Sarhad to report to officials. To make things worse, the interpreter from Tashkurghan decided to return to Sinkiang.

It was an unhappy little caravan that made its way to Sarhad. Tilman had obtained one yak from the headman, and he had one travelling companion who had come with him from Kashgar with the intention of visiting his father in Kashmir. This man, Yusuf, had his own pony. Like Tilman he was visa-less, but assumed that in company with the English sahib he would be all right. The headman was taking no chances. They had not gone far when they were picked up by two men who said that they were police, and insisted on accompanying them.

Sarhad is a frontier town at the crossing of the route from Afghanistan to India, and the Oxus valley route to Sinkiang. It possesses the first arable land of the high Oxus, irrigated by the river emerging from its mountain gorge. Since grain can be bought there it has been a halting place for travellers throughout history—and a place of enforced halts for those who fall foul of the frontier guards. Precisely why they were so suspicious of Tilman was a mystery. True, he had no visa for Afghanistan, but he had a perfectly good passport and he had a reasonable explanation for his presence. Much of the trouble was that he couldn't explain himself because he and the Afghan officials he first met had no common language. Tilman had neither Persian nor Pushtu, and while he knew a fair amount of Hindustani the only Afghanis he met at Sarhad who claimed to understand Hindustani spoke a brand that was as incomprehensible to him as his was gibberish to them. The Afghan–Russian frontier has always been a sensitive area in Central Asian politics, and it is possible that at first he was taken for a Russian spy. When he insisted that he was English he was told that he must be an English spy, though with India just become independent the motives for England's spying on the Afghan border are not obvious.

For whatever reason he was detained—if there ever was any reason apart from general suspicion of strangers—he was made to stay in Sarhad until instructions came from higher authority at Iskashim, about 100 miles away. He was allowed to use his tent, but if he tried to go for a walk two policemen at once made him turn back. On the third day he was told through a Hindustani interpreter that he was to be sent to Iskashim, whence he might be allowed to leave Afghanistan for Chitral if he could satisfy the authorities of his innocence. He had left behind mail and his kit in Gilgit, and to be forced into Chitral meant another long journey. But by this time he was prepared to get out of Afghanistan at any cost.

He left Sarhad on 5 October 1947 and reached Iskashim five days later. It is a journey that few Western travellers have made during this century, and as such it was interesting enough, but on arrival at Iskashim he and Yusuf were put in gaol. He was searched, his diaries and all his papers were taken from him, and the seams of his tent slit to see if anything was hidden in them. An exposure-meter, assumed to be some sophisticated form of radio, aroused the deepest suspicion until a telegraph clerk was able to identify it. Most serious of all, the Chief of Police decided that his appearance did not resemble the photograph on his passport—scarcely surprising, because the photograph was of a clean-shaven Tilman before the war and now he was several years older and had grown a beard.

Although imprisoned in a cell about ten feet square and not allowed to leave it except to go to the outside latrine, he was quite well-treated. He was given a chair, and a piece of carpet was laid on the earth floor. Well-cooked meals were sent to him from the kitchen of the Commissar, the chief official. But his writing materials had been confiscated, he had nothing to do, and he could not find out what was likely to happen. After two days of isolation he went on hunger strike, saying that he would not eat until he had seen the Commissar. When they met, the Commissar was friendly, invited Tilman to join him in a game of cards, and offered him a pull at his *hookah*, but all Tilman could get out of him about his own fate was that he must stay where he was for at least five days. But he was given a pack of cards, and Tilman held afterwards that it was playing patience that kept him sane during his imprisonment.

At last he and Yusuf were allowed to leave, travelling under guard. Tilman was thankful to be on his way, but became more and more unhappy next day, when he realised they were in fact travelling west. This was no possible route for Chitral, and he assumed that he was being sent under guard to Kabul. His maps had been taken from him with the rest of his papers so he could not tell precisely where he was but on 20 October they reached Faizabad, the capital of the Badakshan province of Afghanistan, 135 miles from Kabul and linked to it by a motor road. However, the military commander in Faizabad, who was a general with plenty of authority, and had a son who could speak fluent Hindustani, treated him as well as he could. He was given quarters in the servants' compound of the general's house, and provided with meals from his own mess. He was guarded by an unarmed sentry, and was allowed to sit out of doors or walk in the compound as he liked. Meanwhile the general telegraphed Kabul and said that he could expect his release in three or four days. The three or four days turned into nine because a public holiday intervened, but a telegram came at last and he and Yusuf were sent to the Chitral border, still accompanied by a soldier but now, as the general was careful to explain, as an escort and not as a guard. The unfortunate Yusuf got out of Afghanistan with him, but was unable to proceed to Kashmir because of the war that had broken out over partition. In the end Yusuf returned safely to Kashgar. Tilman always felt a little guilty about him because he had not received the protection expected from travelling with an Englishman. Tilman had got so used to travelling under the power of the British Raj that he took a foolish risk in crossing the Wakhjir Pass into independent Afghanistan. He was lucky to get off as lightly as he did. The conditions of his imprisonment might have been much harsher—and it is not unknown for tiresome strangers on remote frontiers to be shot by trigger-happy guards while "resisting arrest" or "trying to escape".

In 1947 Adeline decided to move from Wallasey to Wales and bought a lovely rambling old house overlooking the Mawddach estuary a few miles inland from Barmouth. The house is called Bod Owen (which means simply Owen's Dwelling, from the name of its original owner) and with it went a considerable area of wooded hillside. This was Tilman's home for the rest of his life, and he grew to love it dearly. He had Welsh ancestry on his mother's side, and for a lover of mountains and the sea there could be no happier place to live than on the beautiful mountain coast of what was then Merioneth and is now Gwynnedd. Bod Owen is on the north shore of the tidal estuary of the Mawddach, and across the river rise range upon range of hills culminating in the summit of Cader Idris, clearly visible when the hills are free from cloud. Tilman was back in England in time to help Adeline settle into their new home, choosing for his sanctum and study a little room on the ground floor with a lovely view over the woods that come up to the garden of the house. He had his desk in the window, and here for the next thirty years he wrote his books, dealt with his massive correspondence, and planned his adventures. Bod Owen was home and he loved it, but nothing could change the pattern of his wandering life— a few months at home, and then a new adventure to some far corner of the earth. By the early summer of 1948 he was again in China.

Tilman's Chinese journey of 1948 was another last of its kind—it would not have been possible after the American break with the China of Mao Tse-tung which came soon afterwards. In the summer of 1948 the Government of Chiang Kai-shek was on its last legs, but its writ still ran in places, among them the northern part of Sinkiang. The Americans had established a wartime consulate at Urumchi, between the Tien Shan mountains and the Bogdo Ola range to the east of them, and Shipton was making the most of his last months as British consul in Kashgar by visiting this remote and fascinating region as their guest. He invited Tilman to join him in an expedition to the Bogdo Ola mountains, a little known range whose heights are somewhat uncertain. There are three main peaks in the Bogdo Ola group, known to Western travellers simply as the East, Centre and West peaks. Merzbacher measured them by trigonometry from Urumchi in 1904, and put the East peak at 21,164 feet, the Centre peak at 21,125 feet and the West peak at 20,787 feet. In 1932, however, a Swedish geological survey assessed the East peak at no more than 18,000 feet. Tilman went into the evidence carefully, and concluded that the Merzbacher survey was reasonably accurate within an error of plus or minus 100 feet, the error allowed by Merzbacher himself. Whatever their precise heights, the Bogdo Ola mountains are exceptionally beautiful, and offer some formidable climbing.

The war in Kashmir made an approach to Sinkiang via India or Pakistan impracticable, so Tilman made his way to Urumchi by crossing the whole of China from Shanghai. He went to Shanghai by air, deploring flying as a means of travel, but accepting it as quick. Of his flight he wrote:

The Chinese saying that the further one travels the less one knows must have been prescient of the air age. Nothing could be truer of air travel. It is about 10,000 miles from London to Shanghai, a journey which, had it been done by sea in a small boat, overland on foot, or even by car, would have provided an education in itself. . . . When it is done by air the traveller is poorer in pocket and no richer in experience.

In spite of this he still needed the aeroplane, for from Shanghai he flew nearly 1,000 miles to Lanchow on the Hwang-ho (Yellow River), whence he could reach Urumchi in a twelve-day journey by postal bus. Tilman's distinction between traveller and passenger hardly applied to Chinese buses in 1948. The traveller, he insisted, is one who uses travel as an end in itself; the bus in China by definition carried passengers, but a twelve-day journey in remote country taking in part of the Gobi Desert is an adventure that can reasonably be considered an end in itself. To put up at "The Inn of the Overlapping Teeth" is an experience that may fitly turn the mere passenger into a traveller, particularly as there was nothing at this inn for even overlapping teeth to bite on, for it was a sleeping inn with no food. Tilman's account of this bus journey in *China to Chitral* is among the most attractive of his writings.

As a climbing expedition the Shipton-Tilman visit to Bogdo Ola was not much of a success, for they failed to climb any of the main peaks. But they had four days together in magnificent mountain country, and climbed a secondary peak at about 17,000 feet from which they had a glorious view of the giants of the Tien Shan some fifty to a hundred miles away to the west. They had a second chance at Bogdo Ola for a curious reason, or rather combination of reasons. The lorry which was to take Shipton back to Kashgar needed repairs, and the American consulate at Urumchi needed ice. Hearing Shipton and Tilman discussing glaciers it occurred to one of the Americans that here was an excellent source of ice. So the two Englishmen used their enforced stay to go back to Bogdo Ola with an American truck to collect ice. Leaving the ice-digging party to get on with the job (which proved surprisingly difficult) they returned to their mountain, arranging to make their own way back to Urumchi in a couple of days. They did not get very far, for Shipton sprained his ankle and his Sherpa servant was unwell, but they reached the axis ridge west of the last snow peak of the range. Tilman wrote that the ridge was broad and smooth, and "the efforts we had made to reach it were well repaid . . . hundreds of miles of Asia lay spread on either hand".

Having returned to the valley they met some Kazak pastoralists who gave them food, but refused to hire out ponies for the eighteen miles to Urumchi. Later a more kindly Kazak insisted on putting them up for the night in his *yort*, a circular felt tent used by nomadic peoples throughout Central Asia. In the morning they were able to hire ponies and got back to Urumchi to find that glacier ice was not a marked success: it was considered useful for preserving food, but was too full of grit to be used in drinks.

Time was running out for Shipton, who had to hand over his consulate in Kashgar to be divided between the Governments of India and Pakistan. The Russian consul in Kashgar was also about to be relieved, so there was a bout of diplomatic entertaining. Tilman endured (and sometimes enjoyed) this for a few days, and then went off to reconnoitre Chakar Aghil, a 22,000-foot outlier of the Hindu Kush some three days' journey to the west of Kashgar. Shipton wanted to climb it before he left, and Tilman hoped to find a possible route.

The doctor to the British Mission in Kashgar, who doubled as Vice-Consul, went with him. He was a fine travelling companion, but in fording a river he had the misfortune to be knocked off his feet by the powerful stream and lost the boots which he had taken off to carry. His only other footwear was a pair of *chaplis* (the sandals of north-west India) and when they came to the mountain sandals were inadequate for walking on glaciers. The doctor did his gallant best and they camped at some 13,000 feet, but his feet were so cut and bruised that he had to stay in camp next day while Tilman went on alone to see if he could work out a route that might lead to the top. He climbed a high valley that he thought should lead to the flanks of Chakar Aghil, but when he got to the head of the valley the mountain disappeared. He could see two peaks in the wrong place, neither of which could be Chakar Aghil, but of the mountain which should have dominated the scene there was no sign whatever. It must have been some trick of light which he was never able to explain, and he could not investigate farther because he had to get back to the doctor. "Certain of nothing except that what must be the north ridge could be reached, I went down," he wrote later.

On the way back Chakar Aghil duly appeared again. It was the best view of the mountain he had had, but it added to his bewilderment for it did not look in the least as he had expected. He duly reported to Shipton, and between them they tried to work out its precise position, and they decided to "have a go".

It was their last climb together, and it is sad that it did not have a happier outcome. They succeeded in finding the right mountain, identified a ridge which they thought would go, and camped at about 17,000 feet. But they had with them a Kirghiz porter who became ill and had to be taken down. Back in Kashgar the man was medically examined, and found to be in apparently normal health. He was a native of high country and had lived for most of his life at around 10,000 feet, yet at 17,000 feet he had suffered so severely from mountain sickness that he began spitting blood. Tilman remained puzzled, and could only conclude that living at high altitude does not necessarily enable the body to acclimatise readily to still higher altitudes, though other mountain people (Sherpas, for example) accommodate to extreme altitudes without great difficulty. He was always interested in this question of acclimatisation because of his own early troubles at height, troubles which, indeed, returned to both him and Shipton on Muztagh Ata. Like sea-sickness, which afflicts some people and not others, altitude sickness is a physiological and psychological problem of great complexity. It cost Tilman and Shipton what might have been a notable summit to add to their joint achievement, but they could not have left a sick man to fend for himself while they went on.

On 1 October Tilman left Kashgar to travel with the mail-runners to Tashkurghan, a five-day journey with ponies. From Tashkurghan he followed a route of his own to Chitral, crossing a number of high passes in the Hindu Kush and being careful this time to stay out of Afghanistan. It was the kind of travel he loved, independent, with his own small caravan, carrying his own *ata* to make bread, and leaving the known track for a lesser-known pass whenever occasion offered. He wanted to enter Chitral by the Darkot pass (15,380 ft) but there was heavy snow and he settled for the lower Boroghil pass at 12,000 feet. Here he met two traders from Gilgit who gave him the surprising news that Pakistan, with (as they put it) her allies Great Britain and the United States, was at war with Russia. Feeling that it was his duty as a soldier to get back as quickly as possible he marched at double stages to Chitral, but after a day he discovered that the news was not true, and he was able to relax. His tour of Central Asia from the Yellow River to the Oxus was attempted before him only by Marco Polo and a handful of the world's greatest travellers, and for political reasons no one has been able to attempt it since.

XI

Nepal and Burma

A GLANCE AT the chronological table on page 357 will show that Tilman made some adventurous journeys, at first by land, later by sea, practically every year for thirty years from 1947. Between expeditions he had a full life, based on Bod Owen: writing books and articles, sometimes lecturing, helping to look after the garden and woodland, visiting friends and having friends to stay, and attending meetings of various clubs and societies. He was an active member of the Himalayan Committee, which succeeded the old Everest Committee in co-ordinating mountaineering activities, and on returning from Chitral at the end of 1948 he was at once involved in planning renewed attempts to climb Mount Everest.

The politics of Everest expeditions had changed. Chinese dominance of Tibet now closed the Tibetan approach to the mountain, and if it was to be climbed by Westerners it would have to be through Nepal. Politics there were sensitive too. The same developments that closed Tibet encouraged some relaxation of the pre-war closure of Nepal, but this was complicated by fears of a possible threat to Nepal's independence after the withdrawal of the British. Her rulers recognised that new diplomatic arrangements were going to be needed, and that the almost total isolation which they had been able to preserve under the indirect protection of the British could not be maintained; but a feudal system of government with a traditional policy of excluding foreigners could not be abandoned overnight. For over a century British-Nepalese relations had been exemplary, and both sides had scrupulously honoured the treaty of friendship which ended war between them in 1816. Nepal remained a sovereign state but accepted a British Resident in Katmandu, who never sought to interfere in internal matters. The policy of excluding foreigners was interpreted so strictly that even the Resident was not allowed to travel outside the *terai* (the lowland country bordering India) and the Katmandu valley. After the First World War, in recognition of the help that Nepal had given to

Britain, and in particular of the magnificent courage of Gurkha soldiers fighting with the British, the status of Resident was raised to Ambassador, which removed even the appearance of Nepalese subservience to Britain. However, Nepal continued to benefit from British rule in India by protection from external threat, by the wages and pensions of Gurkha soldiers recruited into British service, and by the free import of goods through British India.

In 1948–49 the almost total exclusion of foreigners from Nepal was beginning to be relaxed, and there was real hope that a British mountaineering expedition to the Nepal Himalaya might be allowed. Tilman wanted to go to Gauri Sankar (23,440 ft) and thence into the Sola Khumbu region through which Everest could be approached. The Foreign Office, wishing to tread delicately, thought that such a journey across Nepal and far from Katmandu was rather a lot to ask for, and suggested that permission for an expedition to the Langtang Himal should be sought instead. The Nepalese authorities had made it clear that an expedition would have to have an Army escort, and a journey to the Langtang would be easier to keep an eye on. (The escort was not needed for protection, but was required as a political gesture.) It was also suggested that it would help if the expedition undertook some scientific work as well as mountaineering. Since all parts of the Nepal Himalaya have magnificent mountains, then unclimbed and for the most part unknown, Tilman was quite happy to transfer his plans to the Langtang Himal, but he was less happy about combining mountain exploration with scientific research. For the sake of travel anywhere in the Himalaya, however, he was prepared to make concessions, and he undertook to survey the Langtang valley, taking with him a geologist and a botanist. He even agreed that he himself would try to collect a certain species of beetle. Not knowing much about beetles he interpreted this as collecting any beetle that came his way—which he did conscientiously—one of his beetles turning out to be new to science.

Tilman's excursions in Nepal were important to him, and also of some historical importance, for he lighted the way to much climbing in the Nepal Himalaya, and cleared up a number of geographical uncertainties about certain glacier systems. His explorations must be seen in the setting of their time. In his book *Nepal Himalaya* he described Nepal in 1949 as "the largest inhabited country still unexplored by Europeans" but also pointed out that Nepal had been lived and travelled in by Nepalis, Indians and Tibetans for millennia, and that

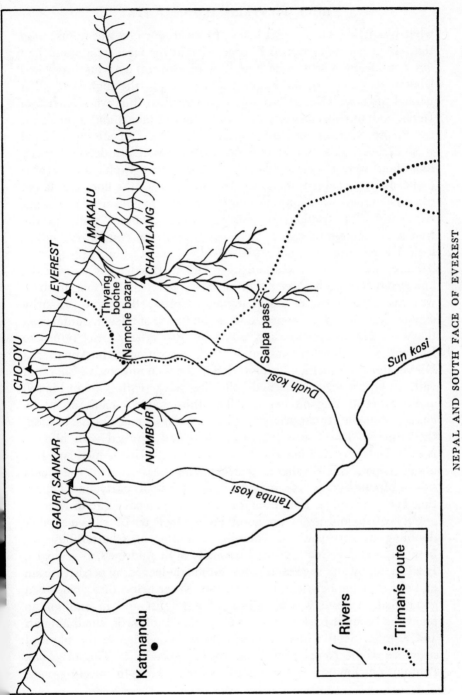

NEPAL AND SOUTH FACE OF EVEREST

CHO-OYU
EVEREST
MAKALU
CHAMLANG
Thyang boche
Namche bazar
GAURI SANKAR
NUMBUR
Salpa pass
Dudh kosi
Tamba kosi
Sun kosi
Katmandu

Rivers
Tilman's route

what was unknown about it before his own journeys was information that either had not reached Europe, or that the local inhabitants had not considered worth recording. Indian Government surveyors had triangulated some of the major peaks in 1850—the highest of all is named after Sir George Everest, who was then Surveyor-General of India. Indian collectors obtained specimens of plants and animals for the British Museum and other scientific bodies. But although Nepal was mapped by the Survey of India the maps were not detailed, many mountains were not triangulated, and much topographical detail was omitted and remained unknown. So with study of the flora and fauna of Nepal—there was information, but it was haphazard. The slight relaxation of restrictions on entry enabled coherent study in the traditions of Western science to be carried out. An American ornithological expedition was permitted to study bird life in 1948–49, and Tilman's own expeditions of 1949–50 added considerably to scientific knowledge. He made three major journeys in Nepal. The first, in 1949, was his exploration of the Langtang Himal; that was primarily exploration, though he hoped to fit in the ascent of a few mountains on the way. The second journey, made in 1950 after a brief return to England, was primarily a mountaineering expedition to the Annapurna Himal, though it included exploration of the then unknown Marsyandi valley, and some scientific and collecting work (with Tilman himself again concentrating on beetles). The third journey came about by chance after the Annapurna expedition, when he met Oscar Houston, the father of Dr Charles Houston (who had climbed with him on Nanda Devi), in Katmandu. Oscar Houston, being American, had obtained permission hitherto denied to the British to visit the Nepal side of Mount Everest. He invited Tilman to join his party, and Tilman thus became the first Englishman to travel the Nepal route to Everest.

On his 1949 journey he was accompanied by Peter Lloyd as a climber doubling as surveyor, O. Polunin, a master at Charterhouse, as botanist, and J. S. Scott, of the University of St Andrew's, as geologist. It was a happy and successful party, although dogged by persistent rain and cloud at the height of the monsoon. Nevertheless they achieved a good deal. Polunin was an all-round naturalist and in addition to plants he brought back a number of specimens of birds, small animals and reptiles. Scott added substantially to knowledge of the physical structure of the Nepal Himalaya. In an appendix to Tilman's book Polunin contributed a valuable study of the region as the meeting-place of plant and animal migration from Kashmir and Afghanistan to the west and from Burma and China to the east.

As headman and cook Tilman recruited the redoubtable Sherpa Tensing Norkay (of later Everest fame) who had spent the war with the Chitral Scouts. Tilman wrote of him in *Nepal Himalaya*:

> Since then he had been to Lhasa with an Italian Tibetan scholar, for whom he had purchased whole libraries—he told me they had brought away forty maunds* of books. Tensing, who gets on well with everyone and handles the local people well has a charming smile, great steadiness on a mountain, and a deft hand for omelettes which he turns out nicely sloppy but firm.

The weather seriously interfered with surveying but they made as thorough a survey of the Langtang valley and its background of mountains on the Tibetan border as infrequent breaks in almost constant rain and mist permitted. They located the position of the majestic Gosainthan (26,291 ft) and were the first Europeans to see a superb unnamed mountain which they called The Fluted Peak because of the exquisite snow fluting "traced", Tilman wrote, "like the ribs of a fan upon its western face". He estimated its height at about 21,000 feet and he, Lloyd and Tensing tried to climb it. They established a camp at around 19,000 feet but were defeated by the weather which made ice-falls extremely dangerous. They climbed a more modest mountain, Paldor (19,451 ft), although wet snow made it hard going. They re-discovered a forgotten pass into Tibet (for them forbidden territory) and worked out the glacier systems and watersheds of the region. For reading when forced to lie up Tilman had equipped himself with Dostoevski's *Brothers Karamazov* and Trollope's *Last Chronicle of Barset*. The weather was so atrocious that he read both three times.

Much of their work, particularly the finding of suitable locations for Peter Lloyd's survey stations, was carried out at considerable heights, though Tilman typically under-stresses the physical difficulties. His diary for 11 June 1949, for instance, records laconically:

> Up at 4 a.m. started 4.30. Snow good. Reached subsidiary ridge 19,000 ft 6.30. Peter did station. The going v. slow after a bad night. Self and Tensing went on to ridge by steep snow, and along it to the

* A maund is an Indian measure equivalent to about 80 lbs.

highest point 20,000. Very thin and soft snow on E side, and corniced. Found two moths dormant in rock crevice at 19,000 ft.

For all his proclaimed hostility to "science" Tilman carefully recorded the trees, shrubs and flowers met at various heights, and any curious bits of natural history he came across. Ten days after finding the moths he recorded seeing some spiders on rocks at an estimated 22,500 feet.

The mountaineering party for the expedition in 1950 was a powerful one, consisting of Tilman, Dr C. H. Evans, J. H. Emlyn Jones, Major J. O. M. Roberts of the 1/2nd Gurkha Rifles and W. P. Packard, a young New Zealander who was a Rhodes Scholar at Oxford. The seniors were all distinguished climbers, and young Packard, who was making his first trip to the Himalaya, had done much climbing in New Zealand. In addition Colonel D. G. Lowndes of the Royal Garhwal Rifles, who had travelled widely in the hills, and spoke Gurkhali, came with them as a botanist. As to scientific purpose, Colonel Lowndes was concerned with flora, Tilman again undertook to collect beetles, and Major Roberts birds. Emlyn Jones, an expert surveyor and Packard a geographer catered for mapping. Four Sherpas were recruited.

The party assembled at Katmandu early in May and left for the mountains on 10 May. They had no definite objective in view but decided to make for the Annapurna Range, whose four magnificent peaks were then still unclimbed. The peaks are known simply as Annapurna I, the highest at 26,492 feet, Annapurna II not much lower at 26,041 feet, III reaching 24,858 feet and IV 24,688 feet. On 3 June, while Tilman and his party were in the Annapurna Himalaya, a French expedition led by Maurice Herzog succeeded in climbing Annapurna I. Their ascent, and more perilous descent in a severe storm (which the Tilman party also experienced, though not in conditions of peril), are a well-known epic of mountaineering history.

The French and British parties did not meet; they were separated by the mountains of the Annapurna chain, and Tilman and his companions learned of the French success only through the mail. Their own activities were as much exploration as climbing for its own sake, and they were probably the first Europeans, certainly the first for a century or so, to visit the Manangbhot district on the Nepal–Tibetan frontier. After casting around for a mountain to climb they selected Annapurna IV, mainly because it was the most accessible for the available time. They established four camps on the mountain, the highest at about 22,400 feet. Evans and Packard seemed to be the fittest pair and they had a go for the summit, but were turned back by a blizzard. On 19 June Tilman, Evans and Packard made another attempt. In *Nepal Himalaya* Tilman described it:

Having climbed for nearly two hours we paused at a small rock outcrop to take stock and to compare our height with that of Macha Puchare [22,958 ft]. . . . It is difficult to judge by the eye alone, but the most hopeful among us dared not affirm that we were much, if anything, above it; which meant that we had risen only 500 ft. After another hour, during which we gained height quicker owing to the steeper slope, the altimeter put us at 23,400 ft. Packard was going strong, Evans panting a little, while the combined effect of age and altitude threatened momentarily to bring my faltering footsteps to a halt. In fact, my goose was cooked, but I was still strong enough to get down alone. Hoping they would move quicker, I persuaded them to leave me. At midday the usual snow scurries began, yet with no threat of worse to follow. I still hoped they might do it, for I had last seen them nearing the shoulder. Alas; presently they reappeared coming down, and before 2 o'clock were back in camp. They had climbed beyond the shoulder to an estimated height of 24,000 ft, where our candid friend the altimeter, which I had urged them to take, registered only 23,800 ft. But Evans had shot his bolt, and Packard, who felt strong enough, was rightly loath to tackle single-handed the last 600 ft of steep and narrow summit ridge.

Tilman was in his 53rd year. Of his own performance he observed, "However well a man in his fifties may go up to 20,000 ft I have come regretfully to the conclusion that above that height, so far as climbing goes, he is declining into decrepitude." Decrepitude did not interfere with another six weeks of energetic exploration, and they brought back new geographical knowledge of a remote area of Nepal, and useful additions to the natural history of the region.

During this exploration Tilman had a nasty accident which, typically, he makes light of, but which would have been serious for anyone less endowed with his remarkable powers of fortitude and self-recovery. Accompanied by two Sherpas he had gone off for a week to explore a glacier descending from the Ladakh range and to have a look at a peak called Himlung Himal. Crossing a ridge of great boulders he slipped and fell backwards about 15 feet. According to his own account:

> If one must move after a fall it is better to do it quickly before the body begins to protest. We had to find water, so with the help of the Sherpas I got down to the hollow, and a little later found myself laid stiff on my back, where I remained for five days, unable even to sit up without help. Throughout it rained steadily, but the Sherpas kept a fire going and went down twice to Bimtakhoti for more food. When I felt strong enough to be carried we got two men up to take our kit while the Sherpas in turn carried me pick-a-back. I dreaded recrossing that ridge but there was no alternative. I sweated freely, and my injured back winced in anticipation as Gyalgen [one of the Sherpas] balanced a precarious way over the boulders, my weight threatening to bring us both down at every step. The rest of the party arrived next day [24 August]. There was nothing they could do except sympathise. . . . As soon as I could rise without help I began to crawl, then to walk, and finally to walk uphill, every day increasing the distance, until on 3 September . . . I climbed to the scene of the accident to collect some flowers.

Annapurna IV was Tilman's last big climb in the Himalaya. He would have liked to have done better, but he was at least as interested in mountain exploration as in climbing as such, and as explorers the expedition had done pretty well. He had intended to go home in September, but the chance of a visit to the Nepal side of Everest changed his plans. The American party consisted of the Houstons, father and son, Mrs Betsy Cowles, an experienced climber, and Anderson Bakewell, who was studying at a Jesuit college near Darjeeling. Tilman's first thoughts, as he recorded them in his book, were not chivalrous: "Hitherto I had not regarded a woman as an indispensable part of the equipage of a Himalayan journey but one lives and learns. Anyway, with a doctor to heal us, a woman to feed us, and a priest to pray for us, I felt we could face the future with some confidence."

It turned out better than he feared. His public misogyny had presumably to be justified, and when he first learned that there was to be a woman in the party he sulked for a few days. The outcome, wrote Dr Charles Houston in a letter, was different: "Betsy was a charming and understanding woman, and within a week they were virtually hand in hand, and I believe were fast friends until she died." Here is Dr Houston's first-hand account of the trip:

My father was not a climber, but a good mountain walker. Just how he obtained permission to cross Nepal I have never been quite sure, but he was the first Westerner (American or European) to go beyond Dhankuta, which was reached by Dillon Ripley [an American scientist with an ornithological expedition] in 1948 and by Hooker [Sir Joseph Hooker, the botanist] in 1860 or so. My father was 67 at the time, a rather sedentary type, but it was the biggest adventure of his life.

I have already told you how Betsy Cowles won Tilman's heart, and after the first few days of sulks they became inseparable. We had perfect Fall weather, and the ten-day walk—really a picnic—was an unforgettable experience, even for Bill: virgin territory, incredible beautiful scenery, a small *bandobast,** and all the world to see. Bill became charming, almost voluble, and our afternoon tea and evenings about the fire were unforgettable.

Bill and I were the first up the ridge to Thyangboche, the first Westerners ever to see that beautiful place. We were royally welcomed, Tibetan tea, devil dances, ceremonies, exchanges of presents —the whole bit. Even Bill was deeply moved. We were lodged in a small stone house liberally ventilated, although this did little to dissipate the smoke from the fire built for us each morning by the monks. They aroused us at dawn with liberal doses of *rakshi* [Nepali rum] served in a huge old-fashioned glass-stoppered pickle jar, still bearing the paper label "Heinz 57 varieties". While Bill and I went up the valley the rest of the party basked in the sun at Thyangboche, enjoying the freshness of Eden.

Tilman and I set our usual fast pace, and what I remember best about the journey is a camp fire at what is now Pheriche. Then it was a wild meadow, with traces of shepherd huts, and ample wood. Bill had a talking jag, and for almost four hours told about his various

* A Hindustani word, meaning "arrangement", but widely used to imply the organisation of anything, from a party to an expedition.

adventures in Sikkhim, Bhutan and elsewhere. How I wish there had been a tape recorder! He told of the virulent malaria which had killed one of his party [in Assam] and almost killed him. . . . He told about river crossings, unclimbed, unnamed peaks, and long dangerous trips up through rain forests. He talked and talked, and even laughed. How can one ever describe such an evening?

Next day we went up the glacier, going quite slowly, because we were not adequately acclimatised. We climbed high on Pumori to look into the West Cwm, but our strength was not enough to let us round the corner. We saw the summit [of Everest], the First and Second Steps, the Yellow Band, and everything that has since become so familiar. We realised that the West Cwm was extremely dangerous, but we cautiously suggested to each other that the route would go, but with great hazard. After many photographs we turned back to Thyangboche, having to carry one of the porters who came down with malaria, and rejoined our friends. There were more ceremonies and exchanges of gifts before we turned back homeward.

This was in the Fall of 1950, when the Chinese had crossed the Yalu, Nepal was in a revolution, and all of the sub-continent seemed about to burst into flame. I remember vividly walking with Bill through the autumn gold, reflecting on what we had seen, and what damage we might have set in train for this innocent, backward country. We were all sad, knowing that this was the end of something unique and wild, and the beginning of a period of great danger and immense change for this wonderful land. All of us felt, I think, a little sad that we had been the instruments.

It is an understandable feeling, but the Houstons and Tilman were scarcely the "instruments" of change in Nepal. Change had to come anyway, and Tilman's travels in 1949–50 were important in demonstrating to the Nepalese that responsible expeditions could be permitted without danger to the State. His personal example, as well as his route-finding and surveying, did much to help the opening of the Nepal Himalaya to mountaineers.

The revolution in Nepal that Dr Houston mentions was a dynastic one conducted in a remarkably civilised manner without bloodshed, and it did not greatly interfere with foreign travellers permitted to enter the country; the revolution was, indeed, part of the political process that gradually relaxed restrictions on entry. It upset neither Shipton's reconnaissance of the Nepal route to Everest in 1951, nor the successful expedition led by Lord Hunt in 1953. The forerunner of these was the Houston expedition in 1950. That was a breakthrough in Himalayan travel, and all later expeditions making the Nepal approach to Everest have benefited from it.

As for Tilman, it took him to the homeland of the Sherpas, whose development as mountaineers he and Shipton had done so much to bring about. Now that the Nepal route to Everest is famous, and "Sherpa" a name synonymous with high climbing, it is hard to realise that barely thirty years ago Tilman's journey with the Houston party to Namche Bazar and Thyangboche was the first impact of the outside world on a region that has since figured in countless mountaineering books. Tilman's *Nepal Himalaya* was the first published account of the Sherpas at home.

In that book he has a touching description of the party's arrival at Namche Bazar:

We were welcomed to the village by an inquisitive but friendly crowd. Namche Bazar, of course, has never ranked as a "forbidden city". It is far from being a city, and it has remained unvisited not because of any very serious difficulties in the way, but because no one has thought it worth the trouble of overcoming them. Nevertheless, it had for long been my humble Mecca. As we rode in I shared in imagination a little of the satisfaction of Burton, or of Manning when he reached Lhasa.

Tilman's description of the Thyangboche monastery is a pleasing footnote to mountaineering history:

Thyangboche is a very small counterpart of Rongbuk monastery on the Tibetan side of the mountain, not a quarter of its size and having only a handful of monks. Yet its abbot, a shy, smiling youth, of reputedly great spiritual power, is held in little less reverence, and its situation is incomparably more beautiful and less austere. It is much less austere inside, too, for they produced a beaker of *rakshi* for our lunch, and when we returned a few days later we found they had the pleasant custom of fortifying their guests with a snorter before breakfast.

There was no time for a full reconnaissance of the Nepal approach to Everest, and from what they saw of the mountain Tilman was not enthusiastic about an attempt to climb it from the Western Cwm—one of the few occasions when his instinctive judgment of mountains was wrong, for this was the route by which Everest was climbed in 1953. In a sense Tilman here was a victim of history: his own attempt to climb Everest had been from the Tibetan side, and all the Everest lore in which he was steeped concerned the approach from Tibet; it was hard to believe that victory would come from a radically new approach. But although Tilman cannot be said to have contributed directly to the final ascent of Everest, indirectly he contributed a great deal. The good relations he and the Houston party established with the Sherpas in their homeland helped Shipton's reconnaissance in 1951 and the victorious expedition two years later. And by getting at least within striking distance of Everest from Nepal he showed that the journey to Thyangboche was not difficult.

That the journey to Everest through Nepal was the last of Tilman's visits to the Himalaya was a deliberate choice. The concluding lines of *Nepal Himalaya* give his reasons:

The best attainable should be good enough for any man, but the mountaineer who finds his best gradually sinking is not satisfied. In an Early English poem attributed to one Beowulf we are told,

Harder should be the spirit, the heart all the bolder,
Courage the greater, as the strength grows less.

If a man feels he is failing to achieve this stern standard he should perhaps withdraw from a field of such high endeavour as the Himalaya.

This was Tilman approaching his 53rd birthday. His scepticism of his own achievement and of the tremendous powers he still had is typical of his habit of self-depreciation—preferable to arrogance, but sometimes as maddening. From his time as a young subaltern on the Western Front, Tilman's performance was consistently cool, decisive, untroubled by second thoughts. But communing with himself, he lacked self-confidence in a curious way. In his diaries, rough working notebooks, sometimes in his letters, quite often in his books he is absurdly hard on himself, feeling that he ought to have done better,

248

or set about tackling something differently. For all his love of the Himalaya he could be despondent, as this note from his diary of his last Everest trip shows: "Thursday 9th November—above Bung 7,500. Drop steeply 2,500 ft to Hongu Khola. Food trouble. Must send ahead to give time to collect. . . . Very slow progress. Fed up with Nepal."

However, a despondent moment might be followed by a "memorable bathe", the view of some magnificent, distant peak, and the sheer joy in travel would surge back. Despondency is mostly edited out of his books, but of self-depreciation there is sometimes too much. In the words of Charles Houston:

My favourite picture of Bill will always be the spare tough nutbrown man in the ragged hat, baggy torn brown sweater, faded khaki shorts over gnarled legs and heavy climbing boots. Uphill or down, he walked at slightly under four miles per hour. I kept up, but barely. He spoke little, but always worth hearing. . . . He was a deep and private man, with an immense willpower and strength, and an incredible sense of humour which he reserved for greatest effect, and one of the toughest men I ever knew. One sometimes felt that he courted disaster, longed for trauma, and he never did things the easy way if with a little effort they could be made to be impossible. He was certainly one of the great influences in my life.

Having said goodbye to the Himalaya Tilman spent most of 1951 at home writing, sailing in the Mawddach estuary, and enjoying life at Bod Owen with his sister. Sailing became steadily more important to him. He bought a 14-foot dinghy for sailing in the estuary, and in addition made two passages to Ireland in a friend's four-tonner. These were recreations. Work was writing, lecturing, and an occasional talk for the BBC. He was always a fluent writer, and at this time of his life his output was considerable, including articles for many periodicals as well as his book on Nepal. He could and did earn money by writing, but money was not his prime impetus—the prodigious effort that went into his letters to friends, and often to strangers who had written to him about something, could have produced a shelf of books. He wrote, as he travelled, because he wanted to. And he wrote for fun—his enchanting letters to *The Times* on various occasions about the yeti giving him as much pleasure to write as they gave others to read.

The Abominable Snowman had cropped up again on the Everest

trip. Tilman was told that yetis exist in considerable numbers round Namche Bazar, especially in winter when the cold drives them down from the higher slopes of the surrounding mountains. In *Nepal Himalaya* he describes how a Sherpa, Lakhpa Tensing, had been so badly mauled by a Snowman the year before (1949) that he died: "By running downhill, which is, of course, the only way a man can run at these heights, one can usually get away from these creatures whose long hair, falling over their eyes, hampers them; but the unfortunate Lakhpa had apparently tripped, and lying half stunned by the fall became an easy prey."

Did he really believe in the Abominable Snowman? His views were summed up in a talk he gave for the BBC in 1949, "I am at a loss to express a definite opinion. I merely affirm that tracks for which no adequate explanation is forthcoming have been seen, and will no doubt continue to be seen, in the Himalaya, and until a better claimant is found we may as well attribute them to their rightful owner, the Abominable Snowman." His experience in Nepal in 1950 at least fitted in with this opinion.

He took a practical interest in everything to do with Bod Owen, particularly in the thinning and replanting of woods on the hillside. He wanted to replace conifers with ash, partly because ash-trees looked more fitting, partly because he believed that ash is immune to rabbits, and he wished to avoid the cost of rabbit-fencing for the land. Full of plans for the garden, he was at home, busy, and happy.

But his restlessness was not stilled, and towards the end of the year he sailed for Burma for the only salaried job outside the Army that he ever attempted—that of British Consul in Maymyo. It was a curious phase of his life, and his reasons for entering the Consular service can only be guessed at. Probably Shipton's influence was partly responsible. Tilman had undoubtedly enjoyed diplomatic life when he stayed at Kashgar. More, Shipton had been able to use some of his time there for travel to fascinating places he would never have got to without his diplomatic standing. Maymyo is not far from Mandalay in central Burma, a legendary land that appealed to the romantic that was always strong in Tilman. From the Foreign Office's point of view he seemed uniquely qualified for the job. After becoming independent in 1948 Burma chose to leave the British Commonwealth, and in 1951 a left-wing coalition called the Anti-Fascist Freedom League gained power. There were various rival movements, and it was important to the British Government to know what was happening in order to protect remaining British interests. Moreover, Burma has a long frontier with China, where Tilman had travelled widely, and his war-time record also showed that he could get on well with all sorts and conditions of men. He was too old for an established post in the Consular service, but short-term postings on contract were available to men with particular qualifications. In addition to what seemed the intrinsic interest of the job Tilman may also have felt that he needed the salary to help meet the post-war cost of living. He had inherited his father's concern for financial stability, and in the uncertain 1950s a diplomatic salary undoubtedly had attractions.

He loved remote and wild places, and he enjoyed those journeys in Burma that took him away from his consulate, but he did not much enjoy the official side of a Consul's life. There was more paperwork than he had bargained for, he had to do a lot of entertaining, and he was expected to be active in social life, none of which appealed to him. His letters from Maymyo to his sister are far more about Bod Owen than about Burma; they are full of suggestions for the garden, and advice on planting trees. Curiously he rather liked motor cars—he did not enjoy tinkering with engines, but he liked driving. New cars at that time were difficult to get in England and he took advantage of his service abroad to buy a new Humber and have it sent out to Burma.

Mr E. F. Given, then serving in Burma and later British Ambassador in Bahrein, has contributed the following account of Tilman in his Consular days:

This strange, taciturn, and at first sight unimpressive man was on closer acquaintance a remarkable personality. From his career no one could doubt his courage and resourcefulness, but it was only after meeting him that one appreciated his sterling character, so impressive that after spending some time in his company, or even receiving a letter from him, one felt uplifted by knowing him. This was in spite of the fact that his taciturnity was so extreme that one learned more about him from his books than from his conversation, which was frequently non-existent.

I think he must have been down on his luck in 1951 to accept the job of Consul for Upper Burma with residence at Maymyo, a post for which he had no evident qualifications other than his experience of travel in difficult places.* At the time most of Burma was infested with bandits or political insurgents, and the writ of the Government ran only in the principal towns and occasionally along the main roads and the railway. Only the Shans of the non-Burmese peoples seemed not to be in rebellion; fortunately Maymyo lies at the edge of their territory, but in their remotest state they harboured the remains of a KMT army which was already setting up an opium growing and smuggling enterprise in what was later called "the golden triangle". The previous Consul had been able to travel about only by using a car painted bright yellow with a large Union Jack on the side, and by letting it be known that he carried no arms or money. . . . These precautions made him not worth attacking.

Although Bill's reputation had preceded him, I think we were all taken a bit aback when this small, spare, grey figure, usually clutching a pipe, turned up in Rangoon. His attitude was in almost every respect different from that of the diplomats. One example will serve. He was staying with one of us about eight miles from the Ambassador's residence, and declined the offer of a car to take him home from a dinner at the Embassy; he preferred to walk on a sticky Rangoon night. I do not suppose it ever entered his head that he might be mugged on the way.

Not long after his arrival in Maymyo a new Humber Hawk motor car arrived for him in Rangoon; he had bought it on the export quota as permission to do so was one of the perks of the service abroad, and he could hardly lose money on the transaction. Understandably he did not wish to leave it to moulder in Rangoon, and typically he decided to take the unusual course of driving it up to Maymyo instead of sending it by river to Mandalay. People had used the road from time to time, but it could hardly be regarded as a popular means of transport. Indeed, foreigners on it were so rare that the police did not bother to check departures from Rangoon by this route, although they could be quite difficult about people going up country by air. Bill wrote to ask me if I would help him drive the car to Maymyo, and not realising how ill-attuned he was to motor transport, I was glad to accept the proposal as a means of seeing part

* He was not in any way down on his luck, though Mr Given's assumption of his reasons for going to Burma is understandable. Tilman was reluctant to discuss his own motives for doing anything.

of Burma I was not likely to be able to visit otherwise. The previous Consul, a hearty extrovert, had got through to Rangoon and back a couple of months before by shaking off his military escort, and had maintained that it was safe enough for a car unaccompanied by the military, who would surely suffer an ambush from bandits anxious for weapons or ammunition.

Bill came down in the Yellow Ford Pilot with the Union Jack, accompanied by a driver and bearer. He had no trouble on the way but we were a bit concerned about the ground clearance of the Hawk. I remember driving not far out of Rangoon over a Bailey bridge which had no approach ramps, with Bill lying flat on the ground in front watching lest the bridge girders should hit some vulnerable part of the car's underneath. Luckily there was no damage except to his nerves. We drove most of the way together in the Hawk, and he was more communicative than I have ever known him. After we had been going for two or three hours we passed through a little town called Nyaungglebin, where there was a market. Bill said, "Let's stop and buy some bananas," so I pulled up, expecting him to go to the nearest fruit stall and come back with a handful of fruit. Nothing of the sort; he walked the length of the market inspecting what was on offer, until he got just the kind he wanted. As we drove off he explained that when he was living at Eldoret in Kenya in the 1930s, where at 10,000 ft altitude he could maintain his acclimatisation for the Himalayas, his mother had been taken seriously ill in England. The farming business was not good, and he could not afford the fare. He therefore rode his bicycle from Eldoret to Kribi on the coast of Cameroon, living almost entirely on bananas which are a staple item of food in Central Africa. On the journey he acquired a connoisseur's taste in bananas, and now had to have just the right sort. . . .*

Arriving at Toungoo Bill declared that it was lunchtime, and instructed my driver to find the best restaurant. The restaurant picked out was certainly adequate, but no doubt it was the one which offered the driver the best free meal for himself as commission. We suffered no ill effects. The day was drawing on, and it was essential to reach Pyinmana where we had arranged to spend the night in the rest house before dusk, otherwise we should probably be

* Tilman's account here of his bicycle ride across Africa in 1933 was more romantic than accurate.

shot approaching the town. We were hastened on our way by the sight of a charred and still-smouldering wooden bridge which some ill-disposed person had evidently tried to destroy. We made Pyinmana—just—and were hospitably entertained by the District Officer, who rarely had such exotic guests. In the rest house Bill declared that he never used a camp bed and was quite happy to sleep in the lumpy-looking object provided by the rest house keeper. He regretted his decision, as even his hardened hide suffered badly from bed bugs during the night.

By this time we were well out of the forest and made good speed across the plain to Meiktila, where the road bridge over the river was still down as a result of the famous battle in 1945. Gangs of men with chains were standing by ready to pull cars through the river for the extortionate sum of 100 rupees. Bill was all for paying, but I thought they would damage his beautiful new paintwork, so I persuaded him to come with me down the river to see what other people were doing. We were able to spot a route being used by trucks and duly set off about a quarter of a mile upstream on very soft sand, which gave us some uneasy moments. We then turned into a shallow part of the river and drove back along a good firm sandbank to a point almost opposite the place where we had come down the bank. The next channel was the tricky bit: the front of the car went down until the water was running along the tops of the wings, and I could feel Bill's confidence oozing out even faster than mine (I was driving). Fortunately, as I reached the point of despair the front lifted, and we rolled up the narrow track to safe level ground without incident. Unfortunately, the Ford with its distributor low down failed to make it, and we spent a couple of hours drying it out before making good smart time up to Mandalay.

When we got to Maymyo we were bidden to drinks by the Anglo-Burman Commander of North Burma District, Brigadier Blake. He declared he was delighted to see us—"I have always said that road was perfectly safe." He then let fall that ours was the first civilian saloon car to make the journey since the troubles broke out four years before. Had I known this sooner I should have been less keen on the journey, but then I should not have had such an insight into Bill's character and personality.

From Maymyo Tilman could send mail to London by diplomatic

bag, and his sister kept him supplied with English stamps so that letters could be posted in London for him by the Foreign Office. Of his surviving letters many are concerned with events at Bod Owen, but he gives his sister glimpses of his life in Burma:

24 June 1952. I was away all last week on my railway journey to Mohnyin from Sagaing. It was hard travel, for even the so called Upper Class carriages have wooden seats, and I had to spend five days and nights in one. The journey each way was only about 250 miles, but the train accomplishes only about 100 miles in the course of the day, and then lies up for the night. . . . The insurgents planted one of their mines on the line on our return. It was a home-made job, which only disturbed the ballast and charred two sleepers. . . . The most horrid threat hanging over me now is the preparation of the Quarterly Account at the end of June—a most complex matter with vouchers in triplicate, schedules, votes 1, 2, 3 etc. and God knows what.

29 July. Rangoon was a change but not really a pleasant one. I never got to bed before midnight owing to the party habit they have and the house I stayed at was on a main road and noisy. I should have got back on Sunday in the Anson (a small four-seater) but after flying for two hours in cloud we had to go back, being unable to find Maymyo. We then ran out of petrol and the pilot was just about to put us down in a paddy field when he was told on the W/T of a strip at Pegu nearby on which we landed safely, and gave thanks. Petrol was sent up from Rangoon by road and we flew back that evening. . . . Could you send via the F.O. a small parcel of flower seed for autumn sowing? They should be in by September, lark-spur, carnation, delphinium, clarkia, lupin, phlox, sweet peas, etc. etc.

11 August. I got my sampan yesterday. It arrived about 6.30 and at 7 p.m. I was up to my neck in the lake trying to moor it, when I should have been at the Club, where a film was being shown on our projector. However, I was well out of it, as the projector failed, and everyone got very bored. We have one dicky projector. The American Information Service in Mandalay has 12 and 2 mobile cinema vans. But the Russians in Rangoon have gone one better by taking over a whole cinema where nothing but Russian films are shown. . . . I have ordered a radiogram of all things, with long

255

playing records. This is to help out the appalling cocktail parties with soft or loud music.

28 August. I have fished a lot without success as yet, either with fly or bait. One sits in the boat and scatters bread upon the water which is soon boiling with feeding fish, until at last the bread is all gone, except for the piece at the end of one's line with a hook in it.

29 September. The garden seeds have not come yet. . . . I'm afraid it's a bit late. The rains appear to be over, though everyone says that October is usually wet. . . . I look like staying put until mid-October owing to a variety of happenings—a book exhibition here and at Mandalay which we have to run, threatened visitors from Rangoon. . . . I am still without the handbook for the Humber, without which one or two adjustments cannot be made. It looks so glossy and gorgeous that if I leave it anywhere urchins cannot refrain from scratching on it. However, glossiness is not vital, and can always be revived if needed. Meanwhile it goes well, and is a pleasure to drive.

9 October. No seeds yet. . . . I went to Mandalay yesterday to attend the opening by the American Ambassador of a new US Information Service library. They spend more money on the information service in Mandalay than we do in the whole of the East. He seemed a nice chap. Much easier to get on with than our man.

10 November. I have to invigilate for a GCE exam (University of London) which I foolishly arranged should be held, the British Council having backed out at the last minute. However, invigilating is easier than sitting. . . . No seeds have come. I think someone must have pinched them.

20 November. I hoped the seeds would turn up by the last Bibby boat, but I'm afraid they have been taken. However, the gardeners save all last year's seeds, so I am not without young stuff now coming on. My sweet peas are about a foot high.

His contract of service with the Foreign Office was due to expire in March 1953 and in December he was told that it would not be renewed. He was not particularly disturbed, but he was annoyed at being, as he put it, "sacked". On 22 December he wrote to his sister:

I felt all along that I was wasting my time and HMG's money in this job. . . . Expect me about April. This solves one problem, but opens

Above: H. W. T.
Mischief's skipper

Right: Mischief on
her return from the
Antarctic, 1967

The Calvo glacier leading to the Patagonian ice-cap

H. W. T. in *Mischief*'s saloon, 1966

Ice off Bylot Island

Above: The galley on *Mischief*

Below: Penguins and elephant seals on Possession Island (in the Crozet group)

Patanela on the way to Heard Island

Above: Sea Breeze in the Needles Channel, 1970

Below: Sea Breeze in Torssukatak Fjord, West Greenland, 1970

Above: Crew of the *Sea Breeze*, 1970; *l. to r.* Colin Putt, Andrew Harwich, Bob Comlay and Iain Dillon

H.R.H. The Duke of Edinburgh presenting H.W.T. with the Fellowship of the Royal Institute of Navigation

Left: Sea Breeze in ice off West Greenland

Below: Baroque in Magdalena Fjord, North-west Spitzbergen, 1974

many others. What does Willy do next? Go to sea, I expect, or perhaps some new line. I should not blurt this out at once, but begin dropping a few hints that my time expires in the Spring and may come home then. I am rather pleased, because the thought of sitting here for another year was a little daunting, but I would rather the initiative had come from me than from them.

He had still a few months of Consular life, which he performed conscientiously but without enthusiasm:

6 January 1953. The Ambassador's visit begins to loom large. I have already had two or three telegrams of 500 words in connection with it. We have to arrange a party for him in Mandalay, and another on a smaller scale here. . . . My long-playing records were landed at Aden! They may arrive in a month or so. Meantime I have borrowed some.

By early March the forthcoming Everest expedition under Lord Hunt was getting publicity, and the *Sunday Express* invited Tilman to report it. He declined, observing to his sister, "There is more than enough published already about Everest." He sold his radiogram and his car; he had to pay duty on the car before selling as it was imported under diplomatic privilege, but as he explained to Adeline, "In the end I shall break nearly even, and have had six months' use of it."
He was relieved by Mr D. F. Parkinson, CMG, who wrote of him:

In the short time he had served in Upper Burma he had certainly made his mark, and I found he was remembered everywhere I travelled, with affection and also a profound respect for his fitness and feats of prowess in the hills. He would set out to climb any hill worth the name, usually barefooted, and reach the top in times which were remembered with awe.

XII

The Sea

TILMAN WENT TO sea as a form of physical adventure that an ageing mountaineer could practise when high climbing was beyond him. But there was one thing he had not reckoned on—he fell in love. *Mischief*, an elderly Bristol Channel Pilot Cutter, forty-eight years old when he bought her in 1954, won his heart in a way that no woman could, and for fourteen years he served her and she served him with unqualified devotion. When she was lost in the ice off Jan Mayen in the Arctic in 1968 he was as bereaved as a husband who has lost a beloved wife, and the obituary he wrote of her and had printed privately is a strange and moving document. There were other boats in his life: he respected their qualities and enjoyed sailing them, but they did not—could not—give him the emotional relationship he had with *Mischief*.

There was a moment in time when *Mischief* became his, when he bought her at Palma, Mallorca, but she did not enter his life so much as infiltrate it. It was not love at first sight—it began (as do many love affairs) with a good deal of frustration, familiar to anyone who has ever bought and fitted out a boat. There were sordid matters of surveys, and looking for rot in her timbers. *Mischief* triumphed over everything, and as she and Tilman got to know each other it was clear that this was a sea-marriage made in heaven. It may seem romantic to consider a boat as a sentient thing, but anyone who has had much to do with boats knows that they can be good, bad, indifferent or even vicious creatures, and while of course it is the man or men in a boat that determine her behaviour, that behaviour is also influenced by subtle qualities of design and building that often cannot be analysed. *Mischief* and Tilman, she only eight years younger than he, were as if made for each other. In fourteen years he sailed some 114,000 miles in her, in Arctic and Antarctic seas, taking her to remote and desolate places where few men—and certainly no amateur-manned sailing boat—had been before. He added a remarkable chapter to the long history of British seafaring. And he left *Mischief*'s name on the map—two mountains and

258

a cape have been officially named after her. The mountains are Mont du Mischief on Ile de la Possession in the French Crozet Islands in the South Indian Ocean, and Mount Mischief, so called by the Canadian Survey, on Baffin Island in the Arctic. The cape named after her, another charming gesture by the French, is Cap Mischief on Kerguelen Island in the Southern Ocean.

In his last letters to his sister from Burma he wrote that he was contemplating going to sea, and he had been thinking of the sea as an alternative to climbing for some time. His first known experience of sailing was at Bari, on the Adriatic coast of Italy, during the war, when he filled in time between leaving Albania and being posted to serve with the partisans in northern Italy by doing some dinghy sailing with John Mullins, his niece Joan's husband, who was then in the RAF. He enjoyed it, and in 1946 he suggested to John Ross, who had served with him in Italy, that they should do some dinghy sailing together. Ross was at Cambridge, having returned to his medical studies interrupted by the war, and Tilman and his sister had rented a cottage at Aberdovey on the Welsh coast at Cardigan Bay while Adeline was house-hunting. Ross was ready enough to go sailing with Tilman. It was December but in Tilman's view the week before Christmas was a fine time for a sail. Dr Ross has written this account of the adventure:

He [Tilman] had probably been planning to learn to sail for some time, believing that he was getting too old for serious climbing and that the challenge of the seas would be a suitable alternative. The estuary at Aberdovey was suitable for this project as the Outward Bound Association had a centre there with a schooner and several dinghies, but late December was a poor time to choose for two novices to venture on to the sea. I arrived on 14 December after a miserably wet journey on my 1931 motorbike and was surprised to find Bill flattened by a bad cold—a rare event with him. Sailing was therefore postponed. . . .

Bill had recovered the following day. . . . After breakfast we had our first outing in *Dot*, a clinker-built 14 ft dinghy, horribly heavy out of the water but robust in it. We were lucky that it was calm that day, and we somehow taught ourselves the basic manoeuvres with and against the wind. There were three further days of sailing.

. . . I can remember few details, but do have some memories of sailing reefed with the wind towards the open sea on a bitterly cold morning, thinking we were fine sailors—until we turned back and had a miserable struggle to reach land. I felt only slightly reassured by the sight of some Army DUKWs [amphibious vehicles] exercising a few miles away. I doubt if they would have noticed us if we had turned over.

The evenings were occupied with crossword puzzles, taking it in turns to cook supper, and preparing the morning's porridge from some peculiarly tough rolled oats which Bill favoured; hours of preparation barely softened their gritty texture. Conversation (as always) was limited, but I was accustomed to this. I left on 20 December. . . . I had learned little about sailing from Bill as he knew no more than I, but I did learn more about self-reliance.

Tilman was devoted to the crossword puzzle in *The Times* and unless he was somewhere out of reach of newspapers he was ill at ease without a daily crossword puzzle. As for cooking, he regarded bread, and to some extent porridge, as connoisseurs regard wine, recording in his diary any bread that particularly pleased him—and bread that he considered vile. Bread (often made by him), butter, rice and other grains, accompanied when possible by yoghourt, were the staples of his diet. He enjoyed a good dinner but he never felt deprived as long as he could get what he considered honest bread.

On coming home from Burma in 1952 he set about serving an apprenticeship in sail. He was fortunate in being able to make two voyages to the Mediterranean with that fine sailor Robert Somerset, passages on which he learned much. He had not quite admitted to himself that he had given up high climbing—he never wholly gave up climbing—but the heights to which he climbed inevitably diminished. The spur to his first long voyage, and in fact to the purchase of *Mischief*, was a project suggested to him by his friend the Reverend Wynn Rhys, who had occupied some of the dreary hours while he was a prisoner of war in Germany devising it. This was to cross the Patagonian ice-cap, the origin of the great glaciers flowing down to the sea on the coast of Chile. It had been crossed from the Argentine side but not from the Pacific, and much of the region was attractively marked on maps as "unexplored". To reach the ice-cap, let alone cross it, required hard climbing, but the heights in the Southern Andes are not on a Himalayan scale, and the crossing would not mean going above about 10,000 feet, easily within Tilman's ceiling. The ice-cap could be reached from the east by travelling across Argentina, but the approach from the Pacific side must be by sea. And the best way to get to the remote inlets of the Chilean coast would be in a boat of one's own. Tilman's impetus to find a boat capable of reaching the Pacific coast of South America came from his enthusiasm for exploring the Patagonian ice-cap.

In January 1954 he heard of a possibly suitable boat for sale, then lying at Palma, Mallorca, and as he was going to be in the Mediterranean with Robert Somerset he could have a look at her. He did, and found *Mischief*, built at Cardiff in 1906 as a Bristol Channel Pilot Cutter. She was 45 feet overall, with a beam of 13 feet, drew 7 feet 6 inches aft, and had an auxiliary engine. She got her name from her first owner, a pilot working out of Cardiff nicknamed "Billy the Mischief". For the first twenty-one years of her life she had been a working boat but as the sailing cutters were replaced by steam pilot boats she and her kind were no longer needed. In 1927 *Mischief* had been sold for conversion as a yacht. Her heavy build (registered tonnage 13·78, displacement 55 tons) and massive gear were not ideal for yachting as it developed between the wars, and between 1927 and 1954 *Mischief* had nine owners—Tilman was to be the tenth. Her scarcely yacht-like construction did not worry him; indeed, her massive timbers and rather old-fashioned appearance appealed to him, and for taking him across the world to Patagonia solidity and sturdiness were positive advantages. Before he could buy her however, she had to be slipped and surveyed, and it was a month before a slip at the yard was vacant. Tilman was hoping to sail for Patagonia by the end of July, to be there in time for the southern midsummer, but he was not yet used to the time-scale that seems to affect everything concerned with boats. It has been observed that no boat that has ever sailed has been completely ready for sea. Like most such universal observations this is not wholly true, but there is a lot of truth in it, and there was much work to be done on *Mischief*. In the spring of 1954 he was still hopeful of sailing for Patagonia that summer. On 30 March from Palma he wrote the first of many hundreds of letters to his sister headed "On board *Mischief*": "I had an uneventful flight. . . . The boat had been slipped only the day before, and they had spent the day removing the inside ballast. It is complete chaos, and we live as in a slum. Today we scraped tons of barnacles off the bottom, and tomorrow, with any luck, they will start removing the cement which is the most important item of the survey."

Mischief carried a foot of concrete ballast, useful in that it does not shift, but a possible source of danger in old boats in case there is rot in the timbers underneath it. To examine the timbers it is necessary to drill through the depth of concrete ballast, and *Mischief*'s cement, put in when she was built, was iron-hard. So, it was found, were her timbers. On 3 April Tilman wrote home:

> The surveyor, backed up by Bobby [Robert Somerset], thinks that there is nothing wrong with *Mischief*'s hull. In fact, in spite of its 50 years, the wood seems as sound as ever. The trip is therefore on, and the only remaining doubt now is whether the work that has to be done on her will be done in time. If the survey is anything to go by they [*sic*] won't, but possibly when the yard knows what has to be done and gets a deposit paid they will put more hands to work and get cracking.

Tilman wanted to stay with *Mischief* throughout her fitting-out, but he had to be in Scotland on 29 June for the conferment of an honorary degree. The University of St Andrew's had provided a geologist for Tilman's Nepal expedition in 1949, and had also helped with a grant. His relations with the university were cordial, and the honorary Ll.D awarded him was a tribute to the academic value of his exploration. Professor A. A. Matheson, Professor of Scots Law, ended his felicitous oration:

> Surely there is a special tract in Paradise sacred to explorers, with meet guerdon for the brotherhood of the tireless limbs and questing spirits and gallant hearts. May it be long indeed before the graduand betakes himself thither to join his peers. But would you, sir [the Vice-Chancellor], here and now ensure that when he does so he should be greeted by Stanley as "*Doctor* Tilman I presume?"

The expedition to Patagonia did not take place as soon as Tilman had hoped. The yard at Palma did well, and the cost was probably half what it would have been in England, but payment was a problem. On board *Patanela* ten years later, Tilman wrote a piece for the ship's newspaper describing how he managed to pay for *Mischief*'s repairs. It was called "Foreign Exchange", and though the copy it was intended for could not be produced because of shortage of time on the homeward run, Warwick Deacock has sent the article from Australia. Tilman had to pay the yard £100 a month on account and £500 in final settlement. In 1954, the UK economy being in what he called "its usual fragile state", the individual's foreign exchange allowance was only £75 a year. There was no problem for small sums, because of the fortunate proximity of Gibraltar, which is in the sterling area:

. . . One who combined the profitable occupations of bar and brothel keeper would accept my bearer cheque for £100, and in due course, after one of his friends had had time to go to Gibraltar and back, he would give me the amount in pesetas. No doubt when these cheques turned up in England my bank might wonder who the "bearer" was and of what sex, but no inquiries would be made. . . .

However, the final £500 was too large an amount to be raised through the "usual channels", and Tilman returned to London with the name of a contact who, he had been promised, would oblige. Back in England,

. . . the whole infringement of strict currency regulations appeared in a different light to what it had in the easygoing atmosphere of Palma. The penalties in the way of fines and imprisonment seemed extremely harsh. . . . However I seemed not to be under police surveillance so, feeling like the criminal I hoped to become, I went to the address given.

His contact, "some kind of Middle European", demanded a cheque for £500 without offering any satisfactory assurance that the required pesetas would be forthcoming. "Too much faith on my part seemed to be required", Tilman commented, and so he confided his problem to a friend in the City, who gave him a telephone number he could use provided he did not mention his informant's name.

When I rang this number (and for all I knew it might have been Scotland Yard) the chap at the other end naturally asked how I knew it, and I had to tell him. He sounded reassured, and made an appointment for next morning.

The sumptuous West End flat proved to be owned by two excessively fat and genial Greeks. They looked like the brothers Cheeryble. . . . When I told Cheeryble Senior that I wanted to do a deal in currency he seemed quite shocked. "My dear sir, you are a respectable man, my brother and I are respectable men, yet you come and ask us to break the law." Then followed a brief lecture on business ethics and moral principles, while I stood shuffling from one foot to the other like an errant schoolboy. "Dear Mr Tilman, go to the Bank of England and ask them. Honesty is the best policy." I slunk out.

In the end, and more in character, he did solve his problem in the straightforward way by going to the Bank of England. It was also the advice of a sailing friend. He found the bank co-operative and was duly authorised to obtain £500 worth of foreign exchange to pay for *Mischief*'s renovation. Thus finding £500 in pesetas did not materially delay the Patagonian expedition. What did was trouble with *Mischief*'s crew.

Tilman recruited a crew of four, including a married couple, the husband an experienced yachtsman who was to act as skipper. They sailed from Palma for Gibraltar at the end of July, and it was not a happy voyage. Precisely what went wrong is unclear, but ten days from Palma to Gibraltar (a slow passage) were enough to show that this was not a crew to sail together to the ends of the earth. In "*Mischief*" in Patagonia Tilman explained:

On passage relations between Grace Darling [the name he used for the woman on board] and myself had been strained although I had been self-effacing, as an owner should be, and silent as usual. Perhaps one of the few remarks I ventured had not been well chosen. We took it in turns to cook, and the day after Grace Darling's turn, when one of the crew who knew how to cook was officiating, I thanked God aloud for having on board one whose presence ensured our having good meals on at least one day in five. Besides a clash of temperaments there may have been other factors; we were late in starting, were bound for a rude climate, and in spite of all that had been done we were not in every respect ready for sea.

On arrival at Gibraltar the crew made it plain that not only were they not going on to Patagonia but that they were not willing to sail *Mischief* even to England. To add to Tilman's embarrassment the Admiral at Gibraltar invited him and his crew to lunch and he had to explain that they were no longer on speaking terms.

This was a serious setback and he decided to postpone Patagonia for a year. He did not want to stay in Gibraltar, but getting *Mischief* to England was not easy. He had one staunch shipmate in David Drummond, an instructor at the Outward Bound Mountain School at Eskdale who joined him at Gibraltar for the ice-cap expedition, and was a climber, not a sailor. "He knew nothing about the sea but being a mountaineer he would stand by me and not desert like the yachtsmen," Tilman observed rather bitterly.

It was not until mid-September that he was able to leave Gibraltar, with a scratch crew obtained by advertising in a local newspaper. This passage was as disastrous as the first. On rounding Cape St Vincent they met rough weather, and two of the crew demanded to be put ashore at Oporto. The entrance to the harbour is hazardous, with fierce tidal streams and a dangerous bar. As they tried to enter the harbour authorities fired a cannon to warn them off, but Tilman was not sure what it meant. Was it perhaps a kindly salute to a yacht? Mercifully a man at the end of a jetty frantically waved a newspaper at them to shoo them away. Tilman put *Mischief* round, she bumped twice but did not run aground, and he was able to anchor for the night outside the bar. In the morning a pilot came out to take them in, and they learned of their peril. The pilot said that if they had tried to cross the bar *Mischief* would certainly have been lost. Tilman was now stranded at Oporto. In October the ever-helpful Humphrey Barton, mentor to whole generations of British yachtsmen, flew out with a friend and rescued him.

This seemed an inauspicious start to Tilman's career with *Mischief* but as things turned out it was just as well that before sailing for Patagonia she went to the yard at Lymington with which Humphrey Barton was associated, for when she got to England it was discovered that her bowsprit, topmast and gaff all needed replacing. Another ominous discovery was that when a man jumped from a jetty on to the deck the planking sagged—and whatever the kinetic energy generated by even a heavy man jumping from a jetty it was nothing compared with a few hundred angry tons of Atlantic. At first he feared that the deck would have to be replanked but Humphrey Barton suggested that the trouble might be cured by putting supporting posts under the deck beams. This was tried, it worked, and *Mischief*'s deck was restored to safety.

The crew for *Mischief*'s first great voyage with Tilman was a happy one. Tilman had so little experience of ocean voyaging under sail that he wanted to find a man who could act as skipper. Through a friend he was put in touch with W. A. Procter, a retired civil servant and experienced sailor, who agreed to join him. Through the Royal Artillery Yacht Club he found Lieutenant M. R. Grove who was granted a year's unpaid leave for the expedition, and another gunner, Major E. H. Marriott, a good climber and member of the Alpine Club, was also recruited. John Van Tromp, a dairy farmer in Sussex and an acquaintance of W. A. Procter, was so keen to sail to Patagonia that not only did he volunteer to be cook but he sold his farm in order to go. They were a likeable and able lot. Having arranged to pick up Marriott and Grove at Falmouth, Tilman, Procter, Van Tromp and a friend of Van Tromp's worked *Mischief* out of Lymington River on 27 June 1955 under her engine. "The engine did not start immediately, but it did as soon as we turned on the petrol," Tilman observed later.

Mischief came of a family in many ways like Tilman's own: able, unpretentious, supremely good at their jobs. The Bristol Channel Pilot Cutter is a working sailing boat whose design grew out of her job—to keep the sea in all weathers, to heave-to efficiently, to be fast, to be handled economically by a man and a boy. The Bristol Channel Pilotage Act of 1861 which made pilotage compulsory for ships proceeding to the Bristol Channel ports created keen competition among licensed pilots (and sometimes a few unlicensed ones). By tradition it was first come, first served, and pilots would go far out to sea to pick up a ship making for the Bristol Channel—they would stand around off Ushant or go well into the Atlantic, patrol the English Channel and sometimes the North Sea. If two or more pilots saw a ship in the distance they would race to reach her, which is why the cutters needed to be fast. Having put the pilot on board a ship the cutter would then be worked home, perhaps over some hundreds of miles, by the man and boy left on board her. The cutters were built at local yards on both coasts of the Bristol Channel, and *Mischief* was built at Cardiff. Around the turn of the century there were some 200 cutters in service, but with the First World War steam completely replaced sail, and after the war the remaining cutters lost their jobs as pilot boats, turned to fishing, or were sold off to anyone who would buy them. They were too heavily built for inshore yachting, but they made magnificent cruising yachts, their sturdy sea-keeping making for safety, their relative roominess below, with no hold to get in the way or to be converted expensively into cabin space, making for comfort. Sadly, they are a breed that is all but extinct, although their lines have influenced the design of a number of later cruising yachts. *Mischief*'s family were among the handiest and most efficient of sailing boats ever built, and her own performance in old age was as remarkable as Tilman's.

On the advice of a compass-adjuster at Falmouth Tilman replaced *Mischief*'s ancient compass with a new one, and on 6 July, having picked up Marriott and Grove, they took their departure from Falmouth for Las Palmas in the Canaries. They made a good landfall, and anchored off the Las Palmas Yacht Club on 23 July. On the passage Tilman put in much practice at taking and working out sights, gradually developing that sixth sense which later put him in a class by himself as a navigator in the Arctic and Antarctic. Procter and Marriott both navigated, and used different methods, so Tilman had plenty of opportunity to compare results. Procter used the Air Navigation Tables, whereas Marriott preferred the older practice of logarithms and mathematics. On the advice of Robert Somerset, Tilman used tables published by the United States Hydrographic Office (H.O. 211) which in combination with a Nautical Almanac gave him all he needed. The other members of the crew also practised taking and working out sights, so there was a fine array of averages for the plotting chart. The result was admirable.

After six days at Las Palmas they sailed on 29 July for the Atlantic crossing, picked up the Cape Verdes on 6 August and crossed the Equator on 29 August in long. 28 deg. W. They had a tiresome few days in the Doldrums but Tilman had put in much homework on the recommended routes for sailing ships and they were not held up for long. On 28 September they made their landfall on Cabo Polonio in Uruguay and on 1 October dropped anchor at Montevideo. Their passage of sixty-four days from the Canaries was not fast, but it was good steady going, and they had every reason to be pleased with *Mischief*, who proved herself sea-kindly as well as robust.

There was a good deal to be done at Montevideo before sailing south. In the South Atlantic and Patagonian channels they would need neither *Mischief*'s topsail nor her big genoa, so it was sound seamanship that her topmast should come down. Striking the topmast was not difficult, but stowing it was—it took up so much room on deck that they contemplated leaving it at Montevideo and collecting it on the homeward run. Fortunately as it turned out they had second thoughts, mainly because they did not want to return by Montevideo but to complete the circumnavigation of South America by sailing home via the Pacific and the Panama Canal. So in spite of the deck space it occupied they took the topmast with them; it proved an unexpected blessing when *Mischief* was in dire trouble later. Other work done at Montevideo included various repairs to sails, and the handstitching (for greater strength) of all the mainsail seams. They also had to take on stores.

Unfortunately Marriott, who had hurt his shoulder, decided at Montevideo that he was not fit enough to make the next leg of the voyage to the Magellan Strait and that he would have to rest, going on by steamer to rejoin them at Punta Arenas, the southernmost town of mainland South America. They would have to call there anyway on their passage of the Magellan Strait. The remaining four could sail *Mischief* well enough, but it would mean harder work and more watchkeeping, and Tilman accepted the offer of a young German to take Marriott's place.

The passage from the River Plate to Punta Arenas, a sailing distance of some 1,200 miles, was a slow one, flat calms alternating with the sudden fierce gales that lash out from the vast pampas of southern Argentina. The engine helped in the calms and *Mischief* behaved so well in the gales that they had no particular anxieties, though the average of 56 miles made good for each day of the passage was dispiriting. There were many new birds and fishes to appease Tilman's insatiable curiosity about natural surroundings—he was as keen an observer of wild life at sea as he had been in the Himalaya. They saw their first penguins and met their first killer whales. Passing Penguin Island off the desolate coast Tilman's retentive memory from his vast reading identified it as the place where the birds were first so called by a Welshman sailing with Sir Thomas Cavendish in the sixteenth century, *pen gwyn* being Welsh for white head.

At last, at two o'clock in the morning of 5 November, they picked up the light from Cape Virgins that marks the westerly entrance to the

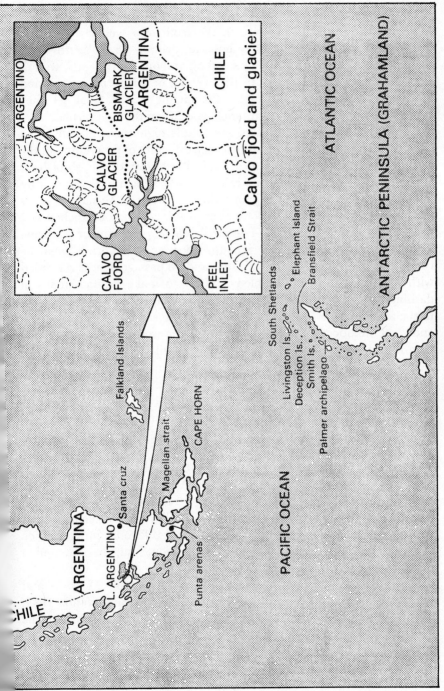

CAPE HORN AND CALVO FJORD

Magellan Strait. But they were in the teeth of a westerly gale and could make no progress, so they hove to, drifting slowly southwards. For the next thirty-six hours they stood off and on, "darning the water" as the sea-phrase has it, until in the evening of 6 November the wind moderated and with the help of the engine and a tidal set they succeeded in entering the strait, anchoring when the tide turned.

The Magellan Strait is a sailing-master's nightmare, not so much from difficulties of navigation as from the difficulty of proceeding in the right direction at all. Time and again in the history of sail, ships have almost made the passage of the strait only to be blown back out of it by a fierce wind springing up against them. Provided the navigation is watched however, the Pilot Book offers a fair selection of anchorages, and Tilman followed the time-honoured practice of sailing or motoring when he could move in the right direction and anchoring when he could not. For the final leg of this stop-and-go passage he was rewarded with a fair wind which enabled *Mischief* to make Punta Arenas in dashing style—a little too dashing, for she bumped a shoal on the way to the anchorage, a mishap that did no damage to her sturdy timbers, and went unnoticed by admirers on shore who were much taken by the flamboyant way in which the English yacht sailed in and rounded-to.

They spent nearly three weeks at Punta Arenas, longer than Tilman wanted to, but they could not leave until the 26th, because he had to wait for the steamer bringing Marriott. The delay turned out to be a godsend, for he learned of a young Chilean mountaineer, Jorge Quinteros, who wanted to join his party for the attempted crossing of the ice-cap. Since he was short of climbers and Marriott's fitness was dubious, Tilman agreed without meeting him to let the young Chilean come. Quinteros was able to get to Punta Arenas by air and arrived on 24 November. Tilman's gamble of taking on an unknown climber paid handsomely. Quinteros (like Sir Edmund Hillary a bee-keeper, a fact that quite irrationally influenced Tilman in his favour) proved a fine mountaineer and a staunch companion; without him, the Patagonian expedition would have failed.

The crossing of the Patagonian ice-cap by Tilman, Marriott and Quinteros had none of the dramatic impact of climbing Nanda Devi, but it was one of Tilman's most remarkable mountain journeys. The ice-cap, the watershed between the Pacific and Atlantic oceans, is one of the most desolate regions of the world. Its comparative lack of height is offset by the severity of its storms, the broken nature of the ground, and the multiplicity of crevasses, hidden by snow until someone falls through. Exploring on the ice-cap is made even more difficult by a total lack of human facilities of any sort. The higher slopes of the Himalaya, the Karakoram or the Hindu Kush may be inhospitable, but the valleys are not wholly unpopulated and offer some, albeit scanty, sources of food. On the ice-cap there is nothing. Its slopes support no human life of any kind and a climber is utterly on his own: everything he needs, every morsel of food, has to be carried. There is no one to come to his help if anything goes wrong. Tilman and his party took supplies for seven weeks, a total weight of some 475 lbs of which about 300 lbs was food. This was carried by three men. Of course the weight diminished as food was eaten and paraffin consumed, but the loads remained heavy throughout the trip. Since these loads could not be carried at one go, stocking the first camps required relays over steep, crevasse-riven, dangerously-broken ground.

Hard as it was, the actual crossing of the ice-cap was only part of the task—first the shore had to be reached through miles of ice-fields, changing in extent and stability with every shift of wind and tide. Tilman's plan was to navigate the maze of Patagonian channels where the southern Andes reach the sea to land on a glacier up which he could hope to climb to the ice-cap. This was where *Mischief* came in, for without a boat the ice-cap could not be reached at all from the Pacific coast—there are no land bases from which a party could march, for the glaciers fall to the sea. He selected Peel Inlet, about 180 miles north of Cape Pilar at the Pacific end of the Magellan Strait which, from the map, looked as if it might lead to a convenient glacier. Unfortunately the glacier proved totally unapproachable, because *Mischief* was stopped by ice from getting anywhere near it. He then tried an extension of the inlet trending north to the Calvo Fjord. Here there were several glaciers, one of which he called the Calvo Glacier and from what he could see of it from *Mischief*'s deck he reckoned that it might provide a route to the top. The shore was beset by ice, but narrow leads kept opening (and closing) as wind and weather changed, and by taking considerable risks, fending off floes with boathooks, he managed to take *Mischief* by her engine to within about fifty yards of a small cove. In his book *Mischief in Patagonia*, he wrote: "As anchorages go this one was more spectacular than safe. Within a stone's throw of us there was on the one hand a fantastically furrowed cliff of sapphire blue ice; on the other, and equally close, a heavily forested cliff; while around us lay a slowly circling mass of floes, some of them as big as a cottage with the garden thrown in."

Mischief and the dinghy were battered, but the scrapes were superficial. Manoeuvring in the dinghy was laborious: it was seldom possible to row more than a few yards and the normal method of progress was to drive an ice-axe into a floe and haul on that. A brief reconnaissance on shore suggested the Calvo glacier as a possible route, but there was not time to explore far for they had to get back to the ship. After another night on board it was clear that the most pressing need was to get *Mischief* away. Tilman summed up:

> On the whole, despite the inconclusive nature of our reconnaissance, it seemed best for us to gamble on finding a route to the ice-cap by way of what we now called the Calvo glacier, for there are few icefalls which time and perseverance will not overcome. The essential thing was to get the ship away as early as possible. The morning's inrush of ice had forced her perceptibly nearer the shore and the night's happenings emphasised strongly that this was no place to linger. About midnight an appalling crash alongside brought us all on deck with a run. We were in time to see the water still boiling and surging and blocks of ice shooting up from below. One of our bigger neighbours had capsized and broken up with all the turmoil and upheaval that would accompany the death throes of a stricken whale.

By daylight the ice had cleared sufficiently to get ashore in the dinghy. Van Tromp stayed on board to look after *Mischief* while the rest went ashore to carry loads to their first camp. With the stores landed, Procter and Grove went back to *Mischief*. Tilman's instructions were precise and realistic. It was now 17 December. The ship's party were to sail to Puerto Bueno, a secure anchorage in the Patagonian channels much used in the days of sailing-ships, and wait there until 1 January, collecting supplies of petrol and paraffin the Chilean Navy had promised to try to get for them. On returning to the Calvo Fjord *Mischief* was to cruise around far enough offshore to be reasonably clear of ice and look for any signs of the ice-cap party—there was wood on shore to make fires, and the yellow tents should be visible from a considerable distance. If there were no sign of the shore party *Mischief* was to find a safe anchorage from which to come back to the Calvo

Fjord every Sunday until 12 February. If nothing were seen of the shore party by then the ship's party was to wait a week, and then return to Punta Arenas.

Tilman had supplies for seven weeks, and he hoped to complete the crossing of the ice-cap in six weeks. *Mischief*'s early return in the first week of January was to provide insurance against some mishap which might mean that the ice-cap venture had to be abandoned. Food for seven weeks could if necessary be spun out by cutting rations, but if the party had not shown up by 12 February they would have been on their own for eight weeks, and food would be getting low. A week after that there could be little hope for them, and it was *Mischief*'s job to get the ship's party back to England. An air search for the missing climbers would doubtless have been undertaken from Punta Arenas, but in the desolate and crevassed region of the ice-cap it is unlikely that they could have been found. *Mischief* could not wait off the Calvo glacier because of the danger from ice—she could only sail away and come back at intervals. And with *Mischief* gone Tilman's party would be on their own, beyond reach of any effective help.

Procter and the ship's party would have had an appalling decision to make if Tilman and his companions had not turned up by 19 February; it would have been agonising to obey Tilman's instructions and sail away for Punta Arenas. Happily, it was not a decision they had to face, for Tilman, Marriott and Quinteros achieved the double crossing of the ice-cap and were back on the beach by the Calvo glacier on 27 January, two days before the first Sunday rendezvous. But they nearly missed being taken off because *Mischief*'s propeller had been damaged by ice and the engine could not be used. *Mischief* herself had the narrowest escape from shipwreck.

Tilman's party also had some narrow escapes. First, the ice-cap expedition nearly had to be abandoned after an apparently minor mishap. Tilman fell into a crevasse, but he was roped to his companions, not much hurt and soon pulled out again. In the fall however, his snowglasses fell off and vanished in the unknown depths of the crevasse. And through his austere insistence on trying to keep down weight by taking as little as possible for himself he had no spare glasses. Fortunately Quinteros had a second pair—without glasses Tilman would have suffered so severely from snow blindness that he could not have gone on. The next threat to the expedition was more serious: Marriott's feet became so painful that it was doubtful if he could continue climbing. They had two tents and he could have been left with food and shelter while Tilman and Quinteros carried on, but Tilman decided that the crevasses were too dangerous for a two-man team. After a night's rest Marriott pluckily said that his feet seemed good enough, and he carried on to the end saying little or nothing of the pain he endured. The state of his feet after the crossing was such that it seemed miraculous that he had climbed at all.

These hazards dealt with, there were the normal dangers of climbing in cruel conditions. On the glacier the going was so bad that more than once they felt that they might have to admit defeat, but determination slowly gained them height, and by carrying loads from camp to uncomfortable camp they won their way to the ice-cap. Then it was a matter of descending on the other side, a little—but not much—easier than getting up. Their goal was Lake Argentino, on the Argentine side of the Andes, and they got to it by going down the Bismarck Glacier. It was extraordinary country. Tilman described it in his book:

> The strangest feature of the Bismarck glacier was the proximity of ice and forest, their line of contact being marked by broken branches and fallen trees. The moraine, where it existed, was a ridge a few feet high littered with stripped tree trunks and apparently as fresh as if deposited only recently. At times the ice almost brushed the living trees. We could walk through open forest of tall Antarctic beech on a carpet of yellow violets, while through the trees, only a few yards off, loomed a monstrous wall of ice.

The final stage of the descent to Lake Argentino was relatively easy, but the lake itself was a disappointment—no expanse of shimmering blue water, but a steep bank of earth, covered with nettles, falling to a sort of refuse dump of ice and dead trees. The tongue of the glacier extended far into the lake and every few moments there would be a thunderclap as a fresh avalanche of ice fell into the water. True to his tradition of "memorable bathes" Tilman decided that he must celebrate his arrival at Lake Argentino by going in, but his companions did not join him. He wrote of the occasion, "Accordingly I rose alone from my bed of briars and nettles, stripped as best I could without getting scratched or stung (there were clouds of virulent horse-flies) and bathed. Bathed is, perhaps, an extravagant term for an act which took less than a few seconds to complete, for hard by an ice-floe nestled close against the bank."

On the way back across the ice-cap they had the narrowest of escapes from disaster. On the way across they had been so oppressed by their loads and so anxious to hurry on that they dumped a pile of food and supplies for the return journey. Soon after they started back a violent snowstorm blew for two days, during which they had to lie up in their tents. When they set off again everything was blanketed by deep snow, and a continuing thin blizzard cut visibility to a couple of hundred yards. With food for only one more day they had to find the dump—and couldn't—all landmarks had been blotted out by the blizzard, and they could see so little that the compass bearings they had taken did not help. After looking around in vain Tilman called off the search, feeling that they must go on while they had strength in the hope of reaching one of the other camps where they had left supplies. At the last moment, after they had shouldered their packs to go on, the mist thinned a little and Marriott spotted something that looked like the corner of a box. It was. They camped there and then, and were soon replete with pemmican and biscuit.

For the descent to the beach at Calvo Fjord they did not follow the glacier by which they had climbed up but took a more direct route down thickly-forested cliffs. They had considered this for the ascent but concluded that it was impossible to carry loads up cliffs so steep through trees and undergrowth. Coming down was another matter, and after a wild scramble of some 2,000 feet they reached the shore scratched but safe. It was 27 January, six weeks and one day after they had been put ashore.

On getting to the beach they found a note which gave news both good and bad. The good news was that although the next Sunday rendezvous was on 29 January they could expect to be taken off the next day, for the practice of the ship's party was for someone to row ashore on Saturdays and stay on shore overnight. That meant they had only one day to wait. The bad news, which far out-weighed the good, was that *Mischief* had been nearly wrecked and was now engineless because the propeller had been broken. She was anchored off another cove only four miles away, but there was no getting to her along the broken ice of the coast. They had to wait until Grove came with the dinghy next day. The ice was so thick that it took him four hours to cover four miles; with more manpower for hauling from floe to floe with the ice-axe, it still took three hours for the return trip.

Mischief's disaster had been to hit a hidden reef and then be trapped by ice. Her tough old timbers took the reef without much damage but she was fast aground, and as the tide fell she keeled over. Procter, Grove and Van Tromp saved her from falling over and being wrecked by using the topmast as a leg to hold her up—without this heavy spar it is doubtful if she could have been saved. When the tide turned and she righted again they tried to kedge her off the reef, but she was fast and would not budge. She was also in grave danger of being struck by drifting ice-floes, and there was even greater danger that a floe would knock away her supporting topmast-leg. There were some tree-trunks on shore and they managed to tow one of these out with the dinghy and rig it as a second leg. Then came the heavy job of unloading several tons of pig-iron ballast to lighten the ship in the hope that she would float again. Since the ballast would be needed if they could get her afloat, all the iron had to be ferried ashore in the dinghy and stacked where it could be recovered, a task that took 36 hours of non-stop work. At last she floated and they hauled her into deeper water. The ballast had to be brought back and re-loaded, with someone standing by to fend off ice-floes all the time—another two days' work.

The most serious damage was to the propeller, which had one blade torn away by ice. The engine was intact, and when the ballast had been re-loaded and re-stowed they thought that they could get away by running the engine at its slowest speed. But as soon as the broken propeller began to turn, water poured in through the propeller shaft, and the engine ran reluctantly, making a horrible knocking sound and frequently stopping. The crew decided that the propeller was unusable, and *Mischief* began drifting slowly back towards the reef on which she had struck. God helps those who try to help themselves: miraculously, a little wind sprang up and *Mischief* was saved by her sails. It was far from an ideal wind for it almost headed them, but *Mischief*'s lovely sailing qualities were never shown to better purpose; by constantly going about they gained a little ground with every tack, until they were able to anchor in relative safety. After a night at anchor the wind changed to a fresh following breeze and they sailed out of danger to an anchorage where they could wait for the shore party. They saved the ship—and the lives of the expedition.

Back on board *Mischief* Tilman had to decide what to do. He had relied on the engine to navigate the intricate channels of the broken Patagonian coast; to try to navigate them under sail was another matter. The safest plan was to sail back to Punta Arenas, but that would have meant abandoning the circumnavigation of South America. He determined to carry on with the voyage, and took the seamanlike course of making for the open Pacific by the easiest route. It meant getting out to sea farther south than if they could have used the channels, but given sea room *Mischief* could carry on to Valparaiso, where she could be hauled out and the damage to the propeller shaft repaired. The most serious casualty now was Charles Marriott, one of whose feet was swollen with blood poisoning that seemed to be advancing up his leg. He was successfully treated with antibiotics.

Mischief romped into the Pacific cheerfully enough, but for three days they were so beset by headwinds that Tilman again contemplated retreating to the South Atlantic by way of Cape Horn. He decided to hang on for a few days more and was rewarded by a change of wind that took them northwards at a steady clip. A problem now was to find out where they were. The deck watch, which was their chronometer, had not been checked for a couple of months. It had not been needed in the Patagonian channels, where navigation was a matter of pilotage from the chart, and several times in their various troubles they had forgotten to wind it. The charging engine had broken down, the battery was flat, and they had no way of getting radio time signals. Without accurate time the working out of longitude was beyond them, but they could get a reasonably good estimate of latitude by guessing local noon and averaging a series of sights taken before and after assumed noon. (They appear not to have thought of lunar navigation which can provide longitude without an accurate chronometer.) Tilman cheerfully went back to the navigation of the days before chronometers, when mariners made for the latitude of wherever they wanted to go and then ran down the latitude until they got there. He decided to make for the latitude of Valparaiso and close the coast when they reached it.

Helped by the Humboldt current they made a fair passage to Valparaiso, old-fashioned navigation working so well that they picked up the Punta Angeles light on the south side of Valparaiso Bay fine on the bow on the night of 23 February. In port everyone was kind and helpful. *Mischief* had to wait until the middle of March for her turn in the dry-dock, but the hospitality of Valparaiso made their stay a pleasant one, and they went in turns to Santiago to visit the home of

Jorge Quinteros. Marriott was still far from well, and Tilman recruited another young Chilean to join the crew for the passage back to England.

Mischief came through her docking with flying colours. Her scrape on the reef had done no damage to her hull—instead, it had scrubbed her almost clean of weed and barnacles! The propeller needed repairs but the shaft itself was found to be undamaged—the leak had been caused by the fracture of a fitting securing the stern-tube for the propeller to the hull. They sailed from Valparaiso on 23 March and after calling at Callao and visiting Lima, completed the circumnavigation of South America by crossing through the Panama Canal. Having returned to the Atlantic they sailed for Bermuda and then home on 1 May, and on the night of 5 July picked up the Bishop Light, a year and a day after leaving Falmouth. The last days of Tilman's first great voyage in *Mischief* were spent groping up-Channel in dense fog, but on 9 July they slipped safely into Lymington River.

This voyage earned Tilman The Blue Water Medal of the Cruising Club of America. The Royal Cruising Club recognised his sailing achievement by giving him its Goldsmith Award.

XIII

To the Far South

MISCHIEF DID MORE than change Tilman's life; she enriched it hugely. He turned to the sea as a second-best form of physical adventure, and bought *Mischief* because he needed a boat capable of taking him to the Patagonian ice-cap. He still considered himself a mountaineer first and a sailor a long way second. His derogatory remarks about yachtsmen in his first book about *Mischief* were typical of his feelings. His first long voyage in *Mischief* was selected because it was a difficult expedition, and because the heights on the Patagonian ice-cap were still within his ceiling at the age of 58. *Mischief in Patagonia* is a fascinating study of a man falling in love, for as the book proceeds *Mischief* takes over—his account of his feeling for her when she was battered by ice, unemotional and dry as he tries to make it, is that of a man who suffers when he fears harm for his beloved. As his feelings for *Mischief* deepened, his whole attitude to the sea changed; from being a sailing mountaineer he became a sailor who would enjoy a climb when he could, and then a man who sought the lonely seas of the Arctic and the Antarctic because he loved them for their own sake. He had lived for mountains and, since discovering in Kenya the austere joy of high places, climbing had given him a purpose in life. It had not given him a life. He had lived for mountains; but you can scarcely make a home at 25,000 feet. You can live for, on and with the sea, and *Mischief* gave him a faithful companion with whom to share it.

His long relationship with *Mischief* was not all honeymoon. An old boat can be as capricious (and as expensive) as a young mistress. There were times when, with his contempt for any form of self-indulgence, he worried about the money he spent on her. He seriously considered selling her at least once, and went as far as advertising her for sale. But he was ill at the time, depressed by an old head injury (later successfully treated), and although he could have sold her, he could not at the last moment bring himself to go through with the sale. He observed afterwards that he was thankful that she could not read advertisements.

In the winter of 1963 there was a crisis in their relationship. On returning from a voyage to Baffin Bay and the Arctic he had *Mischief* surveyed, and the surveyor's report was that she was no longer fit for deep-sea voyaging. That seemed to be that. He left her in her mud-berth at Lymington while he considered what to do. During this miserable period he paid a brief visit to the United States to attend a mountaineering reunion, and while there he saw the American maritime museum at Mystic, Connecticut, where fine examples of old sailing craft are kept afloat. This gave him the idea of trying to find somewhere where *Mischief* could be maintained as an example of the Bristol Channel Pilot Cutter but there seemed to be nowhere in Britain. He had almost made up his mind to replace *Mischief* with another boat, and was on his way to look at one on offer, when a chance meeting in a pub with a man who was having an old ketch rebuilt made up his mind for him: why not rebuild *Mischief*? At least he would find out whether this was possible. *Mischief* was hauled out and came through with flying, if somewhat bedraggled, colours. Her underwater timbers were still sound, and although a lot of work was needed on the upper parts of her old frames it was work that could be done. It would be expensive, but it would be less costly than buying another boat. He showed his faith in her by sailing her to the harsh waters of East Greenland in 1964. She took and returned him safely. She made several more great voyages, and when the end of her life came in 1968 it was not because of old age—she was crushed by ice, and even then she might have been saved had not a pump failed when she was being towed through rough seas. She was gallant to the last: she sank in the end but she took no one with her, giving those on board time to leave.

In the fourteen years of his companionship with *Mischief* Tilman made a series of immense voyages to lonely latitudes unmatched in maritime history, and unlikely to be repeated. It is difficult to define his achievement because he offers no comparison. He sailed farther than most amateur seamen, perhaps farther than any, but he attempted no records, and although he recorded some notable "firsts" in the ascent of unclimbed mountains in the Arctic and on Antarctic islets the adventure was mostly in reaching them; there were none of any great height, and he made so little of his successes that they attracted next to no publicity. He would slip out of Lymington River for a voyage of 20,000 miles with as little fuss as if he were going for a weekend cruise.

He did not himself *think* that he was doing anything out of the ordinary. If he is to be compared with anyone perhaps the nearest comparison is with the Elizabethan seaman John Davis, who "lighted Hudson into his strait, lighted Baffin into his bay".* Like Davis he took small boats into some of the most inhospitable seas of the world by determination and seamanship. Unlike Davis, who at least hoped to make some money by finding a North-West Passage to the trade of the East, Tilman sought nothing except the contentment that he found in remote and desolate places.

On returning to Lymington from Patagonia in July 1956 he retired to Bod Owen to write his book and at once started planning another voyage to the far south. He was attracted by the Crozet Isles in the Southern Ocean, barely fifteen hundred miles north of the Antarctic Circle, partly because they were uninhabited, and partly because the Admiralty *Pilot* gave the largest of them (Ile de la Possession—the group belongs to France) a 5,000-foot mountain with permanent snow cover. The mountain was of course unclimbed, and at the end of June 1957 he sailed from Lymington to climb it. He did not get there. Some 500 miles out of Cape Town, a severe gale carried away *Mischief*'s dinghy, and without a dinghy there was no means of landing on an uninhabited island. Instead, he circumnavigated Africa, sailing home by the Red Sea and the Suez Canal (a tricky business after the Suez war in 1956) and brought *Mischief* safely back to Lymington in July 1958 with another 21,000 sea miles added to her cruising log. Unfortunately, she also came home badly worm-eaten by the teredo worm which lives in tropical seas. This was largely Tilman's fault. He had grudged the cost of reliable anti-fouling paint (in 1957 £12 a gallon, and *Mischief* needed three gallons) and used instead a drum of paint that had been given him in Valparaiso. As he ruefully put it, when he had learned the lesson of this false economy, it might as well have been face powder.

He did not accept the defeat of his projected sail to the Crozet Isles. He had *Mischief*'s worm-eaten timbers replaced, and in the summer of 1959 he sailed again for the Southern Ocean. Bill Procter, who had accompanied him to Patagonia, volunteered to join him again, and he

* Sir Clements Markham, secretary to the R.G.S., who sponsored Captain Scott and a number of other explorers.

got the rest of his crew through an advertisement in the personal column of *The Times*, "Hand (man) wanted for long voyage in small boat. No pay, no prospects, not much pleasure."

He had between twenty and thirty replies, ranging from the lunatic to the useful, but he deliberately limited his field of choice by refusing to drive what he regarded as too far to interview candidates. He was lucky in his crew for this trip, luckier perhaps than he deserved from his somewhat haphazard method of selection, and luckier than he was going to be on some future occasions. In addition to Procter his crew included Roger Tufft, who had just come home from working with the Antarctic Survey and understood conditions in the far south, and John Lyons, a retired schoolmaster who had once played the double-bass in the ship's orchestra on the *Queen Mary* and who volunteered for the galley. He proved to have "a cheerful and likeable disposition", and a fund of good stories.

The flow of letters to Adeline began when fitting out at Lymington:

> Two more things I have overlooked, though you may not be able to find them. One is a cylindrical cardboard box with a wind-measuring gadget inside, and I think on the outside of the box it is called "Ventmeter". Probably on a shelf in the study. The other is more tricky, as I have no idea where it is, if anywhere—i.e. a stopwatch which I thought I brought back last time but may not have. It looks like a watch and has a large hand—may be on the shelf of the bookcase behind my chair.

The faithful Adeline duly found and sent the stopwatch, but the Ventmeter was elusive; her reply brought a request for "the plane for planing wood which should be in one of the drawers in the little chest in the bothy. It will go in quite a small cardboard box. No urgency."

There were the usual last minute things to be done:

> We are getting on with things but one bad snag has arisen. In over-hauling the WC they discovered the skin-fittings on the hull should be renewed. They are under water, so it means we shall have to move to the town quay to lean her against the wall so that the fittings can be replaced at low water. I suppose it is really my fault for not telling them to look at the fittings when she was on the slip. More money down the drain, but I'm getting callous.

They got away at the end of July and had a good passage to the Canaries. On 17 August he wrote to his sister from Las Palmas:

We got in here yesterday. . . . We had a better passage than at one time seemed likely. It took four or five days to clear the Channel, and then the expected northerly winds along the Spanish coast failed altogether. But off St Vincent the real trades started and we then did 120 miles a day. As you can imagine, the first few days were bad, all except Procter and myself were sick.

Old Double-Bass does well in the galley. He's had a bad time of it with Primus trouble. I put all the paraffin into what used to be one of the petrol tanks, and it seems to be full of rust and water. Yesterday, after we arrived, Procter and Tufft got the tank out from behind the engine with great difficulty. We shall probably have to junk it, and carry the paraffin in small tins. Meantime all three stoves are full of dirt and give trouble. Besides cook, he is the life and soul of the party, full of quips and quotations, very well read and knowledgeable. The trouble is his knowledge does not seem to extend to Primus stoves, and he always has to call in Tufft, who does understand them.

The long haul to Cape Town went well, and on 1 November he wrote to Adeline:

We are now running along the Cape Peninsula with Table Bay about 15 miles to the NE, a fine sunny day, and Table Mountain and the peaks along the coast look very well. It has been a faster passage than I expected, thanks to few calms, and favourable winds. . . . But it has been surprisingly cold, and I am not the only one to think so. Nevertheless, Roger Tufft and I have kept up the early morning bucket bathe to the last. Yesterday I had the misfortune to lose a bucket (the one I made at home) over the side, the lanyard on the handle coming undone. The distance logged is 6,150 miles and the only land we sighted was South Trinidad, an island some 300 miles off the Brazil coast. We made a point of going close to it, as it is a most wild, picturesque, uninhabited place.

Letters from Adeline were waiting for him at Cape Town—whenever he was within reach of a postal service she contrived to get mail to him—and her letters always delighted him, and cheered him up if he was feeling depressed. He was not depressed on this visit to Cape Town. The Cape people were always nice to him, and he made a particular friend in Bob Hinings, a mountaineer who opened his home and his heart to him. In *Mischief Among the Penguins* Tilman wrote of him:

> So long as *Mischief* remained in Cape Town the firm for whom Bob Hinings worked, or at least his department of it, might as well have closed down; he was either out with me drinking coffee, or down at the Yacht Basin to see if we wanted anything done. Knowing Cape Town and speaking Afrikaans he was useful in all kinds of ways, from knowing where to have climbing boots nailed to bullying a laundry into paying for a pair of my trousers they had lost. We met frequently at his flat to dine off steak and eggs and to drink the fine mellow brandy which he kept in a large medicine bottle marked "Poison".

Tilman called at Cape Town on several voyages, enjoyed much hospitality, and repaid it by giving lectures to schools and local societies.

Mischief anchored off Ile de la Possession in the Crozets on 27 December after a strenuous passage of gales and near-gales from Cape Town. After the struggle to get there he found a landing on a good sandy beach easier than he had expected. The king penguins, albatrosses, sea elephants and other wild life fascinated him. From the Crozets he went on to Kerguelen Island, to the east and a little south, where there was a French scientific mission. The French were extremely friendly, and they stayed until the beginning of February 1960. On 20 February he summed up the visit to his sister:

> I'm thankful to say we pulled it off this time visiting not only the Crozets but Kerguelen as well. We had the dirty weather one expects in the Forties, cold, wet, gales, but no prolonged storms with the seas building up to dangerous heights like they did in 1957. Altogether it was much easier than I had expected once we got used to the conditions. We anchored at Possession on 27 December and stayed there only 15 days, during which Roger Tufft and I cleared up what peaks there were. They were disappointing. We were led to

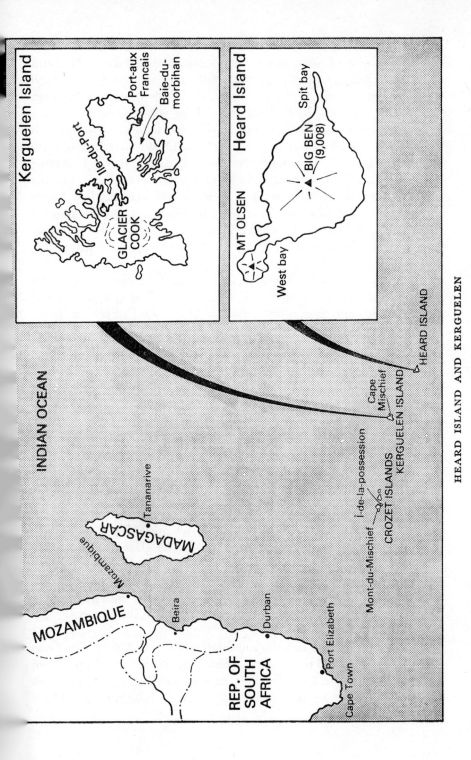

HEARD ISLAND AND KERGUELEN

believe in 5,000 ft snow-covered mountains in the *Antarctic Pilot* and in fact the height was only 3,200 ft and the little snow only temporary. There were two others of 3,100 and 2,700 but there was no climbing. The wild life compensated for this. There was a penguin rookery (king penguins) of several thousand on the beach, one had to brush them off with one's feet to get anywhere. On the beach, too, were hundreds of sea elephants, great creatures like slugs, hardly bothering to open their mouths and bellow unless one kicked them. On the grass slopes above albatross and giant petrels were nesting. Roger ringed over 200 of them. Their eggs and penguin eggs make good omelettes, and we also knocked off the odd penguin to eat. The meat is not bad. The vegetation is very scant, but we collected what there was.

Having exhausted this so soon we went on to Kerguelen 700 miles east in Lat. 49. It is a big island, no danger of missing it, with lots of lovely fjords and little islands, something like the Patagonian fjords. Along the west coast is an ice-cap called Glacier Cook on the chart, which sends down glaciers nearly to the sea on both sides. No height is given, and I don't suppose anyone has set foot on it before. We found an anchorage on the east side and a glacier leading up to it, and spent 10 days there. We crossed it but were unable to go right down to the sea on the west owing to low cloud. The height was only 3,600 ft, surprisingly low for a field of ice 12 miles across and 25 miles long in a latitude as low as 49 deg.

After that we sailed round to the SE coast where the French have their base in the Baie du Morbihan. We had a great welcome, had to have all our meals (and what meals they were!) with them, and when we left they gave us loads of food and ten gallons of red wine. There are 67 men there, including 15 scientists. Their huts have central heating and hot and cold water. Under glass they manage to grow lettuce, tomatoes, potatoes, they have a piggery and some cows, and on a nearby island run several hundred sheep. The mutton was the best I've ever had. Thus they live almost entirely on fresh food. There is a small, privately-owned factory for processing sea elephants for the oil. . . .

We left there on 2 February and I went due north for about 1,000 miles to get clear of the westerlies. Since turning west for Cape Town in Lat. 35 we have had fair winds, and are now less than 2,000 miles away. Yesterday we did a run of 148 miles. With luck, we should get there by mid-March. I hope we shall get away by the end of March, and will come by St Helena and the Azores. It should be much quicker than the Red Sea and the Med. The crew and self are all well, though naturally getting a bit bored with each other. . . . Am looking forward to Cape Town and having your news, and to getting started on the run home. The old boat has stood up to it very well. What to do with her is the problem.

That voyage to the Crozets and Kerguelen lasted eleven months, added 20,000 miles to *Mischief*'s log, and was one of the happiest of his long cruises. The French liked, respected and appreciated him. A year after his visit they made a new survey of Ile de la Possession and officially named its mountain *Mont du Mischief*. They also put Cap Mischief and Glacier Tilman on the map of Kerguelen. *Mischief Among the Penguins*, Tilman's book about the voyage (including an account of his earlier circumnavigation of Africa) has a gaiety that is rare in his writing; all his books have plenty of dry humour, but gaiety is a rarer vein, and makes this book delightful reading. He solved the problem of what to do with *Mischief* simply. He kept her.

For the next five years he sailed *Mischief* north to Greenland and the Arctic, but he made two more great voyages in the Southern Ocean. The first (November 1964 to March 1965) was not his own expedition, and was the only time until his last voyage in 1977 that he made a long voyage in a boat not his own. He was invited by Major Warwick Deacock, an Australian who had been deeply involved in adventure training and the Outward Bound movement, to skipper the 63-foot auxiliary-engined schooner *Patanela* on a voyage to Heard Island, an uninhabited islet some 300 miles from Kerguelen, and attempt to land a party to climb a 9,000-foot peak called Big Ben. How this came about is described by Major Deacock in a letter:

I first met H.W.T. at a lecture he gave at the Royal Military Academy, Sandhurst—greening trilby, diminutive figure, 20 slides with Newton rings, and his dry Tilmanesque humour, with a totally absorbing account of one of his *Mischievous* voyages. A cadet raised his hand:

"Please sir, how do I get on an expedition?"

"Put on your boots and go," was the not unkind reply.

Next was an Alpine Club meeting where Jimmy Mills and I

sought a goal for a planned Himalayan expedition. H.W.T. put us off Gosainthan as (a) "it was probably in Tibet" (b) "I got lost with Tensing in the jungle trying to find the damned thing."

My next contact was in early 1964. I was then an assistant grave-digger at Katherine, Northern Territories, working my way round Australia on a home-made survey, complete with wife Antonia, Kate (3) and Nick (1), a van, eight foot square of canvas, and two billy cans. I had in the Sub-Antarctic season of 1962/3 very nearly perished in an ice-cave close to the summit of Mawson's Peak on Big Ben, Heard Island. I wanted to return and finish off Big Ben, and printed some notepaper with my last £1.7s.6d., headed Australian New Zealand Antarctic Climb (ANZAC!). Later, at the request of Lord de L'Isle, VC, the Governor General on whom I called to seek support, this was changed to South Indian Ocean Expedition to Heard Island. Writing to ten friends to invite them to come along I indicated that I had no money nor means of achieving the island. 1962 had been via *Nella Dan*, the Australian National Antarctic Research Expedition. Back in Melbourne, Dr P. G. Law, director of ANARE, indicated that he knew of a suitable vessel—if I could get her—out of Strahan, West Tasmania: *Patanela* (Tas-manian aboriginal for Spirit of the Storm) a 63ft gaff-rigged schooner that had been to Macquarie Island. I looked at her, fell for her, and wrote to H.W.T. to see if he would come as skipper.

"Dear Deacock. I will be in Sydney by mid-October 1964. Sincerely, etc. Tilman."

I did not know that he had checked out the vessel with a fellow member of the Royal Ocean Cruising Club, nor that he had checked my credentials at the Alpine Club—presumably to find the vessel at least had sound lines; after all I was only to be the ship's cook.

Major Deacock succeeded in enlisting sufficient support to make the Heard Island expedition possible. Before discovering that he could charter *Patanela* he had thought of asking Tilman if the expedition could sail in *Mischief*, but the long preliminary voyage to Australia ruled this out. *Patanela*, a steel vessel, had been built as a yacht, but after a voyage under sail to Macquarie, another remote Antarctic islet, she had been converted for crayfishing, and a powerful Rolls-Royce diesel engine installed. Tilman had grave doubts when he first saw her, as he explained in a letter to Adeline dated 21 October:

We had an uneventful flight with rather too many stops—Rome, Athens, Teheran, Delhi, Singapore, Djarkarta, Darwin, Sydney. After leaving Delhi I had a good sight of both Nanda Devi and Everest—never thought to see them again. We met here about 8 a.m. and we came on board. *Patanela* is lying off one of the better yacht clubs, with showers and hot water. The boat looks all right as far as sailing is concerned, but the accommodation at the moment is almost non-existent. The cabin and galley combined is aft, and about the size of half *Mischief*'s saloon. They want to sleep six here. In the fo'c'sle there are 4 berths, but no light of any kind (bar electric) and according to their own report it is a hell of a place when in any sea. There are no drawers, lockers, or fittings of any kind anywhere. She was used for fishing, and nothing much has been done to alter her. The crew are pretty good, most of them engineers or with some craft, and are capable of doing anything in the way of alterations or repairs. I don't see how we can possibly sail by 1 November. She is far more backward than I expected, in fact an awful shambles. It looks as if the midships hold, where they kept crayfish in seawater, and which was to be used for oil fuel, will have to be made into bunks. I told them I didn't think we could sleep six in the cabin as suggested. I don't think you have any opinion of *Mischief* as a standard of comfort—you should see this!

On 27 October he wrote:

The boat is still one hell of a mess. I'm writing this sitting on an oil drum on deck with my suitcase on my knees. The fo'c'sle where I've been sleeping is having an asbestos lining. The cabin-cum-galley is chock-a-bloc, ditto the wheelhouse. We've got the sails in the last week, but as yet there are no cleats or ring-bolts to tie anything to. There is no compass mounted yet, and when it is the helmsman won't see it.... The engine, a big Rolls Royce job, is, I imagine, very reliable, and we shall have to use it a lot. . . . They still talk of getting off next Sunday 1 November, but I doubt it.

In spite of these morose comments, Tilman worked away, looking after most of the rigging, while others dealt with essential carpentry and the loading and stowing of stores. Although they did not get away on

289

1 November, they sailed four days later. On 5 November there was a last-minute scribble:

This looks like the big day when we should get away. We swung the compass yesterday and at first it looked likely that we should have to find a new place to put the compass, or a new compass, or both. In fact the old chap who was doing it had decided to give up, but I got him to have another go. The compass then seemed to settle down, and instead of errors of about 30 degrees we were getting errors of only 1 or 2 degrees. So we could then give a firm time for sailing, and no doubt there will be an enormous gathering, escorting motor boats, the Press, TV, the lot. Quite terrible. I think the boat herself is all right, but living conditions are so poor that I'm wondering how it will affect the crew, self as well. . . . Writing this standing at my diminutive chart-table.

Patanela turned out to be a happy ship, and the expedition was thoroughly successful. Tilman was in command of the schooner, Deacock of the expedition, and with good sense on both sides the arrangement worked well. Tilman respected Deacock for taking on the uncomfortable and often thankless task of cook—and he came to respect Deacock's cooking, and the quality of their food ("much better than I fare on *Mischief*"). This was partly due to the generous gifts of food by many firms and organisations, partly to the fact that *Patanela* had a big refrigerator. But it was mainly due to Deacock's hard work, and his understanding that an army marches (or sails, once it has overcome seasickness) on its stomach.

Heard Island (53.10 S 73.35 E) is a tiny dot less than 1,000 miles north of the Antarctic Circle. It was first sighted by Peter Kemp, a British sealer in 1833, but gets its name from the captain of an American sealer who rediscovered it about twenty years later. There is no safe anchorage, and landing through the heavy surf is always difficult, usually dangerous, and often impossible. The Australian Government maintained a weather-station there until 1954, when it was abandoned. To get there from Sydney meant sailing some 1,800 miles to round Cape Leeuwin, at the SW tip of Australia, and then another 2,200 miles to the island. But those 2,200 miles could not be sailed direct, for they meant crossing the Roaring Forties, where strong westerly winds head a vessel trying to sail west. To get to Heard Island Tilman decided first to sail north to about 33 deg S and make all his westing in that latitude, where he could expect moderate and variable winds. He did not turn south until he had gone north to a point that brought him within 1,000 miles of Madagascar. It was excellent navigation, and it worked well, though it made a round voyage of over 10,000 miles.

The first leg of the passage was also against headwinds, and to Tilman's annoyance (though he accepted the necessity) they used the big diesel much of the time. From Albany, not far from Cape Leeuwin, he wrote to his sister on 20 November:

We got here yesterday, a fortnight out from Sydney. It will be our last call in Australia, and shall be here a few days as there are some jobs to be done on the boat. We had reasonable weather on the way, with most of the expected westerly winds and one blow during which we hove to. This was one of the few times we had the sails up, and were going pretty fast, with help from the engine as well. We got a green sea over amidships which chucked me against the deckhouse, and did my lower ribs no good. I still feel it, but expect it will be all right in time. One didn't really enjoy it, motoring most of the time with the constant noise and rolling and pitching, but it's quick. We were doing 140 and 160 miles a day. As time is short I think we shall have to motor most of the way there if we have enough fuel. We can use the sails on the way back. Living conditions are very cramped, and we take our meals picnic fashion either on deck or in the cabin as there is no room to sit at the table. The food, however, is good, and there is plenty of it. Warwick Deacock, the leader, is making a good job of cooking, with the help of a big Calor gas stove. Motoring makes things easy. One can turn in at night with no fear of having to get up to change sails, and as one is generally on course and not tacking navigation is easier.

This is only a small place of about 15,000 people. A very good harbour, but I had an awful job getting alongside yesterday evening with a strong wind blowing, and made a mess of it. She handles very well if you know how, and I shall have plenty of practice here, as we shall have to move to get oil. The people are very friendly, and we all had showers and a meal last night. . . . I don't think I shall be able to write letters to anyone. There is no room to sit, and not much time.

With Tilman on the Heard Island expedition were Warwick Deacock (leader and cook), Dr Grahame Budd (scientific officer), John Crick (quartermaster), Dr M. C. Hay (ciné-photographer), Antony Hill (ship's mate), Dr R. Pardoe (medical officer), Colin Putt (engineer, who later sailed with Tilman on *Sea Breeze*), E. J. Reid (radio) and Philip Temple (entomologist). He developed a high respect for all of them and they all liked him. Temple wrote a book about the expedition, *The Sea and The Snow*, full of praise for Tilman's handling of the schooner and the accuracy of his navigation. Tilman was 67, far older than the others, and the difference in age might easily have made for awkwardness. It didn't. The crew enjoyed the humour that spiced his taciturnity ("The skipper never spoke to excess," Temple observed) and Tilman liked their zest and readiness to work.

On 31 December 1964 they put in at what Tilman thought was an uninhabited cove on Kerguelen, well away from the French base at Port aux Français (Baie du Morbihan). They wanted several days at anchor to sort out stores and equipment for the climbing party to be landed on Heard Island. Tilman and the ship's party would have to come back to Kerguelen for a month while the climbers were on Heard, because there was no nearer safe anchorage. He intended to call on the French then, but since his last visit the French had established a summer base near his secluded cove, and the ship had not been in long before there was an invitation to lunch on shore. Deacock has a nice story about a return visit by the French. Tilman invited them to join him in "un coup de Scotch": "He poured generously, and added water. Unknown to him the latter was seawater, in a milk jug. 'Santé' from all, appreciative sips, and, 'Est dur, ce Tilman'."

The climbing party—Deacock, Budd, Crick, Putt and Temple— were put ashore on Heard Island, making a difficult landing in inflatable boats, one of which overturned in the surf. They were wearing skindivers' suits, and those thrown into the sea managed to get ashore without harm. On the island all five climbed Big Ben. Tilman and the remaining four of the crew took *Patanela* to Kerguelen, where they spent a pleasant month with the French. Tilman was invited to sleep ashore, but he felt responsible for the schooner in case she met any emergency, and he would never leave her at night. On 10 February he was back at Heard Island, where the climbing party was safely re-embarked after an anxious struggle with the surf in their landing craft. They saved their film and scientific specimens, but had to abandon most of their equipment. Tilman's entry in *Patanela*'s log wasted no words, "Shore party came off minus kit. Got anchor. Course south."

They had a fine run back to Australia, though they had to use the engine from time to time to meet a Press schedule for their arrival. On 4 March the watchkeeper broke into doggerel and wrote in the log:

> We traverse the seas with effortless ease
> No sheets to harden, no sheets to ease
> No halliards to haul, no sails to hoist
> God bless Rolls, God bless Royce.

Later watches through the night tried to match this entry. Tilman, inspecting the log in the morning, was not pleased. He wrote:

> Attention is drawn to the entries for 4 March
> That the log should be written in seamanlike prose
> Is a rule that every seafaring man knows
> Only a crew of jerks or worse
> Will mar this book with any more verse.   HWT

In his last letter written on *Patanela* just before she got back to Australia he wrote of his companions, "They have been a very good lot to be with, all young or youngish, tough, cheerful, willing and knowledgeable. . . . In spite of the rotten crew's quarters and the crowded state of the galley-cum-saloon (where Deacock and I also slept) there were never squabbles or any signs of temper."

They made Sydney on 13 March 1965 and on 19 March Tilman flew back to London. His luggage was a kitbag, one small suitcase, his sextant and a star-chart.

In contrast to the successful cruise to the Crozets and the happy expedition in *Patanela*, the last of his southern voyages in *Mischief* was a miserable affair. His object was ambitious: to land if possible on Smith Island in the South Shetlands, five hundred miles south of Cape Horn and only sixty miles or so off Graham Land, now called the Antarctic Peninsula. Smith Island was first sighted in 1819 by William Smith, a sealing skipper, and in 1820 another sealer, James Weddell, managed to land on it. So far as is known nobody has landed there since. There is no safe anchorage, and the cliffs and surf are formidable.

Tilman hoped to try his luck at getting ashore with a climbing party to ascend either Mount Foster (6,900 ft), Mount Pisgah (6,000 ft) or both. *Mischief* could not stay off Smith Island while a climbing party was on shore but would have to make for Deception Island, another of the South Shetlands, where there were British, Chilean and Argentine scientific bases. To handle *Mischief* while he hoped to be ashore on Smith Island he recruited David Shaw, a master mariner who got a year's leave of absence from the shipping company he worked for to make the voyage. They sailed from Lymington on 14 July 1966, bound for the Antarctic on his old track to Punta Arenas by way of the Canaries and Montevideo. Tilman was in his 69th year.

On 27 September, on the passage from the Canaries to Montevideo, David Shaw was lost overboard. The tragedy is entered in *Mischief*'s log :

Saturday, 27. Day of disaster. Went on deck at 07.40 to find helm lashed, ship on course, and no sign of David. Called hands and gybed 07.50 2 hrs on ENE course with all hands up rigging. Having found log had stopped and rotator was missing we acted on the assumption that D had grabbed at it and broken it. The log had stopped at 31¼ [mileage reading] which indicated that he had gone overboard at 06.15 as the last reading of the log at 06.00 was 30. The binnacle light was still on and Tom [another member of the crew] had not been called at 07.00. Having run the distance we handed sail and started motoring N and S across course, working back to the west. Roughish sea and white horses made it unlikely to spot a man, even if we were in the right area. All hands stuck in the rigging throughout altho' this was hard work as without any sails she rolled and pitched a lot. Small school of porpoises playing all day round ship, this day of all days, leaping and turning somersaults. Happy as possible, contrast with us. At 18.30 I thought no more could be done so we hoisted main and stays'l and hove to for the night.

No reason for David Shaw's disappearance was ever discovered. He was a fine seaman, and the lashed helm was possibly explained by the fact that he took much interest in experimenting to try to make *Mischief* sail herself. He had no obvious reason to leave the cockpit, and although *Mischief* was heeled during his watch there was nothing exceptional about the weather. Tilman's assumption about the time

Shaw went overboard is probably right. It was the log line that was broken, not merely the rotor torn off. Rotors are not infrequently taken by sharks or other big fish, but a log line is broken more rarely. The broken line here suggested that Shaw had grabbed at it as he went overboard, and that it had broken from his weight, perhaps combined with a sudden heave of the ship. Tilman and his companions did everything possible, sailing back on a reciprocal course, and then zig-zagging across it. If the estimated time of the tragedy was anything like right, it was a forlorn search. Shaw had been in the water for nearly an hour and a half before he was discovered to be missing, and in the time *Mischief*, with her helm lashed, would have covered several miles. And there was no way of telling what leeway she may have made. Tilman sailed back to cover all the distance that *Mischief* could possibly have travelled, and then searched to each side of the direct course. He continued the search throughout the day, the crew looking from the rigging to gain more height than a lookout from the deck. In well over 100,000 miles of ocean voyaging, Shaw was the only man lost from *Mischief* under Tilman's command.

After the tragedy Tilman had to decide whether to go on or to go home. He consulted the crew, who seemed to want to go on, and decided to continue the voyage. He would have been wiser to go back, for at Montevideo two of the crew changed their minds and left. He was now short-handed for the rough seas south of Cape Horn but the streak of stubbornness in him refused to accept defeat. He recruited two unknown men from a Salvation Army hostel and sailed on to Punta Arenas, where a third hand offered himself, and was accepted. He had only two of his original crew left, and the newcomers were of mixed nationality and experience. Nevertheless he went on, and it is scarcely surprising that the voyage was not happy. He sighted Smith Island, though there was now no question of trying to land there, because there was no one else capable of taking charge of *Mischief*, and went on to Deception Island. For reasons that are obscure, but may have had something to do with the behaviour of some members of his crew, the people at the British base were not disposed to be friendly, though he got a more kindly reception from the British research vessel *Shackleton* which put into the base while he was there. Feeling unwelcome he moved over to the Chilean base, where they were rather nicer to him, and two members of his crew were given medical treatment for boils. On 3 January 1967, he gave himself a day off and climbed a snow slope to 1,800 feet, the highest point of the island. He wanted to sail for Cape Town, which would have been his best route home, but a Uruguayan member of his crew, who now wanted to leave *Mischief*, refused to consider being put ashore in South Africa. So he made instead for South Georgia, hoping that he might find a ship at the whaling station there which would take the Uruguayan back to South America. There wasn't, there were arguments and more trouble, and in the end he had to go back to Montevideo, to the annoyance of other members of the crew who wanted to go to South Africa. At Montevideo the whole crew left him, though one later agreed to help him sail back to England. He had a wretched time trying to recruit volunteers for the homeward passage, made worse by the theft of most of his cash and travellers' cheques. In the end he advertised in a local newspaper and had a flood of applicants, most of them totally unsuitable and without either passports or money. He did, however, collect a crew of sorts, and by sheer determination got *Mischief* home to Lymington on 15 July 1967 after a horrible voyage of 20,400 miles.

One can admire Tilman's determination without approving his methods of crew-selection, and he was certainly not always tactful in handling his crews. His Army training and his own instincts required total loyalty to any cause he served—as when he refused to sleep ashore in the comfortable French base on Kerguelen because he felt it his duty to stay with the schooner *Patanela*. What he himself gave, he expected in others, and sometimes he asked rather a lot. *Mischief* was his boat, his expeditions in her were his own passionate interest, remote fjords in the Arctic or the Antarctic were the places his soul loved. He himself was content with his pipe and whatever might be going in the way of food, happy enough with bread or rice, and if there was a bit of curry to go with the rice, so much the better. He fed his crews adequately rather than well, and when there was some curry left over from supper he saw no reason why it should not be finished up at breakfast. When one of the crew complained about this he thought it unreasonable, and in *Mischief Goes South*, wrote testily:

A traveller should have the back of an ass to bear all, and the mouth of a hog to eat what is set before him. The curry, appearing at an unusual hour, was still hot enough to inflame him. I caught his drift quick enough when he violently voiced his disgust at being expected to eat curry for breakfast. This chap, who had eagerly volunteered to come on this voyage, who would have been disappointed if he had been refused, who was now enjoying a free holiday, had apparently persuaded himself that he was doing me a favour. It is a question whether those who contribute nothing towards the expenses of a voyage have any right to complain.

It is equally a question whether the contribution of free labour is to contribute nothing towards the expenses of a voyage. Tilman was not a hard-driving shipmaster of the old school enforcing his orders with a belaying pin, but he would have approved the adage

> Six days shalt thou labour and do all that thou art able,
> The seventh, holystone the deck and scrape the cable.

He might have got on better with some of his crews if he had been physically fierce, instead of expressing displeasure with a muttered sarcasm.

There was a similar problem over his austere approach to the risks of the sea. He was a careful seaman, and when risks had to be taken they were calculated risks, but he never pretended that seagoing involves no danger. Of a complaint that he carried no distress signals or life-raft he wrote in the same book:

In my view every herring should hang by its own tail. Anyone venturing into unfrequented and possibly dangerous waters does so with his eyes open, should be willing to depend on his own exertions, and should neither expect nor ask for help. Nor would equipment of this sort be of much use in Drake Passage, where the chances of being picked up are so slim as to be hardly worth considering. A yacht is supposed to carry distress signals, but is not overmuch reliance placed upon them by the owners of small craft? . . . The perils of the sea are less apparent than the perils of climbing, and have to be carefully assessed. In climbing the penalty for a mistake is obvious and is sometimes exacted instantaneously, so that on the whole there are fewer foolish climbers than foolish amateur sailors.

This is a perfectly valid point of view, but it is one to be accepted for oneself and not imposed on others. A life-raft in the wastes of the

South Atlantic may be useless, but if it helps to instil confidence in a crew it may be of psychological value. Tilman's scorn for such things was inherent in his own mental and moral make-up, but his own cool courage in the acceptance of danger is not to be expected of everyone.

Yet for all his quirks and personal austerities he was an inspiring leader. Warwick Deacock wrote of him after the Heard Island expedition, "The whole crew of *Patanela* held him in the greatest affection and respect. He was a gentle man with great humility, ineffable kindness and patience." Men followed him in war, and many of those who sailed with him thought the world of him, and would have gone with him anywhere. Perhaps he was at his best in war, when loyalty to a cause transcends everything else. In private expeditions the kind of loyalty that he expected, and gave, comes from self-discipline. He got on best with those whose own characters were strong and self-sufficient. If he was sometimes unfortunate in his crews it was because not all men were prepared voluntarily to accept his standards.

XIV

The Arctic and the Loss of Mischief

BETWEEN 1961 AND the Heard Island expedition in 1964–65, Tilman made four voyages to the Arctic in *Mischief*. On returning from Australia in March 1965 he at once fitted out *Mischief* for a voyage to Greenland, and after his miserable experiences on the expedition to the South Shetlands in 1966–67 he went back to the Arctic in 1968, on what proved to be *Mischief*'s last voyage.

Both Arctic and Antarctic offered ice, glaciers and remote unvisited fjords. The Arctic had one big advantage—it is much nearer to the British Isles. As Tilman put it, adapting Prince Hal, "It occurred to me that these southern voyages provided an intolerable deal of sea to one half-pennyworth of mountain, while Greenland, excessively mountainous, is only a month's sail away." Proximity made several things much easier—it is easier to recruit a crew for a voyage of four or five months than for a year, and it costs less to store a vessel for a short voyage. Against this, the long sea passage across the world to the Antarctic offered pleasant stretches of trade wind sailing, whereas the North Atlantic, even in summer, is a harsh, gale-swept sea, and unless a very long route is taken to Greenland—south to the Azores or the Canaries to pick up the North-east Trades to go across to America—the prevailing westerlies are likely to mean long periods of beating into the wind, hard on boat, gear and crew. Probably these very difficulties rather attracted Tilman, and he was certainly attracted by the relative shortness of the passage, so after his successful voyage to the Crozets and Kerguelen in 1959–60 he turned his attention to the Arctic. His early northern voyages were to the west coast of Greenland and the eastern seaboard of the Canadian Arctic. They were happy trips, with good crews. The first, in 1961, took him to Godthaab and on northwards to the Umanak region on the west coast, around Latitude 71 deg N. His climbing companion on this trip was his old friend from the Patagonian ice-cap, Major Charles Marriott, who not only climbed but served as *Mischief*'s cook. On 19 July 1961 Tilman wrote to Adeline from Igdlorssuit, not far from Umanak:

We got in here last night. It is a small settlement close to the fjord we hope to go up. I called here . . . hoping to recruit a couple of local Eskimo to come with us. . . . None of us speak Danish, so things are at a standstill. It's an interesting place, with lots of kayaks, huskies, and sledges. There is also a store and a post office. The scenery is magnificent, sea, icebergs, glaciers, and mountains.

I don't know whether we're going to get any climbing. Charles's foot seems to have gone wrong again—it looks like a chilblain that's gone bad. It may or may not come right. I myself am not so hot at the moment. At Godthaab I slipped on an oil patch on deck, fell hard on a winch, and probably cracked a rib. At least it feels like that. I should think that another ten days should see it right, so that if Charles is fit we can still have a fortnight or three weeks ashore climbing, which will be enough.

The weather is quite remarkable. Ever since crossing the Arctic Circle in Lat. 67.30 it has been fine, sunny, almost hot. The only trouble is there is hardly any wind. Yesterday in order to get here we had the engine going for ten hours—without it we should get nowhere. The whole sea yesterday was covered with icebergs: we counted over 200 big ones. They calve off the glaciers coming down from the inland ice sheet. Ship and crew in good heart.

Failure to recruit Eskimo guides did not matter, for to reach mountains they had simply to sail up a fjord. While waiting for time to heal his hurt rib Tilman occupied himself in collecting plants for the Natural History Museum. As therapy it was not ideal, for he was also suffering from what he thought to be lumbago, and bending down to botanise was painful. But his rib improved, and Marriott's foot also got better. So these two elderly men set about climbing, attempting a 6,500-foot summit from sea level in one day. They did not make it, but they reached over 5,000 feet. A couple of days later they established a camp on a glacier at about 1,200 feet and from there achieved a summit of 5,800 feet. From the Kangerdlugssuaq fjord they made a two-day expedition to a peak of 6,370 feet, from which they could see across to the mountains of Disko Island. Tilman was enchanted to find yellow poppies growing at 3,000 feet. He was more excited by them than by the considerable climbing achievements of Marriott and himself. As usual, he thought that he should have done better.

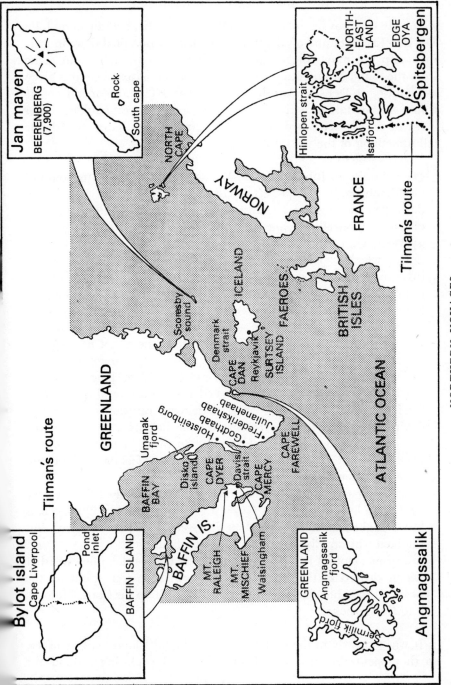

NORTHERN VOYAGES

Jan mayen

BEERENBERG
(7,900)

Rock.
South cape

North
Cape

NORWAY

Scoresby
sound

ICELAND

Denmark
strait

CAPE
DAN

Reykjavik

SURTSEY
ISLAND

FAEROES

BRITISH
ISLES

ATLANTIC OCEAN

FRANCE

Tilman's route

Spitsbergen

NORTH-
EAST
LAND

EDGE
OYA

Hinlopen strait

Isafjord

GREENLAND

Umanak
fjord

Holsteinborg

Godthaab

Frederikshaab

Julianehaab

CAPE
FAREWELL

BAFFIN
BAY

Disko
island

CAPE
DYER

Davis
strait

CAPE
MERCY

Tilman's route

Bylot island

Cape Liverpool

Pond
inlet

BAFFIN ISLAND

BAFFIN IS.

MT.
RALEIGH

MT.
MISCHIEF

Walsingham

GREENLAND

Angmagssalik
fjord

Sermilik fjord

Angmagssalik

For his next voyage in 1962 he followed his Elizabethan hero John Davis to Exeter Sound on Baffin Island. Davis, who sailed there in 1585 in a ship not much bigger than *Mischief*, named a mountain rising from the sound Mount Raleigh. On the modern map its height is given as about 5,700 feet. It was still unclimbed, and Tilman hoped to make a first ascent, taking with him another well-tried companion, Roger Tufft of the Crozet expedition. These extracts from letters to Adeline tell something of the voyage:

Davis Strait. 20 June 1962. . . . We are now about 150 m. south of Godthaab. We've had a better passage so far than last year. On 23 days from Lymington as against 35 we made our landfall 30 m. south of Cape Farewell, having had no westerly wind at all till Long. 27 West. Had three strongish blows, one of them reaching Force 8 during which we hove to, as the wind was foul. Off the Cape we met some icebergs and on closing the land found the Julianehaab Bight full of heavy pack ice and had to stand out again. Two days ago in fog we met some loose pack and had to coast along it for several miles before getting clear. We suffered a hard bump below water but I don't think we did any damage. Anyhow, she is not making any water. Even in a calm sea the pack ice keeps up a menacing growl which can be heard miles away. We saw a seal basking on an ice-floe and a bottle-nosed whale surfaced alongside several times. Near the ice the sea temperature was 34. Air temperature in the fog was down to 35 with the fog freezing on the halyards. We've got the cabin stove going, and I'm beginning to think in terms of winter woollies. Apart from the lethargy of old age I am feeling all right, and have not fallen down and broken anything yet. . . .

A racing pigeon boarded us off Ireland and only left when we closed the land here. It got fat on a diet of lentils and Quaker oats but I doubt if it will survive long in Greenland. Sorry it went, but the boat was rapidly becoming a guano island.

22 June. Got off here [Godthaab] yesterday in thick rainy weather which cleared in the afternoon and showed we were right on the beam. It then blew hard and we had a fast sail up the fjord. Motored into the harbour.

It was too early in the year to make for Baffin Island because of ice, so they spent the next month climbing and exploring around the glaciers descending from the Sukkertoppen ice-cap, north of Godthaab, returning for ice-reports on conditions off Baffin Island. On 25 July he wrote:

Today I got an ice-report from Cape Dyer, Baffin Island, which says the coast is clear, but that 2–5 miles out there is heavily congested ice. Much what I expected so early in the season, but for want of any other plan I think we might as well go over and have a look. One might be able to get round the ice farther south and work up inside it. So we shall probably leave tomorrow or next day, and I doubt if you will hear of us till we turn up, unless we get ourselves reported through Lloyds, or unless we touch at some settlement.

They could not make the coast of Baffin Island, and returned to Holsteinborg (north of Godthaab) in Greenland. But Tilman decided to try again later and used the waiting time to have *Mischief* slipped to see if she had suffered any damage from her bump on the ice. She needed no repairs, but her master did. Ever since his riding accident in Kenya he had had trouble with his teeth, and had to wear dentures. On the attempted passage to Baffin Island he had broken his lower plate; it had been put together with glue and a copper pin, but the makeshift repair did not last. In Holsteinborg there was a young Danish woman dentist who treated him promptly and efficiently: he went to see her in the morning and got back his teeth in the afternoon, though she recommended that he should have a new set made when he could. "I could eat all right without them, but smoking a pipe was the devil," he observed.

In spite of his pessimism about the chances of penetrating the ice to Exeter Sound he got through on his second attempt in the middle of August. He anchored *Mischief* under Mount Raleigh, but was disturbed to notice that the mountain was apparently misplaced on the map, being marked in his view on the wrong side of a glacier. Where Davis's Mount Raleigh should have been was another mountain, which he called "False Mount Raleigh". He and Roger Tufft camped ashore and climbed them both, pleased to discover that "True Mount Raleigh" at 5,700 feet was some 500 feet higher than its "false" neighbour. Later the map was corrected in accordance with his views, and the second mountain was officially named Mount Mischief.

His third voyage north in 1963 was probably his greatest achievement in the Arctic, combining real exploration with the feat of taking *Mischief* into the high latitudes of Baffin Bay. His objective was Bylot Island, north-east of the great mass of Baffin Island, from which it is separated by a strait, Pond Inlet. He set out the attractions of Bylot Island as "being difficult to reach, little known, uninhabited, and mountainous". It had never been crossed, and he hoped to be the first to do so. Since the crossing of some 50 miles through unknown conditions of ice and snow might take up to three weeks, he needed a competent seaman to look after *Mischief* while he and his climbing companion were on shore, and he was fortunate in finding an able volunteer in Ed Mikeska, a Pole who had been a professional seaman and served on a Canadian ice-breaker in the Arctic. His plan was to land on the north shore of Bylot Island near Cape Liverpool and then cross the island to the south coast at Pond Inlet, *Mischief* being sailed round to pick him up. His climbing companion was Bruce Reid, who had been studying at St Andrew's University and had a summer to spare while waiting to join the RAF.

After calling at Godthaab he sailed north to Godhavn on the way to Upernivik, a still more northerly settlement in West Greenland, from which he proposed to attempt the crossing of about 300 miles to Bylot Island. On 6 July 1963 he wrote from Godhavn:

We got in here yesterday, six days from Godthaab. It is the capital of North Greenland, but quite a small place of about 400 inhabitants, 40 of them Danes. . . . We have had no reports on ice yet and I am in doubt what to do. I think we are too early, but if we get to Bylot only in August we shall not have time to cross it, but will have to content ourselves with a journey inland and perhaps a mountain. . . . Ice conditions change quickly, so that unless one is on the spot chances are missed. It's about 300 miles across Baffin Bay from Upernivik. Up there the compass is useless, so we shall have difficulty in steering a course. However, if there is enough sun we shall probably manage to find a way, and the target is a large one,

A particular difficulty of navigation in high latitudes is proximity to the magnetic pole, which makes for wild behaviour in the compass. He carried no gyro-compass to offset this difficulty, contenting himself with the reflection that John Davis and other Elizabethan

Adeline (Mrs Reid Moir) with Toffee, 1973

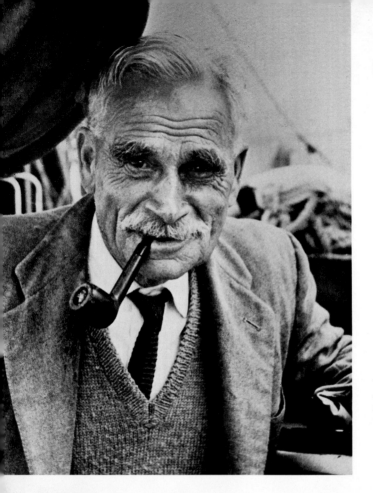

Left: H. W. T. on board *Sea Breeze* in 1971

Below: Baroque off Angmagssalik, East Greenland, 1976

Above: The Mawddach estuary with the house Bod Owen (ringed) in the trees

Below: Bod Owen

The last voyage: the departure of *En Avant* from Southampton, August 1977

seamen had navigated in high latitudes without modern aids, and that he ought also to be able to manage. He was in fact better off than Elizabethan seamen in that he had a sextant and chronometer to help him to find out where he was. Even so, his navigation in those inhospitable ice-packed seas was remarkable.

He decided to go on to try his luck, and on 12 July wrote from Upernivik:

Four days from Godhavn. Not very nice weather, cold and dull until we closed the land, when it became sunny and cloudless like we have had on previous years. . . . The store manager and his wife entertained us last night to coffee and beer. We came back at midnight with the sun well up in the sky. Tonight we go to one of the radio men, who has an English wife. He is a keen sailor. There is no water here. Ice is chipped off ice-floes stranded in the harbour and delivered by truck to each house, where it is put in a tin bin and left to melt. This is the farthest north Greenland town, though there are settlements on the coast as far north as Thule, which the store people here visit in winter by sledge along the sea-ice. There is a hospital here, and a weekly local steamer calls in summer with mail and stores. In winter there is no communication at all. We have yet to get any ice-news. Might get some here but I doubt it, as no one is interested in the state of ice between here and Baffin Island. We shall just have to sail out west till we meet the pack and then hope to find free water to the north of it. August is the earliest one can expect it in normal years, so unless we are lucky we may have to wait. All are well.

He was lucky, and on 23 July he wrote from Bylot Island:

We made the north side of the island today, two miles south of Cape Liverpool. It was, of course, foggy, and we only saw the land when 200 yards away. It was quite a surprise. It has been a tedious passage from Upernivik. We had to go north to Lat. 75 to avoid the ice of the Middle Pack, and even so we kept coming upon straggling rafts of floes. But the real trouble was the lack of wind and we used up a great lot of fuel to get here. Owing to the presence of the ice the sea was like a mirror most of the time—like sailing on a pond. Tomorrow we motor on about 20 m. or so up Lancaster Sound to the jumping off place for the crossing, where Bruce Reid and I take off. The boat will go round to the police post at Pond Inlet. There is also a Hudson Bay store, a post office, and Mission there.

He could not get to his planned "jumping off place" because of ice, so he and Reid started from where they were, near Cape Liverpool. He took food for eighteen days, and was so concerned about the weight they had to carry that although there were polar bear tracks along the shore he did not take a rifle that he had been given in Greenland.

They made the crossing in fifteen days, and for the most part it was an unpleasant journey, because of soft snow into which they sank waist-deep. They nearly came to a still more unpleasant end, for when they got to the Bylot shore of Pond Inlet there was no *Mischief* to be seen. They had arranged to make smoke signals, and were relieved to find a sort of heather that could be burned, and a good deal of drift-wood. But *Mischief*, after a gruelling passage through the ice, had had to shelter on the Baffin Island shore, about ten miles away, and no one saw their signals. They had brought food for eighteen days, fifteen of which were gone. If *Mischief* failed to reach the Pond Inlet settlement no one would know that there were two men on Bylot Island, and once the food they had with them was eaten there was no chance of anything more. They saw tracks of Arctic hares—but had nothing to shoot with.

They were marooned for four days, lighting fire after fire, without attracting any response. They contemplated using an air-mattress as a makeshift raft for the ten-mile crossing of Pond Inlet, but fortunately when they were down to their last biscuit some Eskimos saw their smoke and came over in canoes, powered by outboard motors, to investigate. The Eskimos soon had them on board *Mischief*. When he got to the other shore and saw the haze over Bylot Island, Tilman could understand why their signals had not been seen.

Mischief added to her own laurels by being the first vessel of the season to make the settlement at Pond Inlet. The supply steamer followed a few days later. The community at Pond Inlet were so hospitable, and gave *Mischief* so many gifts of food, that she left Baffin Island better stocked than when she had left Lymington.

On coming home from the Bylot Island voyage Tilman was met by the crisis of *Mischief*'s survey, which condemned her as unfit for further deep-sea sailing. Having refused to accept this verdict (as has been related) and having had the 57-year-old vessel restored to seaworthiness he showed his confidence in her by turning to east Greenland. The west coast is fairly dangerous for a small boat, but it is hospitable compared with the grim wilderness of the east. There, an ice-bound shore stretches down from the Arctic Ocean, a desert of polar ice through which it is often impossible to reach land at all. There are a few settlements, of which Angmagssalik, a little south of the Arctic Circle, is the most important, but whether or not it can be reached by sea depends on the capricious behaviour of the ice. The old whalers and sealers which once sailed in these ice-blocked waters were strengthened against ice, and tried to sail in company, so that help from one vessel would be at hand if another was nipped or struck. Tilman was naturally attracted by this desolation, and his decision to go there in his restored but still ancient *Mischief* was the same in kind as the decision which took him to the Alps thirty years earlier after being told that he would never climb again.

The voyage he planned for the summer of 1964 was to Skjoldungen, a mountainous and little-known islet lying between two long fjords about 100 miles south of Angmagssalik. Nowadays Angmagssalik can be reached readily enough by air, but the approach by sea remains hazardous and sometimes impossible. Acting on the principle that he could not know whether he could get there without trying, Tilman set out.

The year 1964—in which he turned 66—was a year of tremendous sailing activity for him. Summer in the northern hemisphere was filled by his trip to east Greenland, and he then flew to Australia to take *Patanela* to Heard Island in the southern summer. He sailed for Greenland by way of the Faeroes and Iceland, where he had two interesting experiences. The first was to land on Surtsey, a volcanic islet which had just appeared off the south coast of Iceland, erupting from the seabed; Tilman was not the first person to set foot on Surtsey because some Icelanders had already been there, but he could fairly claim that he and his companions from *Mischief* were the first British people to visit the newly-arrived islet. Shortly afterwards, he saluted and was saluted by the Royal Yacht *Britannia*, which was taking Prince Philip on a visit to Iceland. He described this in a letter to Adeline from Reykjavik on 1 July 1964:

307

Yesterday was a big day for old *Mischief*. The Royal Yacht was due in at 4.30 pm so we sailed out with a blue ensign flying at the peak. We had to wait about, but when she arrived near the outer buoys, with an Icelandic gunboat and HMS *Malcolm* astern, we let draw and sailed past and dipped our ensign. Prince Philip came out on the maindeck and waved, and then they dipped their great white ensign. We were the only boat out there.

He did not make Skjoldungen, but reached Angmagssalik, which was a considerable feat. It might have been better if he hadn't, because he got through the ice only by following a 3,000-ton cargo steamer and a local boat built for working in ice, and the wash from the steamer prevented him from keeping near enough before the floes closed up again. Several times the local boat came back to help him out, but then *Mischief* got caught between two floes and sprang some planks. He was able to beach her at Angmagssalik and a local shipwright helped with repairs. On 19 July he wrote:

We've had quite a lot of trouble with the leak. Since arriving here we've had *Mischief* on the beach lying over six times. A good shipwright carpenter gave us a hand, and we are now back at anchor with the leak cured. . . . There is not much to do here. One sort of café place, where they sell biscuits and coffee, and beer can be bought at the Greenland Trading Co. store. We did not discover until too late that beer is not sold on Friday, Saturday or Sunday, the idea being to prevent the pay packet drawn on Friday being squandered immediately on beer. . . . Crew's morale and temper has now recovered. We were all (especially self) getting a bit edgy with hauling her on and off without apparently doing any good.

Ice continued to block the entrance, so he did some local climbing, with two members of his crew, on "a very nice looking peak" of some 3,380 feet. Alas, *Mischief*'s leak started again. They tried to cure it by passing buckets of sawdust under the hull, in the hope that inflowing water would force sawdust into the leaks. This worked to some extent, but a bout of 'flu depressed him, and he decided to abandon Skjoldungen and go home. By 9 August ice-conditions had improved, and he was able to get out to sea. They had a rough voyage home, which did not improve *Mischief*'s leaks, on top of which they had trouble with one of the pumps, though they managed a makeshift repair. He took *Mischief* into Barmouth, where they had a warm reception from the local people and all hands "proceeded in relays to Bod Owen for baths and food". The pump was mended and *Mischief* returned safely to Lymington, after which her master set off for Australia and Heard Island.

Tilman's stubbornness would not accept defeat over Skjoldungen, and as soon as he got back from Australia in the spring in 1965 he was off to the north again. This time he stayed a little longer in Iceland, sailing for East Greenland rather later in the summer. There was still plenty of ice, but he made both Angmagssalik and Skjoldungen and, with Brian Holloway, a young New Zealander, achieved an attractive peak of some 3,000 feet, which they climbed from sea-level. It was a fine sunny day, and coming back he had what he described as "a brief and icy bathe" in an East Greenland tarn.

1966 and 1967 were taken up by his miserable voyage to the South Shetlands and in 1968 he decided to go to the Arctic again, with the ambitious aim of making for Scoresby Sound, 600 miles north-east of Angmagssalik in Latitude 70°N, taking in the island of Jan Mayen, in roughly the same latitude but some 300 miles off the East Greenland coast on the way. Jan Mayen is a desolate island, with savage surf that at times makes landing impossible, but it had a particular attraction for Tilman in an extinct volcano called the Beerenberg rising to some 7,900 feet, which he hoped to climb. It had been climbed before, but is so remote and inaccessible that Tilman thought it a good prize, though it would not be a first ascent. Jan Mayen is uninhabited save that the Norwegians maintain a weather station there.

After calling at Iceland he made a landfall off the South Cape of Jan Mayen on 18 July and on the next day anchored off what had been the old Norwegian base on the west coast of the island. In a normal year Jan Mayen is free of ice by mid-July, but 1968 was a bad ice-year, and although there was no pack in the immediate vicinity of the anchorage off the west coast, there was heavy pack a few miles to the north. Tilman landed from the anchorage and walked across the island, finding that the Norwegians had established a new base on the east coast. The commandant of this station suggested that he should sail *Mischief* round to a small bay near the new base. They moved on

20 July, rounding South Cape in fog, and having to tack twice to weather it. It was then night, the wind dropped, and having got an offing about two miles clear of the east coast Tilman handed the sails to let *Mischief* drift. He took the midnight to 2 a.m. watch himself. It was a filthy night of cold, wet fog, and thinking that *Mischief*, with no steerage way, was not moving, he sat below, going on deck every 15 minutes. He told his relief at 2 a.m. that he could do the same.

Mischief was in fact drifting north at about half a knot, and at about 3.50 a.m. she struck an isolated rock about half a mile offshore. There was a slight swell, which bumped *Mischief* hard against the rock. The engine got her off quickly. She was making a lot of water but two pumps kept the leaks under control and Tilman made for the shore. With fog and a lot of inshore ice about, he had trouble in finding the bay off the Norwegian base, but he got there and anchored at 7 a.m. He rowed ashore in the dinghy to tell the Norwegians of his trouble. It was agreed that the only thing to do was to beach *Mischief*, to try to get at the leaks to repair them. The Jan Mayen beach shelved steeply, and there was a rise and fall of tide of only about three feet. *Mischief* drew 7 feet 6 inches aft, so they could get only at her forward quarters.

The Norwegians supplied tar, felt and copper to cover the likeliest sources of leaks, and a bulldozer to haul round *Mischief* so that they could get at her other side. No very serious damage could be seen. Tarring, felting and coppering certainly reduced the leaks, and a spell at the pumps every two hours kept the inflow of water under control. Tilman was sure that he could sail *Mischief* back to Iceland.

Then the ice struck. The wind changed and heavy floes were blown on to *Mischief*. The Norwegians dynamited one big floe that was threatening her rudder, but there was a limit to what could be done to break up ice with explosives without damaging *Mischief* herself. Tilman and his helpers tried everything they could to haul *Mischief* clear of the ice that was most immediately threatening her, but the ice battered a hole in her hull and she was soon one-third full of water.

The Norwegians were as eager as Tilman to save *Mischief* and the next plan was to use bulldozers to haul her right out of the water. All her ballast was taken out and a bulldozer managed to move her a couple of yards, but the beach was too steep, and the stricken *Mischief* lay helpless in the breakers. These efforts to save her went on for ten days. On 30 July it was decided that her only remaining hope was to have a big patch put on the hole in her side so that she could be towed to Norway. The Norwegian supply ship *Brandal* was due at the base for a two-day visit on 2 August. The Norwegians got in touch with her by radio and her master agreed to attempt a tow. He also arranged to lend *Mischief* a petrol-engined pump, and an electric pump to reinforce the petrol pump during the tow. At 8 p.m. on 4 August *Brandal* sailed from Jan Mayen, with the battered and patched *Mischief* in tow, with Tilman and three of his crew on board her. They could communicate with *Brandal* by walkie-talkie, and in addition to the tow-rope a cable was slung from *Brandal* to provide power for the electric pump.

They met rough weather from the start. No current could be obtained from the power-cable for the electric pump, and they were wholly dependent on the petrol pump. The end of the story is fittingly taken from "*Mischief's* Last Days", a pamphlet with a black border, like an In Memoriam card, which Tilman wrote and had printed to send to his friends:

With water sloshing about inside sleep was hardly possible and for food we made do with hard tack and a cup of tea. Just before midnight I learnt that the pump had given up; the engine was running, but it was not pumping. Three of us were ready enough to quit and I confess that the skipper and owner, who had so much more at stake, had no longer the will to persevere, a fortnight of toil, trouble and anxiety having worn me down. *Brandal* had already been told. She lay to about a cable away and told us to bring off only our personal gear. So we collected our gear, launched the life-raft, and abandoned *Mischief*. She had then about three feet of water inside her. Paddling over to *Brandal* we went on board while three of the crew returned in the raft to salvage the two pumps and telephone. The electric pump, which was very heavy, we had already hoisted on deck through the skylight. The pumps met with scant ceremony, being thrown overboard on the end of a line to be hauled through the sea to *Brandal*. While *Brandal* got under way I remained on deck watching *Mischief*, still floating defiantly, until she was out of sight. We were then about 30 miles east of Jan Mayen.

For me it was the loss of much more than a yacht. I felt as one who had deserted a stricken friend, a friend with whom for the past fourteen years I had probably spent more time at sea than on land, and who when not at sea had never been far from my mind.

Tilman blamed himself for *Mischief*'s loss: he felt that had he not spent part of his own watch below when he thought that she was more or less at a standstill after rounding Jan Mayen's South Cape, and if he had not told his relief that he could do likewise, she would never have struck the rock. He felt that "the disaster, or sequence of disasters, need not have happened; and that more might have been done to save her". It is hard to see how. In freezing fog even the sharpest of lookouts might not have seen a solitary rock, and even if it had been seen *Mischief*, without steerage way, was not under command. Perhaps the engine could have been started in time, perhaps not. And it was not the rock that sank her. Her old timbers stood up well to pounding on the rock, and after makeshift repairs to the leaks Tilman was probably right to think that he could have sailed her back to Iceland. It was ice that destroyed her; once trapped by heavy floes against the steep-to beach of Jan Mayen on which she could not be hauled out, nothing more could be done. The tow was a desperate last hope. Whether she would have survived the tow if the pump had not failed is doubtful; a towed vessel in rough seas is under enormous strain, and the water-logged *Mischief* did not have much chance. Tilman did everything possible for her, and tried to do what was barely reckoned possible. She was sixty-two, he was seventy; in the prime of youth neither man nor boat could have behaved better.

XV

After Mischief

TILMAN MADE "MISCHIEF" immortal—with Joshua Slocum's *Spray*, the first boat to be sailed singlehanded round the world, and a few others, she remains for ever in those paradisal seas whose mariners renew the inspiration to sail and explore from generation to generation. He wrote five books in which she is the sole heroine, and a sixth which is dominated by her although it begins by describing her loss and goes on to describe adventures with her successor, *Sea Breeze*. The five *Mischief* books are *Mischief in Patagonia*, C.U.P., 1957, *Mischief Among the Penguins*, Hart-Davis, 1961, *Mischief in Greenland*, 1964, *Mostly Mischief*, 1966, and *Mischief Goes South*, 1968. The sixth to which she gives her name, though she is not wholly the subject, is *In Mischief's Wake*, 1971; these last four were published by Hollis & Carter.

They are not strictly chronological. *Mischief Goes South*, describing his miserable voyage to the South Shetlands in 1966–67 also has an account of her much happier circumnavigation of Africa nine years earlier. *Mostly Mischief*, recounting three voyages to the Arctic in 1963, 1964 and 1965, includes a section on his voyage to Heard Island in *Patanela* in 1964–early 1965. His style is a plain, seamanlike English in the school of those clean, clear if sometimes rather pessimistic ("on no account should this entrance be attempted without local knowledge") writers who compile the volumes of the Admiralty *Pilot*. Tilman's writing has something in common with that great seaman and hydrographer Captain James Cook, whose qualities of coolness and quiet competence in everything he undertook he also shared.

Tilman knew precisely what he wanted to say, and in this is one of his defects as a writer—he wanted to say too little. It is an uncommon fault in a world bedevilled by wordiness and self-importance, but it can be maddening. Tilman has no highlights; he is so afraid of attracting attention that he dismisses some really outstanding performance, about which the reader longs to know more, in a few laconic lines. It has been said of him that one has to be a mountaineer really to

appreciate his climbing books, a small-boat sailor properly to understand his writing about the sea. There is something in this—the
mountaineer will feel in his bones just what is happening when Tilman
drily remarks on the difficulty of negotiating some crevasse, and one
who, like the present writer, has had the experience of being trapped in
ice in a 44-foot cutter off Greenland, will have a sharper sense of what
is happening when Tilman recounts his own struggles with ice. But to
say that he seldom tells the whole story is not to say that he does not
tell a marvellously good story. He can hypnotise the reader as well
as Coleridge's *Ancient Mariner*, and with a lot more humour. His
accounts of his great journeys in Nepal and Central Asia are good
travel writing, still fresh and readable. His *Mischief* books are unique,
a magical record of a long love affair with an old boat. They are
intrepid exploration too, but what gives them their peculiar quality is
that the lonely landfalls and desolate beaches, the gales and the seas
are suffused by the love of man for boat. They have a niche of their
own in marine literature.

Most of us are a tortured complex of thoughts and second thoughts, of
action and inaction, of unfulfilled wishes and sometimes regret for
those that have been fulfilled. Tilman was uncommon in his consistency; from childhood he seems never to have acted out of character.
Having devised a way of life that suited him—a long summer in the
Arctic, winter at home with his sister at Bod Owen, writing and seeing
friends—he was not going to change it because of ice at Jan Mayen, or
because he had turned seventy. There could be only one *Mischief*, and
he grieved for her always, but his whole tradition was that grief is a
private thing, never to affect action. And there was still the sea. After
the loss of *Mischief* he needed the sea more than ever, above all he
needed the strange solace he had found with her in ice and lonely
latitudes. Within a month of coming home after the loss of *Mischief* he
was negotiating the purchase of another boat.

Sea Breeze found him. Her first appearance in his life was a telegram
from her owner, "Regret loss of *Mischief* can I offer you *Sea Breeze*."
Like *Mischief* she was a Bristol Channel Pilot Cutter, but she was even
older, having been built at Porthleven in 1899. Her rig was similar to
Mischief's but she was a little bigger, three feet longer, one foot more in
beam, and with a Thames Measurement tonnage of 33 compared with

Mischief's 29 tons. Naturally she appealed to Tilman as the sort of boat he could sail, and in spite of a somewhat critical surveyor's report he bought her. She needed a lot of work, and as it was then the end of September 1968, and he proposed to sail her to the Arctic the following June, it had to be done quickly. *Sea Breeze*'s first voyage to the Arctic under Tilman was in fact her shakedown cruise.

It was not one of his happier voyages. He recruited a crew in his usual haphazard fashion, and in spite of having a good cook ("a noble curry and duff for our first night at sea") they were not an altogether happy family. The voyage began badly. Before he left the Solent he noticed water coming into the galley and found that a foot or two of caulking between two of her waterline planks had come out. He put back for repairs and it was found that *Sea Breeze* needed to be re-caulked throughout. That cost him a fortnight's delay in starting. While still in the Bristol Channel *Sea Breeze* lost her topmast and her bowsprit. Tilman had no great love for topmasts (*Mischief*'s was normally stowed) and he could have borne the loss, but he could not sail without a bowsprit. Appledore was only about 25 miles away downwind and he put in there for repairs, making the difficult entrance successfully (without a large-scale chart). While a new bowsprit was being made two of his crew decided to leave, and he had to recruit replacements at short notice. An untried boat and a hastily collected crew did not deter him from making straight for Iceland—and *Sea Breeze* made a remarkably good passage to Seydisfjord on the east coast of Iceland in eleven days.

This brisk sailing raised his spirits and encouraged him to think again of high latitudes and Scoresby Sound. At least one of his crew had had enough and wanted to go home, but the Icelanders of Seydisfjord were nice to them, and after a pleasant short stay no more was said. Tilman and the cook (Brian Potter, a retired bank manager who became a valued friend) climbed Strandertinder (3,310 ft) from sea level. They duly sailed for Scoresby Sound and sighted Cape Brewster in Lat. 70°N, at the southern entrance to the sound. There was a lot of ice and Tilman wanted to poke about to see if they could get into the Sound, but these ideas were brought to an end by what he called "a polite mutiny". The man who had wanted to go home from Iceland again wanted to go back, and two other members of the crew agreed with him. Brian Potter stood by Tilman, but felt that he had not enough sailing experience to overcome the objections of the rest of the crew. So that was that. "To give up when so near, in an able boat with ample supplies, was hard to stomach, but with an unwilling crew there was nothing to be done," Tilman wrote later in *In Mischief's Wake*.

Licking his wounds at Bod Owen he had a letter from Colin Putt, who had been on the Heard Island expedition, saying that he was coming to England from Australia, and asking if there was any chance of a voyage in *Sea Breeze*. If so, a friend of his, a young Australian climber called Iain Dillon, would like to come with them. Tilman had the highest opinion of Putt, an engineer by profession and man of many skills, who had proved himself a staunch shipmate on *Patanela*. His letter seemed like manna from heaven, and Tilman at once began planning a cruise to Greenland for 1970. Brian Potter would have come again, but an operation on his hand prevented him, though he came to Lymington and gave what help he could in fitting out. To complete the crew Tilman recruited two young men, Bob Comlay and Andrew Harwich, who were waiting to go to university. Both turned out well, and the crew for his 1970 voyage was among the best he ever had, making the cruise one of the happiest and most successful.

He decided this time to make for south-west Greenland, an intricate coast of fjords and skerries, with many mountains of 5–7,000 feet for the climbers in the party. To understand his achievements on this voyage it is necessary to consider briefly the formation and movement of ice around Greenland.

The huge icefields of east Greenland consist of ice formed on the spot, of polar ice brought down from the Arctic Ocean, and icebergs calved from the east Greenland glaciers. The pack off south-west Greenland is quite different. It consists of what the Danes call "storis" (big ice) and comes from the ice off east Greenland, being carried round Cape Farewell and north up the west Greenland coast by a clockwise current. Being old ice, compressed in the east Greenland pack, it is hard and firm, and the icebergs in it are huge and solid, extending far below the surface. This ice is carried slowly up the west coast in spring and early summer, blocking the entrances to the fjords.

There is another peculiarity. Off the west coast the Greenland current meets a north-going current originating in the Gulf Stream, and therefore of somewhat warmer water. As the ice is carried north it is gradually dispersed by this warmer water, with the curious result that farther north, until the polar regions of north Greenland are reached, ice-free sea is more likely to be found. Only in exceptionally bad years are the approaches to Godthaab encumbered by ice. Tilman had been to Godthaab several times without difficulty, and had sailed on far to the north without much trouble from ice. He also knew of another geophysical oddity which often provides a considerable area of clear water well north in Baffin Bay.

Tilman's previous voyages had been farther north, and he seems not fully to have appreciated the extent of the pack off the south-west fjords. Tilman was caught, and for five days he was carried slowly northwards in the pack. His crew all remained cheerful, and when they could not get out of the pack they moored Sea Breeze to a huge floe, using ice-axes to shape bollards for the mooring lines. They were in danger of being nipped between floes, but they made light of it, stretched their legs on the ice of their floating dock, and kept a vigilant lookout, with boathooks at the ready to try to shove off any tiresome bergy bits that came too near. The letters to Adeline continued:

In the ice. 13 July 1970. You must have been wondering what had happened to us. About a week ago when trying to get through the ice to find an inshore lead we got stuck in the ice and have been in it ever since, moored to a large floe. The drift is carrying us north, and we are already 100 m. north of Julianehaab. The ice is decaying fast now, and I should think in a day or two we should be able to get out and make for Faeringehavn or Godthaab. After that we shall have to try to get south again. . . . I am lucky to have an excellent crew who have been quite unperturbed, and are bearing the maddening delay with great patience. . . . Except for my chronic cough which has not yielded to sea air yet I am pretty fit. Hope this will be posted in the next few days.

They reached Faeringehavn, a fishing port a little south of Godthaab, on 15 July.

Yet another peculiarity of the south-west Greenland ice is that there may often be a lane of more or less clear water, a few miles wide, between the coast and the coastal pack. The fjords themselves may still be blocked by ice that has drifted in, and this lane is not wholly reliable but can be used with caution. Tilman's aim was to find a back-door way to Julianehaab through the mass of skerries and fjords which might not be completely blocked by ice. It was a wonderful feat of boat-handling in narrow, ice-strewn waters. His crew got some climbing, and although not as much as they had hoped it was in excitingly new country. He himself was greatly interested in the archaeological remains of 11th–12th-century Norse settlements round Julianehaab.

Cape Farewell, like Cape Horn, is an island, and Tilman and his crew sailed from the west coast of Greenland to Prinz Christian Sund on the east coast by going through a maze of fjords instead of going out to sea and rounding Cape Farewell. They were met with great hospitality at the Danish weather station at Prinz Christian Sund.

Tilman had still not sailed to Scoresby Sound. Experience of the ice off east Greenland did not put him off; obstinacy, stubbornness, or refusal to accept defeat made him determined to have another go. In 1971 he tried again, with a good crew, including Bob Comlay from the previous year's cruise. There seemed to be a shortage of volunteer sea-cooks, so he advertised for a "cook for a cool voyage", and recruited Marius Dakin, an art student, who not only turned out to be a good cook but decorated Sea Breeze's galley. This time he sailed east about for Iceland via the North Sea, calling at the Faeroes on the way. On 26 June he wrote from Sando in the Faeroes: "Marius the cook is doing very well indeed in spite of a lot of trouble we are having with the Primus stoves. We shall put this right at Thorshavn [the capital of the Faeroes]. Have just been for a walk on shore. . . . Some of the houses and the church roofed with sods, which means they are pretty old."

On 9 July he wrote from Reykjavik, "We had a pleasant enough sail from Thorshavn, twice it blew up a bit, but no gale. On the way we had a close look at Surtsey, the volcanic island on which we landed in '65. It looks enormous now, but there are only a few fumaroles still smoking."

At Reykjavik one of the crew, who had been perpetually seasick since leaving Lymington, decided that he would have to go home. Tilman was pleased with the man for having done his best; in spite of being able to eat next to nothing he had stood his watches, and although he could have given up in the Faeroes he had sailed on to Iceland. He was able to replace the seasick crewman with a young American who had been working on an Icelandic fishing boat, and who also turned out well. It was here that he was amused by a visitor from a cruise ship who asked where they were bound, and on being told "Greenland" replied, "Ah, following in Tilman's footsteps!"

Soon after leaving Reykjavik they had to use the engine for lack of wind and *Sea Breeze* lost her propeller. He put into Isafjord in north-west Iceland, where he was lucky to buy a second-hand propeller that would serve, and even luckier to get a new shaft made and fitted on the spot, in spite of a forthcoming public holiday. Again ice kept him out of Scoresby Sound and he had to retreat, though he did get into Angmagssalik on the way home.

For 1972 he was attracted by Ellesmere Island at the extreme north of Baffin Bay, in that strange area of sea which the old whaling captains called the North Water because for all its high northern latitude it is often free of ice. On the way to west Greenland, however, *Sea Breeze*'s boom was broken in a gale, and he had to make for Reykjavik to get a new spar made. As a result of this delay he changed his plans and decided to have yet another try for Scoresby Sound.

He called at Jan Mayen to pay his respects, not exactly to *Mischief*'s grave, for she lies somewhere on the bed of the Norwegian sea, but to the scene of her disaster. There was no ice off Jan Mayen this year, and he had high hopes of Scoresby Sound. In fact he got to within about ten miles of the entrance, but was again stopped by ice. Again he decided to make do with Angmagssalik, but on the way *Sea Breeze*'s engine failed, and could not be restarted. It would have been wiser to get away from east Greenland forthwith, but Tilman was always fairly contemptuous of engines, and reckoned that plenty of seamen in the past had made Angmagssalik under sail. Ice did not seem too bad and he got within a mile of the shore when the wind died. His crew tried towing with the dinghy, but *Sea Breeze* was a heavy boat and hard to move. While they were lying helpless the tide brought in masses of ice, and then a sudden squall sprang up. *Sea Breeze* still had her sails up; she heeled over and gathered way rapidly, getting within a quarter of a mile of the shore. Fearful that she would hit one of the numerous ice-floes Tilman got the sails off her. There was little room for manoeuvre, and the best hope seemed to be to let her drift, while the crew did what they could to fend off floes. For three hours they went on like this. It was getting late in the northern summer (21 August) and darkness had come back at night, made worse by low cloud and dirty weather. Around midnight a rocky islet loomed up to leeward. Tilman hurriedly got the staysail up to try to clear it. *Sea Breeze* responded to her helm and was beginning to turn towards safety when an ice-floe hit her lee bow and stopped her. A moment later wind and sea drove her broadside on against the rock. He dropped the staysail and all hands pushed and shoved with boathooks to try to get her off, but there was no shifting her against the wind. They were in extreme peril, for she was caught on a ledge of rock, and with the hammering she was taking might slip off and sink at any moment. Tilman gave orders to abandon ship. There was no time to collect much. A bag of food was flung on to the rock, one of the crew succeeded in bringing off a light bivouac tent, and they saved some sleeping bags. Tilman was the last to leave, scrambling on to the rock with a tin of tobacco, a dry box of matches, but no pipe.

At first light they took stock. *Sea Breeze* was gone, and only the top of her mast showed above water. The bag of food had been washed away, and they had nothing but what they stood up in and the little tent. The rock offered only pools of rainwater: they might starve, but at least they were unlikely to die of thirst, and searching the rock for anything that might have come ashore from the wreck, Tilman found one of his pipes. The little tent was made to shelter two climbers, but they squeezed in three men to try to get warmth from their own bodies, taking it in turns to be inside.

Late in the afternoon they saw a small Greenland trading vessel. They had nothing to light a fire with—unless they burned their tent—so they stood on the highest point of the rock waving sleeping bags. The Greenlanders on the boat saw them, launched their dinghy, and brought it stern-on to the rock, taking off the shipwrecked men in turn. On board they were revived with hot coffee. The Greenlander was on her way to deliver forty drums of oil to a settlement up one of the fjords—it was the settlement's winter fuel supply, so she had to get it there. On arrival *Sea Breeze*'s crew helped to unload it—no lying below feeling sorry for themselves.

On the way back to Angmagssalik Tilman and his crew transferred to a bigger ship that had been taking a doctor on his rounds to some outlying settlements. None of the shipwrecked men, not even the 74-year-old Tilman, needed medical treatment. At Angmagssalik they were welcomed warmly and given a room in the hospital. All Tilman's money and traveller's cheques had gone down with *Sea Breeze* but the Danish Administrator at Angmagssalik waved aside formalities and advanced Tilman enough money, on note of hand alone, to charter an aeroplane to fly his crew to Iceland. At Reykjavik the British Consul was similarly helpful, and they all flew back to London.

Tilman, at this time, was the archetype of Tennyson's Ulysses:

> I cannot rest from travel; I will drink
> Life to the lees . . .

In January 1973 he was made CBE, and in the same month he bought another Bristol Channel Pilot Cutter, called *Baroque*. In age she came about halfway between *Sea Breeze* and *Mischief*, having been built in 1902. He bought her at Mylor in Cornwall, had her fitted out there (his friends Colin Putt and Brian Potter rallying round to help), and on 30 May 1973 set off on yet another voyage to west Greenland. His crew included Simon Richardson, a young rock-climber and keen sailor, for whom he came to have great respect. With the usual quota of delays and troubles in dealing with leaks and repairs he had a successful voyage to Umanak fjord, returning to his old berth at Lymington on 6 October after a cruise of some 5,700 miles. Like her predecessors *Baroque* was old, and bits of her were inclined to break, but she proved a fine sea-kindly boat.

If there was a hard way of doing something Tilman always preferred it. Asked why he lived in Wales and kept a boat at Lymington he replied that there were not any good mountains in Hampshire, whereas from Bod Owen he could look out to Cader Idris. During the winter he would pay at least two visits to Lymington, a round drive of some 500 miles. At first he would sleep on board his current boat—a forlorn resting-place, for a laid-up boat, with her floorboards up and everything in her stripped, offers accommodation compared with which a tent on Everest might seem luxurious. But he got a stove going and a good fug, which he considered beneficial for the boat in helping to keep mildew at bay. Later, he was persuaded to stay with friends. He was still writing industriously. *Ice With Everything*, recounting the wreck of *Sea Breeze* and his first voyage in *Baroque*, appeared in 1974. That year brought one of his greatest voyages and the severest blow of his life— the death of his sister Adeline.

The voyage was a circumnavigation of Spitzbergen, taking *Baroque* to Lat. 80°N, astonishing for a seventy-year-old yacht. Fitting out for the Spitzbergen voyage went normally. Adeline was 82, but she was apparently fit, and Tilman had no reason to be worried about her. (She would never have permitted anyone to worry about her—she had all the Tilman qualities of courage and endurance.) The flow of letters back and forth began as soon as he got to Lymington. He had a good crew in Simon Richardson, who had been a tower of strength on the last cruise, Alan Stockdale and Paul Reinsch, two volunteers from Yorkshire, who had climbed and sailed together, and Andrew Craig-Bennett, a Cambridge undergraduate with considerable sailing experience. There was a setback when Simon had to drop out when his father died, but he continued to help with work on *Baroque* at Lymington. He was replaced in Tilman's customary somewhat casual fashion by David White, who heard of the voyage in conversation in a bar and came along to offer himself as a member of the crew. He had no experience of the sea but Tilman was always ready to give young men a chance and he had three good deckhands in the others.

Tilman always tried to have a regular cook, who was exempt from watchkeeping in return for service in the galley. The alternative is for the crew to take turns in the galley, but this has disadvantages, particularly in rough weather when all hands are constantly having to be called on deck, and also, if several people use the same galley nothing is ever put back in the same place. By standing watches himself Tilman was able to have a regular cook, which made for efficiency in the galley and meals on time. Against these blessings is the fact that cooking on a small boat is hard work, and often horribly uncomfortable. Tilman tried to make up for this by having a rule that the cook was exempt from washing-up. Even so, the galley is among the hardest of jobs at sea, and he was fortunate in his cooks, who nearly always turned out well, earning frequent complimentary references in his diaries.

Originally Andrew Craig-Bennett was recruited as cook for Spitzbergen, but he was always giving a hand on deck and after a few days at sea Tilman found him so useful that he transferred him to watchkeeping and asked David White to take on the galley. It was hard on the inexperienced White, and after a week in the North Sea, he asked to be put ashore. Tilman did not want to call anywhere before Bear Island, an outlier of the Spitzbergen archipelago, and refused the request, explaining, in his book about the voyage, *Triumph and Tribulation*:

Quite apart from the replacement problem, probably insoluble, we could not afford to waste days beating to some port in Scotland, still less did I want to visit the complicated Norwegian coast of which I had charts only for the most northerly part. In a small crew the presence of one unhappy, unwilling member may well cause trouble. Happily I had no need to worry about that. The other three had the success of the voyage at heart as much as I had, that, and the safety of the ship, were all that mattered to them.

In the event David White accepted the situation uncomplainingly, and when he had found his feet in the galley became a useful cook and a good member of *Baroque*'s company, even able to make soda bread.

After battling against frustrating headwinds, and after three days of thick weather without sights, they reached Bear Island (Lat. 75°N) on 2 July, making a wonderful landfall with the island ten miles off "smack on the bow" (which says much for Tilman's dead reckoning).

The Norwegians maintain a weather station there, and a party put out in a boat to greet *Baroque* as soon as they saw her. Writing from Bear Island Tilman told Adeline, "Six of them came off for a drink, and we shall get what we want here in the way of bread and water. One of them who had been on Jan Mayen bet his pals that I was on board as soon as he saw the boat."

On 8 July he wrote from Longyearben, the administrative capital of Spitzbergen:

We got here yesterday, and today I collected your letter of 21 June. It's nice for you to have a great-grandson* as company—that is something of an achievement.

We did the 120 miles from Bear Island to Spitzbergen in 24 hours, and then took three days to do another 120 m. up the coast to this place. A very fine coast, too, nothing but glaciers and snowpeaks. Hardly any ice in the sea, but that is the usual state on this west coast. As soon as we got near the land we met with cloudless skies and 24 hours of sunshine, in contrast to the heavy overcast with hardly a glimpse of the sun in the previous ten days. . . . We shall be

* Jonathan O'Grady, born 12 December 1973 whose mother Judy is the daughter of H.W.T.'s niece Joan Mullins. Adeline spent three months looking after the little boy at his home in Ireland while his parents were abroad.

here for a few days before going on north. The engine started playing up yesterday and although Paul Reinsch knows his way around the engine he has not yet found the trouble. There are no doubt diesel experts here, so we shall consult them. . . . On the whole it seems colder than Greenland, unless it is that I am getting old. . . . We have the cabin heater going, and it works well. Of course it's a lot farther north than we have been in Greenland. We are in Lat. 78 now and hope to get up to 80 before we're finished.

Spitzbergen is an archipelago with the Norwegian name of Svalbard. The largest island, containing the capital Longyearben and some coal mines (two of them leased by the Russians), is West Spitzbergen. It is divided from another island, called North East Land, by the Hinlopen Strait. It was West Spitzbergen (commonly called simply Spitzbergen) that Tilman planned to circumnavigate. On 11 July he wrote to his sister again from Longyearben:

We have delayed sailing until today as a boat with mail came in yesterday and there may be some letters for us. The PO is about a mile from the beach, and two of them have gone there now (10 a.m.) to see. . . . Paul spent three whole days on the engine. A local diesel expert also spent a day on it (at a terrible price) and produced no answer. However, Paul eventually traced the trouble, or thinks he has, and it is running well. Whether this is a permanent cure we shall see and will make our plans accordingly. . . . We got enough stores from the coal company to see us through the voyage. Bread is a problem. What we get here will probably keep only for two or three weeks. They have no black bread (rye) which we could get in Greenland, and which lasts more or less indefinitely. I'm toying with the idea of calling at one of the Russian-owned mines, as I'm pretty sure that they would use black bread. Failing that we shall have to make soda bread. We have enough flour but it takes a long time on the Primus and uses a lot of paraffin.
(Later) Waiting was rewarded with your letter of 2 July.

Sailing northwards, he called at another settlement at Ny-Alesund, and wrote from there on 16 July:

This place is about 60 m. up the coast from Longyearben. There is a weather station. There used to be a coal mine, but that has been abandoned after an explosion. Consequently it's quite a place, with a number of buildings, about 30 Norwegians, and at the moment members of a French expedition and a large Cambridge geological expedition. A ship calls once a week, so we can post letters.

We got no change, or rather black bread, from the Russians when we anchored there a few days ago. The night we arrived they showed great interest, and a number were on the beach taking photographs. I got a promise of ten loaves of *schwarzbrod* for next morning (morgen fruh) from a chap who spoke German. But I think some political commissar must have reproved them for fraternising, because next morning we were left severely alone, and after waiting a couple of hours for something to happen we gave up and pushed off.

The Norwegian in charge here says he was Commandant at Jan Mayen in '68 when we lost *Mischief*. He knew me, but I completely failed to recognise him. The bread situation is partly solved as we got ten boxes of Lifeboat biscuits off the Cambridge party in exchange for a bag of flour, dried egg, and spuds. We got 24 loaves of ordinary bread baked at Longyearben, which will probably go mouldy long before we have eaten it.

Paul and Alan have gone off for the day on a long ridge climb. I climbed a 2,000-ft hill close by, two hours up and one hour down, mostly on snow. I had no axe but used a stout pole instead. The two days we have been here have been wonderfully fine and warm. I did my climb in shirtsleeves. . . . We have just filled up with water and oil, and will push on tomorrow.

On 26 July he wrote what was probably his last letter to his sister. Chatty and matter-of-fact as always, it was to bring to an end a correspondence that began in his schooldays, seventy years before. It is written from Magdalena fjord, near the north-west tip of Spitzbergen:

The number of cruise ships in these parts is astonishing. This fjord is supposed to be one of the Spitzbergen beauty spots. A French ship came in the day we arrived and disgorged a number of tourists to walk about the beach. A party of Swiss climbers camped here told us that another ship which was to pick them up was expected today, so I'm writing this on the chance that we may get it away by this means. . . . We were to have left today, but it has been thick weather, mist and rain, so we have stayed put. . . . When we leave here we shall be homeward bound—there is nothing much in the way of mountains on the north and east coasts, and I fear we have been here long enough. It's an interesting place, but not equal to Greenland. The crew are all well. . . . We have not started on Mrs Jones's cake yet—are reserving this until we reach our farthest north, where I hope we shall be in the next few days.

He signed his letter as always, "Best love, Bill".

They reached their farthest north—80°.04′N—on 28 July. They were about 60 miles off the north coast of Spitzbergen and Tilman reckoned that he could probably have reached 81°N before being stopped by ice, but since he was not attempting any record he turned east to round the point of Verlegenhuken at the entrance to the Hinlopen Strait. The wind forced them south of east and he made the land still west and about ten miles south of the point. They had to beat to round it and stood into the entrance of Hinlopen Strait on 29 July. The wind was now in their favour, but as soon as they rounded the point they met ice. The floes at first were fairly scattered, but the ice ahead looked ominous. They found a secure anchorage on the west (Spitzbergen) side of the strait.

Hinlopen Strait is a fearsome place and many ships attempting it have been forced back by ice. The strait begins by running roughly north to south, but as it goes on it widens and trends easterly. On 30 July the wind went round to the south. There was too much ice about for beating in the narrow strait, so Tilman stayed at anchor in the hope either of a northerly wind, or no wind at all for *Baroque* to proceed under power. On 31 July the wind dropped.

He made good about 40 miles that day, using the engine, and anchored off the Foster Islands, a group of rocky islets towards the shore of North East Land. Next day brought a favourable northerly wind, and they reached Von Otter Island, near the southern end of the strait. No cruise ships—few ships of any sort—come to this desolate eastern end of the Spitzbergen archipelago. While anchored off Von Otter Island they saw a polar bear come down to the beach—the first polar bear Tilman had seen on all his northern voyaging. The bear took no notice of *Baroque*, jumped calmly into the sea and swam past her about thirty yards away. There was practically no darkness and on watch that night Alan Stockdale saw a female polar bear with two cubs.

There are two fairly large islands off Spitzbergen south of the Hinlopen Strait, Barents Island and Edge Island. Between Barents Island and "mainland" Spitzbergen there is a narrow sound, but a fierce tide running up to eight knots hurls ice through it and it was far too dangerous to attempt in *Baroque*. Between Barents Island and Edge Island the sound—Freemansund—is somewhat more navigable, but it is rocky and far from attractive to a navigator. Tilman had to decide whether to attempt Freemansund or to sail east to go outside Edge Island altogether. The prudent course was to make for the open sea, which was what he decided to do, but they were stopped by a barrier of pack ice. Unless they turned back and abandoned the circumnavigation of Spitzbergen they had no choice but to go through Freemansund.

It was difficult but not foolhardy navigation, for both the Admiralty chart and a Norwegian chart that Tilman had on board showed a line of soundings with a least depth of 6 fathoms near the eastern entrance, increasing to 24 fathoms at the western end. The difficulties were the scattered rocky islets, and the currents round them. Tilman was at the helm, proceeding cautiously under power when the tide carried *Baroque* between two islets, about a mile apart. There was an invisible shoal between them, and she ran aground.

It was four o'clock in the morning, but daylight. In *Triumph and Tribulation* Tilman described what happened:

If the crew thought the old man had taken leave of his senses, as they must have done, they studiously refrained from comment. As soon as the tide slackened a bit we ran out a kedge astern bringing the warp forward to the winch. The engine as we knew had no power astern and the winch alone failed to budge her. Circumstances had combined to make things as difficult as they could be. Although the ebb had been running for an hour or more we must have gone on at or near the highest level of water; it was three days after full moon so that the tides were taking off. The difference between high and low water proved to be only about 2 feet which in one way was a good thing because the boat remained more or less upright. What happens, I think, is that when the ebb starts running west the water piles up in the narrow 22-mile-long strait, and thus continues to rise, or at any rate maintains its level at the eastern end when it should be falling. Something similar occurs at the eastern end of the Magellan strait where the water is pent up in the First and Second Narrows, with the result that the west-going and east-going streams continue running in the channel for three hours after high and low water by the shore. There, too, as we found in Freemansund, the duration of slack water is barely noticeable.

There was nothing for it but to throw out ballast. When *Mischief* had run aground off Patagonia the crew laboriously ferried ashore the pigs of iron ballast, so that it could be put back when she floated. With *Baroque* that was not possible. She was about half a mile from the nearest islet, and in the tide, with no appreciable slack water, it would have been dangerous and time-wasting to try to row a dinghy heavily laden with bars of pig iron. The ballast had to go over the side. The sea stayed calm, so *Baroque* was not in danger of doing herself further injury by pounding, but when the west-going stream started it brought in quantities of ice. Really big floes drawing more than six or seven feet grounded on the shoal, but smaller ones—which might weigh half a ton or more—were hurled in at a rate of several knots. They were too heavy and going too fast to be fended off. Twice *Baroque's* rudder shuddered as a floe struck it. And there was not much respite when the tide turned, for the floes that had gone past one way simply came back the other.

All the ballast, and all the fresh water except for a small emergency supply, had to go, and so did a spare mainsail.

"The crew worked like heroes, Paul groping away in the bilge prizing out the slimy chunks of pig-iron—some weighing 80 to 90 lbs— from the filthy bed where for years they had lain undisturbed. In no time all were coated in black oily sludge," wrote Tilman in his book. As *Baroque* lightened she began to float a little and all effort was now directed to trying to pull her head round so that the engine, which had no power in reverse, could help to push her off. Andrew Craig-Bennett took the big Fisherman anchor, weighing about one hundredweight, in the dinghy and dropped it where pulling on the cable could exert a turning movement on the bow. Tilman's account continues:

In the course of the night by heaving away on the firmly embedded big anchor, little by little we brought her head round until at last she pointed in the right direction. The westerly wind still blew vigorously out of the strait. It seemed to be an almost permanent local feature, and later when we were trying to make headway through the strait we had good reason to curse it. As they say in Africa, cross the river before you start reviling the crocodile's mother, and at this juncture, twenty-four hours after the first stranding, we wanted a west wind, the more the better. So with the whole mainsail and staysail set and drawing, the flood tide making, the engine flat out, the kedge warp quivering under the strain of the winch, and a subdued cheer from the crew, she began to move.

The big Fisherman anchor was cut loose and abandoned—they were not going to risk going aground again in trying to recover it. A moment later, however, they were aground again, trapped against a big ice-floe on the edge of the shoal. They had one spare kedge on board, a little anchor of only 25 lbs. Small as it was this little anchor gripped well enough to take the strain of the winch, and once more wind, sails, engine and tide helped to get her off. Again the anchor was abandoned leaving only the 60-lb plough-type anchor which was normally used.

Baroque was afloat and under command, but they were not out of danger. They had thrown overboard three tons of ballast and almost all their drinking water. In that Arctic desert of East Spitzbergen there was nowhere they could put in for supplies or repairs. The shores of Freemansund, however, offered stones and an occasional stream, and they put into a small bay to see what they could find. There were stones in plenty in a variety of sizes, and a trickle of water which Tilman decided could be dammed to provide what they needed. But they were anchored 400 yards off shore, and soundings taken from the dinghy showed that the water shoaled almost from where they were, and that they could not move in closer. So they tackled the back-breaking job of ferrying stones and water there and then.

They had two dinghies: the normal pram carried on deck and an inflatable rubber dinghy. Using both they toiled for a day and got the job about half done. Tilman finished the story in his book:

For most of the next day the wind proved too strong for the tide and it was not until after supper that ferrying began again. By midnight,

329

when only one load of stones and two of water were needed to complete the job, a brief puff of wind discouraged the crew. I was set on getting away on the morning tide, and the crew, seeing my disappointment, fell to work again. By 2 a.m. we were getting the dinghies on board for the last time. Ever since the stranding they had cheerfully given all they had in back-breaking wet and grimy toil to retrieve a bad situation.

On 10 August they were through Freemansund, the westerly wind at last relenting a little, as if it acknowledged defeat by this indomitable ship's company. They made straight for the North Atlantic and home, deciding to avoid the North Sea by going round the British Isles west about. Their bread was finished, and they made do with Lifeboat biscuit. Neither the 76-year-old skipper nor anyone else in *Baroque*'s company seems to have contemplated making for the nearest port in Norway. At one time they thought of calling at the Faeroes, but when they got there the wind was fair for Scotland, so they carried on to Stornoway which they entered on the night of 6 September.

On Saturday, 7 September, Tilman telephoned Adeline at Bod Owen from Stornoway to report their safe arrival. Her own news (or what she chose to tell him on the telephone) gave no cause for concern, and he sailed on for Lymington. Adeline died at home the day after he had telephoned. In keeping with her life of devotion to others she slipped away with the minimum of trouble for anyone else. Dressed to go to church that Sunday she sat down in a chair for a moment before leaving home, and died.

Her daughter and son-in-law, Pam and Brigadier Derek Davis, did everything they could to get the news of Adeline's death to Tilman at sea. He carried no radio transmitter so it was not possible to call *Baroque* directly, but they hoped that other shipping might be able to contact her, and they tried to get in touch with him through the coastguard service. They failed, and Tilman knew nothing of his bereavement until he reached Lymington on 24 September, when a friend met *Baroque* to tell him.

In a letter to me on 2 October Tilman wrote, "I feel I have lost my sheet anchor."

XVI

Climber and Sailor

ADELINE INDEED WAS Tilman's anchor for over forty years, but he had lost anchors in dangerous seas off Spitzbergen without losing control of his ship, and grievous as the loss of his beloved sister was he did not let it change his life. He continued exactly as before, spending the winter at Bod Owen, planning a voyage to high latitudes for the following summer. In the intervals of planning his next voyage he had much to do—writing a book about the last adventure, taking the dogs that had always been part of the family at Bod Owen for long walks, working in the garden. He had many friends round Barmouth and he saw them regularly. The Rev. Wynn Rhys, an old friend, had retired and come to live near Barmouth and he called at least once a week. On Sundays there was church—Tilman did not parade his religion but he remained faithful all his life to the Anglican creed in which he was brought up and when he was at home he never missed a Sunday service unless he was ill. Adeline's death brought one change in his preparations for sailing to the Arctic—he had to arrange for the dogs to go into kennels. It made them all the happier to greet him when he got back. When he was away his niece Pam kept an eye on Bod Owen, and when he went to Lymington to visit *Baroque*, or to London, he would stay with Pam and her family in Hampshire on the way.

He was never lonely because he had always been self-sufficient, more than capable of looking after himself, of cooking, baking bread, and brewing his own beer. A typed recipe for what he called "Bod Owen Beer" is among his papers. It runs:

4 gals water
2 lbs Golden Syrup
1 lb brown sugar
3 ozs dried hops
4 lbs Malt Extract
4 ozs dried yeast

331

Put half the hops into each of two muslin bags. Bring water to boil and while it is heating add sugar and syrup and one bag of hops. Allow to simmer for 20 minutes then add the rest of the hops. Boil gently another 20 minutes.

Remove hops, squeezing through colander, and throw away. While liquid is still hot stir in Malt extract having first warmed it. Cool to blood heat or less. Take out a jugful, dissolve yeast in this, and return to main container. Cover and leave to work.

If you cannot boil all 4 gals. use the largest container available for the boiling process and transfer the concentrate to the fermenting vessel which may be of earthenware or glass, and make up to the full quantity with cold tap water.

After two days remove crust and scum and give a stir. After two more days skim again. In 4 to 6 days, depending on the temperature, the working will finish and it is ready for bottling. It will be fairly clear but it helps to stir in finings (islinglass, white of egg) on the third or fourth day.

Use screw top bottles. Prime each with $\frac{1}{2}$ teaspoonful of sugar. Syphon off beer carefully into bottles leaving about $1\frac{1}{2}''$ air space under screw top. Screw top on tightly and give a good shake to help dissolve sugar. Allow to stand for a week or longer. The yeast forms a deposit at the bottom of the bottle so on opening pour into a large jug and continue until dregs start to come over.

In the winter of 1974 his thoughts turned again to the north-west coast of Greenland for the summer of 1975, and he had the nucleus of a crew in John Shipton, son of his old friend who had written to ask if John could accompany him on a voyage. He recruited the rest of the crew in his customary fashion, which he called "leaving things to time and chance". In fact he tried not to leave too much to chance by recruiting friends, or those recommended by friends, but he was usually compelled to rely on chance in the end because at the last moment people often found that they could not come. At 77, with a boat turned 73, he still had no difficulty in getting volunteers to sail with him to the Arctic.

Baroque needed some attention. She had to be re-ballasted, and her rudder required a new heel-fitting. The Spitzbergen stones which had ballasted her on the voyage home were left on the quay at Lymington, whence they soon disappeared among souvenir hunters or cultivators of rock gardens. There must be several rockeries in Hampshire with stones from beyond the Arctic Circle. One stone was taken by the Lymington Town Sailing Club, fitted with an inscribed brass plate, and presented to Tilman. "Weighing some 30 lbs it is on the heavy side for a paperweight but it makes an admirable door-stop," he observed.

The voyage went well, though there was the usual trouble with ice off south-west Greenland. Tilman stood watches as usual, enjoyed the cook's duff, and thought nothing of climbing the rigging to the cross-trees to inspect ice. After calling at Godthaab he went on north, but in a squall off Disco Island *Baroque*'s mainsail-boom was broken. That prevented any attempt to go farther north, but he sailed home successfully with the mainsail set loose-footed, getting back to Lymington in September.

Still he would not give up. He had tried and failed to reach Ellesmere Island to the north of Baffin Bay, and in 1976 he tried again. This was a miserable voyage. *Baroque* suffered some damage in heavy weather in the North Atlantic, and although he himself felt happy enough about rounding Cape Farewell to continue north off west Greenland, a majority of his crew insisted that they should make for Reykjavik for repairs. There one of his crew left, but he found a replacement. He now abandoned hopes of reaching Ellesmere Island and decided to make another trip to east Greenland and Angmagssalik instead. He got through the ice to Angmagssalik successfully, but met disaster coming away. In steering to avoid an ice-floe he ran aground. They were near the entrance to the harbour, off an oil installation, and as *Baroque* was not damaged, it was simply a matter of waiting for the tide to float her off. But on a falling tide she would go over on her side, and to prevent this Tilman ran a warp from her mast to a bollard on the shore. That should have been all right, but the warp he used was nylon, so that instead of keeping her upright it stretched as she went over, and she fell on her side. As the tide came back she was flooded.

The oil company ran a power-line to her and supplied an electric pump, which enabled her to float, but everything was in an appalling mess, and the engine, having been submerged, needed an overhaul. Two of his crew lost heart and left Angmagssalik on a steamer. The other two stood by him, and when *Baroque* was fit to go helped him to sail her back to Iceland. There he recruited two more volunteers for the passage to England, but on leaving they met heavy weather and the head of the staysail blew out. This did not particularly worry Tilman who was concerned simply to mend it, but the crew wanted to put back to Iceland. Even one member of the original crew who had stood by Tilman staunchly through all their previous troubles now felt that they ought to put back—he explained later that this was out of concern for Tilman, who, after the strain of the voyage, seemed far from well. Back in Reykjavik this man agreed to stay, and Tilman once more set about finding volunteers to make up a crew. Unable to do so, *Baroque* had to be laid up at a yard in Iceland.

Was it time to call it a day? He didn't want to, but he was beginning to fear that he might have to, and he considered selling *Baroque*, though he had no intention of leaving her in Iceland and was determined to bring her home. Increasing deafness was tiresome, but there were still plenty of interests in life. On 15 February 1977 he wrote to Miss Mabel Pugh, who had sent him a card for his 79th birthday, "You must have a computer memory to remember these obscure anniversaries." She had worked for Barclay's Bank in Liverpool where he kept his account, and had asked for his autograph when he called at the bank after leading the Everest expedition in 1938. He gave it at once, and later he used to send her postcards and letters from his various expeditions. So much for the alleged misogyny in practice. Like other women whom he actually met, Miss Pugh found him the soul of courtesy and consideration over nearly half a century.

Letters from friends were always important to him, and they became increasingly so after Adeline's death. There was the crossword puzzle in *The Times*. Then there was the Three Peaks Race. This is an arduous yacht race from Barmouth to Fort William during which two members from the crew of each competing boat must climb Snowdon, Scafell and Ben Nevis, the highest peaks in Wales, England and Scotland. The origin of the race is described in a letter from Dr Robert Haworth, of Barmouth:

The Barmouth to Fort William Three Peaks Race was started in 1977 by a group of people in this area who formed a completely autonomous committee. H. W. Tilman was involved from the beginning, his enthusiasm for the idea of the race as well as his advice in planning were a great help. The Merioneth Yacht Club has representatives on the race committee and have helped, but they do

334

not control the race. In the Spring of 1977 a small technical committee met several times to draw up the rules of the race. HWT was fully involved at all these meetings, giving us the benefit of his enormous experience. Competitors get little help during the race, they cannot use mechanical means of transport—in fact, the Spartan attitude of HWT is very much reflected in the rules.

The first race sailed from Barmouth on 25 June 1977 and the boats came into Barmouth on or before 24 June so that the crews could meet. The main attraction for many of the crews was to meet HWT—he spent hours on the Friday and Saturday mornings talking to them. After going out to the start of the race HWT came ashore again at Barmouth, then left for Fort William to see the finish. The race was tough, only four boats finished, though some which dropped out motored to Fort William for the celebrations.

In 1978 the committee presented the H. W. Tilman Trophy for the boat which gave the best account of the race based on the ship's log. We felt that this combined sailing, mountaineering *and* writing, so that the trophy was worthy of his name.*

There were also the lifeboats. Tilman was president of the Barmouth branch of the Royal National Lifeboat Institution, and the "Lifeboat Suppers" he gave annually were memorable. These were hot-pot suppers for the lifeboat crews, for which he provided both the food and the drink, joining afterwards in the singing that was always a feature of the occasion.

He was saddened by the departure of old friends. In a letter he wrote to the author on 1 May 1977 he observed, "I am paying the penalty of living too long with the loss of contemporaries and friends. Eric Shipton died recently of cancer, and I did not even know he was ill." He could not really blame himself for not having known about Shipton, for his illness was brief. In spite of their close relationship they did not correspond much, and the letter from Shipton in 1975 asking if his son John could crew on *Baroque* was the first that Tilman had heard of him for some time. Theirs was a deep but not outwardly expressive friendship—it had no need to be.

* The first H. W. Tilman Trophy was won, appropriately, by *Cannonade*, entered by 103 Air Defence Regiment, Royal Artillery.

To bring *Baroque* home, Tilman arranged for a crew including Frank George, a friend from the Royal Institute of Navigation, to fly out to Iceland, and arrived at Reykjavik himself on 17 May 1977. *Baroque* had to be rigged, and food and stores bought. There was much to do. Extracts from his diary record:

21 May. Finished aloft. Self did most. Safety harness when sitting on cross trees. Got bowsprit on with a struggle. Had generator on most of the day but not enough battery to start.

22 May. Engine going and charging. Rain in night and drips. Porridge boiled over. Started bending mainsail but too much wind to finish. SE gale. The weather has been consistently foul.

23 May. Buying food, etc. Up to £56 at the supermarket.

24 May. Cooked breakfast. F volunteered to wash up. A fine day for a change.

25 May. Bad weather report. High bringing easterlies Force 5–6. Went to the Met. Office and got charts. Went to the supermarket for meat and butter. Go, or stay? Finally decided to go, and sailed 3 pm.

It was a wet trip home. They called at Holyhead on 9 June and reached Lymington on 14 June. He was at Bod Owen in good time for the start of the Three Peaks Race.

* * *

It would have been tidier to attempt an assessment of Tilman as a climber after the last of his great land journeys, but it would have been out of focus, for he himself did not fit tidily into any pattern. Although the sea came to fill a large part of his life he never ceased to climb, going up mountains in the Arctic into his late seventies. He might dismiss them as a "mere" 2–3,000 feet, but these were climbs from sea-level and would have seemed formidable to many other men. In him climbing and seafaring went together, the one, in origin, at any rate, being an extension of the other. I have therefore left an assessment of him both as climber and sailor to this chapter. Peter Lloyd, president of the Alpine Club, who climbed with Tilman on Nanda Devi, on Everest in 1938, and explored with him in Nepal, writes:

On the way through Sikkim in 1938 we were entertained at a formal dinner by the Maharajah of Gantok. Bill made a short speech, the keynote of which was a quotation from Thoreau's *Walden* in praise of the simple life. In retrospect this was significant, for simplicity was the characteristic of most if not all his journeys. The equipment for his Himalayan travels was essentially boots, ice-axe, rope, tent, sleeping bag, Primus stove. Such devices as wireless sets, crampons, oxygen equipment he preferred to dispense with. As a concession to the age he lived in he had a camera, but, in my experience, rarely used it.*

The essence of Himalayan travel is logistics, and recollections of expeditions tend to centre on camp life, transport and provisioning problems, food. In this field Bill had a style of his own. He got a reputation for austerity and under-provisioning but in the main this followed from the quest for mobility and economy. (Apart from Everest all his other journeys were privately financed.) He would rather dine off eggs and potatoes bought at the last village than off a hamper of delicacies from Fortnums. He took great pride in the tinned farmhouse cheddar cheese which he always brought out from England. He learned to bake and in Nepal in 1949 took great delight in baking a cake or a loaf in an improvised oven, using the dried yeast which was a key item in his provision list. Another key item was a bag of chillies, invaluable for making dull food more palatable.†

As a companion Bill was taciturn, but never, save when ill, grumpy. In spite of the eventful life he had led he seldom talked of past achievements or experiences. (It is a curious thing that in this respect Eric Shipton, with whom Bill is often bracketed, was so totally different: he could hardly have been more talkative.) But he was neither silent nor inarticulate and had both a splendid sardonic humour and a capacity for puncturing an overstated argument with devastating common sense. Nor was he a solitary person; he was always ready to pass the time with a game of chess or picquet.

As a climber he was competent rather than spectacular, and the qualities I associate with him are determination, endurance, and dependability. But above all he had the feeling that in the mountains he was at home, that while others were visitors he belonged there, knowing how to adjust, how to live in comfort in a hard environment. His most remarkable quality, without doubt, was his natural authority. This

* In fact Tilman took a large number of photographs, primarily to illustrate his writings. But he used a camera as a duty rather than a pleasure.

† On his voyages he insisted that every galley should be equipped with Tabasco sauce.

came out most emphatically on the Nanda Devi expedition of 1936. We started off as a group of climbers, four British and four American, including some who were more experienced and others more technically qualified, and without formal leadership. At the outset, on the approach march, Bill was the inevitable organiser because he alone knew the country and spoke the lingo.* But though on the mountain these qualities were no longer relevant we quickly realised the need for a recognised leader, and the inevitability of selecting Bill for this role. It all came about perfectly naturally and painlessly.

Bill's conduct of the 1938 Everest expedition (about half the size of previous ones!) was in my view exemplary. It is true that we achieved no records, but we were halted by objective difficulties to which there was no answer. His greatest achievements as a mountaineer, however, were the exploration (1934) and the ascent (1936) of Nanda Devi.

His return to Everest with the Houston party of 1950 had an element of sadness in it for two reasons, first because it was the end of his time in the big mountains, secondly because he made the mistake of reporting too gloomily on the prospect of access to the South Col up the Khumbu icefall, which now seems to be followed twice a year. But he was right to draw back, for this was perhaps the beginning of the more organised and mechanised climbing of a later generation. His era was over. And who would have thought that he would rebound from this setback to enjoy another quarter century of adventurous travel in a style of his own invention?

This is an able firsthand account of Tilman as a climber or mountaineer in the accepted sense of the word. But he was much more than climber or mountaineer; he was a combination of mountaineer, explorer and traveller in the classical sense of one who travels as an aim in itself to learn about the rest of the world. Herodotus was the archetype of such travellers, and Tilman had something in common with him—insatiable curiosity. And it was his mountain explorations with Shipton in the Karakoram and his crossing of the Patagonian ice-cap that were unique. The great expeditions to the North and South Poles that dominated exploration in the first decade of the century were more protracted efforts at human survival, but they were of a different order;

* He had taken pains to learn some Urdu and Hindi on his expeditions with Shipton.

they were mounted with greater resources, involved larger parties, and did not require particular climbing skills. Shipton and Tilman, and later Tilman alone, showed that you can go to the ends of the earth by putting on a pair of boots and going. In their earlier partnership Shipton, although ten years younger, was by far the more experienced mountaineer, and Tilman readily accepted his leadership. Later Shipton came to rely on Tilman in a relationship based on mutual respect and understanding.

Tilman's mountain navigation was uncanny; he seemed to know by instinct whether a route would "go" (and where it went). Francis Chichester, another great navigator, once described navigation in conversation with the author as "the summing up of everything". The navigator is constantly having to make judgments, to allow for this, to take account of that, to assess the probable behaviour of wind and weather (in mountains the probable condition of ice and snow as well) over the next few hours or days. Tilman had this quality of judgment. In the regions of his great land journeys maps were sparse and often wrong; a pass might or might not be in the expected place, it might or might not lead to the right valley. When Tilman chanced his arm in deciding whether to continue or abandon some particular route he was usually right. He was a "lucky" navigator, but it was not really luck; his navigational skill was based on the rare quality of applied common sense joined with self-discipline, scrupulous recording of time and estimated distance, and the ability "to sum up everything". He never acted on wishful thinking, never assumed that he was in a particular place because that was where he *hoped* he was. He sought facts, collected as many as he could, added and subtracted, and acted on the outcome of his practical arithmetic.

The self-discipline, mental control and ability to assess a situation that made him a great explorer were equally displayed in war. He understood guerilla warfare in the mountains of Albania and northern Italy because instinctively he sought the facts about it in order to act as effectively as possible without illusions. He *knew* that for all their courage, the Italian band with whom he fought in 1944 were allowing themselves to be caught in a trap on Le Vette. But he was a British liaison officer, not their commander, and when they decided to stand and fight he stayed with them, knowing that this would mean disaster. That it was less of a disaster than it might have been was due in considerable part to his understanding of mountains and his correct

339

assessment of what the Germans would do after the engagement. Tilman the traveller and explorer was Tilman the soldier in different clothes. His qualities in war and in travel were the same blend of determination, self-control and common sense.

Physically, mentally and morally he had great strengths, but he also had some weaknesses, perhaps best described as "political" in the widest dictionary meaning of politics as "the science or art of government". He detested administration in the Army, and held that an expedition which cannot be planned on a half-sheet of notepaper is scarcely worth going on. This reflects an admirable self-reliance but it also betrays a certain lack of concern for the organisational problems of others. He needed so little himself that it seems not to have occurred to him that what he dismissed as unimportant might be felt as essential by someone else. Both by training and by instinct he had genuine sympathy for the human needs of those he commanded in the Army and he had a compassionate understanding of the difficulties of those with whom he fought in Albania and Italy, and of peasants in Africa and Asia whom he met on his travels. He never knew poverty himself, but his sympathy for the poor was real. He had no use for Communism as a political creed but he respected the courage of those who risked their lives for it during the war and he understood their desire to liquidate their oppressors. But he was better at dealing with peasants and soldiers than with volunteer companions. If they were content wholly to accept him on his own austere terms he was a magnificent leader; if they had doubts or grievances that needed putting right he was inclined to feel hard done by. Perhaps for all the power of his mind he lacked imagination; it may be significant that in his voluminous writings he seems never to have attempted fiction.

None of this detracts from his personal achievement. His record as traveller and explorer on land and sea is so extraordinary that it can scarcely be overstated. By his time there was little of the earth's surface left to be discovered; had there been he would surely have discovered it. Compared with the acclaim of getting to the Poles, his crossings of Bylot Island and of the Patagonian ice-cap seem small beer, and he himself did nothing to attract publicity save for his ascent of Nanda Devi, which made news in 1936 for the fortuitous reason that it was the highest mountain then to have been climbed. But Nanda Devi was only one incident in his career. The problem in trying to assess his performance is that it was so diverse. The world likes its Einsteins to be mathematicians, its Shackletons to be identified with the Antarctic, its Livingstones with Africa. Tilman travelled and explored wherever he could, from the Congo forest and the fever-ridden marches of Assam to the high slopes of the Himalaya, from China to Chitral, from Baffin Bay to Patagonia. There is a case for regarding him as the greatest *individual* explorer of the twentieth century.

For the following distinctive assessment of Tilman as a seaman I am indebted to Colin Putt, who knew him at sea as well as anyone, having sailed with him on *Patanela* and *Sea Breeze*, and gave him much help in fitting out for several voyages. Colin Putt wrote from Australia:

I first met Bill Tilman in the flesh when he came to Australia to take command of *Patanela* for the Heard Island voyage. In a way I felt I'd known him for years even at that stage, from his mountaineering writings. His approach to mountain exploration had seemed to us singularly appropriate to our own case; when I started climbing in New Zealand a lot of the high country was still unmapped and unexplored; we used to go into new country for several weeks at a time and make maps of what we found there, and because we were so thoroughly isolated from any effective help or rescue we found much more virtue in steadiness, hardiness and sound judgment than in any technical brilliance. To us the idea of mountaineering from hotels, with the aid of guides and even porters, was incredible, and of mountaineering authors who wrote up to the end of the thirties only Tilman and Shipton seemed to us to make sense: particularly Tilman— his Spartan ways, such as taking only one shirt for a six months' expedition, showed us that he was a sound bloke who knew what makes a pack too heavy to carry in safety.

Tilman held strong, and nowadays unconventional views about getting into trouble at sea, being rescued, and the responsibilities involved. Nobody has any right to expect to be rescued if he gets into trouble, and trouble becomes mentionable only after you have fought your way out of it. He went to sea with an appreciation and an acceptance of any risks involved, and expected his crews to do the same. He didn't carry a radio transmitter, and the ship's boat was suitable only for expeditions ashore in a calm harbour; he put a tremendous amount of thought, money and effort into what he considered the most

341

effective means of safety at sea, the preparation of the ship herself and of the navigational information for the voyage.

In *Patanela* in the Roaring Forties, the dinner-table conversation once turned to the fact that Phil Temple couldn't swim. Some seemed to see this as a distinct disadvantage at sea, but the Skipper said to him, "You're lucky, you'll have an easier time than the rest of us would, if you go overboard." It brought home to all of us the fact that in a place like the Southern Ocean, things like a raft, a lifejacket, or the ability to swim will only prolong the agony. Rescue by others was seen as yet another false hope, in the same class as these.

I consider Bill Tilman to be the most highly intelligent man I've ever known. The true depth and breadth of his understanding of things like navigation were astounding, but of course he never made any sort of show of this. . . . In making a decision, on a matter of navigation or a matter of life and death, he would take all the time available to consider the facts and reach his conclusion. Again and again he would come up with the best possible decision at the last possible moment, clearly and concisely announced. This required of his crews real faith in him and in his judgment. . . . In an increasing wind and sea, he would stand on deck for hours at times, watching the ship's reactions, and ready to act quickly if necessary to make and implement his decision on what to do at the change of watch, when there was a double watch available to do the job. Going into close and heavy pack ice, with no immediate threat of the ice closing up, he would advance to the very last place where the ship could be turned round at all before deciding to turn and come out. This business of taking as long and going as far as is safe, even when success appears unlikely, is a piece of mountaineering wisdom too; it is the way to get your peak when conditions are adverse. It is also a military virtue—"time spent in reconnaissance is seldom wasted".

I think his main motivation in forever going to new and remote places and doing new and difficult things had little to do with being first. He had a genuine love of new sights, new experience and new knowledge of any kind. It seemed to give him as much delight to discover an unlikely ledge above the glacier, supporting a profusion of wild flowers, as to reach the summit of a peak. Sea birds and sea creatures that were encountered were always a matter of great interest, and he spent much time and effort, on the voyage and after it, identifying them. The most commonplace voyage was always much better if

342

made with some new variation to visit some previously unvisited place on the way.

He would learn any skill for which he had a real need. Thus, he became very good at splicing wire rope rigging, and when *Mischief*'s deck required completely relaying he learned enough of shipwright's work to do a sound job himself. When modern yacht chandlers degenerated to offering blocks in stainless steel and nylon, hopelessly unsuited for use in a Bristol Channel Pilot Cutter, he set about making his own from beech wood and galvanised iron sheaves, and made a nice job of them too.

To understand Tilman's attitude to his ships, crews and voyages, it would help if we understood just what he was trying to achieve. This was in fact exactly the same thing as in his earlier travels ashore; he was after the greatest possible size and quality of new and difficult things actually done, using the slenderest resources. . . . He had a much clearer insight than anybody else into the need to recognise the tools with which he did a job as the tools only, not the main object of the exercise. A ship, particularly, although only a tool for use in voyaging, can so easily become the object of so much effort and attention that the original purpose suffers or even gets lost; once his ships were up to the requisite standard of seaworthiness Tilman quietly, politely but firmly resisted all attempts to elaborate, improve, or further equip them. He knew that so far from helping with the main objective, these things would take up time, effort and attention which were needed for the main, simple job he had in hand. Similarly, in his own words, he "eschewed publicity". He asked his crews for no contribution beyond their part in working the ship, and in return he claimed the right to set the objectives for each voyage as well as to set the standards for victualling, accommodation, and safety. Simplicity in seafaring was his watchword, for these very good reasons. Where a system that he wanted to use was available, fully developed, and had already stood the tests of time and use, he would use it exactly as it stood, trying to avoid even minor alterations to it because he knew they were unnecessary and because he rightly feared the unconsidered consequences of such changes. The position-line method for navigation was such a system that he understood and used well.

He was a navigator rather than a pilot—it's hard to be a pilot when you are forever visiting places you have never seen before. Astronomical fixing of position was his speciality, and he would use this method for preference even when within sight of the shore and its landmarks, only stopping his sun and star observations when the land blotted out the necessary horizon. The tools he used were basically those of Cook, with minor adaptations to suit modern conditions. Sextant, chronometer and nautical almanac were what he relied on, but he did accept the innovations of the Air Navigation Tables, to ease the burden of manual calculations, and a radio receiver to correct his chronometer-watch. Through the Tables, of course, he used the position-line method of fixing position, and he had learned that in high latitudes, where decent sights of sun and stars can be rare, it pays to take a sight on anything in the sky that offers, at any time. Thus he did not really make a daily fix of his position in the formal way, but rather used any new position-line he could get, whenever he could get it, to update his position on the chart in a semi-continuous manner. Sights taken fleetingly through flying mist, from a small vessel in big seas, are not always highly accurate, and he had a rather mysterious way of assessing the probable accuracy of each observation, applying this to his determined position, and arriving at a sort of intuitive appreciation of the distribution of his possible and probable positions about the one actually marked on the chart. You could do this, if you were a good enough mathematician and programmer, with the aid of a respectable-sized computer, but the Skipper did it all in his head.

To him, the compass was a useful and nearly essential means for keeping the ship's head pointed the same way for the duration of the watch, and that was all. When he sailed to Pond Inlet, and the compass pointed substantially the wrong way, it didn't inconvenience him at all, so long as the thing was consistent in its lying.

He never had much luck with patent logs, at his ships' low speeds they were inaccurate, and on a long voyage the supply of spare rotors would be used up by the denizens of the deep before he had got far. After that, he would train the crew to judge the ship's speed, using a Dutchman's log,* and then have them estimate the speed and distance made good over each watch. He never even considered taking to sea such things as radio direction finding or other electronic navigational aids; he just didn't have a use for them.

Coming home from Greenland in the autumn of 1970, we struck some rough weather around Denmark Strait which broke the gaff and

* Throwing a chip overboard from the bow and timing how long it takes the ship (of known length) to pass it.

344

sprung a plank (both of which we repaired), and inundated and stopped the chronometer, which we could not get going again. Tilman continued to use his normal methods of navigation, but changed over from the now useless chronometer to a wrist watch, which was corrected as often as possible by radio time-signals. It was most interesting to note that at the same time and without fuss, he introduced a back-stop in the form of the pre-Cook navigation methods, as used for instance by Dampier. He set a course down the Atlantic to arrive well to the west of the Scillies, and began to take noon sights and Pole Star sights. In this way he placed us accurately on the latitude of the Bishop Rock and some 60 miles to the west of it . . . and then sailed due east, carefully checking and maintaining the latitude. The Bishop Rock light turned up in due course, in fog, right ahead and rather unpleasantly close, proving that the old method works perfectly (but has its limitations).

Homeward bound from Heard Island in March 1965, we ran into thick haze derived from bushfire smoke off the West Australian coast, and it was clear that identification of our landfall was going to be uncertain. Our last sight of land had been Heard Island, a fortnight before, and good sights had been few and far between in the interval while running down our easting. During the night before our expected landfall the wind died and we started motoring. I came on deck at daybreak next morning to find the ship motoring through thick smoky haze over a calm sea, with the Skipper in charge and keeping a sharp lookout. As the light grew, we realised that there was land close at hand on both sides, with a clear channel ahead. He had put us right in the middle of Vancouver Sound, the great fjord-like channel that leads in to Albany! This could have been just luck, but I saw him repeat the performance in 1970 in Davis Strait. We were in a storm in the Strait, then in fog and among ice as we closed the coast in the vicinity of our objective, Arsuk Fjord. Good sights had been sparse, and once in the ice we had even experimented with a home-made artificial horizon in an attempt to get a sight when we could just see the sun, but not a water horizon. Very late in the evening the fog began to clear a little and we could at last see the land; we were square in the middle of the broad entrance of Arsuk Fjord!

His bible in this regard was Lecky's *Practical Wrinkles in Navigation*, first published in the 1870s; he always carried a copy with him on voyages, and took any opportunity that offered to try out the methods described and recommended. In the later 1800s Lecky and others were trying to do what Tilman was trying to do in the late 1900s, to navigate accurately and safely using limited and simple equipment, supported by a lot of common sense and hard work. In his writing, Tilman dwelt on his rare mistakes in navigation almost to the exclusion of his habitual successes; here he gives a false picture of himself.

Tilman's three ships were all Bristol Channel Pilot Cutters, and the schooner *Patanela* which he skippered on one long voyage was of a similar type. They were working sailing vessels, not yachts, of fairly heavy displacement with long straight keels, big rudders, great depth and little freeboard, strongly constructed, and with a short broad gaff rig. None of these ships was fast, and this was a key factor in their ability to survive the worst of sea conditions. Waves generally don't hit ships; ships hit waves and thus damage or destroy themselves. Tilman would crack on as much sail as he possessed when conditions were favourable, but he was very careful never to abuse a ship by pushing her too hard. Modern yachting, and especially racing, consists very largely of pushing the ship at all times as hard as she will take, using efficient but unseamanlike devices such as spinnakers and huge head-sails to do so; Tilman's seamanship and the way in which he used it to nurse an old and shaky ship along are almost unimaginable to a modern yachtsman. As wind and sea increased, he was on the watch for the first tiny sign that the ship might be starting to labour, a distinct impact with a wave, water coming aboard hard, the deck starting to bury in the water regularly, or complaining sounds from the hull or rigging. His response to these warning signs was to reduce sail, just enough to ease the ship but not enough to stop her. If it looked as if really bad weather was on the way, he would include in the earlier stages of shortening sail the complete removal of sail from the bowsprit, so that nobody would have to go out on it in rough conditions. He was particularly careful not to drive a ship hard to windward, where damage is most easily done and the compensating benefit of distance gained is most hard to achieve. If headed by the wind in any but the finest weather he would prefer to heave to and wait for a shift of wind, avoiding a testing experience for ship and crew. He thus came to depend heavily on the now unfashionable ability of a ship to heave to; and the old long-keeled gaff-rigged boats were very good at this. Their huge lateral area underwater, when stalled as a hydrofoil, gave a very small rate of drift, so that he was in the place he started in when the shift of wind came. They were stable and could be left to their own devices when hove to, and their great displacement made them comfortable and sea-kindly as they lay, unlikely to throw a man overboard or damage themselves. When hove to in phosphorescent water I have watched the way in which the long keel, stalled in the water, sheds great eddies from alternate ends, and how these eddies, moving away to windward of the ship, trip up the waves as they rear up above her and bring them crashing down harmlessly a few feet from the weather rail.

Sometimes a sudden deterioration in conditions would catch the Skipper with some sail up that he wanted handed, but that there might be some danger in handling. He was perfectly clear on the right course of action here, which was to leave the sail to its fate. When we were hit by a sudden cold front and consequent storm while trying to land on Heard Island, we first hove to under the gaff foresail alone. After a few hours the wind suddenly shifted and increased further, towards force 12, "that force of wind no canvas can withstand". Some of us began to consider how to hand the sail before it blew out, but the Skipper stopped us firmly. "We may have lost that sail," he said, "but I don't want to lose any men with it."

The one disadvantage of all this heaving to in gaff-rigged vessels was that he broke a lot of spars. When a big sea had built up, and especially when the wind had started to moderate, the old gaff-rigged cutters, reefed down and hove to, would start to back-roll into the approaching seas, snatching and jerking at their booms and gaffs unmercifully. Kicking tackles reduced the movement a bit, but probably increased the stresses in the spars. On a number of occasions after a big blow, Tilman unrolled the reefs from the bottom of his mainsail to find the boom in two pieces, and at least once the gaff failed instead. I think he lost more spars this way than through unintentional gybes when running, which are the usual cause for worry with inexperienced crews.

If anybody ever knew how to deal with chafe in a sailing ship's gear on a long passage it was Tilman. His approach was simple, get rid of the contact at which chafe occurs if possible, otherwise use chafing gear. Nothing was allowed to touch his sails once they were set. Lee topping lifts and backstays were provided with hooks at the lower end, so that they were simply unhooked and triced back alongside the standing rigging. This meant that you had to set them up again before going

347

about but the old cutters were slow in stays and gave plenty of time for this. He worked away at the leads of halliards until they ran clear of all other items. This left only the sheets to chafe against main rigging or guard rails, and once set up these were armed with scotsmen cut from an old sail. He had little use for baggywrinkle and the like, preferring to keep his sails off the standing rigging altogether. To this end, he seldom let the main sheet out very far even when running, but often used to top the boom up instead so that the upper part of the mainsail would swing out wide. This avoided contact of the lower part of the sail with the stays and at the same time it kept the boom, which was very long, out of harm's way in a big sea. If a seam showed signs of chafe or weakening, let alone broken stitches, he would be on to it straight away with needle and palm, having learned that at sea a stitch in time saves 9 to the power of 9. *Sea Breeze* was still fitted with the old original deadeyes in her main rigging, and the Skipper went to a lot of trouble to get the right sort of tarred hemp rope and Stockholm tar and set up the lanyards in the correct manner. The result served very well too, while an intruder of a rigging-screw on the inner forestay came undone one dark night and caused no end of trouble.

When shortening or making sail at sea, Tilman would usually run the ship off before the wind with sheets hauled in, and would take the helm himself to minimise the chances of a gybe while the crew were working on the lower spars. This trick reduced the apparent wind and gave the vessel an easy, quiet motion while sails were being muzzled and reef pendants and points dealt with, a delightful contrast to the madly flapping canvas, screaming wind and sharp motion which are associated with shortening sail on the wind. The only time he ever let her gybe in the middle of this manoeuvre I was on the end of the bowsprit, and can say only that the resulting jolt was less serious than the sort of thing you can expect with every other wave if the ship is crashing into a head sea.

That was not the sort of thing you could do on a lee shore, of course, but Tilman agreed with Conrad—the true peace of God is found a thousand miles from shore. To him, the deep sea was a safe, restful and enjoyable place, only to be left with regret. Distant and poorly charted coasts were exciting, but the crowded waters and detailed protocol of home harbours made him more than a little uneasy. In such places you seem to be expected to manoeuvre your ship with a powerful engine and with skill acquired by going alongside a thousand docks; Tilman would arrive in Lymington at the end of a year's voyage, often with the engine out of action altogether, and at sea this had been of no account. He came perilously close to demolishing a number of rickety jetties in different harbours of the world as his ponderous ships failed to answer his command to stop at close quarters.

He placed great value on a really sharp lookout, to be maintained at all times by those on deck. Sailing as he did in the heavily frequented North Atlantic, and in waters where floating ice is common, he was quite right in this. The man on watch, or on anchor-watch, had to be on deck and able to see his sails and his horizon, he could only take such shelter as these requirements allowed. Self-steering gear seemed worse than useless to him, because with a crew of five or more steering the ship gave some necessary occupation, and because steering pins the man down to a job on deck, to the exclusion of sheltering elsewhere. Oil-lamps on a small vessel are not highly visible at sea, and once off soundings he would stop using his navigation lights, thus enabling the crew to see better, unaffected by odd patches of light in their foreground. The lights would be brought into use, and backed up with a powerful torch, if anything hove in sight. He had reason to know how poor is the design of oil lamps intended for use on deck at sea, especially those made for small craft, where the lampmaker seems to think that strength and reliability can be of no importance, and generally produces something rather like a toy lamp. He was always experimenting with different fuels, wicks, wind-baffles and so on in an attempt to extend the range of wind strengths in which a lamp would function. Some of these experiments were carried out at sea, and others, in winter, on the slopes of Cader Idris. At one stage he produced a stern-lantern which worked perfectly in strong winds, but would go out if confronted with a calm!

. . . [His books] are written in such low key, full of such understatements, that anybody who doesn't know the things about which he is writing, from personal experience, may easily think that nothing is happening at all. I remember talking about Tilman's books with a man who was an experienced mountaineer-expeditioner, but who at that time had never been to sea. He remarked that it was peculiar that while Tilman's mountaineering books were full of action and packed with interest, in his sailing books nothing ever seemed to happen. He had the ability to read between the one set of lines, but not the other. I think that this sort of thing applied not only to the Skipper's writing, but also to a lesser extent to his conversation. He had travelled as far and read as much as any man, and what's more he had understood what he had seen and read. He could and did contribute to any conversation with well informed views and comment, but if the other chap showed a lack of interest he would dry up, for he was a little shy, and wait for him to raise another subject. He found talking pleasant enough if it held some meaning, but not essential. His quiet sense of humour shows clearly in all his writings, but it may surprise some to hear that often on voyages, mealtimes and other foregatherings with the crew were occasions of almost continuously rollicking mirth. He had an endless fund of droll quotations and anecdotes to suit every occasion. He was a learned man, and would swap Latin puns and palindromes with those who were able.

As for his attitude towards women, he would talk with them, climb with them or sail with them, just like anybody else, if they were intelligent and sensible. He didn't always suffer fools gladly, regardless of their sex. He got on well with children, treating them gravely as people who, though small, were of some consequence. I particularly remember with gratitude how he looked after my own small deaf son at a picnic, where he had been unable to make proper contact with the other children, and how when the boy was bigger he lent him a dinghy to learn to row in.

In *Patanela* he was caught by a boarding sea and thrown heavily against the deckhouse, breaking some ribs. The expedition's surgeon strapped them up and this was the last we heard of it. Only now, as I write this with broken and strapped ribs, do I realise what pain and unease this injury involves, even in the sheltered world of home, car and office. In a small bucking ship the Skipper carried on his navigation and watchkeeping duties as if nothing had happened to him, and I think that, by his standards, nothing had.

Tilman kept extensive and detailed records of all his voyages. The ship's log was kept on the chart table and was entered up every hour by the man on watch, with course, speed, wind and sea conditions, changes of sail and so on, in concise and formal terms. The brevity of the required entries was a great comfort when your hands were pain-fully frozen and paper and pencil were wet. Stores were always stowed with the aid of a stores listing, the quantity of each item and its exact place of stowage were entered in an exercise book, and as stores were taken out and used they were crossed off the list. The Skipper kept a sort of amplified diary in another exercise book, in which he wrote a page or two almost every day. This was the raw material for his books, and in it he wrote not only the bald account of the day's events, but also the associated descriptions, comments, thoughts, quotations and so on which would later be made into a book. He was a dutiful if not an enthusiastic photographer, he made sure that he had photos of anything of importance or interest, handling the camera rather like a small and unfavoured piece of artillery. Again, the details of each photo taken were carefully entered in a book. All this carefully prepared material was taken back to Bod Owen at the end of a voyage, where it enabled him to produce books of great factual accuracy.

A final word about Tilman's amazing steadiness under fire; when the chips were down, and real, not merely imagined, danger was there, his cool steadiness was an inspiration to others. In *Patanela* the wind rose through force 12, the interface between air and water began to become diffuse and indistinct, and the little steel ship rang like a boilermaking shop to the blows of the great waves. When this had been going on for some hours and seemed to be reaching its peak, the Skipper remarked quietly, "Thank God we have a sound ship under us." A remarkably reassuring statement, which put new heart into all of us. When *Sea Breeze* was beset in the storms in 1970, and again when she was leaking too badly for the pumps to cope in a North Atlantic storm, you could see him carefully thinking through from the problem to the possible solutions, with a powerful mind unimpeded by fear or haste, and it became obvious, then, that your best hope for safety lay in following this man. He was a very great gentleman. One thing about the Heard Island expedition that he never made the slightest mention of was that he, by far the best mountaineer of us all, had to stick with the ship and forego any opportunity to take part in the climbing. It was unfortunate but inevitable, so he put the thought aside and we were able to learn another detail of how a gentleman behaves.

XVII

The Last Voyage

TILMAN EXPRESSED A whimsical hope that he might spend his eightieth birthday in the Arctic, but as his birthday came in February he accepted that as impracticable. Then came an invitation which made it possible that he might celebrate his birthday in the Antarctic, towards the end of the Antarctic summer of 1978. His young friend Simon Richardson, who had crewed for him on *Baroque* in 1973, and for whom he had a high regard, was fitting out a steel tug, converted to a gaff-rigged cutter, for an expedition to Smith Island in the South Shetlands, and he invited Tilman to join it.

Smith Island and the climbing of Mount Foster were the objectives in Tilman's unhappy voyage in *Mischief* in 1966–67. He was glad to have an opportunity to return, but was conscious of his age and disabilities. "I don't see myself being of much use beyond standing watches," he wrote to Michael Richey, director of the Royal Institute of Navigation, but he decided to go. Simon, whose home at Stockbridge in Hampshire is not far from Lymington, had frequently helped in fitting out *Baroque*. Simon's concept of the expedition was similar to Tilman's ten years earlier. Smith Island is notoriously difficult to land on, but he proposed to try to land a climbing party with provisions for three months, while his boat *En Avant* returned to Deception Island, thence putting in if possible some exploration of the Antarctic Peninsula (Graham Land). *En Avant* was to go back to Smith Island early in February 1978, thus making it at least theoretically possible for Tilman to spend his eightieth birthday on 14 February on Smith Island, if not on Mount Foster.

En Avant sailed from Southampton early in August 1977 and after calling at Las Palmas in the Canaries in September reached Rio de Janeiro on 25 October. Tilman wrote letters from Rio to a number of friends, and among them one to Frank George, who had helped him to bring back *Baroque* from Iceland:

352

26 October 1977. We got in here yesterday evening, 54 days out of Las Palmas. It's about 3,500 m. so we did not do so badly. After picking up the SE trades in Lat 4 N we knocked off 100 miles a day for a week. The so-called SW monsoon between the two trade wind belts failed, or produced mostly southerly winds and not much rain. The crew are in good shape and still on speaking terms with each other and with Simon, the skipper. Fifty-four days cooped up together is not a bad test, though of course it was all pleasant weather and easy sailing. They are a much better lot than any I have had, and between them have a number of special skills, navigation, electrics, machinery, woodwork, welding, etc. Mountaineers are the lack, and I can't see us doing anything on Smith Island even if we can land there.

We're lying stern on at one of those super luxurious yacht clubs that the Latin races delight in. . . . The only notable event of the voyage was the catching of a 5 ft shark on rod and line, but he had to be shot through the head before he could be landed. I lead a very easy life, doing practically nothing beyond standing a watch. We have a very competent ex-Merchant Navy chap who does the navigating. The big plotting charts I got and your small ones for plotting stars (he takes 6 or 7 at a time) are very useful. Remember me to Michael [Richey] whom I will overlook this time, as you can give him the news. I think I told you *Baroque* was sold and is now lying in St Katherine's Dock. Kindest regards to you both. Yours, Bill.

The lack of mountaineers in the party was to be made good by picking up two New Zealand climbers at Port Stanley, in the Falklands. *En Avant* sailed from Rio bound for the Falklands on 1 November 1977. The rest is silence.

H. W. Tilman has no known grave. In A. E. Housman's words, "He wears the turning globe".

ختام سخن

BIBLIOGRAPHICAL NOTE

H. W. Tilman's own books are

The Ascent of Nanda Devi (Cambridge University Press, 1937)
Snow on the Equator (Bell, 1937)
When Men and Mountains Meet (Cambridge University Press, 1946)
Mount Everest – 1938 (Cambridge University Press, 1948)
Two Mountains and a River (Cambridge University Press, 1949)
China to Chitral (Cambridge University Press, 1951)
Nepal Himalaya (Cambridge University Press, 1952)
Mischief in Patagonia (Cambridge University Press, 1957)
Mischief among the Penguins (Rupert Hart-Davis, 1961)
Mischief in Greenland (Hollis and Carter, 1964)
Mostly Mischief (Hollis and Carter, 1966)
Mischief Goes South (Hollis and Carter, 1968)
In Mischief's Wake (Hollis and Carter, 1971)
Ice With Everything (Nautical Publishing Company, 1974)
Triumph and Tribulation (Nautical Publishing Company, 1977)

Other books that have been particularly helpful in the writing of this biography include

Nanda Devi, by Eric Shipton (Hodder and Stoughton, 1936)
That Untravelled World, by Eric Shipton (Hodder and Stoughton, 1969)
The Sea and The Snow, by Philip Temple (Cassell Australia, 1966)
The Story of Everest, by W. H. Murray (Dent, 1953)
The Albanians, by Anton Logoreci (Gollancz, 1977)
No Colours or Crest, by Peter Kemp (Cassell, 1958)
The First World War, by A. J. P. Taylor (Hamish Hamilton, 1963, Penguin Books, 1966)
English History 1914–1945, by A. J. P. Taylor (Oxford University Press, 1965, Penguin Books, 1970)

In addition, there are many articles by Tilman, and many references to him, in newspapers and magazines over more than half a century. The *Geographical Journal* Vol. XCII No. 6 and the *Himalayan Journal* Vols. VII, IX, X, XI and XV are directly relevant.

CHRONOLOGICAL TABLE

1898   Harold William Tilman born 14 February at Wallasey, Cheshire.

1909   Berkhamsted School.

1915   (January) Royal Military Academy, Woolwich. Commissioned 28 July into Royal Field Artillery.

1916   (January) Began active service on the Western Front. Battle of the Somme. Wounded, but went back to the front.

1917   Wounded January, immediate award of Military Cross, evacuated to hospital in England. Returned to front in May. Battles of Nieuwpoort, Ypres, Passchendaele. Awarded bar to MC. Promoted Lieutenant, transferred to Royal Horse Artillery.

1918   Took part in German spring offensive and Allied advance into Germany.

1919   Resigned commission, went to Kenya to be a planter.

1926   In partnership with father, bought more land in Kenya.

1930   Started climbing in East Africa with Eric Shipton (Kibo, Mawenzi, Kilimanjaro, Mt Kenya).

1932   Holiday in England. Serious accident in Lake District. Told he could never climb again. Went on his own for mountain tour in the Alps (July).

1933   Prospecting for gold in Kenya. Climbed Kilimanjaro alone. Crossed Africa by bicycle from Uganda to West Coast. Returned to England.

1934   First visit to Himalaya. Nanda Devi reconnaissance with Shipton.

1935   Everest reconnaissance.

1936   Ascent of Nanda Devi with Odell.

1937   Exploring in Karakoram with Shipton.

1938   Leader of British Everest expedition. Crossed Zemu Gap.

1939   Attempted to climb Gori Chen in Assam Himalaya (spring).

357

Seriously ill with fever. Returned to England to rejoin Army.

1940   Fought in France. Evacuated from Dunkirk.

1941   Briefly with Army in India, then in Iraq.

1942   With 8th Army in Western Desert.

1943   Volunteered for parachute training and special service behind enemy lines. Parachuted into Albania as liaison officer with Partisans.

1944–45 Service with Italian Resistance in Northern Italy. Awarded DSO and Freedom of Belluno. Retired from Army.

1946   Broke arm in climbing accident in Scotland. Short trip to Switzerland.

1947   With Swiss expedition to Rakaposhi. With Shipton in Kashgar. Attempt to climb Muztagh Ata. Arrested in Afghanistan. Returned to live with sister at Bod Owen, Barmouth (to be his home for the rest of his life).

1948   Central Asian journey from China to Chitral. Attempted climbs: Bogdo Ola, Chakar Aghil.

1949   Exploring in Nepal.

1950   With expedition to Annapurna IV. Travelled Nepal route to Everest with Houston expedition.

1952   Consul at Maymyo, Burma.

1953   Home. Sailing at Barmouth.

1954   Bought *Mischief* at Palma, Mallorca. Awarded Hon. Ll.D by University of St Andrew's.

1955–56 Sailed *Mischief* to Patagonia, crossed Patagonian ice-cap, completed circumnavigation of South America.

1957–58 Circumnavigated Africa.

1959–60 Sailed *Mischief* to Crozet Islands and Kerguelen.

1961   Sailed to West Greenland (Godthaab, Umanak Fjord).

1962   West Greenland and east coast of Arctic Canada.

1963   Baffin Bay, crossed Bylot Island.

1964   East Greenland (northern summer).

1964–65 Navigated schooner *Patanela* for Warwick Deacock's Heard Island expedition. Later 1965 sailed *Mischief* to East Greenland.

1966–67 Sailed *Mischief* to South Shetlands, South Georgia.

1968   Jan Mayen. Loss of *Mischief*. Bought *Sea Breeze*.

1969   Sailed *Sea Breeze* to Iceland, East Greenland coast.

1970   In *Sea Breeze* to West Greenland, fjords around Julianehaab.

1971   *Sea Breeze* to East Greenland.

1972   To East Greenland. Shipwreck, loss of *Sea Breeze*.

1973   Awarded CBE. In *Baroque* to West Greenland (Godthaab, Umanak).

1974   Circumnavigation of Spitzbergen in *Baroque*.

1975   West Greenland in *Baroque*.

1976   East Greenland in *Baroque*. Trouble after grounding. *Baroque* left to winter in Iceland.

1977   Brought *Baroque* home from Iceland. Sailed from Southampton in *En Avant* with expedition to Smith Island in South Shetlands led by Simon Richardson. 1 November *En Avant* left Rio bound for Falklands. Nothing known since.

INDEX

361